6

A Communicative Course in English

Sandra Costinett
with Donald R. H. Byrd

Donald R. H. Byrd *Project Director*

Anna Veltfort *Art Director*

Prentice Hall Regents
Englewood Cliffs, NJ   07632

Contributing Writer: Gerry Strei
Composition: Don Williams
Cover Design: Roberto de Vicq
Interior Concept and Page-by-Page Design: Anna Veltfort

ACKNOWLEDGMENTS

Illustrations: Pages 62, 73, 110, 111, 116, 117, and 136 by Anna Veltfort; pages 14, 21, 36, 37, 44, 80, 81, 98, 112, and 113 by Anne Burgess; pages 32, 33, 45, and 46 by Hugh Harrison; pages 4, 5, 10, 24, 54, 89, 92, 99, and 118 by Randy Jones; pages 58, 59, 96, and 97 by Eileen McKeating; pages 7, 20, 31, 34, 51, 52, 60, 64, 66, 72, 79, 102, 106, 107, 124, 128, and 132 by V. Gene Myers; pages 69, 70, and 109 by Charles Peale; pages 30, 35, 38, 39, 50, 82, 94, 122, 126, and 127 by Bot Roda; pages 25, 26, 40, 55, 56, 75, 84, 85, 93, and 95 by Arnie Ten.

Photos: Page 1 by Photofest; page 2 by NASA; page 9 by Bill Anderson/Monkmeyer Press; page 11 by Reuters/Bettmann; pages 12, 13 (bottom) and 100 by UPI/Bettmann; pages 13 (top) and 121 by AP/Wide World Photos; page 18 (top) by Donna Jernigan; page 18 (middle) by Daemrich/The Image Works; page 18 (bottom) by Michael Newman/Photo Edit; pages 19 and 78 (middle right) by Bill Bachmann/Photo Researchers, Inc.; page 22 by Jerome Wexler/FPG International; page 23 (top) by Beryl Goldberg/Monkmeyer Press; page 23 (bottom) by Howard Dratch/The Image Works; pages 28 and 29 (top left) by Porterfield/Chickering/Photo Researchers; page 29 (top right) by Hugh Rogers/Monkmeyer Press; pages 29 (bottom left), 77 (middle), and 104 (box 3) by Chester Higgins, Jr./Photo Researchers, Inc.; page 29 (bottom right) by Ken Ross/FPG; pages 41(left), 49(top), and 120 (left) by Bettman Archives; page 41 (right) by Victor Englebert/Photo Researchers, Inc.; page 42 (top) by Louise L. Serpa/Photo Researchers, Inc.; page 42 (middle) by Kenneth Murray/Photo Researchers, Inc.; page 42 (bottom) by Mark Antman/The Image Works; page 48 (top) by Collections of the Library of Congress; page 48 (bottom) by Arlene Collins/Monkmeyer Press Photo Service; page 49 (middle) by The Makers of Armstrong's Linoleum; page 49 (bottom) by Maria Pape; page 65 by Mark Lennihan; page 71 by *Xplora 1: Peter Gabriel's Secret World* ©1993 Real World Multi Media Ltd.; page 76 (top left) by Mark Humphrey/AP Photo; page 76 (top right) by Jacksonville Symphony Association; page 76 (bottom left) by Sergio Penchansky/Photo Researchers Inc.; page 76 (bottom right) by Randy Matusow/Monkmeyer Press; page 77 (top) by Star File; page 77 (bottom) by Mimi Forsyth/Monkmeyer Press; page 78 (top left) by David Powers; page 78 (top right) by Carol Rosegg/Martha Swope Associates; page 78 (middle left) by Boris Erwitt/FPG International; page 78 (bottom left) by John Moore Photography; page 78 (bottom right) by Joel Gordon Photography; page 86 (top left) by Ann Holmes/Photo Researchers, Inc.; page 86 (top right) by Dick Davis/Photo Researchers, Inc.; page 86 (bottom left) by George Holton/Photo Researchers, Inc.; page 86 (bottom right) by F. Sacristan/Gamma-Liaison, Inc.; page 87 by R. Matusow/Monkmeyer Press; pages 90 and 91 by Frank LaBua; page 101 (top) by Gamma; page 101 (bottom) by NBT; page 104 (box 1) by Rhoda Sidney/Monkmeyer Press; page 104 (box 2) by A. Albert/The Image Works; page 104 (box 4) by Peter Menzel/Stock Boston, Inc.; page 104 (box 5) by Doug Plummer/Photo Rearchers, Inc.; page 119 (top left) by Spencer Grant/Monkmeyer Press; page 119 (top right) by Jay Berndt/Stock Boston, Inc.; page 119 (bottom left) by Michael Kagan/Monkmeyer Press; page 119 (bottom right) by Roberta Hershenson/Photo Researchers, Inc.; page 120 (right) by Martha Swope Assoc.

Realia: Pages 3, 5, 6, 8, 9, 15, 16, 17, 33, 42, 43, 45, 47 (top), 52-53, 57, 61, 63, 65, 67, 70, 71, 83, 84, 87, 88, 90, 94, 96, 108, 115, 118, 120, 125, 126, 127, 131, 133, 134, and 135 by Siren Design; pages 19, 26, 28, 29, 35, 36, 39, 47 (bottom), 50, 60, 62, 98, 104, 105, 128, and 129 by Anna Veltfort.

Permissions: Pages 12-13: ©1980 by The New York Times Company. Reprinted by permission. Pages 22-23: Reprinted by permission of *Psychology Today* magazine. ©1984, American Psychological Association. Page 32: ©1981 by The New York Times Company. Reprinted by permission. Pages 42-43: Written by Murray Rubenstein. Originally published by *Science Digest.* Page 52:©1984 by The New York Times Copmpany. Reprinted by permission. Page 61: Reprinted with permission of Science Digest, ©1985 by The Hearst Corporation. Page 67: Adapted with permission of Collier Associates from Unlocking Opportunity by Catherine Lilly and Daniel Martin, ©1985 by Catherine Lilly and Daniel Martin. Page 80: Reprinted with permission of *Working Woman* magazine, ©1985 Hal Publications, Inc. Page 90: Reprinted by permission of *The Futurist,* published by The World Future Society. Pages 100-101: Nuestro magazine, June/July 1982. Pages 110-111: WGBH-Boston, NOVA ©1985 Addison-Wesley, Reading, MA. Pages 120-121: ©1984 by The New York Times Company. Reprinted with permission. Page 129: Repritned with permission of *Psychology Today* magazine, ©1985 American Psychological Association. Page 131: Reprinted with permission of *Woman's World* magazine. Page 133: ©1985, USA TODAY. Reprinted with permission. Page 135: Reprinted with permission of *Psychology Today* magazine, ©1985 American Psychological Association.

The editors have made every effort to trace the ownership of all copyrighted material and express regret in advance for any error or omission. After notification of oversight, they will include proper acknowledgment in future printings.

CONTENTS

UNIT	PAGES	THEMES	FUNCTIONS
1 Lessons 1 – 5	1–10	Arguments Regrets Hopes and wishes	Debate an issue Support an argument Express regret Talk about hopes and wishes
2 Lessons 6 – 10	11–20	Descriptions Recommendations	Describe yourself Describe someone else Make a recommendation
3 Lessons 11 – 15	21–30	Shopping Workplace situations	Convince someone Inform someone Make a purchase
4 Lessons 16 – 20	31–40	Instructions Explanations Hobbies	Give instructions Explain something Talk about interests
5 Lessons 21 – 25	41–50	Descriptions Sizes Comparisons Problems	Describe something Talk about dimensions Make comparisons Describe a household problem
6 Lessons 26 – 30	51 – 60	Reasons Consequences Proposals	Give reasons Talk about consequences Make a proposal Talk about people
Review of units 1 – 6	61 – 68	Review	Review

S E Q U E N C E

INTRODUCTION

A complete course. The new edition of *Spectrum* is a six-level course designed for adolescent and adult learners of English. Levels 1 and 2 of *Spectrum* are appropriate for beginning students and "false beginners." Levels 3 and 4 are intended for intermediate classes. Levels 5 and 6 are for advanced learners. The student book, workbook, and audio cassette program for each level provide practice in all four communication skills, with a special focus on listening and speaking in levels 1 to 4, and on reading and writing in levels 5 and 6.

Real communication from the beginning. *Spectrum* is "a communicative course in English," and is based on the idea that communication—the exchange of information—is not merely the end-product of language study, but rather the very process through which a new language is acquired. To this end, *Spectrum* has three basic aims:

- to provide motivating materials that teach students to function in real-life situations;
- to teach only authentic English that stimulates natural conversation both in and outside the classroom; and
- to give students a feeling of success and achievement as they learn the language.

From the very beginning, students practice language that can be put to immediate use. For example, students learn to ask for information, make suggestions, and apologize. They learn the appropriate language for different situations, such as formal speech used with strangers and informal speech with friends. Most importantly, they are encouraged to express their own ideas and feelings, and to give their own opinions.

Language learning the natural way. *Spectrum* acknowledges that students can understand more English than they are able to produce. In other words, their ability to comprehend language (to listen or read) naturally precedes their ability to produce it (to

speak or write). To this end, *Spectrum* places great emphasis on comprehension. Students in the beginning and intermediate levels begin each unit by listening to and reading conversations that provide rich input for language learning. Many of the functions, grammatical structures, and vocabulary items in these conversations become "active" and are practiced in the lessons that follow. However, some of the functions and structures in these conversations are "receptive"—they are intended for comprehension only—and do not become productive until later units or levels.

At the advanced levels (levels 5-6), each unit begins with an authentic text for reading and discussion, and provides cultural and thematic input. In addition, a realistic conversation provides context for active practice in the pages that follow.

A carefully graded syllabus. As they engage in a variety of exercises that practice basic linguistic functions, students are guided toward the use of correct grammatical structures. Both the functions and the structures in the *Spectrum* syllabus are carefully graded according to simplicity and usefulness. Grammatical structures are presented in clear paradigms with informative usage notes.

Sometimes students encounter and use grammar and expressions that are not formally introduced until later units or levels—for example, when language items are needed to perform a given function appropriately. The goal is to provide students with a continuous stream of input that challenges their current knowledge of English, thereby allowing them to progress naturally to a higher level of competence. In the beginning level, for instance, students learn expressions such as "Could you spell your last name?" and "May I take a message?," although the modals *could* and *may* are not analyzed systematically until the intermediate level. In the advanced level, the same structures are expanded further. This system of preview-review works as follows:

- the structures are previewed—introduced formulaically.
- they are then analyzed—examined and practiced systematically.
- when appropriate, they are reviewed—recycled for further practice.

Changes in the new edition. Heeding the insights and suggestions of reviewers and long-time users of *Spectrum* around the world, significant changes have been made in the new edition of *Spectrum*.

- The first four levels of *Spectrum* are available in split editions—1A, 1B, 2A, 2B, 3A, 3B, 4A, and 4B—as well as full editions.
- Each student book contains a substantial amount of new material accompanied by color illustrations and photographs.

- Each unit begins with a summary of the language that is featured and practiced. In addition, there is a preview task on this page that relates the theme of the first lesson to the students' own experiences or prepares the students for the cultural material in the lesson.
- The student book is divided into self-contained one- and two-page lessons, each with its own thematic focus. The workbook is divided into corresponding lessons.
- A greater range of exercise types, including interviews, role plays, and information-gap activities, has been included to challenge students.
- There is an increase in the number and variety of listening activities in the course.
- Reading selections in each unit are more challenging. They are often longer and include pre-reading tasks as well as strategies for reading in English.

REVIEWERS AND CONSULTANTS

For the preparation of the new edition, Prentice Hall Regents would like to thank the following long-time users of *Spectrum*, whose insights and suggestions have helped to shape the content and format of the new edition: Motofumi Aramaki, Sony Language Laboratory, Tokyo, Japan; Associação Cultural Brasil-Estados Unidos (ACBEU), Salvador-Bahia, Brazil; AUA Language Center, Bangkok, Thailand, Thomas J. Kral and faculty; Pedro I. Cohen, Professor Emeritus of English, Linguistics, and Education, Universidad de Panamá; ELSI Taiwan Language Schools, Taipei, Taiwan, Kenneth Hou and faculty; James Hale, Sundai ELS, Tokyo, Japan; Impact, Santiago, Chile; Instituto Brasil-Estados Unidos (IBEU), Rio de Janeiro, Brazil; Instituto Brasil-Estados Unidos No Ceará (IBEU-CE), Fortaleza, Brazil; Instituto Chileno Norteamericano de Cultura, Santiago, Chile; Instituto Cultural Argentino Norteamericano (ICANA), Buenos Aires, Argentina; Christopher M. Knott, Chris English Masters Schools, Kyoto, Japan; The Language Training and Testing Center, Taipei, Taiwan, Anthony Y. T. Wu and faculty; Lutheran Language Institute, Tokyo, Japan; Network Cultura, Ensino e Livraria Ltda, São Paulo, Brazil; Seven Language and Culture, São Paulo, Brazil.

SPECIAL ACKNOWLEDGMENTS FOR LEVEL 6

Kevin McClure, ELS, San Francisco, CA; Elise Klein, ELS, New Haven, CT; Monica Haupt, ELS, Oakland, CA; Maureen Daly of New Haven, CT.

Components of the course

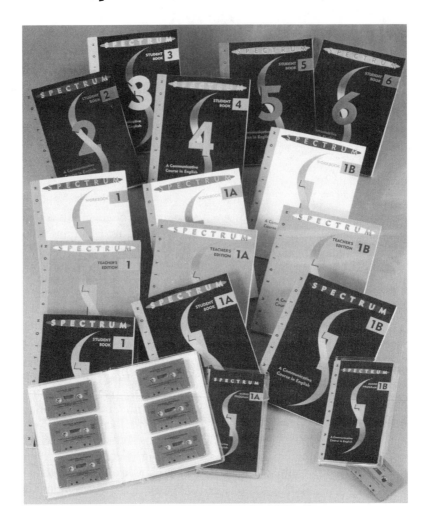

Flexible design. The new edition of *Spectrum* has been designed to be used in a variety of instructional programs and teaching situations.

- The full editions of the student books for levels 1-4 consist of fourteen units divided into one-, two-, or three-page lessons. The split editions contain seven units each. There are review sections after every three or four units. Levels 5 and 6 are available only in full editions. For these levels, the student book consists of twelve units. There are review sections after the first six units and after the last unit.
- The workbooks are divided into lessons and review sections which correspond to the lessons in the student books. The workbook lessons can be used in class or assigned as homework.
- There is an audio cassette program to accompany the student book and workbook at each level. For the first four levels, each full edition has a six-cassette program and each split edition has a three-cassette program. Levels 5 and 6 each have a five-cassette program.
- The teacher's editions provide a wide range of suggestions for using the various components of the course.
- A testing package includes a placement test for the six-level course and two achievement tests for each level.

Variable course length. Each full edition of the student book for levels 1-4 contains approximately sixty hours of instructional material (approximately fifty hours for each of levels 5 and 6). Class time can be expanded to approximately ninety hours (eighty hours for levels 5 and 6) by using the optional activities in the teacher's edition and by using the workbook lessons as a regular classroom activity. Using sections of the audio cassette program for practice in the language laboratory can also increase the length of the instructional program.

Each split edition of the student book contains approximately thirty hours of classroom material. Class time can be expanded to approximately forty-five hours by using the optional activities in the teacher's edition and by incorporating the workbook lessons into the classroom program.

THE STUDENT BOOK

Each unit of the student book begins with a preview page which gives an overview of the language in the unit and a preview of the reading in the first lesson.

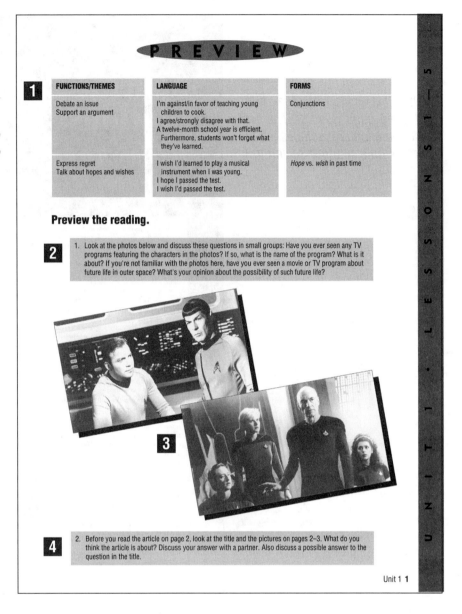

1. Each preview page gives a concise summary of the functions, themes, language, and grammatical structures taught in the unit.

2. Discussion questions encourage students to think about the theme and relate it to their own lives. Students may discuss these questions in English or in their native language.

3. Illustrations or photographs introduce students to the theme and setting of the first lesson.

4. Pre-reading questions invite students to speculate what the title of the reading means and what the article is about.

Each unit is divided into one-, two-, and three-page lessons. The first lesson in each unit establishes the theme with a reading selection.

1.

Space Stations:

Do they have a future?

Life on the space shuttle.

1 Many years from now, when people regularly take their vacations in outer space, they will look back on the twentieth century and try to date the beginning of the space age. Some will say it all started with the launching of Sputnik in 1957, others will point to Neil Armstrong's first steps on the moon in 1969, and still others will mention the birth of the space shuttle—a spacecraft that could be used more than once to make space travel much less expensive. But at least a few will emphasize that the true beginning was the creation of populated space stations.

2 A space station will actually be a home in space. It is designed so that many people can live and work for a longer time than they would be able to in an ordinary, crowded spacecraft. Through the doors of a space station, spacecraft will leave for the moon or even Mars at a fraction of the cost of launching them from Earth. In the space station's "rooms," astronauts and scientists will conduct important experiments in fields ranging from astronomy to chemistry.

3 The space station will have facilities for sleeping, bathing, exercising, eating, and relaxing. When it's time to sleep, astronauts will zip up in sleeping bags that hang from the wall. To shower in space, feet are strapped down, water is hosed on, and then the water is sucked up by a device like a vacuum cleaner. This water is then purified and recycled, as is the water for washing clothes. Astronauts will use a variety of exercise equipment to stay in shape, exercising about two hours a day. Food will be stored on the space station in one of two forms—dried or frozen. When astronauts want to eat, they will add liquid to dried food, or heat frozen food in a microwave oven. New supplies and fresh fruits and vegetables can be brought to the stations by shuttles. Astronauts will relax by watching videos, using the computer, reading, and talking to friends and family on Earth via radio.

4 Many experiments can be conducted on space station laboratories. Animals will be brought up into space to study the effects of weightlessness. Some will be living in the same conditions as the astronauts, while others will inhabit an area that is kept spinning to achieve a centrifugal force equal to Earth's gravity. These animals can then be studied to observe similarities and differences among the two groups in space and a control group on Earth. The lack of gravity in space also has benefits, mainly in the area of technology and manufacturing. Perhaps new alloys can be created from metals that do not mix on Earth. Computers and solar cells use crystals that could grow better in space. In the area of medicine, there is hope of new drugs being created that are purer and easier to manufacture.

5 And if space stations are successful, the next step may very well be space cities. Scientists believe that the benefits of space cities will far outweigh their costs. These space cities will help solve today's most pressing problems, among them overpopulation, the energy crisis, and pollution.

6 Not everyone agrees that we even need a space station, let alone space cities. Some scientists think that much experimentation and study must be done here on Earth before space stations are workable. They aren't sure that we should spend billions of dollars on a project whose technology is not yet established and whose benefits to the human race are still in question. These scientists think that the money could be better spent on shorter-range scientific research.

7 Nevertheless, an international partnership made up of the U.S., Japan, Canada, and ten European nations has been working on plans for Freedom—a space station designed both as a place for experimentation and research and as a spaceport for peopled trips to Mars. Begun in 1984, the program is struggling to continue despite criticism and budget cutbacks. Over the next few years, important decisions about the future of the Freedom space station, and the future of space exploration as a whole, will be made.

2 Unit 1

1. The readings are recorded on cassette in natural spoken English. Recorded material is always indicated by the symbol ▭.

2. The readings are authentic newspaper or magazine articles that have been carefully selected to increase comprehension and to encourage and stimulate oral discussion.

3. The context of each reading is enhanced by illustrations or photos related to the story.

4. The functions and structures introduced in the readings are primarily for recognition as students listen to and read the articles.

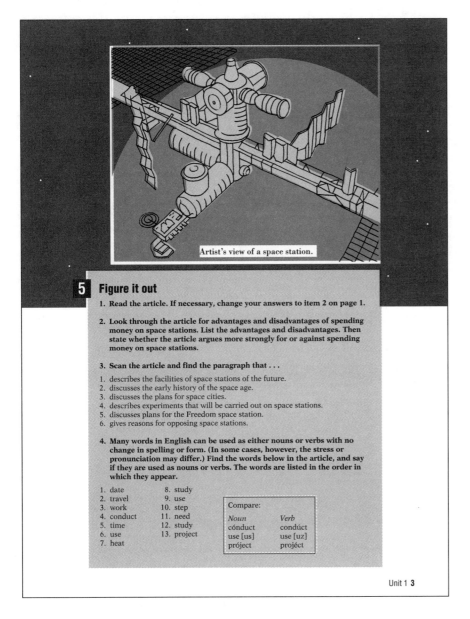

Artist's view of a space station.

5 Figure it out

1. Read the article. If necessary, change your answers to item 2 on page 1.

2. Look through the article for advantages and disadvantages of spending money on space stations. List the advantages and disadvantages. Then state whether the article argues more strongly for or against spending money on space stations.

3. Scan the article and find the paragraph that . . .

1. describes the facilities of space stations of the future.
2. discusses the early history of the space age.
3. discusses the plans for space cities.
4. describes experiments that will be carried out on space stations.
5. discusses plans for the Freedom space station.
6. gives reasons for opposing space stations.

4. Many words in English can be used as either nouns or verbs with no change in spelling or form. (In some cases, however, the stress or pronunciation may differ.) Find the words below in the article, and say if they are used as nouns or verbs. The words are listed in the order in which they appear.

1. date	8. study
2. travel	9. use
3. work	10. step
4. conduct	11. need
5. time	12. study
6. use	13. project
7. heat	

Compare:

Noun	Verb
cónduct	condúct
use [us]	use [uz]
próject	projéct

5. Students can read and listen to the article several times, each time focusing on different information. The exercises in the **Figure it out** section focus on reading for the main idea, reading for specific details, drawing inferences, summarizing, and vocabulary development.

Next, two thematic lessons stress listening comprehension of a conversation followed by related productive practice through real communication.

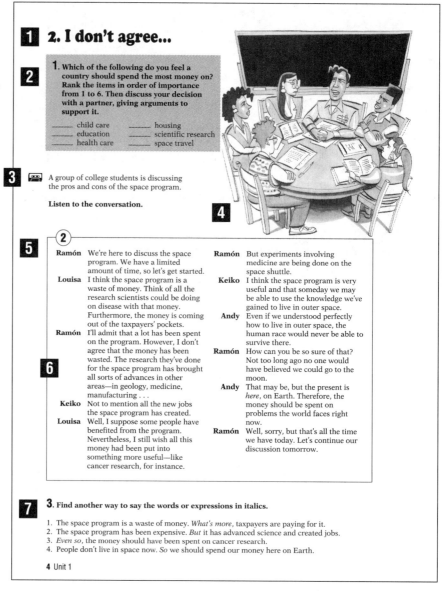

1 **2. I don't agree...**

2 **1.** Which of the following do you feel a country should spend the most money on? Rank the items in order of importance from 1 to 6. Then discuss your decision with a partner, giving arguments to support it.

____ child care	____ housing
____ education	____ scientific research
____ health care	____ space travel

3 🔊 A group of college students is discussing the pros and cons of the space program.

Listen to the conversation.

4

5

②

Ramón We're here to discuss the space program. We have a limited amount of time, so let's get started.

Louisa I think the space program is a waste of money. Think of all the research scientists could be doing on disease with that money. Furthermore, the money is coming out of the taxpayers' pockets.

Ramón I'll admit that a lot has been spent on the program. However, I don't agree that the money has been wasted. The research they've done for the space program has brought all sorts of advances in other areas—in geology, medicine, manufacturing . . .

6

Keiko Not to mention all the new jobs the space program has created.

Louisa Well, I suppose some people have benefited from the program. Nevertheless, I still wish all this money had been put into something more useful—like cancer research, for instance.

Ramón But experiments involving medicine are being done on the space shuttle.

Keiko I think the space program is very useful and that someday we may be able to use the knowledge we've gained to live in outer space.

Andy Even if we understood perfectly how to live in outer space, the human race would never be able to survive there.

Ramón How can you be so sure of that? Not too long ago no one would have believed we could go to the moon.

Andy That may be, but the present is *here*, on Earth. Therefore, the money should be spent on problems the world faces right now.

Ramón Well, sorry, but that's all the time we have today. Let's continue our discussion tomorrow.

7 **3.** Find another way to say the words or expressions in italics.

1. The space program is a waste of money. *What's more*, taxpayers are paying for it.
2. The space program has been expensive. *But* it has advanced science and created jobs.
3. *Even so*, the money should have been spent on cancer research.
4. People don't live in space now. *So* we should spend our money here on Earth.

4 Unit 1

---

1. A general theme serves to naturally group together important functions and structures in each one- or three-page lesson.

2. The second lesson of each unit begins with a warm-up activity which prepares the students for the conversation that follows.

3. Conversations are recorded on cassette in natural spoken English. Sound effects help give the conversations authenticity.

4. The context of the conversations is enhanced by art which illustrates the story.

5. Opening conversations present natural language set in authentic situations students can relate to.

6. New functions and structures are introduced initially for recognition only as students listen to and read the conversations. Time is allowed for the new language to be absorbed—to "sink in"—before it is actively practiced. Most of the functions, structures, vocabulary, and expressions taught in *Spectrum* are systematically previewed in this way.

7. Students can listen to the conversations several times, each time focusing on different information. The exercises which follow the conversations are intended to test the students' comprehension of the conversations and increase their awareness of new functions and structures.

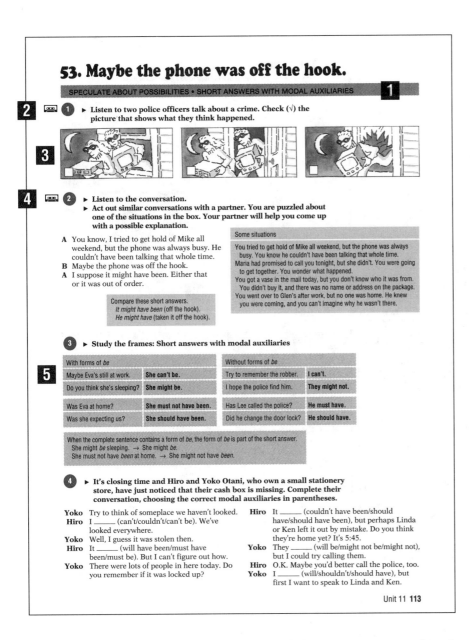

1. A clear and colorful design divides each lesson into major teaching points. Important functions and grammar points are clearly highlighted so the teacher and the student know the goals of each lesson.

2. Task-based listening activities give students practice in hearing, understanding, and responding to spoken English.

3. Photographs, illustrations, or realia provide the context for meaningful language practice.

4. Natural spoken models of the new language are recorded on cassette and provide aural input before students practice on their own.

5. After they are practiced in context, structures are analyzed formally. Special usage notes for grammatical structures, functions, and vocabulary are given when appropriate.

The thematic lessons are followed by exercises which involve free conversation and listening comprehension.

19. Your turn

1 Look at the pictures, and then try to find out how to do at least one of these activities. Bring your notes to class and, working in groups, share your instructions with your classmates. They will ask you questions when they don't understand.

2

3

▭ **Listen in**

Look carefully at the recipe below. Then listen to an interview in which the well-known chef, Martine Beck, explains how to make her dish, "Adam's Apple." You may wish to take notes while you listen. Then complete the recipe.

Adam's Apple
🍎 🍎 🍎 🍎 🍎

_____ large _____ , peeled and sliced
_____ tablespoons water
1/4 cup _____
_____ teaspoon cinnamon
_____ cup butter
1/2 cup _____
_____ eggs
_____ cup flour
_____ teaspoon baking powder

_____ , preheat your oven to 350° and butter a 2-quart baking dish.
_____ you are waiting for the oven to heat, combine the apples, the water, the 1/4 cup of sugar, and the cinnamon.
_____ , pour the apple mixture into the baking dish and set it aside.
_____ preparing the apples, in another bowl, mix the butter and the 1/2 cup of sugar until the mixture is fluffy.
_____ , add the eggs and beat well.
_____ , add the flour and baking powder and mix well.
_____ , spread the batter over the apples and bake in the oven for 50 minutes.
_____ the dish is ready, serve it hot with vanilla ice cream on the side. It serves 4 to 6 people.

🍎 🍎 🍎 🍎 🍎

1. Working in groups, students draw on their imaginations and personal experiences to communicate freely, using any language they have learned so far. This exercise personally involves the students in an activity related to the themes or functions of the unit.

2. A variety of photographs, illustrations, or realia suggest different topics for discussion.

3. The **Listen in** exercise is a short, unscripted listening activity—for example, an "overheard" conversation, telephone recording, radio broadcast, or public announcement. This activity provides valuable additional listening practice and tests the students' comprehension of oral language which expresses the themes or functions of the unit.

10. On your own

1. Write a two- or three- paragraph letter to the Kozinskis, the family who would like to host a foreign student. In the letter, describe the FSPS applicant that you have chosen to stay with them. Tell why you have selected this applicant.

2. Choose one of the following tasks.

1. You have been placed with the Kozinski family. You plan to live with them while you study in the United States. Write them a letter describing yourself.

2. You have been assigned a pen pal in an English-speaking country. Write a letter to him or her describing yourself.

The last lesson of each unit is an activity which provides students with the opportunity to practice in writing the function or theme which is the focus of the unit.

1. Students are given a situation or a problem and are asked to respond to it in writing.

2. Illustrations, photos, realia, or listening passages are used as stimuli for a second writing activity.

After every six units, there is a review section. The reviews reinforce material taught in the preceding units.

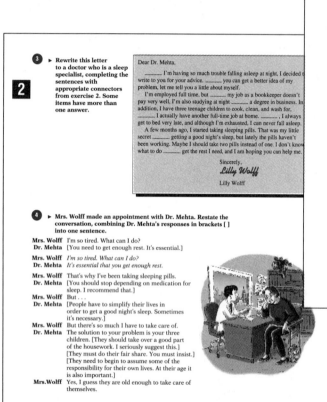

1. The review section consists of four different readings, each followed by a set of thematically related exercises.

2. Most of the review exercises require productive use of the language being reviewed.

THE WORKBOOK

The workbook can be used independently by students at home or as additional work in class. It is divided into lessons which correspond to the lessons in the student book. There are also corresponding review sections.

Lesson 7

1 ► Mrs. Reilly is interviewing David Mitchell and Mark Robinson for a job as a drugstore clerk. Listen to the interviews. Choose *a* or *b*. Then complete each sentence.

First interview

1. One reason David wants the job is that he *has to help out at home* .
   a. wants to save money for college   (b.) has to help out at home
2. David enjoys _____.
   a. working with people   b. telling other people what to do
3. David seems to be _____.
   a. unfriendly and reserved   b. friendly and outgoing
4. David considers himself _____.
   a. reliable   b. irresponsible
5. David thinks Mrs. Reilly would find him _____.
   a. honest and hardworking   b. untrustworthy and unambitious

Second interview

6. One reason Mark wants the job is that he _____.
   a. likes to talk to people   b. enjoys responsibility
7. Mark considers himself _____.
   a. cooperative and patient   b. easygoing and creative
8. Mark _____ imagine himself making things.
   a. can   b. can't

2 ► If you were Mrs. Reilly, would you hire David or Mark? Complete the paragraphs.

If I were Mrs. Reilly, I'd hire _____ because _____
_____
_____
_____
_____

I wouldn't hire _____ because _____
_____
_____
_____
_____

8 Unit 2

Lesson 10

► For which position do you consider yourself best suited? Write a short paragraph describing yourself and telling why you would be the right person for the job.

WANTED

INSURANCE SALESPERSON

Good verbal skills; must get along well with people and enjoy challenges. This is a real opportunity for the energetic person. The Acme Insurance Company

KINDERGARTEN ASSISTANT

Must like children and have a patient, helpful manner. Early morning hours needed. Kinderguard Center

HOSPITAL TECHNICIAN

A responsible person needed for independent laboratory work. Must have a good eye for details. This work requires someone who is careful. Institute Humana

SHOE STORE MANAGER

The right person will advance rapidly if he or she is ambitious, hardworking, and neat. Must be a good dresser with an eye for current fashion. Elite Footwear

3 NAME _____ COMPANY _____
_____
_____
_____
_____
_____
_____
_____
_____

12 Unit 2

---

1. The workbook provides additional listening practice, including exercises that focus on comprehension and interpretation of spoken language.

2. It provides writing practice on the functions, grammatical structures, and vocabulary introduced in the student book.

3. The last lesson of the workbook unit is either a guided or a free writing activity. The writing task is usually related to the theme of the last lesson of the student book unit.

THE TEACHER'S EDITION

The teacher's edition provides a wide range of suggestions for using the components of the course. The recommendations for teaching each exercise in the student book can be adapted to suit individual teaching styles and to meet the needs of particular students.

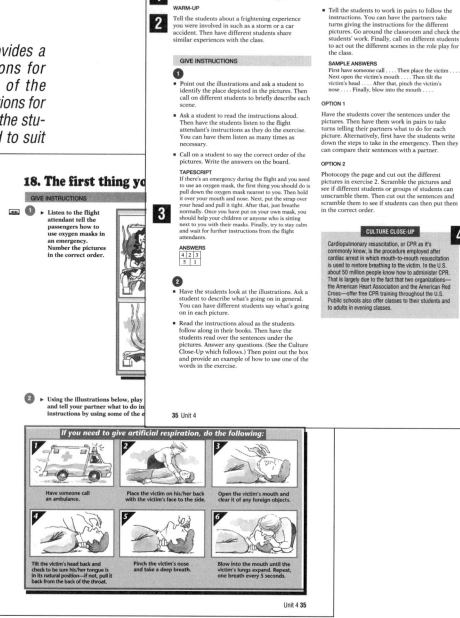

1. The teacher's edition features page-by-page instructions conveniently interleaved with duplicates of the student book pages. Also included is the scope and sequence chart from the student book. The answer key for the workbook exercises and the scripts for the workbook listening activities are located at the back of the book.

2. Suggested warm-up exercises and optional activities are provided for each lesson and can be used when time is available.

3. Included in the instructions are answer keys for exercises and scripts for the listening activities.

4. Background information, including notes on language and culture, is given for readings and conversations as well as for certain exercises. Notes concerning methodology and pronunciation are also provided.

THE AUDIO CASSETTE PROGRAM

For each level, there is a set of audio cassettes that may be used with the student book and its accompanying workbook. Material that is recorded on cassette is preceded by the symbol ▭.

1. Four cassettes in each set contain material from the student book and feature all the conversations, model dialogues, and listening activities, as well as a dramatization of the reading selection in each unit. These realistic recordings have been done by professional actors and include music and sound effects.

2. One cassette in each set is to be used with the workbook and contains additional listening activities.

3. Complete scripts for the recorded material from the student book and workbook are located in the teacher's edition.

THE TESTING PACKAGE

A placement test for the six-level course and two achievement tests for each level are available to programs using *Spectrum*.

The placement test has been developed to allow teachers and administrators to place students in the appropriate level of *Spectrum*. The two achievement tests can serve as mid-term and final exams in programs that use the full editions of the student book. They can be used as final exams in programs using the split editions.

GENERAL TEACHING CONCEPTS

Although specific suggestions are given for each pair and group activity in the page-by-page teaching notes of this teacher's edition, some general teaching concepts are particularly applicable to the successful use of *Spectrum*. These include ways to stimulate classroom interaction through problem-solving, role-playing, and other communicative practice in groups and pairs. Also included are ideas for using games and songs, and evaluating students' progress.

Paired practice and group work. Students need to interact freely with others in order to achieve the communicative goals of the course. Many of the exercises in *Spectrum* have been specifically designed for practice in pairs or small groups, thus allowing all of the students to be actively involved at the same time. This type of practice gives students a chance to use new language without the pressure of performing in front of the class, thus encouraging a favorable attitude toward English and promoting a feeling of success and self-esteem.

- Before having the students work in pairs or groups, act out part of the exercise with a volunteer to demonstrate how to do the exercise.
- While your students are practicing, it is a good idea to move from pair to pair to offer assistance where necessary and to discourage students from using their native language.
- After acting out the conversation once, students should exchange roles and, if possible, choose new partners. Changing roles and partners is especially valuable in conversational exercises where students ask for personal information, because with each new partner the conversation will be slightly different, thus providing a new challenge.
- To conclude the practice, sets of students can volunteer to go through the exercise for the whole class.

It is possible to divide students into groups or pairs at random according to how they are seated in the classroom. Some teachers, however, find it effective to place students into groups based on their individual needs and abilities. At times it is better to put students of similar abilities together so that more proficient students can challenge each other and less proficient students can take the time they need to concentrate on difficult areas. In this way, all students can work at their own pace. At other times it is advantageous to have strong students work with students who are progressing more slowly in order to provide encouragement and serve as peer models.

For those class situations where it is difficult to have students work in groups or pairs, you can present an exercise by practicing it with several individual students. After the students are familiar with the exercise, call on pairs to practice it together. Each new pair of students should add new vocabulary or give personal information if appropriate.

Problem-solving and information-gap activities. Communication is most authentic when there is an actual exchange of information between students, with neither speaker knowing in advance what the other will say or how he or she will say it. Many of the activities in the new edition of *Spectrum* incorporate this element of unpredictability. Such tasks as locating places on a map, identifying people's occupations based on a series of clues, conducting interviews, or asking for directions require the students in a pair or group to seek information they do not have—to collaborate, examine alternatives and options, and exchange opinions.

Problem-solving and information-gap activities are extremely valuable. By focusing the students' attention on a problem to be solved, they are provided with an opportunity for real communication. More important than the actual completion of the task are the interaction skills the students use to reach their goal. During an activity, you should be prepared to:

- assist students in using functions necessary for pair or group interaction, such as asking for a meaning, interrupting politely, asking for and giving an opinion, and asking for clarification; and

- move from pair to pair or from group to group, noticing whether one or two students are dominating or whether someone is interrupting in an inappropriate manner.

By observing the process of communication, you can give the group suggestions on how to improve the interaction.

Role-playing and dramatization. Role-playing activities and dramatization of conversations and situations can make language come alive and can add variety, spontaneity, and fun to the classroom. These activities can be enhanced, whenever possible, by the use of real objects as suggested by the artwork in the text, such as items of clothing, currency, fruits and vegetables, theater tickets, and so forth. Such supplementary materials provide a multi-sensory experience for the student. To make a role-playing activity effective and useful, you should:

- encourage students to move about and respond physically in the roles they are playing. For example, positioning themselves in groups can make conversations seem more natural and feel more "real."
- have them use facial expressions and gestures that reinforce meaning. If a formal introduction is taking place, students should smile and shake hands. If a student is giving directions, he or she should point the way.
- encourage students to use vocal expression to convey meaning. For example, when saying "I'm tired," fatigue should be apparent in the voice.
- be sure they use voice quality to convey characterization. For example, a person acting out a phone call can be portrayed as a young child, as a teenager in trouble, or as an older person who has some wonderful—or terrible—news to tell.
- be sure they make the distinction between formal and informal language when appropriate.

- point out appropriate intonation and stress. For example, when correcting or verifying an item, heavy stress is on the part of the sentence being corrected:
Student 1: Is this 2845?
Student 2: No, it's 2835.
- point out different expressions that convey the same language function or meaning when appropriate. For example, in greeting someone, students can say *Hi, Hello, How do you do?* and *Good morning.* They can use an expression such as *O.K.* to mean *I agree, I feel fine, Yes,* or *I accept.*

Games. Games provide an enjoyable way to change the focus from language learning to language use. They heighten the learner's interest and can be used both for amusement and to stimulate learning. They create an environment in which students interact to reach a goal while following rules that limit and guide their behavior. The student book contains a number of problem-solving activities that can be made into games simply by designating groups as teams and setting rules and time limits.

You can devise your own games from ones you already know, such as Hangman, Tic–tac–toe, Bingo, and Twenty Questions. Twenty Questions, for example, can be used to encourage real communication. A student who is "it" chooses a well-known historical or popular personality and plays the role of that person. The other students ask up to twenty questions about the person's talents, abilities, place of residence, country of origin, or other facts, adapting language learned from the textbook. Students should ask only yes-no questions and must listen to all the questions and answers in order to guess the identity of the famous person. The student who guesses correctly is then "it."

Songs. Songs are an important aspect of culture, representing the history, folklore, and current idiom of a country. They have universal appeal and can provide enjoyment, relaxation, and a sense of community. Singing can build students' confidence by allowing them to enjoy a degree of fluency in English before they have achieved it in speaking. Songs can also serve as memory aids for learning vocabulary and internalizing stress and rhythm patterns. If an appropriate song cannot be found, you may wish to write new words for a familiar melody, using structures from the lesson. It is helpful to explain the context of a song before students listen to it or learn it.

Error correction. Making errors is an unavoidable part of the language-learning process. At the same time, most people agree that a fear of making errors can inhibit students from speaking and keep them from getting essential oral practice. It is important to correct students in a way that is supportive, yet clear, direct, and focused, so they will learn to monitor themselves and express themselves more appropriately.

Language errors fall into many different categories. There are errors of meaning, appropriateness, grammar, and pronunciation. Generally speaking, it is most important to correct errors that really affect communication and those that relate to the focus of an exercise or activity. If an exercise emphasizes a specific grammar point, errors related to that point should be corrected. If an exercise covers an aspect of pronunciation, the emphasis should be on pointing out the relevant pronunciation errors. If the students are engaged in more open-ended practice—such as a problem-solving or role-playing activity—grammar and pronunciation errors become less important than meaning and appropriateness.

- It is usually most effective to give students a chance to correct themselves first before you supply a correction. You can give a hint by saying what type of error has been made, such as "word order" or "tense."
- Students can also benefit from correcting their own and one another's errors in homework assignments. One or two students can write the homework on the board and the entire class can check it for errors, making corrections on their own papers.

- Develop a sense of timing when correcting errors or supplying needed structures and vocabulary. If a student is struggling to express an idea and is searching for a word, it may be best to assist him or her immediately so that the idea can be expressed. On the other hand, if a pair of students are engaged in free conversation and are communicating well except for a few errors, it could be distracting to interrupt them. During such practice you can note the errors that students have made frequently and point them out at the end of the activity.

Evaluation of students' progress. Tests and other methods of evaluation, such as carrying out a task or participating in a role-play activity, are an important part of the language-learning process. Students can see what areas they need more practice in, and teachers can use the results for planning future lessons. The review sections in the student book have been expressly designed for the purposes of evaluation and review. However, if you want to check your students' progress more often, you can prepare your own informal tests by designing items similar to those used in the textbook. The ideas suggested below show how various types of test items reflect the learning objectives of *recognition, recall, transfer,* and *creative use* of language.

- For testing *recognition,* students can demonstrate their understanding of information by:
  1. matching items, such as parts of conversations;
  2. selecting an item from three or four choices, such as choosing the appropriate answer to a question;
  3. organizing information, such as rearranging lines from a known dialogue, putting words into the correct order to form a sentence, and alphabetizing names; or
  4. listening to dialogue lines and identifying the speaker.

- For testing *recall,* students can demonstrate that they have acquired specific knowledge by:

1. filling in blanks with the appropriate response, such as the correct verb form, a word which describes a picture, or the words missing from a dialogue;

2. saying or writing the expected response after listening to a dialogue or piece of information;

3. writing sentences for pictures; or

4. writing sentences or paragraphs from dictation.

• For testing *transfer* of knowledge, students can show they are able to apply known information in different situations by:

1. paraphrasing or summarizing a passage they have heard or read;

2. editing a passage to change one tense to another;

3. transforming a dialogue from a formal to an informal register;

4. providing expressions appropriate in a given situation, such as two people being introduced to each other; or

5. writing the missing words in a passage (the cloze method).

• For testing the *creative use* of English, students can show their proficiency by:

1. relating an experience, either orally or in writing;

2. answering questions about a reading passage;

3. writing original sentences based on information that has been provided; or

4. performing specific tasks, such as giving information about themselves, expressing opinions, asking questions, and creating dialogues.

PAGE-BY-PAGE TEACHING INSTRUCTIONS

PREVIEW

*The chart at the top of the **PREVIEW** page in the Student Book lists the "productive" language introduced in the unit—these are the language items that students will practice actively in the exercises following the first lesson. In each unit there is a certain amount of "receptive" language as well—items intended for comprehension only. "Receptive" language is introduced mainly in the readings but may appear in the opening conversations as well. Some examples of receptive language in Unit 1 are:*

...zip up
...the effects of weightlessness
...solar cells use crystals
...shorter range scientific research
...budget cutbacks
...out of taxpayers' pockets
Not to mention...

Before you begin teaching, go over the functions/themes, language, and forms in the chart. This will give you a preview of what you will encounter as you guide the students through each unit.

As you progress through the book, both you and the students can use the chart for reference or to review the language that has been practiced.

Preview the reading.

This pre-reading activity provides background information to help students understand the opening reading and relate it to their own experience.

- Tell the students to look at the photos. Ask different students to describe what's happening in each picture.

- Have the students follow along in their books as you read aloud the instructions for item 1. Then have the students work in small groups to discuss the questions. Go around the classroom and join in the discussions. Then call on different students to share their answers to the questions with the class. (See the Culture Close-Up which follows.)

- Ask a student to read aloud the instructions for item 2. Have the students answer the questions and then compare their answers with a partner. Call on a student to share his or her answers with the class.

CULTURE CLOSE-UP

Star Trek is the most popular adult science fiction series ever created for U.S. television. The original series began in 1966 and ended in 1969, but reruns of the series continued until 1987 when a new series was launched. The original series was set in the 23rd century aboard the space ship *Enterprise*. The mission of the crew was to "seek out new life and new civilizations" in the universe. The main characters were Captain James Kirk and Officer Spock, a creature born of a father from the planet Vulcan and a mother from the planet Earth. The original TV series inspired five Hollywood movies featuring the Star Trek characters and different voyages of the *Enterprise*. In 1987 a new series, *Star Trek: The Next Generation,* was created. It is set in the 24th century and has as its main characters Captain Jean-Luc Picard, Commander William Riker, and Lieutenant Commander Data, an android. *Star Trek* has many loyal fans (known as "Trekkies"). The fans have regular conventions where they gather to exchange anecdotes about the series, listen to guest speakers talk about Star Trek themes, and buy and sell Star Trek merchandise such as T-shirts and buttons.

PREVIEW

FUNCTIONS/THEMES	LANGUAGE	FORMS
Debate an issue Support an argument	I'm against/in favor of teaching young children to cook. I agree/strongly disagree with that. A twelve-month school year is efficient. Furthermore, students won't forget what they've learned.	Conjunctions
Express regret Talk about hopes and wishes	I wish I'd learned to play a musical instrument when I was young. I hope I passed the test. I wish I'd passed the test.	*Hope* vs. *wish* in past time

Preview the reading.

1. Look at the photos below and discuss these questions in small groups: Have you ever seen any TV programs featuring the characters in the photos? If so, what is the name of the program? What is it about? If you're not familiar with the photos here, have you ever seen a movie or TV program about future life in outer space? What's your opinion about the possibility of such future life?

2. Before you read the article on page 2, look at the title and the pictures on pages 2–3. What do you think the article is about? Discuss your answer with a partner. Also discuss a possible answer to the question in the title.

1.

Space Stations:

Do they have a future?

Life on the space shuttle.

Many years from now, when people regularly take their vacations in outer space, they will look back on the twentieth century and try to date the beginning of the space age. Some will say it all started with the launching of Sputnik in 1957, others will point to Neil Armstrong's first steps on the moon in 1969, and still others will mention the birth of the space shuttle—a spacecraft that could be used more than once to make space travel much less expensive. But at least a few will emphasize that the true beginning was the creation of populated space stations.

A space station will actually be a home in space. It will be designed so that many people can live and work for a longer time than they would be able to in an ordinary crowded spacecraft. Through the doors of a space station spacecraft will leave for the moon or even Mars at a fraction of the cost of launching them from Earth. In the space station's "rooms," astronauts and scientists will conduct important experiments in fields ranging from astronomy to chemistry.

The space station will have facilities for sleeping, bathing, exercising, eating, and relaxing. When it's time to sleep, astronauts will zip up in sleeping bags that hang from the wall. To shower in space, feet will be strapped down and water hosed on. Then the water will be sucked up by a device like a vacuum cleaner. This water will then be purified and recycled, as will the water for washing clothes. Astronauts will use a variety of exercise equipment to stay in shape, exercising about two hours a day. Food will be stored on the space station in one of two forms—dried or frozen. When astronauts want to eat, they will add liquid to dried food, or heat frozen food in a microwave oven. New supplies and fresh fruits and vegetables could be brought to the stations by shuttles. Astronauts will relax by watching videos, using the computer, reading, and talking to friends and family on Earth via radio.

Many expectations could be conducted on space station laboratories. Animals will be brought up into space to study the effects of weightlessness. Some will be living in the same conditions as the astronauts, while others will inhabit an area that is kept spinning to achieve a centrifuge force equal to Earth's gravity. These animals could then be studied to observe similarities and differences among the two groups in space and a control group on Earth. The lack of gravity in space also has benefits, mainly in the area of technology and manufacturing. Perhaps new alloys can be created from metals that do not mix on Earth. Computers and solar cells use crystals that could grow better in space. In the area of medicine, there is hope of new drugs being created that are purer and easier to manufacture.

And if space stations are successful, the next step may very well be space cities. Scientists believe that the benefits of space cities will far outweigh their costs. These space cities will help solve today's most pressing problems, among them overpopulation, the energy crisis, and pollution.

Not everyone agrees that we even need a space station, let alone space cities. Some scientists think that much experimentation and study must be done here on Earth before space stations are workable. They aren't sure that we should spend billions of dollars on a project whose technology is not yet established and whose benefits to the human race are still in question. These scientists think that the money could be better spent on shorter-range scientific research.

Nevertheless, an international partnership made up of the U.S., Japan, Canada, and ten European nations has been working on plans for Freedom—a space station designed both as a place for experimentation and research and as a spaceport for peopled trips to Mars. Begun in 1984, the program is struggling to continue despite criticism and budget cutbacks. Over the next few years, important decisions about the future of the Freedom space station, and the future of space exploration as a whole, will be made.

1. Space Stations: Do they have a future?

*The first lesson of every unit begins with a **reading** that presents a particular theme or topic which is then further explored in one or more of the subsequent lessons. Students focus on the receptive task of reading so they can absorb new language items without feeling pressure to speak. The **Figure it out** exercises are designed to test and enhance comprehension without requiring students to use the new language actively. This does not mean that you should discourage students from speaking. It simply means that you should give them this time for the new language to "sink in" if they need it. Active practice begins on p. 4.*

PROCEDURE

■ Point out the pictures on pp. 2 and 3 and read aloud the captions as the students follow along in their books. Answer any questions students have about the pictures and the captions.

■ Have the students read through the article. Tell them not to stop to look up every unfamiliar word during the first reading, but rather to try to get the general meaning of the article.

■ After the students have read through the article a first time, you may want to have them summarize it. Then they can read the article again. You may also want to play the cassette or read the article aloud. As they read a second time, have them find the meanings of any unfamiliar words by asking a classmate or by looking the words up in a dictionary.

Figure it out

1. Read the article.

- Tell the students to work with a partner to discuss any changes they made to item 2 on p. 1. Then call on different students to share any changes with the class.
- Help the students with unfamiliar vocabulary or structures. (See the Methodology Note which follows.)

METHODOLOGY NOTE

When students have problems understanding unfamiliar grammatical structures at any point in the book, you can use one or more of the following procedures:

1. Draw a diagram on the board to indicate the verb tense(s) or time sequence involved.
2. Provide several one-sentence examples.
3. If appropriate, act out the meaning of the structure.
4. Make reference to a similar structure in the students' native language.

For unfamiliar vocabulary items:

1. Refer students to the surrounding context for clues to the meaning of the items.
2. Write new words on the board. Then, if appropriate, act them out or use the following techniques and materials to help students understand the meanings: gestures, realia, visuals graphics, and charts.
3. Explain unknown items with words already understood by the student.
4. Allow students to consult with their classmates for information about new words and to share word meanings.
5. Have students use dictionaries to find the meanings of words which are still unknown at this point.
6. For items still not understood, allow for translation from the native language.
7. Have students keep written logs and make audio tapes of new words and their definitions for home study.

2. Look through the article for advantages and disadvantages of spending money on space stations.

- Tell the students to read through the instructions. Answer any questions about the procedure.
- Have the students do the exercise on separate paper. When they finish, tell them to compare answers with a partner. Next call on different students to each read their answers aloud.

POSSIBLE ANSWERS

advantages
Many experiments can be conducted on space station laboratories.
Benefits may result in the areas of technology, manufacturing, and medicine.

disadvantages
Money may be wasted on a project whose technology is not yet established and whose benefits to the human race are still in question.

The article argues more strongly *for* spending money on space stations.

3. Scan the article and find the paragraph that...

- Read the instructions aloud and have different students read the exercise items. Answer any questions. Make sure the students understand what it means to "scan the article." (See the Methodology Note which follows.) Point out the paragraph numbers in the article.
- Have the students do the exercise and then check their answers with a partner. Then call on different students to say the answers.

ANSWERS
1. 3   2. 1   3. 5   4. 4   5. 7   6. 6

METHODOLOGY NOTE

Scanning is a reading technique in which the reader samples the text rather than reads word for word. Scanning involves first knowing which specific information to look for. To teach students to scan, tell them to read over the text quickly and look only for the information they have been asked to find. For example, in the first exercise item above, students should be told to look specifically for the word *facilities*.

4. ...Find the words in the article, and say if they are used as nouns or verbs.

- Ask a student to read aloud the instructions. Then have the students repeat the words in the list and those in the box after you. If necessary, review the difference between a verb and a noun.
- Tell the students to do the exercise and then compare answers with a partner. Then call on different students to share their answers with the class.

ANSWERS
1. verb	5. noun	9. verb	13. noun
2. noun	6. verb	10. noun	
3. verb	7. verb	11. verb	
4. verb	8. verb	12. noun	

OPTION

Have the students use the words in the box in sentences that show they know the meanings of the words. For example:

Acceptable
The teacher said my conduct shows I know how to behave well.
Unacceptable
He talked about conduct.

They can also use the words in the list, first as verbs and then as nouns, in sentences. Tell them to write their sentences on separate paper. When they finish, have them compare sentences with a partner. Finally, call on different students to read their sentences aloud and write them on the board for you to check.

FOLLOW-UP

Students can use the six items in exercise 3 to write a brief summary of the article.

WORKBOOK Lesson 1, p. 1. *Upon completion of the Student Book lesson, assign the corresponding Workbook page or pages.*

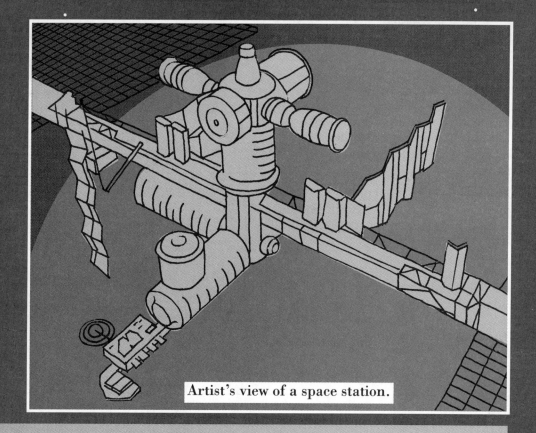

Artist's view of a space station.

Figure it out

1. Read the article. If necessary, change your answers to item 2 on page 1.

2. Look through the article for advantages and disadvantages of spending money on space stations. List the advantages and disadvantages. Then state whether the article argues more strongly for or against spending money on space stations.

3. Scan the article and find the paragraph that . . .

1. describes the facilities of space stations of the future.
2. discusses the early history of the space age.
3. discusses the plans for space cities.
4. describes experiments that will be carried out on space stations.
5. discusses plans for the Freedom space station.
6. gives reasons for opposing space stations.

4. Many words in English can be used as either nouns or verbs with no change in spelling or form. (In some cases, however, the stress or pronunciation may differ.) Find the words below in the article, and say if they are used as nouns or verbs. The words are listed in the order in which they appear.

1. date
2. travel
3. work
4. conduct
5. time
6. use
7. heat
8. study
9. use
10. step
11. need
12. study
13. project

Compare:

Noun	Verb
cónduct	condúct
use [yus]	use [yuz]
próject	projéct

2. I don't agree...

1. Which of the following do you feel a country should spend the most money on? Rank the items in order of importance from 1 to 6. Then discuss your decision with a partner, giving arguments to support it.

_____ child care   _____ housing
_____ education   _____ scientific research
_____ health care   _____ space travel

 A group of college students is discussing the pros and cons of the space program.

Listen to the conversation.

Ramón We're here to discuss the space program. We have a limited amount of time, so let's get started.

Louisa I think the space program is a waste of money. Think of all the research scientists could be doing on disease with that money. Furthermore, the money is coming out of the taxpayers' pockets.

Ramón I'll admit that a lot has been spent on the program. However, I don't agree that the money has been wasted. The research they've done for the space program has brought all sorts of advances in other areas—in geology, medicine, manufacturing . . .

Keiko Not to mention all the new jobs the space program has created.

Louisa Well, I suppose some people have benefited from the program. Nevertheless, I still wish all this money had been put into something more useful—like cancer research, for instance.

Ramón But experiments involving medicine are being done on the space shuttle.

Keiko I think the space program is very useful and that someday we may be able to use the knowledge we've gained to live in outer space.

Andy Even if we understood perfectly how to live in outer space, the human race would never be able to survive there.

Ramón How can you be so sure of that? Not too long ago no one would have believed we could go to the moon.

Andy That may be, but the present is _here_, on Earth. Therefore, the money should be spent on problems the world faces right now.

Ramón Well, sorry, but that's all the time we have today. Let's continue our discussion tomorrow.

3. Find another way to say the words or expressions in italics.

1. The space program is a waste of money. _What's more_, taxpayers are paying for it.
2. The space program has been expensive. _But_ it has advanced science and created jobs.
3. _Even so_, the money should have been spent on cancer research.
4. People don't live in space now. _So_ we should spend our money here on Earth.

2. I don't agree . . .

1. Warm-up Activity

This activity is always related to the conversation which follows. It helps prepare students for the conversation by getting them personally involved in an activity which is similar to the situation or topic of the conversation.

- Have the students follow along in their books as you read aloud the information and instructions in the box. Then have them work with a partner to discuss their decisions.

- Go around the classroom and check the pairs' work. Then call on different pairs to share their decisions and discussions with the class.

2. Conversation

BACKGROUND

A group of college students is discussing the pros and cons of the space program. The discussion is being led by a student named Ramón.

LANGUAGE

...coming out of the taxpayer's pockets. is an idiomatic expression usually used when referring to wasteful spending by the government. It's another way of saying "being paid by the taxpayers."

...all sorts means *many different kinds.*

Not to mention really means the opposite of what it says. It's another way of saying "In addition, I should mention."

...put into is another way of saying "spent on."

Even if we understood is another way of saying "Although we may someday understand."

That may be is short for *That may be true.*

...right now means *at the present time.*

...that's all the time we have is another way of saying "we don't have any more time (to spend)."

PROCEDURE

- As the class members examine the illustration, point out the students and the setting. Ask a student to describe what's happening in the picture.

- Play the cassette or read the conversation aloud as the students follow along in their books. (If you are reading the conversation aloud, speak at a normal speed and perform each role as realistically as possible. Show the change in speakers by shifting your position or by pointing to the appropriate character in the illustration.) If appropriate, read the conversation aloud with a student. Students can listen to the conversation as many times as they need to in order to understand the language introduced.

3. Find another way to say the words or expressions in italics.

- Call on different students to read aloud the exercise sentences. Answer any questions.

- Tell the students to do the exercise and then compare answers with a partner. Then call on different students to read the answers aloud. Ask a student to write the answers on the board for you to check.

ANSWERS
1. Furthermore
2. However
3. Nevertheless
4. Therefore

OPTION 1

Point out the characters in the illustration and have class members guess the names of the different students (Ramón, Louisa, etc.). Tell the class members who guess to give a reason for their guesses.

OPTION 2

Have the students work in groups of four to continue the conversation. Go around the classroom and join in the discussions. Finally, call on different groups to share their continued discussions with the class.

CULTURE CLOSE-UP

Space exploration in the U.S. is administered by a government agency called NASA, which stands for the National Aeronautics and Space Administration. NASA was formed in 1958 and is an independent civilian agency directly responsible to the president. NASA's biggest breakthrough in space exploration was to put a man on the moon, achieved during the Apollo Program in the 1960s. Other projects include the Skylab space station, the Viking Mars landers, and the Voyager probes of the outer planets. NASA is also responsible for conducting many other space and earth-science programs. In the late 1970s, NASA developed the reusable space shuttle to make access to space cheaper and easier.

FOLLOW-UP

Students can write out the arguments they used to support their answers to the question in exercise 1.

WORKBOOK Lesson 2, p. 2

3. I disagree with that.

Have the students make up compound sentences with *but* to express contrasts. Write an example on the board:

A space program costs a lot of money, but it can help us in the future.

Call on different students to say their statements.

DEBATE AN ISSUE

- Tell the students to read over the conversation. Answer any questions. Then have them listen to the conversation. You can act it out with five students.

- Point out the box and ask different students to read the opinions aloud. Then read aloud the second set of instructions. Next point out the words *Besides, Even so, but,* and *so* in the conversation. Ask a student to substitute *What's more* for *Besides* in B's line and read it aloud.

- Have the students work in small groups to act out similar conversations. Go around the classroom and listen in, giving help when needed. Finally, call on different groups to act out their conversations for the class.

- Call on two students to read aloud the Editorial and the Editorial Rebuttal. Answer any questions students have about the vocabulary and structures. Then read aloud the first set of instructions.

- Point out the box on the left and ask different students to read the questions aloud. Then point out the box on the right and have the students repeat the expressions after you. Answer any questions.

- Have the students work with a partner to write their editorials. Go around the room and answer any questions the pairs have about their work.

- Read aloud the second set of instructions. Then have the pairs exchange editorials and write their rebuttals. When they finish, tell the pairs to exchange rebuttals. Finally, call on different pairs; have one partner read their original editorial and the other the rebuttal.

OPTION

Stage a class debate. Work with the students to come up with a controversial issue which class members will be more or less equally divided about in their opinions. Divide the class into teams A (in favor of the issue) and B (opposed to the issue). Tell the team members to work together to prepare statements which support their positions. Next call on alternate team members to state their positions. Encourage team members to counter the opposing team's arguments and to draw conclusions.

3. I disagree with that.

 1
- ▶ **Listen to the conversation.**
- ▶ **Act out similar conversations, using one of the opinions in the box or a different opinion. Use** *what's more* **or** *besides* **when you support an argument,** *but* **or** *even so* **when you counter an argument, and** *so* **when you draw a conclusion.**

A I'm against teaching young children to cook. They usually make a mess and waste food.

B I agree. Besides, children can hurt themselves.

C Even so, I think children *should* learn how to cook. Everyone should learn to be self-sufficient.

D That's how I feel. Cooking isn't dangerous if children are taught safety rules.

E Well, I'm in favor of teaching girls to cook, but it's a waste of time to teach boys.

F I strongly disagree with that. Everyone eats, so everyone should know how to fix a meal.

Some opinions
Children should(n't) learn to cook.
Children should(n't) make their own decisions.
People should(n't) have to retire at a certain age.
Employees should(n't) call their bosses by their first names.
A person should(n't) get married before the age of thirty.

2
- ▶ **Read the Editorial and Editorial Rebuttal below. Then find a partner who agrees with you on one of the issues in the box. Work together and write a short editorial supporting your point of view.**
- ▶ **Exchange your editorial with a pair of students who took the other point of view, and write an answer to their editorial. Use some of the expressions in the box.**

Are you for or against . . .
a twelve-month school year?
building more nuclear power plants?
spending more money on scientific research?
more child-care programs for working parents?
free university education for all students?
universal government-sponsored health coverage?

Some expressions	
First of all . . . Furthermore/Moreover . . .	◀ support an argument
But . . . However . . . Nevertheless . . .	◀ counter an argument
Therefore . . .	◀ draw a conclusion

Editorial

Time for a Twelve-Month School Year

The time has come to extend the school year to twelve months. If students attend school all year, they won't have the usual three months of summer vacation to forget what they've learned during the previous nine months. Moreover, there will be less risk of students' getting into trouble because they have too much unstructured time. Furthermore, a twelve-month school year will allow us to make full use of our public school facilities. We taxpayers should not have to pay for the upkeep of buildings that go unused for three months every year. Students may not like the idea of going to classes all year round. However, teachers and taxpayers will agree that it makes more sense than the traditional academic year.

– Alberto Campos

Editorial Rebuttal

Let's Keep the Nine-Month School Year

The twelve-month school year proposed by Alberto Campos in last week's paper may sound like a good idea to tired parents and dissatisfied taxpayers. Nevertheless, there are a lot of people who would be adversely affected by it. First of all, many students use the three months of summer vacation to earn the money they use to pay for books, clothing, and other necessary items during the school year. There are also many businesses whose customers are students on summer vacation. If the school year is extended to twelve months, summer camps for young people, like the one we operate, would be forced to close, and all of our employees would be out of work. The nine-month school year has worked well for a long time. Therefore, let's not try to fix what isn't broken.

– Carol and Roger Jenkins
Rolling Hills Summer Camp

3 ▸ **Study the frames: Conjunctions**

A twelve-month school year is efficient.	What's more, Besides Furthermore, Moreover,	students won't forget what they've learned.
A nine-month school year gives students longer vacations.	However, Even so, Nevertheless,	school buildings go unused for three months.
A nine-month school year gives students longer vacations,	but	school buildings go unused for three months.
A nine-month school year has worked well for a long time.	Therefore,	we should keep the traditional academic year.
A nine-month school year has worked well for a long time,	so	we should keep the traditional academic year.

Furthermore and *moreover* connect two ideas that support each other. These words mean *and*.

However and *nevertheless* connect ideas that counter each other. These words mean *but*.

Therefore introduces a logical conclusion.

In formal writing, do not start a new sentence with *but* or *so*.
If you are connecting two short ideas with the other conjunctions, you may use a semicolon (;) rather than start a new sentence.
   A nine-month school year has worked well; therefore, we should keep it.

 4 ▸ **Listen to the conversations. Does the second speaker in each conversation** *support the argument* **or** *counter the argument* **of the first speaker?**
Check (√) the correct column.

SUPPORTS THE ARGUMENT   COUNTERS THE ARGUMENT

1. _____   _____
2. _____   _____
3. _____   _____
4. _____   _____
5. _____   _____

5 ▸ **The principal of a high school is going to give a speech to the students. Rewrite the speech, using at least three of these conjunctions:** *furthermore, moreover, however, nevertheless,* **and** *therefore.*

It has recently come to my attention that some students have not been attending classes regularly. This is a very serious situation. You cannot get good grades if you do not attend classes. You cannot qualify for a good job. It's true that many employers don't look at grades. Employers do want employees who are well educated, responsible, and have a positive attitude. I've heard several students say that classes are boring. If you have a positive attitude toward the material, you will see that it can be interesting. A good education is the most valuable of all possessions. I urge all of you to attend classes regularly.

DEBATE AN ISSUE • SUPPORT AN ARGUMENT • CONJUNCTIONS

- Have the students examine the frames as you call on different class members to read aloud the possible sentences. Answer any questions.

- Point out the boxes and read aloud the information in them as the students follow along in their books. Answer any questions.

OPTION

On the board, write the following incomplete sentences:

All students need time to relax; therefore,
Watching too much TV hurts the eyes; furthermore,

Tell the students to complete the sentences. Then call on different students to read aloud their completed sentences for you to check.

Have the students write similar incomplete sentences of their own, using the conjunctions in the frame and appropriate punctuation. Then have them exchange sentences with a partner and complete their partner's sentences. Next have the partners read over and check each other's sentences. Finally, call on different pairs to read aloud their sentences and write them on the board.

METHODOLOGY NOTE

To help students understand the structures in the frames from this and other exercises throughout the book, it may be useful to have them locate occurrences of these structures in the opening reading and the conversation from lesson 2.

- Read aloud the instructions. Answer any questions about the exercise procedure.

- Have the students listen to the conversation and check the appropriate column. You can have them listen as often as necessary. Finally, call on different students to say the answers.

TAPESCRIPT

1. **A** You know, I'm all in favor of a 12-month school year. For one thing, my kids won't forget all the math they've learned the year before. What's more, they won't get into trouble with less free time on their hands.
   B Nevertheless, you have to consider some of the disadvantages. Just think of all the kids who get full-time jobs in the summer to pay for their expenses during the school year. They'll be out of luck. Moreover, . . .

2. **A** I think the more money we spend on scientific research, the stronger we become as a nation. Furthermore, scientific breakthroughs that result from this research make our lives easier.
   B That's right, and besides, we need research to find solutions to the many problems we have.

3. **A** I'm all for free university education. After all, education is a basic right that should be accessible to everyone. And furthermore . . . free university education means a better educated society.
   B Even so, just think of the cost. We may end up with a better educated society, but we'll be poorer at the same time!

4. **A** I don't like the idea of universal health coverage. It'll mean more government intervention in our affairs and more red tape.
   B That's for sure! What's more, it'll mean higher taxes for all of us.

5. **A** I'm really in favor of that new proposal to have criminals do service in the community instead of just having them spend all their time locked up in a jail cell.
   B I agree. Besides, that way we tax payers will get something in return for all the money it's costing us to house those criminals. The only thing is . . . I'm not so sure hard-core offenders should be allowed to participate in the program. Other than that, it sounds good to me.

ANSWERS

	SUPPORTS THE ARGUMENT	COUNTERS THE ARGUMENT
1.	___	✓
2.	✓	___
3.	___	✓
4.	✓	___
5.	✓	___

- Ask a student to read aloud the instructions. Answer any questions about the procedure. Then have the students read over the speech. Answer any questions. Next have the students rewrite the speech.

- Tell the students to compare their rewritten speeches with a partner. Next call on a different students to read aloud the sentences from the rewritten speech.

ANSWERS

. . . You cannot get good grades if you do not attend classes. Moreover, you cannot qualify for a good job. It's true that many employers don't look at grades. Nevertheless, employers do want employees who re well educated, responsible, and have a positive attitude. I've heard several students say that classes are boring. However, if you have a positive attitude toward the material, you will see that it can be interesting. A good education is the most valuable of all possessions. Therefore, I urge all of you to attend classes regularly.

- Have the students examine the frames as you call on different class members to read aloud the sentences in them.

- Read aloud the information in the boxes. Answer any questions students have about the use of *hope* vs. *wish* in past time. If necessary, review the past perfect tense.

OPTION

Have the students work in pairs to write down sentences of their own like those in the frames on the left. When they finish, have them exchange papers with other pairs and write matching sentences with *hope* and *wish* like those in the frames on the right. Then call on different pairs to read aloud their sentences and write them on the board.

- Have the students read over the conversation. Answer any questions. Then have them listen to the conversation. You can have two students act out the conversation and complete it.

- Point out the box and ask different students the questions in it. You can also call on different class members to ask their classmates the questions.

- Read aloud the second set of instructions. Then have the students work in pairs to act out similar conversations.

- Go around the room and listen in on the conversations, giving help when needed. Finally, call on different pairs to act out their conversations for the class.

- Point out the illustration and ask a student to describe it. Then read aloud the first set of instructions.

- Tell the students to read over the exercise items. Have a student tell the class which exercise item the illustration pertains to (item 1). Point out the pothole in the illustration. Answer any questions about the exercise items. Then have the students do the exercise.

- Tell the students to compare answers with a partner. Then call on different students to read aloud their answers and write them on the board.

POSSIBLE ANSWERS
1. Eileen wishes she'd watched where she was going.
   She hopes she didn't damage her car.
2. Marie hopes Stella got the letter.
   She wishes she'd written to her sooner.
3. George hopes no one took his briefcase.
   He wishes he'd remembered to take it with him.
4. Masa wishes he could have kept working full time at his company.
   He hopes he gets the job at the other company.

OPTION

Have the students write down five "hopes" and five "wishes" they have. Remind them to use the words *hope* and *wish* in past time. Collect the sentences and in your spare time, make note of any errors by simply checking (✓) or circling them. Then return the sentences to the students and have them rewrite them to include any necessary corrections.

Call on different students to read aloud their sentences. You can have the class members report on the hopes and wishes they hear. For example:

Student A says "I hope I passed the last English exam."
The class members write "(*Student's name*) hopes he/she passed the last English exam."

FOLLOW-UP

Students can write complete sentence answers to the questions in the box in exercise 7.

6 ▶ **Study the frames:** *Hope* **vs.** *wish* **in past time**

Past time
I might have passed the test.
Tom might have quit his job.

▶

| I hope | I passed the test.
Tom didn't quit his job. |
| --- | --- |
| **Past tense form** | |

Use *hope* to talk about something that possibly happened.
    I *hope I passed* the test. (I possibly did.)

Past time
I didn't pass the test.
Tom quit his job.
I couldn't take a vacation.

▶

Past perfect form	
I wish	I had (I'd) passed the test.
Tom hadn't quit his job.
I could have taken a vacation.

Use *wish* to talk about something that's contrary-to-fact.
    I *wish I'd passed* the test. (I didn't.)

 7 ▶ **Listen to the conversation.**
    ▶ **Act out similar conversations with a partner. Use the information in the box or your own information.**

A I wish I'd learned to play a musical instrument when I was young. I love classical music, and I've always wanted to play in an orchestra.

B Well, it's not too late. I know you have a busy schedule, but maybe you should consider taking music lessons. What instrument would you learn to play?

Do you wish you . . .
had learned to play a musical instrument?
had majored in a different subject?
had known your grandparents (better)?
had stayed in touch with your old friends?
hadn't moved when you were young?
hadn't taken your current job?

8 ▶ **Read about these people, and say what they hope and wish about the past.**
    ▶ **Compare your answers with a partner.**

1. Eileen O'Brien wasn't paying attention while she was driving, and she hit a big pothole. She is afraid she might have damaged her car.
   Eileen wishes _____ .
   She hopes _____ .

2. Marie Laporte finally wrote to her friend Stella after three years. Two months later, she still hadn't gotten an answer, and now she's afraid Stella may have moved.
   Marie hopes _____ .
   She wishes _____ .

3. George Burke gave a speech yesterday. When he got home, he realized he'd left his briefcase in the auditorium.
   George hopes _____ .
   He wishes _____ .

4. Masa Asato wanted to keep working full time, but his company asked him to retire. Masa had an interview to be a part-time consultant at another company.
   Masa wishes _____ .
   He hopes _____ .

4. Your turn

Read the newspaper articles. The highlighted words are important for understanding the articles. Try to guess the meaning of the words from the context of the articles. As you read, form your own opinion on these issues: censorship of violence in video games, physical punishment of children in school, and government funding for the arts. Then, working in groups, argue for or against one or more of the issues. Try to support your argument with information in the articles or with your own examples.

VIOLENCE IN VIDEO GAMES

White Pine, Wyoming, usually a quiet town, was the scene of controversy last weekend as a parent group tried to ban the sale of violent video games.

Twenty parents, carrying signs saying "Stop the Violence Before It Begins" and "Protect Our Children Now," demonstrated in front of several stores where video games are sold.

The parent group said that video games have become increasingly violent because of advances in computer technology. "The violence in video games is worse than the violence on TV," one member of the group said. "When children are playing these games, they are actively participating in violent acts." For example, in one popular game whose goal is to become the world's best fighter, the characters' heads are torn off and their hearts are ripped out.

Teenagers who were interviewed outside one store were outraged by the demonstration. "To assume that young people will do whatever they see doesn't say much for their intelligence," said Greg Bryant, 16. "I should be able to buy any game that I choose," said Shelly Woods, 18. "If the demonstrators are against violent video games, they shouldn't buy them for their children. Censorship is not the answer."

🔊 Listen in

Read the statements below. Then listen to a radio discussion. Based on the opinions you hear, decide which person would be more likely to make each statement. Say *Ms. Young* or *Dr. Torres*.

1. Children who move all the time may have trouble in school.
2. People who move a lot are more tolerant and open-minded.
3. Children who move a lot find it easier to get used to new situations later in life.
4. Moving frequently can put a lot of stress on a couple's marriage.

4. Your turn

The **Your turn** activity provides the students with productive practice of some of the functions and structures introduced in the unit.

The **Listen in** activity gives students the opportunity to "overhear" an authentic conversation in English. A listening script is not provided in the student book in order to help prepare students for real-life listening experiences.

- Point out the headlines in the articles on pp. 8 and 9 and call on different students to read them aloud. Have the students guess what the articles are about. Point out the places named in two of the articles—White Pine, Wyoming and San Francisco, California. Point out the architecture in the photo on p. 9. (See the Culture Close-Up which follows.)

- Read the instructions aloud as the students follow along in their books. Answer any questions about the procedure. Then have the students read the article.

- Call on different students to say what they think the highlighted words mean. You can write the correct meanings on the board. Next have the students form their own opinions on the various issues. You can tell them to write down their opinions on separate paper.

- Have the students work in groups to argue for or against one or more of the issues. Remind them to support their arguments with the appropriate information. Go around the room and join in on the discussions. Finally, call on different groups to present their arguments to the class. Encourage class discussion. (See the Methodology Note which follows.)

METHODOLOGY NOTE

This is a fairly unstructured activity and allows for a certain amount of free conversation. For group work involving free conversation or discussion, it is a good idea to assign roles to certain students—for example, the "captain" to ensure that each group member participates; the "noise monitor" to make sure that the group does not disturb other groups; the "secretary" to write down the group's conclusions or findings; and the "reporter" to report the group's work or findings to the class.

CULTURE CLOSE-UP

Wyoming is one of the Mountain States of the western U.S. It's the tenth largest state in area but the least populated state in the nation. Wyoming is rich in energy resources. Its name comes from an Indian term meaning "at the big plains." Its nickname is the "Equality State," earned in 1869 when the women of Wyoming became the first in the U.S. to win the right to vote. The capital of Wyoming is Cheyenne, founded in 1867 as one of the state's earliest permanent settlements.

San Francisco is sometimes called the nation's most beautiful city. Located in western California on a peninsula between the Pacific Ocean and the San Francisco Bay, San Francisco has one of the world's most beautiful natural harbors. The city is a very popular tourist destination because of the spectacular views from its 43 hills, its fascinating architecture, and its famous restaurants.

Listen in

- Read aloud the instructions as the students follow along in their books. So they know what to listen for, have the students read over the statements in their books before they listen to the radio discussion.

- Play the cassette or read the tapescript aloud with two students. If you read the conversations aloud, be sure to use appropriate stress and intonation. After they listen, have the students decide which person would be more likely to make each statement. Then call on different students to share their answers with the class.

TAPESCRIPT

Host Today on *Two-Minute Topics* we're talking to author Ethel Young and the well-known psychologist, Dr. Ramón Torres. Ms. Young, in your book, *On the Move*, you say that frequent moves are good for a family. Don't most experts disagree with you?

Ms. Young It's not a popular opinion, but nevertheless it's true. Living in different places makes kids grow up faster. Furthermore, people who move a lot tend to be more cosmopolitan.

Host What would you say about that, Dr. Torres?

Dr. Torres Well, it's possible that frequent moves might make some people more cosmopolitan; however, a lot of moves can also make families unstable.

Ms. Young I can't agree with that. My family has made thirteen moves in the last twenty years, and we're a very happy and stable family.

Dr. Torres That may be true, but studies have shown that frequent moves are not good for family members, especially children.

Ms. Young Well, I think that if a family is stable to begin with, a change of location can only serve to make the children's lives more interesting. And, as I point out in my book, frequent moves can also help broaden one's horizons.

Host I wish we could talk more on this topic, but our time is up. I want to thank you both for joining us today.

ANSWERS
1. Dr. Torres
2. Ms. Young
3. Ms. Young
4. Dr. Torres

FOLLOW-UP

Students can write brief summaries of one of the articles on pp. 8 and 9.

WORKBOOK Lessons 3-4, pp. 3-5

Family *Sues* School for Slapping Child

A Westway couple was awarded $15,000 by a circuit judge after their ten year old accidentally had a tooth knocked out when he was slapped by his teacher, Mrs. Gertrude Wells, 47.

In his testimony, Robert Farrington, 10, described how his teacher had slapped him across the face for bringing a live frog into the classroom and "creating a serious disruption."

Mrs. Wells may face suspension, depending on the decision of the local school board.

"I am extremely sorry about the tooth," commented Mrs. Wells, "and I did not mean to lose control. This child, however, was always misbehaving. I was really fed up with him. This was the third time in a week I had lost at least a half hour of class time because of his behavior."

LOW INCOME HOUSING FOR ARTISTS APPROVED

SAN FRANCISCO, CA., May 30—The housing commission has approved the conversion of two apartment buildings on Sunrise Street to low-income housing for artists, writers, and people in the performing arts.

Although some local artists felt the decision was "long overdue," there was a great deal of opposition in the community. "These buildings provided low-income housing for poor families," said one area resident. "They will be forced out into the street."

"I feel sorry for the families who will have to move," commented Sally Fisher, a dancer. "However, if the arts are going to survive, the government will have to support them."

5. On your own

1. **Listen to people's opinions about the different issues in the box below. Then form your own opinions and agree or disagree with the ones stated.**

- a ban on smoking in public places
- a twelve-month school year
- criminals doing service in the community
- universal health coverage

2. **Write an editorial for a newspaper, choosing one of the options below.**

1. Give your opinion on one of the issues you discussed in Lesson 4. Support your arguments, counter any opposing arguments, and then draw a conclusion.

2. Support your point of view on any issue that is of concern to you. Draw a conclusion if possible.

5. On your own

This activity serves as the culminating event for the unit. It provides students with the opportunity to perform in writing the function which was the focus of the unit. Often this activity also has the students practice the auxiliary skills of reading, listening, and/or speaking.

PROCEDURE

- As the students follow along in their books, read aloud the instructions for item 1. Answer any questions students have about the activity. Then ask different students to read aloud the issues stated in the box.

- Have the students listen to the interview as many times as necessary. Then have them write down their opinions. Next call on different students to tell the class their opinions.

TAPESCRIPT

Interviewer Young man, what do you think about the idea of going to school twelve months a year instead of only nine?

Male You must be kidding! I need to work in the summer to pay for the school year. Besides, nine months of studying is enough!

Interviewer Excuse me, ma'am . . . I'd like to know your opinion about the government-sponsored universal health coverage being proposed. . . .

Female I'm totally opposed to it! *That* way I won't be able to choose the doctor I want; the government will do it for me. What's more, we'll all end up paying more taxes.

Interviewer Sir, I'd like to know what you think about the idea of allowing criminals to shorten their time in prison by doing service in the community.

Male I'm all for it! I think that's one way to rehabilitate certain kinds of criminals. And furthermore, it'll save us taxpayers a lot of money.

Interviewer Young lady, I'd like to know what you think about banning smoking in all public places, including restaurants and airports.

Female I'm definitely in favor of it. I like the idea of being able to eat in a restaurant or cafeteria without having to breathe in someone else's smoke.

- Read aloud the general and specific instructions for item 2. Tell the students how long you want their editorials to be. Tell them to make up a title or headline after they've finished writing. Remind them to use appropriate punctuation and capitalization.

- Have the students share and discuss their editorials with a partner. Then go around the classroom and check the students' work. Answer any questions students have about grammar, punctuation, and capitalization. Finally, call on different students to write their editorials on the board and read them aloud for the class.

OPTION

Bring to class (or have the students bring) two editorials from an English-language newspaper. Make copies and give half the class one editorial and half the class the other. Tell the students to write rebuttals to the editorials they received. When they finish, have the students compare rebuttals with a partner in their group. Next have the members of each group exchange editorials with the other group and write rebuttals to the second editorial. When they finish, have the group members compare and discuss their rebuttals with a partner's rebuttals.

WORKBOOK Lesson 5, p. 6. Before assigning the writing task, point out the first sentence of the editorial. Explain that it's the main or "topic" sentence for the paragraph. Remind the students to include topic sentences in their rebuttals.

CULTURE CLOSE-UP

Smoking in indoor public places is becoming extremely rare in the U.S. This is largely due to widespread public awareness of the health hazards caused by smoking itself as well by "second hand smoke"—smoke inhaled by someone who doesn't smoke. The result of such awareness has been the passage of laws in many states which ban smoking in public places such as hospitals, schools, libraries, and government office buildings. In some states, smoking is also banned in non-government office buildings and restaurants.

PREVIEW

Before you begin teaching, go over the functions/themes, language, and forms in the chart. This will give you a preview of what you will encounter as you guide the students through the unit.

Preview the reading.

- Point out the photo and ask a student to describe what's happening in it. Then read aloud the instructions for the first exercise.

- Have the students work with a partner to discuss the questions in exercise 1. Then discuss the questions with the entire class. (The person in the picture is the first black president of South Africa, Nelson Mandela.)

- Tell the pairs to work on exercise 2. When they finish, read the question aloud and call on different students to share their answers with the class.

FUNCTIONS/THEMES	LANGUAGE	FORMS
Describe yourself Describe someone else	How would you describe yourself? I'm a reliable person. I consider myself hardworking. What do you think of him? I can't see him working with kids. He seems too indecisive.	Verbs followed by direct objects + noun, adjective, or verb complements
Make a recommendation	Why don't you go to Mario Zanelli? Mario always cuts my hair however I ask him to.	Question words with -ever

Preview the reading.

1. Work with a partner. Do you know the name of the man in the photo below? He is famous for fighting against discrimination. What does the word *discrimination* mean? In what areas of the world is there discrimination?

2. Before you read the article on pages 12–13, look at the title and the photos. How do you think the article will relate to discrimination? Discuss your ideas with a partner.

Jesse Owens

An Athlete's Life in Retrospect

by Frank Litsky

Jesse Owens receiving a gold medal at the 1936 Olympic Games.

Jesse Owens, whose four gold medals at the 1936 Olympic Games in Berlin made him perhaps the greatest and most famous athlete in track and field history, never received much recognition at the time of his success. The victim of racial discrimination and of the times in which he lived, Owens ultimately created his place in history through his own inner courage and determination. Today Owens is remembered not only as a great athlete, but as someone with great moral integrity who believed in the old-fashioned values of honesty and hard work.

■ Father Was a Sharecropper

James Cleveland Owens was born September 12, 1913, in Danville, Alabama, the son of a sharecropper and the grandson of slaves. The youngster picked cotton until he and his family moved to Cleveland when he was 9. There, a schoolteacher asked the youth his name.

"J.C." he replied.

She thought he had said "Jesse," and he had a new name.

He ran his first race at age 13. After high school, he went to Ohio State University, paying his way as a $100-a-month night elevator operator because he had no athletic scholarship. As a sophomore, in the Big Ten championship games in 1935, he set even more records than he would in his Olympic glory a year later.

A week before the Big Ten meet, Owens accidentally fell down a flight of stairs. His back hurt so much that he could not exercise all week, and he had to be helped in and out of the car that drove him to the Big Ten meet. In an unsuccessful attempt to lessen the back pain, Owens sat for a half hour in a hot tub. He still rejected suggestions that he withdraw and said he would try, event by event.

He did try, and the results are in the record book. On May 25, 1935, Jesse Owens equaled the world record for the 100-yard dash (9.4 seconds), broke the world record for the broad jump (now called the long jump) with his only attempt (26 feet 8 1/4 inches), broke the world record for the 220-yard dash (20.3 seconds), and broke the world record for the 220-yard low hurdles (22.6 seconds).

■ Overcomes Racial Prejudice

The stage was set for Owens's victory at the Olympic Games in Berlin the next year, and his triumph would come to be regarded as not only athletic but also political. Although Adolph Hitler had intended the Berlin games to reinforce the Nazi doctrine of Aryan supremacy, the United States Olympic track team of 66 athletes included ten African-Americans, and six of the individual gold medals in track won by American men were won by black athletes. Owens was the hero, winning the 100-meter dash in 10.3 seconds, the 200-meter dash in 20.7 seconds, and the broad jump at 26 feet 5 1/2 inches. He also headed the United States team that won the 400-meter relay in 39.8 seconds.

Hitler did not congratulate any of the African-American winners, a subject to which Mr. Owens addressed himself for the rest of his life.

"It was all right with me," he said years later. "I didn't go to Berlin to shake hands with him, anyway. All I know is that I'm here now and Hitler isn't."

Having returned from Berlin, he received no telephone call from the president of his own country, either. In fact, he was not honored by the United States until 1976, four years before his death, when he was awarded the Presidential Medal of Freedom. Three years later, he received the Living Legends Award.

There were no big contracts for Owens after his Olympic victories. He became a playground janitor because

6. Jesse Owens: An Athlete's Life in Retrospect

PROCEDURE

- Point out the photos on pp. 12 and 13 and read the captions aloud. Answer any questions.

- Have the students read through the article. Follow a procedure similar to that on p. 2 of this book.

Figure it out

1. As you read the article, look for facts that support each of the statements.

- Tell the students to read the instructions. Then ask different students to read aloud the three statements. Answer any questions. Next have the students do the exercise.

- Have the students compare answers with a partner. Then call on different pairs of students; have one partner read aloud the statement from the book and the other the facts that support the statement.

SAMPLE ANSWERS
1. He worked as a night elevator operator to pay his way through college. Even though he was in great pain, he still ran in the Big Ten meet of 1935.
2. He was not congratulated by Hitler after his Olympic victory in 1936. The president of his own country did not congratulate him, either.
3. He was awarded the Presidential Medal of Freedom in 1976. He received the Living Legends Award in 1979. President Carter issued a statement about him at the time of his death.

2. Based on your interpretation of the article, explain the meaning of the sentence.

- Read the sentence aloud and make sure the students understand the meaning. Then have them explain the meaning in their own words. You can have them write down their answers.

- Call on different students to explain the meaning of the sentence. You can write the best explanation on the board.

SAMPLE ANSWER
Owen's victory and the victories of other African-American athletes meant that the Berlin games did not reinforce the Nazi doctrine of Aryan supremacy, as Hitler had wanted. Perhaps more importantly, however, the U.S. government showed that it was also prejudiced towards African-Americans because Owens was not congratulated by his own president after his victory.

3. Look at the following statements, quoted from the article, that Jesse Owens made.

- Have different students read the three statements aloud. Answer any questions. Then tell the students to prepare their explanations of what the statements say about Owen's attitude toward life.

- Call on different students to share their explanations with the class. You can write the best explanation on the board.

SAMPLE ANSWER
Jesse Owens was the type of person who got great personal satisfaction from his accomplishments. He tried to overcome his personal disappointments and did not let himself become bitter about things he could not change.

4. ...Use five words from the list to write sentences about Jesse Owens.

- Make sure the students understand what it means to "form adjectives from nouns." Then have them repeat the list of adjectives after you. You can ask them to say the noun form of the adjectives. (See the Language Note which follows.)

- Have the students write their sentences about Jesse Owens. Go around the room and answer any questions they have about their work. Then call on different students to write their sentences on the board.

SAMPLE ANSWER
Jesse Owens' *athletic* abilities helped him win four gold medals at the 1936 Olympic Games.
Answers will vary.

OPTION

Have the students write sentences of their own to show they know the meaning of the adjectives. Explain that the sentences do not have to be related to Jesse Owens or the article about him. You can write a sample sentence on the board:

A bank is a financial institution.

When they finish, have the students compare their sentences with a partner. Then call on different students to read their sentences aloud and write them on the board.

LANGUAGE NOTE

The noun forms of the adjectives in the list are *athlete, finance, patriot, person, profession, Olympus,* * *race,* and *politics.*

**Olympic* comes from the Greek place name (noun) *Olympus,* a mountain in Greece, fabled home of the ancient Greek gods.

CULTURE CLOSE-UP

The first Olympic games ever held in the U.S. took place in St. Louis, Missouri, in 1904. Since then, the U.S. has sponsored the games in 1932, in 1984, (both times in Los Angeles, California), and in 1996 (in Atlanta, Georgia). More countries attended the games in 1984 than ever before.

FOLLOW-UP

Students can write down their corrected answers to the questions in item 2 of the Preview.

WORKBOOK Lesson 6, p. 7

he could not find another job. He ended his career as an amateur runner and accepted money to race against cars, trucks, motorcycles, and dogs.

"Sure, it bothered me," he said later. "But at least it was an honest living. I had to eat."

In time, however, his gold medals changed his life. "They have kept me alive over the years," he once said. "Time has stood still for me. That golden moment dies hard."

■ Celebrated as a Speaker

By many, Owens will be best remembered as a public speaker. Despite his personal disappointments, his speeches praised the virtues of patriotism, clean living, and fair play. His delivery was spellbinding, and he was once described as a "full-time banquet guest, what you might call a professional good example."

Jesse Owens died of cancer in 1980, at the age of 66. Although Owens was ignored at the time of his success, his personal triumph over prejudice is perhaps best expressed in this statement, which was issued by [United States] President Carter at the time of his death:

"Perhaps no athlete better symbolized the human struggle against tyranny, poverty, and racial bigotry."

Jesse Owens receiving the Presidential Medal of Freedom from United States President Gerald Ford, 1976.

Jesse Owens in a parade in Cleveland, Ohio.

Figure it out

1. **As you read the article, look for facts that support each of the statements below. When you have finished reading, give at least two facts that support each statement.**

   1. Jesse Owens was a man with a great deal of determination who did not give up easily.
   2. Jesse Owens was discriminated against because he was black.
   3. Over time people's feelings and attitudes toward Jesse Owens changed a great deal.

2. **Based on your interpretation of the article, explain the meaning of the sentence below.**

   Jesse Owens's triumph [in the 1936 Olympic Games] would come to be regarded as not only athletic but also political.

3. **Look at the following statements, quoted from the article, that Jesse Owens made. Then explain in a few sentences what you think these statements as a group say about Owens's attitude toward life.**

   1. "I didn't go to Berlin to shake hands with [Hitler], anyway. All I know is that I'm here now and Hitler isn't."
   2. "Sure, it bothered me [that I couldn't find a better job.] But at least it was an honest living. I had to eat."
   3. "[My gold medals] have kept me alive over the years. Time has stood still for me. That golden moment dies hard."

4. **Both the suffixes -ic, as in athletic, and -al, as in personal, are used to form adjectives from nouns. Use five words from the list to write sentences about Jesse Owens.**

athletic	patriotic	professional	racial
financial	personal	Olympic	political

7. You really surprise me.

1. What kind of person does each of these jobs require? Explain to your partner why you would or would not be the right person for one of them.

an athletic instructor   a department store salesperson   a diplomat
a night security guard   a tour guide   a flight attendant

Bill, a tennis instructor at a community center, is talking to his friend Vanessa.

Listen to the conversation.

② 2

Bill Hey, have you heard? Robert is retiring.

Vanessa Oh, really? Well, maybe you'll be made athletic director. Keep your fingers crossed.

Bill Oh, I hope not. Whoever they choose is fine as long as it's not me. I'm the wrong person for that job!

Vanessa Why do you say that? I mean, what kind of person does it take?

Bill Someone with a more easygoing personality.

Vanessa Oh, come on. You seem like someone who could handle anything.

Bill Me? You've got to be kidding. That job would make me much too nervous. Besides, I'm happy with things the way they are. I consider teaching tennis a challenge. It's a chance to get people interested in sports.

Vanessa You really surprise me. I always thought you were more ambitious.

Bill Not really. I take pride in my work. Whatever I do, I like to do well, but I wouldn't call that ambition.

Vanessa So, you really don't think you're cut out for it?

Bill No, I really don't. I just can't imagine myself managing a staff and worrying about finances. I don't handle pressure too well.

Vanessa You know, that's not the impression I have of you at all. That's how I'd describe myself!

3. Say *True, False,* or *It doesn't say.*

1. Bill thinks the athletic director should be easygoing and able to handle pressure.
2. Vanessa thinks Bill is cut out for the job of athletic director.
3. Vanessa would like the job herself.
4. Bill considers himself ambitious.
5. Vanessa thinks she handles pressure well.

7. You really surprise me.

1. Warm-up Activity

- Ask a student to read aloud the instructions. Then have the class repeat the job names after you. Answer any questions about the jobs.

- Have the students work with a partner to do the exercise. When they finish, call on different pairs to share their discussions with the class.

OPTION

Tell the pairs to come up with additional jobs that they feel qualified or unqualified for. Have them continue their discussions about these jobs. Then tell them to share their discussions with another pair of students. Go around the classroom and listen in on the discussions.

2. Conversation

BACKGROUND

Bill, a tennis instructor at a community center, is talking to his friend Vanessa. Vanessa thinks Bill would be a good candidate for the job of athletic director, but Bill disagrees.

LANGUAGE

...be made (athletic director). is another way of saying "be appointed (athletic director)."

Keep your fingers crossed. is an idiomatic expression used when talking about luck. It's like saying "Hope for the best."

Oh, I hope not. is short for *Oh, I hope I won't be made athletic director.*

...as long as means *with the condition that.*

Oh, come on. is an expression of disbelief. It's like saying, "You must be kidding." (See the next entry.)

You've got to be kidding. is also an expression of disbelief. It's like saying "You must be joking."

...I'm happy with things the way they are. is another way of saying "I'm happy with the present situation."

...take pride in (my work) means to be satisfied with (my work).

...cut out for it means *suited for it.*

...handle pressure is another way of saying "work well under stress."

...at all is used to emphasize *not.* It's another way of saying "whatsoever."

PROCEDURE

- As the students examine the illustration, point out the different characters from the conversation. Ask a student to describe what's happening in the picture.

- Follow a procedure similar to that indicated for the opening conversation in the previous unit.

3. Say *True, False,* or *It doesn't say.*

- Tell the students to read over the sentences. You can also have different students read them aloud. Then have the students do the exercise.

- Tell the students to compare and discuss their answers with a partner. Then call on different students to read the answers aloud. Ask a student to write the answers on the board.

ANSWERS
1. True
2. True
3. It doesn't say.
4. False
5. False

FOLLOW-UP

Students can write down corrected versions of the false statements in exercise 3.

WORKBOOK Lesson 7, p. 8

8. I consider myself hardworking.

Tell the class about an athlete you admire or about an Olympic event you've watched. Then call on different students to share similar information with the class.

DESCRIBE YOURSELF • DESCRIBE SOMEONE ELSE

- Tell the students to read over the partial interview. Answer any questions they have. Then have them listen to it. You can read the interview aloud with a student or have two students read it aloud. It may also be a good idea to model a continuation of the interview for the class.

- Point out the boxes and ask different students to read aloud the sentences. Answer any questions. Next point out the vocabulary items in the box on the right and help students understand the meanings. (See the Methodology Note on p. 3.)

- Have a student read aloud the second set of instructions. Then tell the students to act out similar interviews with a partner. Go around the room and listen in on the interviews, giving help if necessary. Finally, call on different pairs to act out their interviews in front of the class.

CULTURE CLOSE-UP

When someone is interviewed for a job in the U.S., it is expected that the person not only answer questions from the interviewer(s) but also be assertive enough to ask any necessary questions about the job and mention personal accomplishments and strengths.

- Read aloud the information about Bob Morgan on the clipboard. Then act out the conversation with a student as the class members follow along in their books.

- Read the instructions aloud. Then point out that "your notes" refers to the information listed on the clipboard. Next have the students read over the information on the clipboard and in the box. Answer any questions.

- Have the students discuss the job candidates with a partner. Tell them to use the conversation in their books as a model. Go around the classroom and listen in on the conversations. Finally, call on different pairs to act out their discussions for the class.

OPTION

Have the students role play job interviews. Tell them to decide on a job they want to be interviewed for. Then have them tell a partner about the job. The partner should take notes and make up questions for an interview. Next have the partners take turns interviewing each other. Encourage them to use their imaginations. Go around the classroom and check the pairs' work. Finally, call on different pairs to act out their interviews for the class.

8. I consider myself hardworking.

1
- ▶ Listen to part of a job interview.
- ▶ Act out a similar interview with a partner. Describe yourself using the descriptions and characteristics in the boxes or your own information. Remember, at an interview you should mention only your *positive* characteristics.

A How would you describe yourself?
B I'm a reliable person. I consider myself hardworking and creative. I enjoy responsibility and I handle pressure well.

Some descriptions
Positive
I'm a reliable person.
I consider myself hardworking.
I enjoy responsibility/a challenge.
I handle pressure well.
Negative
I can't see/imagine him working with kids.
Kids make her nervous.
His coworkers consider him unreliable.
She seems like someone who wouldn't be a good teacher.

Some personal characteristics	
Positive	**Negative**
ambitious	unambitious
cooperative	uncooperative
creative	unimaginative
hardworking	lazy
independent	indecisive
modest	conceited
outgoing, friendly	unfriendly
patient	impatient
reliable, responsible	unreliable, irresponsible
self-confident	insecure
honest, sincere	insincere

2
- ▶ You have interviewed three people for one of the jobs in the box below. Using the information in your notes, discuss the job candidates with your partner. You may also use the descriptions and characteristics in exercise 1.

A I interviewed Bob Morgan yesterday to be our new physical education teacher.
B Oh, I've seen his résumé. What did you think of him?
A He really didn't impress me. To tell you the truth, I can't see him working with kids. He seems too indecisive.
B Have you heard anything about him?
A Nothing very positive. His coworkers consider him unreliable, and I've heard he doesn't handle responsibility too well.

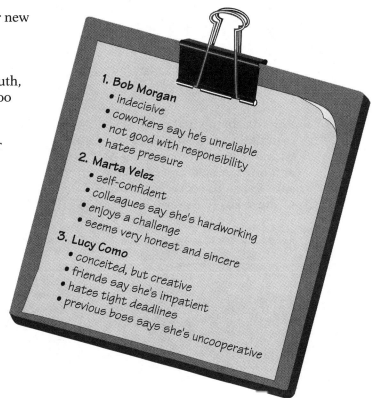

1. **Bob Morgan**
   - indecisive
   - coworkers say he's unreliable
   - not good with responsibility
   - hates pressure

2. **Marta Velez**
   - self-confident
   - colleagues say she's hardworking
   - enjoys a challenge
   - seems very honest and sincere

3. **Lucy Como**
   - conceited, but creative
   - friends say she's impatient
   - hates tight deadlines
   - previous boss says she's uncooperative

Some jobs
a physical education teacher
an art director for the new magazine, *The Great Outdoors*
a sales manager for a computer company
a social director for a large resort hotel
a flight attendant for a major international airline
a nontechnical worker to assist a research team in the Sahara Desert

DESCRIBE YOURSELF • DESCRIBE SOMEONE ELSE • VERBS FOLLOWED BY DIRECT OBJECTS + NOUN, ADJECTIVE, OR VERB COMPLEMENTS

3 ▶ Rate yourself on the chart below. Write *1, 2,* or *3*.
▶ Discuss with a partner why you would or would not be the right person for one of the jobs in exercise 2, using the personal characteristics from the chart.

I think I'd be a good art director because I consider myself creative and outgoing.

1 = very 2 = average 3 = not at all

ambitious	____	modest	____
cooperative	____	outgoing, friendly	____
creative	____	patient	____
hardworking	____	reliable, responsible	____
honest, sincere	____	self-confident	____
independent	____		

4 ▶ Study the frames: Verbs followed by direct objects + noun, adjective, or verb complements

| They | appointed | **him** | **director.** |
| They | made | **her** | **supervisor.** |

▲ noun

| They | consider | **me** | **reliable.** |
| My job | keeps | **me** | **busy.** |

▲ adjective

| I | can't see | **him** | **working** | with kids. |
| They | make | **him** | **lose** | his patience. |

▲ verb

Some verbs and their possible complements

Verb	Noun	Adjective	Base form of verb	Progressive form of verb
appoint	√			
call	√	√		
consider	√	√		
elect	√			
find		√		√
hear			√	√
imagine				√
keep		√		√
make	√	√	√	
see			√	√
watch			√	√

Sense verbs, such as *hear* and *see*, may be followed by either base or progressive forms of verbs.

5 ▶ Rewrite the obituary, completing each sentence with one item from column A and one from column B. Make sure to use the correct tense of the verbs in column A.

Column A	Column B
elect her	doing
watch her	my closest friend
can't imagine myself	laughing and playing
consider her	genuinely sincere
keep me	happy
found her	a lifetime member
make everyone	busy

SONIA MERENDA

Sonia Merenda, who founded the Society for Orphaned Children 62 years ago, died last week after a long illness. For over 60 years, Mrs. Merenda was a dedicated worker at the Society, and last year, the Society *elected her a lifetime member* for her long years of service.

At a memorial service for Mrs. Merenda on Sunday, people expressed their fond memories. "Mrs. Merenda was so good to me as a child," said Claude Duval, now 34. "For many years I _____ . I never lost touch with her, and I would visit her often." Mr. Duval's wife, Miriam, remembers the first time she met Mrs. Merenda. "I _____ , the kind of person everyone likes," she said. "I once _____ with the children for over an hour. She seemed to _____ ."

Sonia Merenda continued to work until several months ago. "My work _____ seven days a week," she said in an interview last year. "But I _____ anything else."

Sonia Merenda will be missed by all of us. Expressions of sympathy may be mailed to the Society for Orphaned Children.

DESCRIBE YOURSELF • DESCRIBE SOMEONE ELSE • VERBS FOLLOWED BY DIRECT OBJECTS + NOUN, ADJECTIVE, OR VERB COMPLEMENTS

- Read aloud the first set of instructions. Point out the chart and explain what it means to "rate yourself." Answer any questions. Then have the students rate themselves on the chart.

- Ask a student to read aloud the second set of instructions. Answer any questions about the procedure. If necessary, model a sample discussion with a student in front of the class.

- Tell the students to have the discussions with a partner. Go around the room and listen in. Finally, call on different pairs to act out their discussion for the class.

- Have the students examine the frames as you and a class member read aloud the sentences. Answer any questions. (See the Language Note which follows.)

- Point out the chart on the right and have the students study it. Read aloud the rule at the bottom of the chart. Answer any questions.

OPTION

Have the students work is small groups to write sentences of their own for the verbs and the patterns outlined in the chart. Remind them to include a direct object—noun or pronoun—immediately after the verb. Write an example on the board:

The teacher considers us responsible.
We elected Paulo class president.

Tell the groups to compare their sentences with other groups. Then call on different group reporters to read aloud their group's sentences and write them on the board for you to check.

LANGUAGE NOTE

The verbs in the frame and the chart can be immediately followed by either direct object pronouns or nouns. For example:

They appointed him director.
They appointed John director.
They appointed your friend director.

- Explain what an obituary is. Then have the students read over the incomplete obituary. Answer any questions.

- Next read the instructions aloud. Point out the words in the columns. Answer any questions.

- Point out and read aloud the sample answer in the first paragraph of the obituary. Then tell the students to rewrite the remainder of the obituary.

- Tell the students to compare answers with a partner. Then call on different students to read aloud the completed sentences and write them on the board. Finally, have a student read aloud the obituary in its entirety.

ANSWERS
considered her my closest friend
found her genuinely sincere
watched her laughing and playing
make everyone happy
keeps me busy
can't imagine myself doing

- Ask a student to read the instructions aloud.
  Then point out the list of characteristics on the
  right and have the students repeat them after
  you. Answer any questions.

- Have the students listen to conversation and
  check the appropriate characteristics. They can
  listen as many times as necessary. Finally, call
  on a student to read aloud the answers.

TAPESCRIPT

Man So, have you thought about who we should
hire for the new sales rep position?

Woman Sure, I've thought about it. First of all,
whoever we hire should be able to work
without much direction.

Man You're right about that. That's why Julie Visk
didn't work out. She wasn't independent
enough.

Woman Another thing—the ideal candidate will be
able to travel wherever and whenever it's
necessary. After all, we have clients all over
the world, and when they want service, we've
got to be there right away.

Man Good point. I think we also want someone
who doesn't mind hard work—you know,
someone who does whatever it takes to get
the job done.

Woman Sounds good. Here are a couple of resumes
that seem like possibilities. Why don't you
take a look?

Man Will do. Let's meet again tomorrow to
discuss them.

ANSWERS
willing to travel
independent
hardworking

- Point out the boxes to the right and read aloud
  the information. Then call on different student
  to read aloud the sentences in the frames.
  Answer any questions.

OPTION

Tell the students to work in pairs to write
additional sentences that have question words with
-ever. Encourage them to write sentences related to
themselves and their own environment. Go around the
room and answer any questions the pairs have about
their work. Finally, call on different students to read
aloud their sentences and write them on the board.

- Have the students read over the conversation.
  Answer any questions. Make sure they
  understand the meaning of the word *hairdresser*.

Then have them complete the conversation,
using question words with -*ever*. Next tell them
to check their answers with a partner.

- Have the students listen to the conversation to
  check their work. You can read the completed
  conversation aloud with a student.

- Tell the students to work with a partner to
  practice the conversation. Remind them to use
  appropriate pronunciation, intonation, and body
  language. Go around the room and check their
  work. Finally, call on a pair of students to act out
  the conversation for the class.

ANSWERS
A Whatever, wherever
A whichever
B however, whenever

OPTION

Have the pairs continue the conversation. Tell them
to pretend that A has just returned from getting his
or her hair cut at Zanelli Hair Stylists and is
describing the experience to B. Encourage them to
use their imaginations. Go around the room and
listen in. Finally, call on different pairs to act out
their conversations for the class. Give a prize for
the most original conversation.

CULTURE CLOSE-UP

In the U.S., it has become increasingly common for
male and female barbers or hair stylists to work
together in the same place of business. Furthermore,
men often have both male and female clients. The
same is also true for women hair stylists.

- Point out the model essay and have the students
  read through it. Answer any questions. Then call
  on different students to read the paragraphs aloud.

- Read the instructions aloud. Answer any
  questions. Then have the students write their
  own essays. Go around the room and answer any
  questions students have about their work.

- Call on different students to read aloud their
  essays. You can select a student to write his or
  her essay on the board. Alternatively, collect the
  essays and in your spare time, mark any errors.
  Then return the essays for the students to make
  any necessary corrections. Finally, collect the
  essays again and check the corrections before
  returning them to the students.

FOLLOW-UP

Students can use the notes in exercise 2 to write
sentences describing each of the candidates.

creative
willing to travel
patient
independent
hardworking

 6 ▶ **Listen to the conversation between two sales managers. Check (√) the characteristics they want in a job candidate.**

7 ▶ **Study the frames: Question words with -ever**

Whoever we hire should be reliable. He gets along with **who(m)ever** he meets.	I get nervous **whenever** I give a speech. **Whenever** I talk to my boss, I get nervous.	Question words with -ever give the idea of "any." whoever we hire = anyone we hire
She enjoys **whatever** she does. **Whatever** I do, I do well.	He's done well **wherever** he's worked. **Wherever** I go, I have a good time.	
We can go to **whichever** movie you prefer. **Whichever** one you want to see is fine.	I go to work **however** I feel, sick or not. **However** I feel, I go to work.	where + ever = wherever

 8 ▶ **Complete the conversation, using question words with -ever.**
▶ **Listen to check your work.**
▶ **Practice the conversation with a partner.**

A My hairdresser is just awful. _____ I ask him to do, he always seems to do something else. I've never had a good hairdresser, in fact. I just seem to have bad luck _____ I go.
B Listen, I know of two very good hairdressers. . . .
A Well, I'd prefer to try _____ one is less expensive.
B Then why don't you go to Mario Zanelli? The name of the place is Zanelli Hair Stylists, and it's at 43 Deco Street.

A That's right near where I work.
B I'm sure you'll be satisfied. Mario always cuts my hair _____ I ask him to. And he's almost always available _____ I want to make an appointment.
A Great! Thanks a lot for the recommendation.

9 ▶ **Often, when you apply to go to a college, to get a scholarship, or for a job, you are asked to write a short essay about yourself. Read the model essay. Then follow the instructions on the application form and write about yourself.**

THE BRUBANK CORPORATION

Name CYNTHIA J. COGGINS

In 200 words or less, describe yourself. What are your strengths? What are your weaknesses?

I am a very reliable and conscientious person. Whenever I have a job to do, I try to do it to the best of my ability. I like responsibility and I enjoy challenges. I try to find creative solutions to problems.

All of my life, I have gotten a great deal of personal satisfaction from my work. I enjoy working with others as well as alone. I am sincere and I am fair. My classmates and colleagues consider me kind and understanding.

Unfortunately, though, I have a major shortcoming. I am not always patient. People who do not do their full share of the work make me angry. I think people in school or at work have a responsibility to others, and I can't see myself working with people who are unreliable.

I realize this description may make me sound somewhat conceited and demanding. Actually, I am a very modest person, but in order to give you an accurate picture of myself, I have tried to be very honest. In any case, I feel that whatever I do and wherever I go, I have the personal characteristics that will make me successful.

9. Your turn

You and a group of classmates work for the Foreign Student Placement Service (FSPS). You have three applications from foreign students who want to live and study for a year in the United States. Unfortunately, you only have one application from a family that would like to host a foreign student. Look at the student information cards below, and read the letter from the family on page 19. Then, working in groups, discuss the different students and decide which one to place with the family.

FOREIGN STUDENT PLACEMENT SERVICE

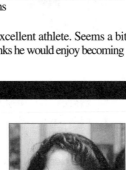

1. **NAME** Paulo Serrador
2. **ADDRESS** Rua da Bahia, 1723/Belo Horizonte, Brazil
3. **AGE** 15
4. **HEALTH** Excellent
5. **FAMILY BACKGROUND** Father, owner of small grocery store; mother, nurse; no brothers or sisters
6. **SCHOOL INFORMATION** Serious student who tries hard, but receives only average grades in all subjects
7. **ENGLISH PROFICIENCY** Speaks excellent English (has many American, British, and Australian friends)
8. **INTERESTS AND HOBBIES** Swimming, soccer, camping; has played in several national soccer competitions
9. **REFERENCES** Four excellent references from teachers (see file)
10. **COMMENTS** Very outgoing and confident, well liked by his teachers and fellow students. Also an excellent athlete. Seems a bit indecisive about his future, but plans to go to college after high school. He isn't sure what he'll study, but he thinks he would enjoy becoming an English teacher.

FOREIGN STUDENT PLACEMENT SERVICE

1. **NAME** Lucia Morales
2. **ADDRESS** Apartado Posal 995/Guatemala, Guatemala, C.A.
3. **AGE** 16
4. **HEALTH** Excellent
5. **FAMILY BACKGROUND** Father, doctor; mother, housewife; sister, 14, in high school; sister, 20, studying accounting in college; brother, 18, works for national airline
6. **SCHOOL INFORMATION** Excellent student, top of her class in chemistry and biology; very good grades in other subjects
7. **ENGLISH PROFICIENCY** Cannot speak English well, but has a good knowledge of grammar; currently enrolled in a private English conversation class after school
8. **INTERESTS AND HOBBIES** Reading and classical music
9. **REFERENCES** Three impressive letters from current teachers and two from the hospital where she has worked as a nurse's aide during school vacations (see file)
10. **COMMENTS** Hardworking student who wants to be a doctor like her father. Very conscientious in her schoolwork and part-time jobs, but shy. Wants to learn English and feels it would be easier to do so living with an English-speaking family.

FOREIGN STUDENT PLACEMENT SERVICE

1. **NAME** Michio Yoshimura
2. **ADDRESS** 66 Banchi/ Aza Kawaguchi/Oaza-Yamashita/ Himeji City, Japan
3. **AGE** 16
4. **HEALTH** Excellent, but walks with crutches (right leg crippled at birth)
5. **FAMILY BACKGROUND** Father, farmer; mother, housewife; sister, 11, in primary school; brother, 22, high-school history teacher and swimming coach
6. **SCHOOL INFORMATION** Very serious student, excellent grades in science and math; average grades in other subjects
7. **ENGLISH PROFICIENCY** Speaks English with difficulty, but would learn quickly if he had more contact with English speakers
8. **INTERESTS AND HOBBIES** Repairs his friends' radios and stereos; president of science club; excellent swimmer
9. **REFERENCES** Excellent references from four teachers (see file)
10. **COMMENTS** Serious student who is ambitious and determined. Would like to become an electrical engineer and wants to learn English well enough to go to college in the United States after he finishes high school. Very energetic and outgoing in spite of handicap.

9. Your turn

- Read the instructions aloud as the students follow along in their books. Then point out the student information cards and the photos on pp. 18 and 19. Next have the students read over the information on the cards and the letter from Mrs. Kozinski. You can call on different students to read the information and letter aloud. Answer any questions.

- Have the students work in groups to discuss the different students and decide which one to place with the family. Go around the room and join in the discussions as you check the students work. Finally, call on different group reporters to share with the class their group's decision and the reasons for it.

OPTION

Have the students work in pairs. Tell them to pretend they are Mr. and Mrs. Kozinski or the Kozinski children. Ask them to write a friendly letter to one of the students featured on p. 18 to inquire about the student's background, school information, English skills, interests and hobbies, etc. When they finish, have the pairs exchange letters with other pairs. Then have the pairs answer the letters. Next tell them to give the letters they've just written to the other pairs. Finally, call on different pairs to read aloud their original letters. Ask the appropriate pairs to read aloud their answers.

CULTURE CLOSE-UP

There are several organizations in the U.S. that help place high-school age students from other countries with American families. These organizations try to match the students with the most appropriate families. They usually look for similarities in hobbies and other interests on the part of a particular host family and a student applicant. Probably the best-known organization of this kind is the American Field Service (AFS). It places students with American families during a year of high-school study in the U.S. Since it was founded in 1914, AFS has placed students from 80 countries in 3000 U.S. communities. The address of AFS is 313 E. 43rd St., New York, New York 10017.

Listen in

- Explain to the students what a horoscope is. So they know what to listen for, have the students read over the possible statements in their books before they listen to the conversation. Answer any questions.

- Play the cassette or read the tapescript aloud with a student. If you read the conversation aloud, be sure to use appropriate stress and intonation. As they listen, have the students choose a or b. When they finish, call on different students to say the answers aloud.

TAPESCRIPT

Steven That was great, Ana! We should come here together more often.

Ana Yeah, well, I have to get back to the office, Steven.

Steven Oh, relax. You worry too much. I'm always late after lunch.

Ana Well, I'm not. I'm too conscientious to take my job so casually.

Steven Hey, listen to our horoscopes from today's newspaper . . . Mine says "You are conscientious and reliable. Success will come to you soon." (*Chuckles*)

Ana What does mine say?

Steven Get this: "You are romantic. Soon you will fall in love with someone nearby."

Ana Gee, I wonder if that means you, Steven.

Steven (*Laughs*) I can't imagine you ever falling in love with someone who's lazy and irresponsible like me. It must mean the waiter. (*Both laugh*)

ANSWERS
1. a
2. b
3. a
4. b

FOLLOW-UP

Students can review the **Your turn** exercise and write down who they would choose and why.

WORKBOOK Lessons 8-9, pp. 9-11

Mr. Steven Compton
Foreign Student Placement Service
870 North Michigan Avenue
Chicago, Illinois 60626

150 Cedar Drive
Naperville, Illinois 60565

Dear Mr. Compton:

I am returning our application to host a foreign student for the coming school year. My husband, John, and I are looking forward to this special visit, and our son and daughter are as excited as we are about sharing our home. We think we have a great deal to offer, both intellectually and socially, to a foreign student.

As you can see from the enclosed application, our family is ambitious and hardworking, but we are also very sports-minded. As we mentioned under "Interests and Hobbies," John coaches the Sacramento Flyers (the high school soccer team) and my daughter, Debbie, is on the high school swimming team. One thing that I forgot to mention on the application is that the entire family goes camping several times a year. We all enjoy the outdoors a great deal.

The application didn't ask for the length of time we have been at our jobs, but I would like to mention that my husband has been teaching English for twelve years, and I have been a nurse at Mercy Hospital for almost four years. Our son, John Jr., works part time also. He has had an afternoon paper route for the past two years. Also, there was no place on the application for me to mention that Debbie won the Freshman Class Science Prize this year. She was extremely pleased and has decided to major in computer electronics when she goes to college.

I think the application covers everything else. However, I did want you to know as much about us as possible. We are all looking forward to hearing from you.

Sincerely,

Beth Ann Kozinski

Beth Ann Kozinski

🎦 Listen in

**Read the statements below. Then listen to the
conversation between Steven Compton and Ana Cruz, employees
at the Foreign Student Placement Service, as they finish lunch. Choose *a* or *b*.**

1. Ana takes her job
   a. seriously.
   b. casually.

2. Ana's horoscope says
   a. success will come to her soon.
   b. she'll soon fall in love.

3. Steven's horoscope says he's
   a. conscientious and reliable.
   b. very romantic.

4. Steven thinks of himself as someone
   a. very reliable.
   b. lazy and irresponsible.

10. On your own

1. Write a two- or three- paragraph letter to the Kozinskis, the family who would like to host a foreign student. In the letter, describe the FSPS applicant that you have chosen to stay with them. Tell why you have selected this applicant.

2. Choose one of the following tasks.

1. You have been placed with the Kozinski family. You plan to live with them while you study in the United States. Write them a letter describing yourself.

2. You have been assigned a pen pal in an English-speaking country. Write a letter to him or her describing yourself.

10. On your own

PROCEDURE

- As the students follow along in their books, read aloud the instructions for exercise 1. Answer any questions students have about the activity.

- Have the students go over their letters with a partner. Go around the room and answer any questions students have about their own writing. Call on different students to write their letters on the board and read them aloud.

- Read aloud the general instructions for exercise 2. Then ask two students to read aloud the instructions for items 1 and 2. Answer any questions.

- Have the students write their letters on separate paper. Go around the room and answer any questions they have about their work. Then call on different students to read aloud their letters and write them on the board.

OPTION

Assign exercise 2 for homework. After the students hand in their letters, mark any errors. Then return the letters for the students to make any necessary corrections. Finally, collect the letters again and check the corrections before handing them back to the students.

WORKBOOK Lesson 10, p. 12. Before assigning the writing task, go over some descriptive adjectives with the students—for example, those in the box at the top of p. 9 in their workbooks. Remind them to use appropriate descriptive adjectives in their paragraphs.

Before you begin teaching, go over the functions/themes, language, and forms in the chart. This will give you a preview of what you will encounter as you guide the students through the unit.

Preview the reading.

- Tell the class to look at the illustration as you have a student describe it. Then read aloud the item 1 information. Answer any questions about the procedure.

- Have the students work in pairs and follow the instructions. Go around the classroom and check their work. Then call on different students to act out their conversations for the class.

- Read aloud the instructions for item 2. Then have the students do the exercise. Next call on different students to tell the class what they thought the purpose of a flea market was before they read the first two paragraphs and after they read them.

  ANSWER
  The purpose of a flea market is the sale and exchange of goods.

PREVIEW

FUNCTIONS/THEMES	LANGUAGE	FORMS
Convince someone Inform someone	I don't really need a footrest. Even so, I suggest that you try it out. You won't find a better buy. It's important that the boss not realize you're behind. It's necessary that we finish the work today.	Some verbs and expressions that require the subjunctive
Make a purchase	I'd like to think it over. I'd like to think about it.	Two-word verbs

Preview the reading.

1. **Student A** You are selling the used items shown in the picture. Student B will ask you some questions about one of the items. Answer the questions and try to give Student B several good reasons to buy the item.
   Student B You are interested in buying one of the used items in the picture. Ask Student A some questions about it. Decide whether or not you want to buy it.

2. Before you read the article on pages 22–23, look at the title and photos and explain what you think the purpose of a flea market is. Then read the first two paragraphs. Does your answer change?

11. Flea Market

by Cree McCree

A typical weekend crowd at a flea market.

① On any weekend at sunrise, while most of the country still sleeps, vans, pickup trucks, campers, and cars crammed with every conceivable item gather in empty parking lots, fairgrounds, and drive-in movie theaters across the U.S. By noon, the scene overflows with thousands of people who have come to bargain and browse at this mad carnival called a flea market.

② People have traded and bartered for centuries. Whatever else the flea market may appear to be, its purpose is the sale and exchange of goods. Whether they are knowledgeable collectors or just plain bargain hunters, people are drawn to the flea market by the enormous amount and variety of merchandise offered. The possibility of finding something truly valuable before anybody else does makes shopping at a flea market a treasure hunt.

③ For many buyers, the ritual of bargaining at a flea market is as much fun as the bargain itself. It's not just the money they save that gives them a warm inner glow of accomplishment; it's the satisfaction of playing an ancient game.

④ Satisfaction also comes from the immediacy of a flea-market exchange. After you negotiate your price, it is "cash and carry"—the dealer pockets your money, you go home with your purchase, and that's that. You got what you wanted, and the dealer got what he or she wanted. In today's world of credit cards, the flea market takes you back to a time when life was simpler and money had more meaning.

⑤ There's magic in a place where anything can happen. The flea market allows us to be children again, to play dress-up and try on funny hats, and to embark on an adventure of discovery and surprise. It also allows us to reclaim items from our past that have been swept away by time, only to reappear again, almost miraculously, at the market.

⑥ The variety of people who set up stalls at the flea market often rivals the variety of the merchandise. These vendors may have nothing in common during their weekday lives, but over the weekend their diversity becomes community. A couple sells embroidered slippers next to a teenager displaying cat's-eye sunglasses across from another dealer's car hubcaps, baby dolls, and plastic potted plants. On the street, they would probably never talk to each other. Here they do.

⑦ What do these "fleas" have in common here? Perhaps

11. Flea Market

- Point out the photos on pp. 22 and 23 and read the captions aloud. Ask different students to describe the photos.

- Have the students read through the article. Follow a procedure similar to that on p. 2 of this book.

Figure it out

1. As you read, look for the answers to the questions.

- Have the students read over the four questions and try to answer them without looking back at the article. When they finish, have them compare and discuss their answers with a partner.

SAMPLE ANSWERS

1. You can bargain with a flea market vendor to lower the price, but you cannot usually do this at a store. Also many different types of merchandise may be placed in the same area at a flea market, and not everything that is for sale is new. In stores, similar kinds of merchandise are placed together, and the merchandise is always new. In addition, unlike at a store, you must pay cash at a flea market, and you cannot place an order for something that is not available.
2. They enjoy bargaining because they can save money and because they are playing an ancient game. They also enjoy the many surprises to be found at flea markets: items they haven't seen in years, funny and unusual objects, the chance to talk with many different kinds of people, and the opportunity to look over many different kinds of merchandise in one place. In addition, they enjoy being able to buy things in such a simple way. At a flea market, you see something you like, buy it immediately, and take it home.
3. The vendors may come from many different backgrounds and nationalities and have different lifestyles. However, vendors are alike because they have similar beliefs. They believe in being independent and controlling their own lives. They would rather have freedom than security. At a flea market, they can sell what they want, and decide what hours they will work.
4. They are well organized, and vendors put a lot of hard work into them. But most important, there is a spirit of cooperation, and everyone helps each other out.

2. Find at least one paragraph that makes each of the main points.

- Have the students scan the article to find the different paragraphs. Then tell them to compare answers with a partner. Next have them use the answers to help check and correct their answers to exercise 1.

- Call on different pairs to read aloud the answers to exercise 2; have one partner read aloud an exercise item and the other the corresponding paragraph number. Then ask different students to read aloud the answers to exercise 1. You can have other students write the answers on the board.

ANSWERS
1. paragraphs 2 and 5
2. paragraph 8
3. paragraph 3
4. paragraph 2
5. paragraphs 6 and 7
6. paragraphs 3, 4, and 5

3. ...Use five words from the list to write sentences about flea markets.

- Have the students repeat each of the nouns after you. Point out that the primary word stress occurs on the third syllable from the end in each of the words. (See the Pronunciation Note which follows.)

- Tell the students to write their sentences on separate paper. When they finish, have them compare their sentences with a partner. Finally, call on different students to read aloud their sentences and write them on the board. Alternatively, collect the students' papers to check their work.

ANSWERS
Answers will vary.

PRONUNCIATION NOTE

The primary stress on nouns that end in -ity usually occurs on the third syllable from the end. Note:

actívity divérsity possibílity commúnity secúrity
   3 2 1

FOLLOW-UP

Students can write down the names of objects one might find for sale at a flea market.

WORKBOOK Lesson 11, p. 13

A woman shopping at a flea market.

A vendor displaying her merchandise.

it is a belief in getting ahead, in becoming economically self-sufficient, and in taking control of their own lives. Vendors willingly give up the security of a nine-to-five job in exchange for freedom: freedom from rigid working hours; freedom from the world of inflation; freedom to choose when, where, and what they will sell; freedom to be what they want to be.

⑧ Yet the flea market is much more than an odd mixture of people selling a hodgepodge of products. "This is a serious enterprise," says vendor Joel Kaufmann of New York. "The amount of labor and organization that goes into an operation like this is phenomenal." Perhaps most important to the flea market's success is the spirit of cooperation among vendors. "At the flea market, everyone is encouraged to be an individual, [but, at the same time,] to help each other out," says Caggie Daniels of Santa Fe, New Mexico. "It's a shame cities aren't run like this."

Figure it out

1. **As you read, look for the answers to these questions. When you have finished, try to answer the questions without looking back at the article. Do exercise 2 before correcting your answers.**

1. How is shopping at a flea market different from shopping at a regular store?
2. What are some of the reasons that people enjoy shopping at a flea market?
3. How are the vendors at a flea market different from each other? How are they alike?
4. What makes flea markets operate successfully?

2. **Find at least one paragraph that makes each of the following main points. Then use your answers to this exercise to help you check and correct your answers to exercise 1.**

1. The variety of merchandise at a flea market offers its shoppers many surprises.
2. Flea markets work so well because everyone cooperates with each other.
3. Many people enjoy the game of bargaining just as much as the money they end up saving.
4. The flea market is, in fact, a business whose main purpose is to sell merchandise.
5. Although vendors may seem to have nothing in common, they share similar beliefs and values.
6. Many people enjoy the flea market because, in various ways, it reminds them of the past.

3. **The suffixes -*ity* and, in some cases, -*ty*, are used to form nouns from many adjectives. Use five words from the list to write sentences about flea markets.**

activity	certainty	community
diversity	possibility	security

12. You're welcome to think it over.

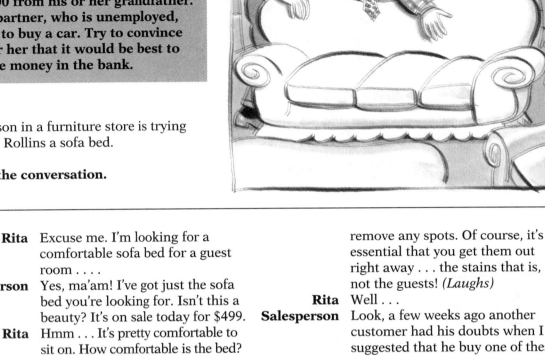

1. Your partner has just inherited $25,000 from his or her grandfather. Your partner, who is unemployed, wants to buy a car. Try to convince him or her that it would be best to put the money in the bank.

 A salesperson in a furniture store is trying to sell Rita Rollins a sofa bed.

Listen to the conversation.

2

Rita Excuse me. I'm looking for a comfortable sofa bed for a guest room . . . .

Salesperson Yes, ma'am! I've got just the sofa bed you're looking for. Isn't this a beauty? It's on sale today for $499.

Rita Hmm . . . It's pretty comfortable to sit on. How comfortable is the bed?

Salesperson Here, let me open it for you to try out . . . .

Rita Yes, the bed's not too bad . . . . I'd like to think it over, though. It's not exactly what I had in mind.

Salesperson I can assure you that you won't find anything more reasonable or more comfortable. And this is the ideal sofa bed for a guest room. It's important that your guests be comfortable, right?

Rita Yes, but I'm worried about the color. White gets dirty so easily, and you know how guests are sometimes . . . .

Salesperson Oh, this fabric doesn't stain very easily. A little soap and water will remove any spots. Of course, it's essential that you get them out right away . . . the stains that is, not the guests! *(Laughs)*

Rita Well . . .

Salesperson Look, a few weeks ago another customer had his doubts when I suggested that he buy one of these sofa beds. But do you think he brought it back? No way! In fact, he called me up and ordered another one.

Rita Well . . . it *is* comfortable . . . Uh . . . but I think I'll look around and then decide.

Salesperson You're welcome to think it over, but I can't guarantee that it'll still be here if you decide to come back.

Rita Oh, is this the only one you have?

Salesperson It's the last one we have in stock. They've been selling like crazy.

Rita Still, I'll have to think about it. It's a big purchase.

Salesperson O.K. I just hope you make the right decision.

3. Check (√) the statements that are stated or implied in the conversation.

____ Rita wants to buy a sofa bed.

____ Rita needs a sofa bed for her living room.

____ The sofa bed in the store comes in white or black.

____ Rita isn't sure she wants to buy the sofa bed.

____ The salesperson says the sofa bed is easy to clean.

____ The salesperson tries to convince Rita by talking about a satisfied customer.

____ Rita buys the sofa bed before leaving the store.

12. You're welcome to think it over.

1. Warm-up Activity

- Read aloud the information and the instructions in the box. Then have the students work in pairs and follow the instructions.

- Go around the classroom and check the pairs' work. Then call on different pairs to share their conversations with the class.

OPTION

Have the pairs change roles. (Student A has just inherited the money, and Student B gives the advice.) Tell Student B to try to convince Student A to put some of the money in the bank and to do something else with the rest (other than buy a car). Go around the class and listen in on the conversations. Finally, call on different pairs to present their conversations to the class.

2. Conversation

BACKGROUND

A salesperson in a furniture store is trying to sell Rita Rollins a sofa bed, but Rita is not ready to make up her mind and buy it.

LANGUAGE

…*just the sofa bed* is another way of saying "the exact sofa bed."

…*pretty (comfortable)* means *rather* or *somewhat (comfortable)*.

…*try out* means *check* or *test*.

…*not too bad* is another way of saying "pretty good."

…*think it over* is another way of saying "think about it."

…*what I had in mind* means *what I had planned on (buying)*.

…*get (them) out* means *remove (them)*.

…*had (his) doubts* is another way of saying "wasn't sure."

No way! is an idiomatic and emphatic way of saying "No."

…*look around* is another way of saying "check at other stores."

…*in stock* means *available* or *on hand*.

…*selling like crazy.* is an idiomatic way of saying "selling very well."

…*just (hope)* means *simply (hope)*.

PROCEDURE

- As the students examine the illustration, point out the characters from the conversation. Ask a student to describe the characters. Have another student tell the class what's probably happening in the picture.

- Follow a procedure similar to that indicated for the opening conversation in Unit 1.

3. Check (✓) the statements that are stated or implied in the conversation.

- Have the students read over the statements. Answer any questions. Then have them scan the conversation to find the statements that are stated or implied.

- Ask the students to compare answers with a partner. Then call on different students to read aloud the correct statements.

ANSWERS
Rita wants to buy a sofa bed.
Rita isn't sure she wants to buy the sofa bed.
The salesperson says the sofa bed is easy to clean.
The salesperson tries to convince Rita by talking about a satisfied customer.

OPTION

Have the students work in pairs to act out the conversation. Then have them make up similar conversations of their own. Tell them they can decide on whatever sale item they want—a house, a car, a vacation package. Encourage them to use their imaginations. Go around the room and listen in. Then call on different pairs to act out their conversations for the class.

CULTURE CLOSE-UP

In cities throughout the U.S., very large warehouse-type stores are becoming popular. In these stores, large quantities of merchandise are available at discount prices—for example, if a customer buys a case rather than a single box of detergent, he or she can save a lot of money. Furniture warehouses are also popular. They feature enormous showrooms of different kinds of furniture at slightly lower prices than one would find in a traditional department store. Furniture warehouses also offer special sales at which certain items are sold at sizeable discounts.

FOLLOW-UP

Students can write yes-no questions for the statements in exercise 3. Then they can write short answers.

WORKBOOK Lesson 12, p. 14

13. I suggest that you try it out.

WARM-UP

Go around the classroom and ask students to volunteer to tell the class about any experiences they've had selling something to someone.

CONVINCE SOMEONE

- Point out the illustrations and have the students repeat the captions after you. (See the Pronunciation Note which follows.) Next have the students read over the conversation. Then point out the boxes, read the headings aloud, and have the students repeat the sentences after you. Answer any questions.

- Ask a student to read aloud the second set of instructions. Then have the students work in pairs to act out similar conversations. Tell them to use some of the sentences in the boxes in their conversations.

- Go around the room and check the pairs' work. Then call on different pairs to act out their conversations for the class

PRONUNCIATION NOTE

Compound nouns receive primary stress on the first noun. Note:

foótrest
compúter desk
vídeo rack
boókcase

2

- Have the students read over the conversation. Answer any questions. Then have them listen to the conversation. You can act it out with a student in front of the class.

- Read aloud the headings in the boxes and call on different students to read aloud the sentences in the box on the left. Read aloud the expression in the box on the right and show the students how they can be made into complete sentences. (See the Option which follows.) Answer any questions.

- Have a student read aloud the second set of instructions. Then tell the students to work with a partner to act out similar conversations.

- Go around the classroom and listen in on the conversations, giving help if needed. Then call on different pairs to act out their conversations for the class.

OPTION

To demonstrate how the expressions in the box on the right are followed by a subject pronoun and the base form of the verb, make each expression into a complete sentence. Say the sentences aloud and write them on the board. For example:

It's important that you be here on time.
It's essential that Paulo get here early.
I strongly suggest that you buy the white sofa bed.
I propose that we have a class party next week.

Next have the students work with a partner to make up their own endings for the expressions. Finally, call on different students to say their sentences aloud.

13. I suggest that you try it out.

  1
► Listen to the conversation.
► Act out similar conversations. You are looking to buy one of the items in the illustrations below. Your partner is a salesperson and will try to sell you the item.

A Hello, I'm looking for an easy chair, preferably in a dark color.
B Well, this one is on sale. It even comes with a footrest.
A Hmm . . . I don't really need a footrest. I have a small apartment.
B Even so, I suggest that you try it out. You won't find a better buy. If you don't like it, you don't have to buy it.
A Well, O.K. Let me try it out.

Some objections	Some suggestions
I don't really need a _____ . It doesn't match my furniture. It's the wrong shape/size for my apartment. The color/style isn't exactly what I had in mind.	Try it out. Look it over. See if you like it. See how it works.

easy chair with footrest   computer desk with chair   TV/VCR cabinet with video rack   bookcase with pull-out desk

  2
► Listen to the conversation.
► Act out similar conversations, using the information and expressions in the boxes. Your partner is a friend who you are concerned about. Try to find out what's wrong and convince your friend to do something about it.

A Is everything O.K., Shelly? I've noticed you haven't been concentrating on your work.
B This job is just so boring . . . .
A I know, but you know that we have to get things done on time here. It's important that the boss not realize you're behind.
B Yeah, I suppose you're right.
A Personally, I think you should work a little later tonight to catch up. It's up to you, though.
B But we were supposed to go to the movies tonight, remember?
A Feel free to cancel if you want. It's more important that you get your work done.

Some situations at work	Some ways to convince someone
Your partner hasn't been concentrating and is behind in his or her work. Your partner dislikes another employee, but the two of them have to work together. Your partner finds the work too difficult, but is too embarrassed to ask for help. Your partner shares an office with someone who receives frequent personal phone calls.	It's important that . . . It's essential that . . . I (strongly) suggest that . . . I propose that . . . ▲ These expressions are followed by a subject pronoun and the base form of the verb.

3 ▶ Listen to the conversation in which one speaker is trying to convince the other. Write the number of each conversation in the appropriate box.

4 ▶ Study the frame: Some verbs and expressions that require the subjunctive

They	recommend suggest insist propose	that	I you he she we they	be plan finish set	on time. a meeting. the work today. a schedule.
It's	important necessary essential crucial				

▲ subject pronoun   ▲ base form

Compare:
They insisted *that we be* on time.
They wanted *us to be* on time.

5 ▶ Rewrite these memos from the manager of a department store to two of his employees, completing them with the correct forms of the verbs in parentheses.

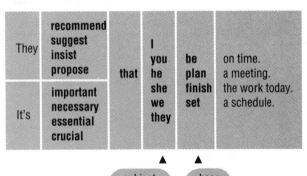

MEMO

Alice,

It is essential that I _____ (hire) another salesperson to help you in the electronics department. The employment agency recommended that I _____ (interview) a Mr. Murray. He will come in tomorrow at 2:00. Although I realize that you _____ (be) very busy, it is important that he _____ (meet) you, so I'll bring him to your department at about 2:30.

Harry

MEMO

TO: John
RE: Flavio Morino

I want Flavio _____ (take) his vacation next month. He hasn't had a vacation for two years because he always says he's too busy. It's crucial that he _____ (get) away from the accounting office for a while. I think you should propose that he _____ (take) four weeks off—two weeks for last year and two weeks for this year.

Harry

CONVINCE SOMEONE • INFORM SOMEONE • SOME VERBS AND EXPRESSIONS THAT REQUIRE THE SUBJUNCTIVE

3

- Have the students look at the illustrations as you call on different class members to describe what's happening in each picture. Then read the instructions aloud. Point out the answer box in each picture.

- Have the students listen to the conversations as many times as necessary. Tell them to check the appropriate boxes. Then call on a student to read aloud the answers.

TAPESCRIPT

1. **Man** Jessica, are you ready to finish up our report? I keep worrying that we won't have it done in time for the meeting.
   Woman Sure, I'm ready. To tell you the truth, I'm a little worried myself. We'll both feel better when it's behind us.
   Man Meet you in the conference room in ten minutes?
   Woman I'll be there.

2. **Man** People waste so much time and money going to doctors. I haven't been to one in five years.
   Woman That doesn't sound too smart. You never know when something might be wrong.
   Man Well, I'm not going to worry about it. I have enough problems already. And doctors are so expensive.
   Woman Look, it's up to you, but I think your health isn't something to take chances with. I strongly suggest you make an appointment for a checkup. Better safe than sorry.
   Man Well, I'll think about it. You might have a point.

3. **Man** Well, that's all the bills paid for this month . . . and look at this! We actually have $500 left over.
   Woman That's great!
   Man Now, what should we do with it? Go away for the weekend? Or maybe buy a new sofa bed for the guest room.
   Woman Wait a minute. You know what I think we should do . . .
   Man You mean, put it in our savings account. But we have lots of years ahead of us to save money. Saving money is boring. Let's have some fun now.
   Woman No, I think it's really important that we start putting some money away. You never know what might happen—repairs to the house, hospital bills . . .
   Man I guess you're right. But I still think it would be more fun to buy something.

4. **Man** Emily, isn't it time to take the cat to the vet for his shots?
   Woman You're right, it is. I had completely forgotten about it.

Man Why don't you get him into his carrier, and I'll call the vet to tell him we're coming. Oh, and we can drop off our dry cleaning while we're in the neighborhood.
Woman Okay, but you know it's never easy to get Felix to go to the vet. . . . Here kitty, kitty, kitty . . .

ANSWERS

4

- Have the students examine the frame as you and some class members read aloud the possible sentences. You can also have the students repeat the sentences after you. Then read aloud the information in the box. Answer any questions. (See the Language Note which follows.)

LANGUAGE NOTE

The subjunctive mood is not very common in English. Note that it is used in noun clauses after a small class of verbs which indicate strong or weak suggestions or degrees of importance or necessity. Verbs in the subjunctive are always in the base form; they are never inflected.

OPTION

Have the students write a sentence for a partner recommending, suggesting, insisting, or proposing something. Tell them to use the subjunctive as in the frame. Then have the students respond orally to their partners' sentences. For example:

Student A writes "I insist that you give me your watch."
Student B says "No, I can't. I need it to know when to leave for the bus."

Go around the room and read different sentences and listen to the responses. Finally, call on different pairs to read aloud their sentences and say their responses.

- Tell the students to read over the memos. Answer any questions. Then have a student read the instructions aloud.

- Tell the students to rewrite the memos. When they finish, have them compare their work with a partner. Finally, call on two students to read the memos aloud. Ask another student to write the answers on the board.

ANSWERS
hire, interview, are, meet
to take, get, take

Unit 3 **26**

- Have the students examine the frames as you read aloud the possible sentences. You can have the students repeat the sentences after you.

- Point out the lists of separable and inseparable verbs and explain how they are used. For example, say "We can say 'Bring back my book' or 'Bring my book back.' We say 'Ask for a raise' but not 'Ask a raise for.'" Then have the students repeat the verbs after you.

OPTION

Have the students use as many of the verbs as they can in original sentences. Tell them to write their sentences on separate paper. Remind them to write two versions of the sentences with separable verbs. When they finish, have them compare their work with a partner. Then call on different students to read their sentences aloud and write them on the board for you to check.

- Point out the expressions in the box and have the students repeat them after you. Then ask different students to use the expressions in sentences. Answer any questions.

- Tell the students to read over the incomplete conversation. Answer any questions. Then ask a student to read aloud the instructions.

- Have the students complete the conversation and then compare answers with a partner. Finally, call on two students to act out the completed conversation for the class. Ask a student to write the answers on the board.

ANSWERS

Salesperson bring it back, run into any major
difficulty with it
Salesperson look it up
Customer think about the cassette player
Salesperson Think it over, ask for me

- Read the instructions aloud as the students follow along in their books. Then ask two students to read the description aloud. Answer any questions.

- Tell the students to write their letters on separate paper. When they finish, have them compare letters with a partner. Finally, call on different students to read aloud their letters and write them on the board.

OPTION

Tell the students to make up their own situations like the one described in the book. (Or they can use real situations they know about.) Have them describe the situation on paper. Then tell them to exchange papers with a partner. Next have them write short letters of advice to the persons in the situations they've been given. After that, tell the students to again exchange papers with their partners. Finally, call on different students to read aloud their situations and letters.

FOLLOW-UP

Students can write out the conversations they acted out in exercise 1.

6 ▶ **Study the frames: Two-word verbs**

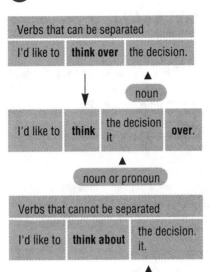

Verbs that can be separated
I'd like to **think over** the decision.

↓ ▲ noun

| I'd like to | **think** | the decision it | **over**. |

▲ noun or pronoun

Verbs that cannot be separated
I'd like to **think about** the decision. it.

▲ noun or pronoun

Some separable verbs		
bring back	look up	think over
call up	pick out	try out
figure out	pick up	turn off
fill in	put on	turn on
fill out	take back	write down
get back		

Some inseparable verbs		
ask for	look for	talk about
go over	plan for	think about
hear from	run into	worry about

7 ▶ **Complete the conversation between the salesperson and the customer, using the items in the box. Pay attention to whether the verb can be separated, and make sure you place the pronouns correctly.**

think about/the cassette player	bring back/it	run into/any major difficulty
think over/it	ask for/me	look up/it

Salesperson Enjoy your stereo.
Customer Thanks. Oh, by the way, what should I do if I have any trouble with it?
Salesperson Well, if you have any trouble during the first three months, I suggest that you just _____ . After that, if you _____ with it, Mitsuyo will guarantee free service and parts for a full year.

Customer O.K. By the way, where's the nearest Mitsuyo service center?
Salesperson Actually, I don't know. But you can _____ in the phone book.
Customer Thanks. And I'll _____ . I'm just not sure if I can afford it right now.
Salesperson All right. _____ and just _____ if you come back. I'll be happy to help you.

8 ▶ **Read the description below about a friend of yours who is planning to get married. Then write a short letter convincing your friend that he or she is making a big mistake.**

A good friend of yours who is very hardworking and very wealthy has decided to get married. The person he or she is marrying is unemployed and never has any money, but likes to dress well, go out to eat all the time, and go dancing at night. During the day, the person sleeps late and spends the rest of the time at the beach or playing tennis.

Although your friend likes to dance and play tennis, he or she is basically very domestic and likes to cook, eat at home, and go to bed early. He or she also likes to work, and often works long hours, sometimes even on the weekends.

14. Your turn

You and a group of classmates would like to take a vacation together. Read the descriptions of the two tours in the ads and look at the photos. Discuss the pros and cons of each trip, and then try to convince the other students in your group to take the trip that appeals to you more.

Listen in

A man is trying to convince a friend to take a vacation in Curaçao. Read the sentences below. Then listen to the conversation and choose *a* or *b*.

1. The man thinks Curaçao is
   a. too far.
   b. not far at all by plane.

2. The man thinks Curaçao is just
   a. a typical tropical island with a beach.
   b. like being in paradise.

3. The woman is
   a. excited about going to Curaçao.
   b. hesitant about going to Curaçao.

4. The man thinks Curaçao is
   a. relaxing because you can do whatever you want to do.
   b. exhausting because there is so much to do.

What kind of vacation do you enjoy? Do you prefer to go to a tropical resort? to the quiet countryside? to visit your relatives? Discuss these questions in groups.

CURAÇAO
GRAND GETAWAY
BARGAIN CHARTER TOURS
ONE WEEK ONLY $749*

This fabulous vacation includes:

- round-trip airfare from Miami, Florida
- bus from airport to hotel
- 7 nights at the Deluxe Beachfront Hotel
- special shopping discounts
- day tour of island
- dinner with a local family
- hotel entertainment

And much, much more!

Departures every Monday until June. Reserve now. Space is limited and tours sell out quickly!

*Vacation price based on double occupancy + 15% of indicated list price as tax and service charge.

Wilemstad, Curaçao

14. Your turn

- Point out the photos on pp. 28 and 29. Call on different students to read aloud the captions and to describe the photos. Next ask different class members to read aloud the information in the ads. Answer any questions.

- Read the instructions aloud as the students follow along in their books. Answer any questions about the exercise procedure.

- Have the students work in groups to discuss the pros and cons of each trip. Remind them that each group member must try to convince the other group members to take one of the trips. Tell the group members to support their arguments. You can provide an example:

  I think we should take the Grand Getaway tour because it's a better bargain and we get to do more things.

- Go around the room and listen in on the discussions. Then call on the different group reporters to summarize the group members' opinions for the class.

Listen in

- So they know what to listen for, have the students read over the exercise items before they listen to the conversation.

- Play the cassette or read the tapescript aloud with a student. If you read the conversation aloud, be sure to use appropriate stress and intonation. After they listen, have the students do the exercise.

- Tell the students to compare answers with a partner. Then call on different students to read their answers aloud and write them on the board.

TAPESCRIPT

Woman I really need a vacation. I just can't decide where to go.

Man Have you ever been to Curaçao?

Woman No, I haven't. It's so far.

Man Oh, come on. In this day and age, nothing is far. Besides, once you get there, it's like being in paradise. I really think you should consider it. In fact, I suggest you ask your travel agent about it.

Woman What's so great about Curaçao? It's just another tropical island with a pretty beach.

Man Just another tropical island, she says. Bright, sunny days with blue water rolling up onto the clean white sand; cool breezes blowing through the palm trees on clear, moonlit nights. Come on, it's a fantastic place to go.

Woman Oh, I don't know.

Man Look. You can go wherever you want, but it's important that you relax during your vacation, and Curaçao is the perfect place for that. I mean, you can do all of the things you like to do—play tennis, swim, read, rest—not to mention eat well and get a gorgeous tan. Why are you so hesitant? Come on! Be adventurous!

Woman You're certainly making it sound better by the minute. O.K. Maybe I'll check it out with my travel agent.

Man I suggest you hurry. This is a very busy time of year, and reservations aren't always easy to get. And it's absolutely necessary that you have reservations.

ANSWERS
1. b
2. b
3. b
4. a

- Ask a student to read aloud the second set of instructions as the class members follow along in their books. Then have the students discuss the questions in groups. Go around the classroom and join in the discussions. Finally, call on different group members to discuss their preferences with the class.

FOLLOW-UP

Students can write down their own answers to the
questions posed at the end of the **Listen in**
exercise.

WORKBOOK Lessons 13-14, pp. 15-17

Wilemstad, Curaçao

Caracas, Venezuela

Curaçao + Fabulous Cruise
Caracas, San Juan, + Bermuda Option

You've never experienced anything like it!
Includes:

- round-trip flight from Miami to Curaçao
- cruise to exciting Caracas, San Juan,* and back to Curaçao
- all meals and entertainment
- swimming pool and health club
- supervised wind surfing and scuba diving available at only a small cost

All this without ever leaving the boat!
7 days/6 nights—Only $1,399**
Every day a new adventure!

*For the truly adventurous, fly from San Juan on to lovely Bermuda for an additional 3 days and 2 nights at the low, low cost of only $499.**
**Tax excluded; Bermuda extension includes return flight from Bermuda to Miami.

San Juan, Puerto Rico

Southhampton, Bermuda

15. On your own

1. Imagine that someone you know is reluctant to take a trip to your city or country. Write the person a letter describing your city or country, and try to convince him or her to come for a visit. Include any necessary information on making reservations. Also mention if it is necessary to make any special arrangements or preparations, such as getting a passport or visa.

2. Choose one of the items in the pictures. Write an advertisement that will convince people to buy that item.

15. On your own

PROCEDURE

- Have the students read through the instructions for the first exercise. Answer any questions they have about the activity. (See the Option which follows.)

- Tell the students to write their letters on separate paper. Then have them go over their letters with a partner. Go around the room and answer any questions students have about their own writing. Finally, call on different students to write their letters on the board and to read them aloud.

OPTION

Before the students begin their letters, write a model letter of your own on the board. To one side of the letter, indicate the different parts by writing the information from the instructions—description of city/country, reasons to come for a visit, information on making reservations, arrangements for getting a visa.

CULTURE CLOSE-UP

When people travel by car within the U.S., they often stay at motels. Motels usually have parking facilities close to where one's room is located. They also tend to be spread out over a large area and usually have swimming pools and garden areas. In the downtown areas of cities, travelers usually choose to stay in hotels. Hotels are usually larger than motels and have several stories of accommodations. Unless it's the tourist season, reservations are usually not needed at most motels. However, in large cities where conventions are often held, it's always a good idea to make reservations ahead of time at both motels and hotels at any time of the year.

- Point out the illustrations and have different students describe them for the class. Then read aloud the instructions for exercise 2.

- Tell the students to write their ads on separate paper. When they finish, have them compare and discuss their ads with a partner. Then call on different students to write their ads on the board and to read them aloud. Check their work—make sure the ads make sense, are grammatically correct, and have appropriate punctuation and capitalization.

OPTION

Bring to class (or have the students bring) magazine or newspaper ads featuring pictures of different merchandise along with descriptive text. Separate the pictures from the text and give only the pictures to small groups of students. Tell them to write ads describing the merchandise so that people will be convinced to buy the item(s). Go around the room and check their work. Next hand out the original texts that came with the ads and have the groups compare their own writing with that from the newspapers or magazines. Finally, call on different group reporters to show the class the ads and different texts.

WORKBOOK Lesson 15, p. 18. Before assigning the writing task, review expressions that are used to convince someone—for example, those in the box on p. 14 and in exercise 2 on p. 15 of the students' workbooks. Remind the students to include some of these expressions in their letters to Lee.

PREVIEW

Before you begin teaching, go over the functions/themes, language, and forms in the chart. This will give you a preview of what you will encounter as you guide the students through the unit.

Preview the reading.

- Tell the class to look at the illustrations as you have different students describe them. Then have the students work in pairs to discuss the questions in the first exercise. Go around the classroom and listen in. Finally, call on different students to share their answers to the two questions with the class.

- Have the students follow the directions for the second exercise. Tell them to guess what the article is about. Go around the room and check the pairs' work. Then call on different pairs to tell the class what they think the article is about. Ask a student what the word *perils* means (*dangers*).

> **CULTURE CLOSE-UP**
>
> There are some areas of the U.S. where travel during certain times of the year may be dangerous. One of these areas is the snow belt, where snow storms and icy roads can make driving extremely hazardous. Another area is the flood plain of the Midwest. During very heavy rains, roads there can become dangerous and bridges sometimes are weakened or even washed out.

FUNCTIONS/THEMES	LANGUAGE	FORMS
Give instructions	First, you have to make the preflight inspection. Then, you start the engine. Once you've started the engine, you continue your checking.	Using time markers to put events in order
Explain something	After you start the engine, you contact ground control. When flying an airplane, you should be careful.	General statements with *before*, *after*, and *when*
Talk about interests	Before taking pottery classes, I used to make things out of leather. After I took flying lessons, I bought a plane.	Specific statements with *before*, *after*, *when*, and *while*

Preview the reading.

1. Work with a partner. What makes each of the trips in the pictures dangerous? Have you ever taken a trip that turned out to be dangerous? Tell your partner about it.

2. Before you read the article on page 32, look at the title and the illustration on pages 32–33. What do you think the word *perils* means? Discuss your ideas with a partner.

Balloonist Recalls Perils on First Pacific Crossing

by Wallace Turner

In its 6,000-mile Pacific crossing, the balloon *Double Eagle 5* hovered near disaster and narrowly avoided crashing into a street of homes in California, just minutes before a desperate landing on a mountain ridge. Ben Abruzzo was making the first attempt to cross the Pacific in a balloon with passengers. Also on the balloon were Larry Newman, 34, and Ron Clark, 41, both of Albuquerque, New Mexico; and Rocky Aoki, 42, owner of a restaurant chain, who financed the voyage.

When asked what the worst part of the trip was, Ben Abruzzo said, "All of it. We had a tough takeoff. . . . We picked up ice and couldn't get rid of it."

The rough voyage began in Nagashima, Japan, on November 10, and, according to Abruzzo, nothing worked as expected. "We picked up ice right away, and the weight [of the ice clinging to the balloon] kept us from getting our altitude," Abruzzo said. "We carried ice all across the Pacific." The crew repeatedly had to lighten the balloon by throwing out ballast—bags of sand that regulate the balloon's ascent and can be poured out to make the balloon lighter. Yet, not only was ballast being used up at a fast rate, but the balloon still couldn't climb because it had picked up more snow and ice. "Halfway across we were down to 4,500 feet when we should have been at 22,500 feet," Abruzzo said.

He said that if it hadn't been for the ice, "we would have made it to Europe easily." The balloonists had intended to land in a valley a few miles inland from the ocean, near Ukiah, California. Because of the ice, however, the balloon could not cross the mountains to the east.

"So we started coming down," Abruzzo said, "and when we broke through [the clouds] we could see this street of homes, with the lights on, and I knew we couldn't come down there." He added that the gondola—the basketlike structure suspended beneath the balloon to hold passengers and equipment—would have destroyed one of the homes.

"It's one thing for us to risk our necks in the balloon," Abruzzo added. "But the thing you don't do is risk any injury to anybody on the ground."

To slow the descent of the balloon, all remaining ballast was dropped from it. "Then we were caught in a whirling spin, and the rate of ascent went to 1,500 feet a minute, the most rapid I ever saw for a helium balloon," Abruzzo said.

After rising, the balloonists were in darkness in the storm again. The balloon reached 6,000 feet, not enough to cross the 8,000-foot mountain peaks ahead. It passed a ridge, and they then decided to make their landing on the other side. They put down the drag ropes—heavy ropes that are thrown out of the balloon just before landing to lighten the load and break the fall. The balloon slowed and the crew saw the mountainside coming up.

The men knew that if they took the balloon up again, there would be no way to stop. So they got ready, and when the gondola touched the ground, Abruzzo fired the separation charge, which deflates the balloon so the wind will not drag the gondola. "The balloon exploded," he said, "and we all ended up in one end of the gondola."

The balloonists landed near Covelo, California. They notified searchers that they were safe for the night, and then, Abruzzo said, he went to sleep for "the best night's sleep since we left Japan," 84 hours and 31 minutes earlier, on the longest balloon ride ever made.

16. Balloonist Recalls Perils on First Pacific Crossing

PROCEDURE

- Point out the illustration and ask a student to describe it. Then point out the map. Have a student locate California on a world map or globe.

- Have the students read through the article. Follow a procedure similar to that on p. 2 of this book.

Figure it out

1. Read the incomplete statements.

- Have the students read over the incomplete statements. Answer any questions they have. Then have them complete the sentences.

- Tell the students to compare answers with a partner. Then call on different students to read aloud the completed sentences. Have other students write the answers on the board.

POSSIBLE ANSWERS
1. Nagashima, Japan / California
2. of the weight of the ice clinging to the balloon.
3. California, homes with lights on
4. descend, ascend
5. notified searchers that they were safe and then went to sleep.

2. Find the highlighted words and say what they refer to.

- Point out the highlighted words in the article. Make sure the students understand the exercise procedure. Then have them do the exercise.

- Tell the students to compare answers with a partner. Then call on different pairs; have one partner read aloud the highlighted word and the other the word(s) it refers to in the article. You can ask a student to write the answers on the board.

ANSWERS
1. the balloon *Double Eagle 5*
2. the trip
3. ice
4. the balloon
5. in the street of homes
6. the balloon
7. the balloon
8. the balloonists
9. the men

3. Rephrase the paragraph about the balloon crossing.

- Have the students repeat the list of words after you. Then ask a student to read the paragraph aloud.

- Tell the students to follow the instructions and rephrase the paragraph. When they finish, have the students compare answers with a partner. Then call on a student to read the rephrased paragraph aloud. Ask a student to write the answers on the board.

ANSWERS
expected, attempt, tough, coming down, narrowly avoided, homes, voyage

OPTION

Tell the students to use the synonyms from the list in sentences which show they know the meaning of these words. They can write sentences such as the following one, based on the information in the article, or make up entirely new sentences of their own.

The balloonists succeeded in their attempt to cross the Pacific.

Tell the students to write their sentences on separate paper. When they finish, have them compare sentences with a partner. Next ask them to write their sentences on the board and read them aloud.

FOLLOW-UP

Students can write five information questions and five yes-no questions based on information in the article. Then they can exchange questions with a partner and answer the questions they receive.

WORKBOOK Lesson 16, p. 19

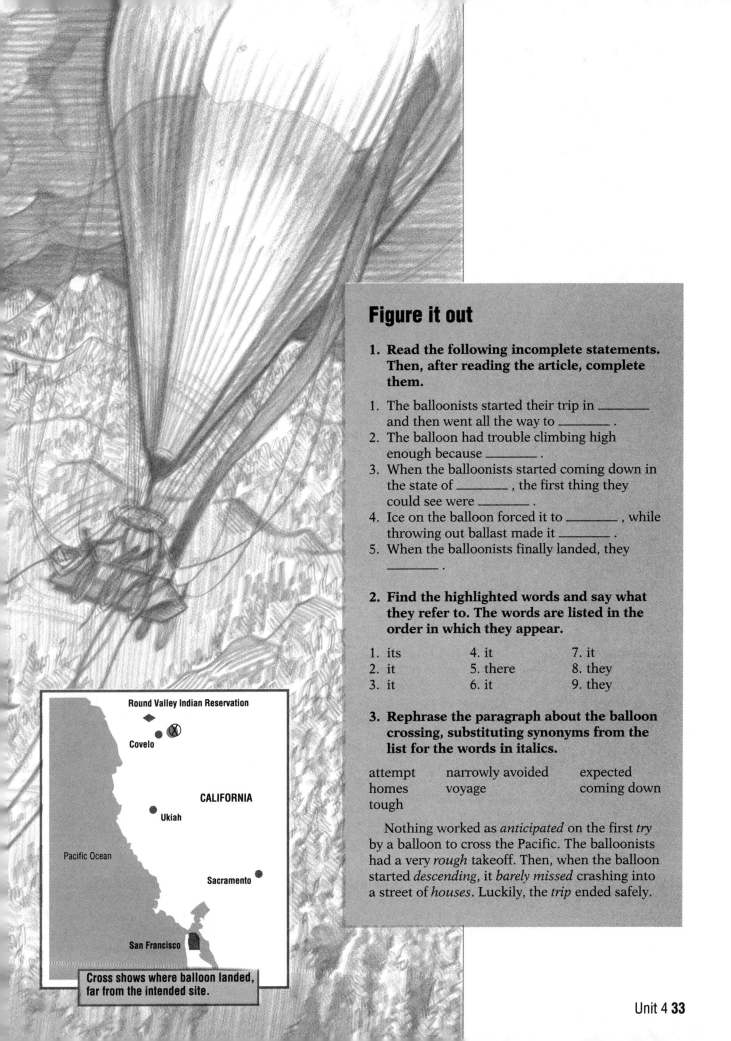

Figure it out

1. **Read the following incomplete statements. Then, after reading the article, complete them.**

   1. The balloonists started their trip in _____ and then went all the way to _____ .
   2. The balloon had trouble climbing high enough because _____ .
   3. When the balloonists started coming down in the state of _____ , the first thing they could see were _____ .
   4. Ice on the balloon forced it to _____ , while throwing out ballast made it _____ .
   5. When the balloonists finally landed, they _____ .

2. **Find the highlighted words and say what they refer to. The words are listed in the order in which they appear.**

1. its	4. it	7. it
2. it	5. there	8. they
3. it	6. it	9. they

3. **Rephrase the paragraph about the balloon crossing, substituting synonyms from the list for the words in italics.**

attempt	narrowly avoided	expected
homes	voyage	coming down
tough		

   Nothing worked as *anticipated* on the first *try* by a balloon to cross the Pacific. The balloonists had a very *rough* takeoff. Then, when the balloon started *descending*, it *barely missed* crashing into a street of *houses*. Luckily, the *trip* ended safely.

Round Valley Indian Reservation

Covelo

CALIFORNIA

Ukiah

Pacific Ocean

Sacramento

San Francisco

Cross shows where balloon landed, far from the intended site.

17. So, what comes next?

1. Tell your partner how to do one of the following:

1. Start a car, back it out of a driveway, and drive forward.
2. Change a flat tire on a busy highway.
3. Play a game or sport popular in your country.
4. Make your favorite recipe or national dish.

Hector Cantor, an amateur pilot, is explaining some of the basics of flying to one of his friends, Ned Lee.

Listen to the conversation.

2

Ned	Tell me something . . . aren't you ever afraid?
Hector	Never. I can't wait to get up there.
Ned	I've always wondered what it's like—flying your own plane. I mean, what do you do exactly?
Hector	Well, before even getting into the airplane, you have to make the preflight inspection. You have to check things like the propeller, the wings, the tires, the fuel tanks . . .
Ned	Yeah, I guess that would be important.
Hector	Yes, it's *extremely* important. In fact, a few times while making the inspection, I discovered some real problems.
Ned	Better than discovering them in the air! So, what comes next?
Hector	Then, you start the engine and contact ground control for permission to taxi onto the runway.
Ned	And after that you're ready for takeoff?

Hector	Not quite so fast. Next, you have to check all of the instruments and controls in the cockpit, as well as some of the other parts of the plane—like the engines while they're running, the wing flaps, the tail rudder . . .
Ned	I never knew it was so complicated! Is that it?
Hector	Yes. Finally, you're ready to fly. So you contact the control tower and ask for permission to take off.
Ned	What about once you're in the air?
Hector	Well, you always have to keep your eyes on the instruments and look around for other aircraft when flying.
Ned	Hmm . . . it sounds a little bit like driving a car. In fact, I think I'll stick to that—it's closer to the ground!

3. Match.

1. Before getting into the plane,
2. After making the preflight inspection,
3. After getting permission to taxi onto the runway,
4. Once you've checked the instruments and controls in the cockpit,
5. When flying,

a. you start the engine and contact ground control.
b. you're ready to fly.
c. you always have to look around for other aircraft.
d. you check the propeller, the wings, the tires, and the fuel tanks.
e. you have to check all of the instruments and controls in the cockpit.

17. So, what comes next?

1. Warm-up Activity

- Read aloud the general instructions in the box. Then ask different students to read aloud the four items. Answer any questions.

- Have the students choose an item and work with a partner. Go around the room and check the students' work. Finally, call on different students to explain to the class the procedure they chose.

2. Conversation

BACKGROUND

Hector Cantor, an amateur pilot, is explaining some of the basics of flying to one of his friends, Ned Lee. Ned is amazed at how complicated piloting a plane is.

LANGUAGE

I can't wait to get up there. is another way of saying "I'm eager to take off and be in the air."

...before even means *before*. The word *even* is simply used to emphasize the fact that certain things have to be done before getting into the airplane.

...what comes next? is another way of asking "What do you have to do next?"

Is that it? is another way of saying "Is there anything else?"

What about once you're up in the air? is short for *What do you have to do once you're up in the air?*

...keep your eyes on means *carefully watch*.

...it sounds a bit like is another way of saying "it seems a little like."

...stick to (that) means *stay with (that)*.

PROCEDURE

- As the students examine the illustration, point out the two characters from the conversation. Ask a student to tell the class what's happening in the picture.

- Follow a procedure similar to that indicated for the opening conversation in unit 1.

3. Match.

- Tell the students the read over the language in the two columns. You can also have different students read the language aloud. Answer any questions. Then have the students do the exercise.

- Ask the students to compare answers with a partner. Then call on different pairs; have one partner say the part of the sentence from the left column and the other the part from the right column.

ANSWERS
1. d
2. a
3. e
4. b
5. c

OPTION

If appropriate, tell the students what you went through on your first airplane flight. For example:

I was very excited and a bit nervous when we first got to the airport. Then when my father pointed out the airplane, I really got worried. . . .

Next ask different students to volunteer to tell the class similar personal stories.

FOLLOW-UP

Students can write down the procedure they chose to describe in exercise 1.

WORKBOOK Lesson 17, p. 20

18. The first thing you should do is . . .

WARM-UP

Tell the students about a frightening experience you were involved in such as a storm or a car accident. Then have different students share similar experiences with the class.

GIVE INSTRUCTIONS

- Point out the illustrations and ask a student to identify the place depicted in the pictures. Then call on different students to briefly describe each scene.

- Ask a student to read the instructions aloud. Then have the students listen to the flight attendant's instructions as they do the exercise. You can have them listen as many times as necessary.

- Call on a student to say the correct order of the pictures. Write the answers on the board.

TAPESCRIPT

If there's an emergency during the flight and you need to use an oxygen mask, the first thing you should do is pull down the oxygen mask nearest to you. Then hold it over your mouth and nose. Next, put the strap over your head and pull it tight. After that, just breathe normally. Once you have put on your own mask, you should help your children or anyone who is sitting next to you with their masks. Finally, try to stay calm and wait for further instructions from the flight attendants.

ANSWERS

4	2	3
5	1	

- Have the students look at the illustrations. Ask a student to describe what's going on in general. You can have different students say what's going on in each picture.

- Read the instructions aloud as the students follow along in their books. Then have the students read over the sentences under the pictures. Answer any questions. (See the Culture Close-Up which follows.) Then point out the box and provide an example of how to use one of the words in the exercise.

- Tell the students to work in pairs to follow the instructions. You can have the partners take turns giving the instructions for the different pictures. Go around the classroom and check the students' work. Finally, call on different students to act out the different scenes in the role play for the class.

SAMPLE ANSWERS

First have someone call . . . . Then place the victim . . . . Next open the victim's mouth . . . . Then tilt the victim's head . . . . After that, pinch the victim's nose . . . . Finally, blow into the mouth . . . .

OPTION 1

Have the students cover the sentences under the pictures. Then have them work in pairs to take turns telling their partners what to do for each picture. Alternatively, first have the students write down the steps to take in the emergency. Then they can compare their sentences with a partner.

OPTION 2

Photocopy the page and cut out the different pictures in exercise 2. Scramble the pictures and see if different students or groups of students can unscramble them. Then cut out the sentences and scramble them to see if students can then put them in the correct order.

CULTURE CLOSE-UP

Cardiopulmonary resuscitation, or CPR as it's commonly know, is the procedure employed after cardiac arrest in which mouth-to-mouth resuscitation is used to restore breathing to the victim. In the U.S. about 50 million people know how to administer CPR. That is largely due to the fact that two organizations—the American Heart Association and the American Red Cross—offer free CPR training throughout the U.S. Public schools also offer classes to their students and to adults in evening classes.

18. The first thing you should do is...

 1 ▶ Listen to the flight attendant tell the passengers how to use oxygen masks in an emergency. Number the pictures in the correct order.

2 ▶ Using the illustrations below, play the role of a first-aid instructor and tell your partner what to do in an emergency. Order your instructions by using some of the expressions in the box.

First . . .	Last . . .
Then . . .	Finally . . .
Next . . .	

If you need to give artificial respiration, do the following:

1 Have someone call an ambulance.

2 Place the victim on his/her back with the victim's face to the side.

3 Open the victim's mouth and clear it of any foreign objects.

4 Tilt the victim's head back and check to be sure his/her tongue is in its natural position—if not, pull it back from the back of the throat.

5 Pinch the victim's nose and take a deep breath.

6 Blow into the mouth until the victim's lungs expand. Repeat, one breath every 5 seconds.

3 ▶ **Study the frames: Using time markers to put events in order**

First,	you have to make the preflight inspection.
Then,	you start the engine.
Next,	you contact ground control.
Last,	you check the instruments.
Finally,	you're ready to fly.

You may substitute *after that* for *then*, *next*, or *last*.
First, you have to make the inspection.
After that, you start the engine.

Once **As soon as**	you've started the engine, continue your checking.
By then, **By that time,**	you're almost ready to fly.
By the time you've finished,	you're ready to fly.

The meaning of *once* is less immediate than *as soon as*.
I'll call Jim *once* I get home. = I'll call him sometime after I get home.
I'll call him *as soon as* I get home. = I'll call him right after I walk in the door.

4 ▶ **Victoria found this note from her mother when she got up Saturday morning. Rewrite the note, completing the sentences with appropriate time markers. Most items have more than one answer.**

Victoria,

I need you to help me today. I have to work until 12:00 and I forgot to tell you before you went to bed last night.

_____, please strip your bed and throw the sheets in the washing machine. The machine is all set for you. Just add 1/4 cup of detergent and close the lid.

_____, Toby needs a bath. The dog shampoo is under the kitchen sink, and there's an old towel on the kitchen counter. _____, brush him well; _____, give him his bath. _____ you've finished, let him go outside so he can run around and dry in the sun. _____ you're done washing Toby (and cleaning the bathtub), your sheets should be done. Put them in the dryer and set the timer for 1/2 hour.

_____, I should be home.

Love,
Mom

- Have the students examine the frames as you and different students read aloud the contents. Then read the information in the boxes. Answer any questions.

OPTION 1

Have the students find examples of the time markers in the conversation on p. 34. Call on different students to read aloud the sentences that contain the markers.

OPTION 2

Tell the students to think about a procedure involved in doing a particular task. Then have them work with a partner to share their thoughts. Ask the pairs to write down the steps involved in performing the task(s). Remind them to use the time markers from the exercise. Finally, call on different pairs to read their procedures aloud and write them on the board.

- Point out the illustration. You can ask different students to describe what's going on. Next have the students read through the note. Answer any questions.

- Next read the instructions aloud. Then tell the students to rewrite the note. When they finish, have them compare answers with a partner. Then call on different students to read aloud the paragraphs from the note. Ask other students to write the answers on the board.

ANSWERS
First, Next, First, then/next, Once/As soon as, Once/As soon as, By then/By that time/By the time you've finished

CULTURE CLOSE-UP

Most people in the U.S. do not have domestic help to do chores around the house. Instead, family members tend to share household responsibilities.

Pets are often treated as parts of the family. Family members often take turns feeding, bathing, and walking house pets.

EXPLAIN SOMETHING • GENERAL STATEMENTS WITH BEFORE, AFTER, AND WHEN

- Have the students examine the frame as you have different students read aloud the possible sentences. You can also have the students repeat the sentences after you.

- Read aloud the information in the box. Answer any questions about the vocabulary and structures in the frame.

OPTION

Have the students form even-numbered groups. Tell the group members to each write a clause or phrase beginning with either *Before, After,* or *When*. Encourage them to use their imaginations. Then have the members within each group exchange papers and complete the sentences they've just received. Next tell them to compare and discuss the sentences they've just completed. Finally, call on different group members to read aloud their sentences and write them on the board.

- Point out the illustration and ask a student to describe what the woman is doing. Find out if any of the students know about what's involved in making pottery.

- Tell the students to read over the conversation. Answer any questions about the vocabulary and the structures. Then have the students listen to the conversation.

- Ask a student to read the instructions aloud. Then have the students work in groups of three to act out similar conversations. Go around the room and listen in, giving help if needed. Finally, call on different groups to share their conversations with the class.

TALK ABOUT INTERESTS • SPECIFIC STATEMENTS WITH *BEFORE, AFTER, WHEN,* AND *WHILE*

- Have the students examine the frame as you have different students read aloud the possible sentences. You can also have the students repeat the sentences after you.

- Read aloud the information in the box. Answer any questions about the vocabulary and structures in the frame.

OPTION

Have the students work in pairs. Tell each partner to write down a clause or phrase beginning with one of the time markers in the frame. Then have the partners exchange papers and complete the sentences they've just received. Go around the room and answer any questions about the students' work. Finally, call on different students to read aloud their completed sentences and write them on the board.

- Tell the students to compare answers with a partner. Then call on different students to read aloud the completed sentences. Ask a student to write the answers on the board.

- Have the students read over the conversation before they listen to it. Answer any questions about the vocabulary and structures.

- Tell the students to read the second set of instructions and to act out similar conversations with a partner. Then call on different pairs to act out their conversations for the class.

FOLLOW-UP

Students can write their own notes modeled after the one in exercise 4.

5 ▶ Study the frame: General statements with *before, after,* and *when*

Before	you get getting	in the plane,	you do the preflight inspection.
After	you start starting	the engine,	you contact ground control.
When	you fly flying	an airplane,	you should be careful.

While is not used very often to make general statements.

6 ▶ Listen to the conversation.
▶ Act out similar conversations in small groups. Find out what hobbies or special interests the members of your group have. Ask a group member to explain how something is done.

A Do you have any hobbies?
B Well, I make pottery.
C Can you tell us a little bit about how you do it?
B Well, first, you take a piece of clay and center it in the middle of a potter's wheel. Then, while the wheel is turning, you shape the clay with your hands. After shaping the clay into a bowl or vase or whatever, you let it dry.
A Is that all? It must be more complicated than that!
B Well, you can decorate the pottery and put a glaze on it. A glaze gives it color and makes it shiny. But before doing this, you have to put the pottery in a very hot oven called a kiln for several hours. This step is called "firing." After firing, you put on the glaze, and then you put the pottery back in the kiln. When the pottery comes out, it's ready to use.

7 ▶ Study the frame: Specific statements with *before, after, when,* and *while*

Before	I became becoming	a pilot,	I was a bus driver.
After	I took taking	flying lessons,	I bought a plane.
When	I graduated	from school,	I left home.
While	I was going going	to school,	I worked at an airport.

When talking about something specific, you should express the subject after *when*.

8 ▶ Listen to the conversation.
▶ Act out a similar conversation with a partner. Ask your partner how he or she became interested in the activity he or she explained in exercise 6.

A Pottery sounds like a fun hobby. How did you get interested in it?
B Oh, I don't know. I've always been interested in arts and crafts. Before taking pottery classes, I used to make things out of leather—mostly wallets and belts. Then one day, while looking around at a crafts fair, I got into a conversation with a professional potter. He convinced me to take one of his classes . . . .

Unit 4 **37**

19. Your turn

Look at the pictures, and then try to find out how to do at least one of these activities. Bring your notes to class and, working in groups, share your instructions with your classmates. They will ask you questions when they don't understand.

19. Your turn

- Point out the illustrations on pp. 38 and 39 and ask different students to describe what's going on in the pictures. You can ask the students if they've ever done any of the activities depicted in the illustrations and to tell the class about their experiences.

- Read aloud the instructions as the students follow along in their books. Then assign the homework: tell the students to choose an activity which they don't know how to do and to find out how to do that activity. Tell them to make notes about the procedure and to bring their notes to the next class.

- Have the students form groups. Tell them to share their instructions with their group members. Encourage the group members to ask questions about any procedure(s) they don't understand.

- Go around the classroom and listen in. Select the procedures which are described most accurately and have them presented to the class.

Listen in

- Tell the students to read the instructions. Then, so they know what to listen for, have them read over the incomplete recipe before they listen to the interview.

- Have the students listen to the interview as many times as necessary. Then tell them to complete the recipe.

- Tell the students to compare answers with a partner. Then call on different students to read the parts of the recipe aloud. Ask a student to write the answers on the board.

TAPESCRIPT

Interviewer Why don't you tell us a little about yourself, Ms. Beck? How did you get to where you are today?

Martine Well, I've always loved to cook—and, of course, eat. So, after finishing high school, I went to a cooking school. During this time I worked as a waitress. It was far from glamorous, I can assure you. Anyway, I used to hang around the kitchen and drive the cook crazy. But my persistence paid off. Before long, I was helping him out, and he got me my first job as a chef.

Interviewer I've always wondered what it takes to be a good cook. I feel helpless in the kitchen, personally.

Martine Cooking really isn't a complicated process. Anyone with common sense who can read can make wonderful dishes. I mean, how complicated can reading a recipe be? We all know the difference between a cup and a half a cup, or a teaspoon and a tablespoon.

Interviewer Could you give our listeners an example of one of your *easy* recipes?

Martine Of course. Well, let's see. . . . Yes. There's a wonderful little dessert called Adam's Apple. And it's really very easy to make.

First, turn on your oven and preheat it to 350 degrees. Then, butter a 2-quart baking dish. While you're waiting for the oven to heat, peel and slice 5 large apples. Next, combine the apples with 2 tablespoons of water, 1/4 cup of sugar and 1/8 teaspoon of cinnamon. Then, pour the apple mixture into the baking dish and set it aside.

After preparing the apples, in another bowl mix 1/2 cup of butter and 1/2 cup of sugar together until the mixture is light and fluffy. Next, add 2 eggs and beat the mixture well. After that, add 1/2 cup of flour and 1 teaspoon of baking powder and mix well.

Finally, spread the batter over the apples and bake in the oven for 50 minutes. Once the dish has finished baking, serve it hot with a scoop of vanilla ice cream on the side. It serves 4 to 6 people, and its absolutely marvelous.

ANSWERS
5 . . . apples, 2, sugar, 1/8, 1/2, sugar, 2, 1/2, 1, First, While, Then, After, Next, After that, Finally, Once

OPTION

Have the students bring their favorite recipes to class. Tell them to work in pairs. Have the partners take turns dictating the steps in their recipes for each other to write down. Then have them exchange papers and check each other's work. Go around the classroom and choose a recipe you think all the class members would like to have. Read it aloud and have the students write it down.

CULTURE CLOSE-UP

Apples are grown in many parts of the U.S., and Americans eat a lot of them. People are reminded of the health benefits of apples by an old saying—"An apple a day keeps the doctor away." The most popular dish made with apples—apple pie—could be called the national dessert in the U.S. When Americans want to label something as typically American, they say "That's as American as apple pie."

FOLLOW-UP

Students can write down instructions for doing any simple task that comes to mind.

WORKBOOK Lessons 18-19, pp. 21-23

🎧 Listen in

Look carefully at the recipe below. Then listen to an interview in which the well-known chef, Martine Beck, explains how to make her dish, "Adam's Apple." You may wish to take notes while you listen. Then complete the recipe.

Adam's Apple
🍎 🍎 🍎 🍎 🍎

_____ large _____ , peeled and sliced
_____ tablespoons water
1/4 cup _____
_____ teaspoon cinnamon
_____ cup butter
1/2 cup _____
_____ eggs
_____ cup flour
_____ teaspoon baking powder

_____ , preheat your oven to 350° and butter a 2-quart baking dish.
_____ you are waiting for the oven to heat, combine the apples, the water, the 1/4 cup of sugar, and the cinnamon.
_____ , pour the apple mixture into the baking dish and set it aside.
_____ preparing the apples, in another bowl, mix the butter and the 1/2 cup of sugar until the mixture is fluffy.
_____ , add the eggs and beat well.
_____ , add the flour and baking powder and mix well.
_____ , spread the batter over the apples and bake in the oven for 50 minutes.
_____ the dish is ready, serve it hot with vanilla ice cream on the side. It serves 4 to 6 people.

🍎 🍎 🍎 🍎 🍎

20. On your own

1. Choose one of the options below.

1. Write the instructions for making your favorite recipe. If you need help, ask a friend or a member of your family.
2. Write about yourself, explaining how you got to your current position in life. First tell what you are doing and then explain how your past experiences led you to this point.

2. Choose one of the pictures and write the instructions.

How to play a videotape.

How to send a fax.

How to make a glass of fresh orange juice.

How to wash clothes.

20. On your own

- Have the students read through the instructions and items in the first exercise. Answer any questions they have about the activity.

- Tell the students to complete their writing tasks on separate paper. Then have them go over their work with a partner. Go around the room and answer any questions students have about their own writing. Finally, call on different students to write their compositions on the board and to read them aloud. Alternatively, assign the activity as homework.

- Point out the illustrations and ask different students to describe the various pieces of equipment for the class. Then ask different students to read aloud the captions.

- Read aloud the instructions for the second exercise. Then have the students write their descriptions. When they finish, have them compare and discuss their descriptions with a partner. Then call on different students to write their descriptions on the board and to read them aloud. Check their work.

OPTION

Bring to class (or have the students bring) pictures of different kinds of commonly used equipment. Have each student choose a piece of equipment and write the instructions for its use on separate paper. Then have the students exchange pictures with a partner and write the instructions for their partner's piece of equipment. Next have the partners compare the two sets of instructions. Go around the classroom and check the pairs' work.

WORKBOOK Lesson 20, p. 24. Before assigning the writing task, point out the time markers in Cliff's note. Remind the students to use time markers in their notes.

PREVIEW

Before you begin teaching, go over the functions/themes, language, and forms in the chart. This will give you a preview of what you will encounter as you guide the students through the unit.

Preview the reading.

- Read aloud the instructions for the first exercise as the students follow along in their books. Then point out the illustrations and read the captions aloud. Have the students do the exercise with a partner. Go around the classroom and listen in on the conversations. Finally, call on different pairs to share their conversations with the class.

- Have a student read aloud the instructions for the second exercise. Then have the pairs do the exercise.

PREVIEW

FUNCTIONS/THEMES	LANGUAGE	FORMS
Describe something Talk about dimensions	What are they like? They were much bigger and heavier than the ones we have today. It's four feet wide and six feet long. Your dining area is only eight feet by eight feet.	
Make comparisons	How much did the old glass milk bottles weigh? They weighed about 14 ounces more than today's paper milk cartons.	Dimensions and weight
Describe a household problem	The linoleum looks so dull and worn. Some of these nice yellow vinyl tiles would make a big difference.	Order of adjectives

Preview the reading.

1. Work with a partner. Wonders are unusually amazing things or events. Tell your partner about ancient wonders in your culture or in a culture you know about. Also tell your partner what you know about the pictures below.

The Aztec calendar

Machu Picchu

2. Before you read the article on pages 42-43, look at the title and the photos on page 42. What do you know about these ancient wonders? Discuss your ideas with a partner.

21. Ancient Wonders

by Murray Rubenstein

The Great Wall of China.

Incan village in Peru.

The Roman aqueduct in Segovia, Spain.

If you stood on the moon and looked back toward Earth, you could see with the naked eye only one structure: the Great Wall of China, which was built in the third century B.C. Today the wall stands as a reminder that modern technology owes a tremendous amount to the accomplishments of ancient builders and engineers. With surprising ingenuity they used the powers of nature to design splendid buildings, bridges, and tunnels. Above all, they passed down to modern engineers their conviction that by hard work the world could be molded and reshaped for the benefit of the people living in it.

By far the best-documented technology of the ancient world was that of the Greeks and Romans. The Greeks had a firm grasp of mathematics and physics, and they used their knowledge to build great buildings, many of which are standing today. The Romans, in turn, applied Greek theory on an even grander scale to build magnificent highways and viaducts, public baths, and elaborate sewage systems. The Romans constructed 56,000 miles of roads and highways; some parts of the Appian Way can still be seen southeast of Rome.

Less well known are the road-building activities of South America's Incas, who flourished during the fifteenth century. The Incas built over 10,000 miles of roads throughout the Andes Mountains, from present-day Argentina to Colombia. Their Royal Road of the Sun, 3,250 miles long, was the longest road in the ancient world—far longer than any Roman road.

The Incas were also great bridge builders. Around the year 1350, they constructed a suspension bridge across the great Apurímac River in the Andes in present-day Peru. The bridge, still in use in 1890, contained neither metal nor wood. Its suspension cables, which were 148 feet long and as thick as a human body, were made by twisting the strong fibers of a local plant.

Yet long before any of these cultures flourished, the ancient Chinese were making the most of their scientific knowledge. The most amazing of all Chinese engineering accomplishments was, of course, the Great Wall. Begun in the third century B.C., the Wall was intended primarily as a defense against invaders from the north. The Great Wall stretches for over 1,400 miles (2,500 miles counting curves) and separates Mongolia from China. Branching off from the main wall are numerous extensions, which were designed to anticipate special military problems. If the Great Wall and all of its branches

21. Ancient Wonders

PROCEDURE

- Point out the photos and ask different students to read aloud the captions and tell the class what they know about the ancient wonders featured in the pictures.

- (Before doing this step, have the students do the first exercise in the **Figure it out** section which follows.) Have the students read through the article. Follow a procedure similar to that on p. 2 of this book.

Figure it out

1. Before reading the entire article, scan the first sentence of each paragraph.

■ Have the students scan the beginning of each paragraph and list the ancient cultures on separate paper. Then have them summarize the article's main point.

■ Have the students compare answers with a partner. Then call on different students to say the answers aloud.

ANSWERS
The Chinese
The Greeks and Romans
The Incas

SAMPLE ANSWER
People through time look back on earlier civilizations with both wonder over the accomplishments made under such primitive conditions as well as with puzzlement over the earlier civilization's failure to develop science further.

2. As you read the article, pay attention to the important points.

■ Have the students read through the exercise items. Then have them do the exercise.

■ Have the students compare answers with a partner. Then call on different students to read aloud the answers. You can have different class members write the answers on the board.

ANSWERS
1. Incas – They built over 10,000 miles of roads throughout the Andes Mountains, and their Royal Road of the Sun was the longest road in the ancient world. Around the year 1350, they constructed a suspension bridge across the Apurímac River in the Andes that was still in use in 1890.
2. Chinese, China, Europe – They developed the world's oldest system of roads around 300 B.C. Canals and rivers were controlled by locks in China seventeen centuries ahead of Europe. Spaghetti, gunpowder, and the process of printing also originated in China. And the amazing Great Wall of China, begun in the third century B.C., shows how fully the Chinese used their technology.
3. Greeks and Romans – The Greeks built great buildings, and the Romans applied Greek theory to build impressive highways and viaducts, public baths, and sewer systems. However, because slaves provided cheap labor, the Greeks and Romans did not apply their knowledge to building machines.

3. ...Rephrase the sentences, using noun modifiers.

■ Make sure the students understand what noun modifiers are and how they are formed. (See the Language Note which follows.) Have them read through the exercise items and then do the exercise.

■ Tell the students to compare answers with a partner. Next call on different pairs; have one partner read aloud the sentence from the book and have the other read aloud the rephrased sentence.

ANSWERS
1. a beautiful handmade chair
2. the highest-paid clerks
3. the best-prepared students
4. a battery-operated watch

LANGUAGE NOTE

Nouns or adverbs can also be combined with the present participle of a verb to form noun modifiers:

He's a salesman who talks fast. = He's a fast-talking salesman.

She's a woman who loves peace. = She's a peace-loving woman.

OPTION

Divide the class into two teams. Tell the team members to work together to come up with five sentences like those in the exercise items and in the Language Note above—sentences with nouns or adverbs that can be rephrased with noun modifiers. Tell the team members to write down the sentences. When they finish, call on a member from one team to say a sentence aloud. See if a member of the other team can come up with the correct rephrased sentence. Continue the game by next calling on a member of the opposing team. Score a point for every correctly rephrased sentence. The team with the most points wins.

FOLLOW-UP

Students can choose a paragraph from the article and write a brief summary of what it says.

WORKBOOK Lesson 21, p. 25

were set in a straight line, they would extend across the Atlantic Ocean from England to the United States.

The Chinese were actually centuries ahead of the rest of the world in many areas. Around 300 B.C. they developed the world's oldest system of roads. The national highway system was carefully maintained, and drivers of horse-drawn wagons caught speeding were arrested and fined.

Regularly during the Middle Ages and Renaissance, Europe became excited over "inventions" that had originated in China centuries earlier and had migrated slowly westward to Europe. Canals and rivers were controlled by locks in China in the third century B.C., seventeen centuries ahead of Europe. When we sit down to have a dish of spaghetti, we are really having a Chinese meal. Spaghetti originated in China, and it was brought back to Italy by Marco Polo. Gunpowder, which finally made its way to Europe in the 1400s, actually originated in China in the eighth century. The Chinese

even developed the process of printing with wood or metal blocks in 600 A.D., over 800 years before Johann Gutenberg printed the famous Gutenberg Bible, the first book to be printed in movable type in Europe.

When we look at the incredible accomplishments of the Chinese, it becomes clear that the Greeks and Romans could have done more with their technology. Perhaps one reason they didn't is that they felt no need for machines. Slaves provided the ultimate cheap labor.

It is likely that 2,000 years from today people will look back on us with a mixture of admiration and puzzlement. Just as we do when we look back on ancient civilizations, future people will marvel at our ingenuity under such primitive conditions. But just as we wonder why the Greeks and Romans failed to develop their science further, people of the future will no doubt shake their heads in puzzlement over our failure to make even better use of our scientific knowledge.

Figure it out

1. **Before reading the entire article, scan the first sentence of each paragraph to find out which ancient cultures the article focuses on. Then read the last paragraph and summarize the article's main point.**

2. **As you read the article, pay attention to the important points that are made about each culture. When you have finished, complete the sentences below with the name of the correct people(s) or place(s). Then find several facts in the article that support each statement.**

   1. Although they were not that well known, the _____ built an incredible system of roads and an amazing bridge.
   2. The _____ made full use of their scientific knowledge. Many inventions originated in _____ centuries before they reached _____ .
   3. The accomplishments of the _____ in building were very impressive; however, they could have done more with their technology.

3. **Many modifiers of nouns may be formed by combining a noun or adverb with the past participle of a verb, as in these examples from the article:**

   - **horse-drawn wagons =** *wagons* that are/were *drawn* by *horses*

   - **the best-documented technology = the** *technology* that is/was *documented the best*

   Rephrase the sentences below, using noun modifiers.

   1. I bought a beautiful chair yesterday that was made by hand. (The modifier is one word.)
   2. I would never take a job at Lou's Bookstore. The clerks that are paid the highest only make $20,000 a year.
   3. It's important to study hard. Only the students that are prepared the best get into good universities.
   4. This is a watch that's operated by batteries. You'll never have to wind it.

22. It belonged to your grandparents.

1. People didn't always travel by car or plane, turn on the water faucet for a drink of water, go to the supermarket for a package of flour, or watch TV for entertainment. What important changes in technology have taken place during your own lifetime or during your parents' lifetime? Describe at least one change to your partner.

 Lisa Scott is helping her parents clean out the attic when she finds something unexpected.

Listen to the conversation.

②

Lisa	Hey, look what I found! What is this ugly old thing? It weighs a ton.
Mrs. Scott	Hold on now. . . . That happens to be a radio, and I used to listen to it when I was just a kid. It belonged to your grandparents.
Lisa	It's incredible! Why would anyone have wanted a radio that looked like this?
Mr. Scott	Well, first of all, there weren't any smaller ones in those days. Furthermore, this radio was considered quite attractive when my mother and father were young.
Lisa	Really? Hmm . . .
Mr. Scott	You know, in those days people would invite their friends over to listen to the radio for the evening.
Lisa	No kidding!
Mrs. Scott	Remember when the first transistor radios came out, Jim? They caused as much excitement as laptop computers.
Mr. Scott	That's the truth. I remember getting a shiny, new silver radio for my birthday. I couldn't believe it was only six inches long and I was able to carry it around in my pocket.
Mrs. Scott	It's not only appliances that have gotten smaller, though. Think of houses, apartments, and cars. Even ceilings used to be several feet higher than those in modern houses.
Mr. Scott	Not to mention doorways! Now if you're over six feet tall, you have to bend over.
Lisa	How tall are you exactly?
Mr. Scott	Six two, unfortunately. (*Rubs bump on head*)

3. Find another way to say it.

1. It fit in my pocket.
2. It was only six inches in length.
3. What's your exact height?
4. That's true.
5. You couldn't find any smaller ones then.
6. It's really heavy!
7. People thought this radio was very good-looking.

22. It belonged to your grandparents.

1. Warm-up Activity

- Have two students read aloud the information in the box. Next, have the students work in small groups to discuss the question. Then have them describe a change in technology to a partner.

- Go around the classroom and join in the discussions. Then have different students tell the class about important changes that have taken place in technology.

2. Conversation

BACKGROUND

Lisa Scott is helping her parents clean out the attic when she finds something unexpected—an old radio. Lisa's parents talk about the radio and changes in technology over time.

LANGUAGE

It weighs a ton. is an exaggeration used to emphasize the fact that the radio weighs a lot— more than most radios weigh nowadays.

Hold on now... is another way of saying "Wait a moment... Be careful about what you're saying."

That happens to be (a radio) is another way of saying "Surprising as it may seem, that's (a radio)."

...just (a kid) means *no more than* or *no older than (a kid).*

...quite (attractive) means *rather (attractive).*

No kidding! is used to express astonishment. It's like saying "You must be kidding!"

...(carry it) around means *(carry it) from one place to another.*

Even (ceilings) is used to emphasize the degree or extent of something—in this case, the fact that not only are appliances, buildings, and cars smaller, but ceilings are also lower.

...to bend over means *to stoop.*

How tall are you exactly? is another way of saying "What's your exact height."

Six two is short for *Six feet and two inches (tall).*

PROCEDURE

- As the students examine the illustration, point out the three characters from the conversation. Ask a student to describe what's happening in the picture.

- Follow a procedure similar to that indicated for the opening conversation in Unit 1.

3. Find another way to say it.

- Call on different students to read aloud the exercise sentences. Answer any questions.

- Tell the students to do the exercise and then compare answers with a partner. Then call on different students to read the answers aloud. Ask a student to write the answers on the board for you to check.

ANSWERS
1. I was able to carry it around in my pocket.
2. It was only six inches long.
3. How tall are you exactly?
4. That's the truth.
5. There weren't any smaller ones in those days.
6. It weighs a ton!
7. This radio was considered quite attractive.

CULTURE CLOSE-UP

Many houses in the U.S., especially those with pointed roofs, have attics. Attics are usually used as storage places. Many people tend to store old items that they are attached to for one reason or another which they hope to someday restore, pass on to their children or grandchildren, or sell.

FOLLOW-UP

Students can write down their answers to the question in the box in exercise 1.

WORKBOOK Lesson 22, p. 26

23. What were they like?

WARM-UP

Play a game to guess the ages of different people and things. Begin by asking different students questions. Encourage other opinions. For example:

T: How old do you think that monument is in the city square?

S1: About a hundred years old.

S2: Oh, I disagree. I think it's only about 50 years old.

T: How old do you think the mayor's husband is?

S1: Gee . . . He must be about 60 years old.

S2: What? You must be kidding! He's got to be almost 80.

Continue the game by calling on different students to ask their classmates similar questions.

DESCRIBE SOMETHING • TALK ABOUT DIMENSIONS

- Have the students follow along in their books as you read the instructions aloud. Then point out the illustrations and ask different students to read the captions aloud and describe the items. Explain that the word *circa* is Latin for *approximately*.

- Have the students listen to the conversations and number the items. Then tell them to compare answers with a partner. Next write the answers on the board.

TAPESCRIPT

1. **A** What in the world is this?
   B Oh, my great-grandmother had one of those in her attic. Before washing machines were invented, people had to scrub their clothes by hand. . . .
   A They used one of these to wash clothes?
   B No, but after the clothes were washed, they used it to squeeze the water out.

2. **A** Grandpa, how were things different when you were a little boy?
   B So many things were different that I don't know where to begin! . . . Well, for instance, I couldn't just walk into the kitchen and get myself a cold drink like you do.
   A Really? Why not?
   B We didn't have a refrigerator. Instead we had a small box used to keep just a few things cold—like meat and dairy products.
   A How was it different from a refrigerator?
   B Oh, it was much smaller and narrower. And it wasn't electric. You had to put blocks of ice in it to keep things cold.

3. **A** Look at this picture. I remember seeing one of these once at a flea market. Have you ever seen one?
   B No, what were they like?
   A Oh, they were much bigger and heavier than the ones we have today. And you had to heat them on the stove before you pressed clothes with them.

B That doesn't sound like too much fun.
A I'm sure it wasn't.

4. **A** Thanks for coming to the antique store with me. I know it's not your favorite thing to do.
   B That's O.K. Believe it or not, I found something I like.
   A What?
   B This.
   A Oh. What is it?
   B People used to play music on it. You put a record here, turned this crank, and the music came out through this trumpet.
   A Huh, I've never seen one of these before. It's a lot bigger than a CD player. How did the music sound?
   B Kind of scratchy, and when it slowed down, you had to turn the crank again. But it looks much more interesting than a CD player, don't you think?

ANSWERS

- Have the students read over the conversation. Answer any questions they have. Then have them listen to the conversation. You can act it out with a student.

- Read aloud the second set of instructions. Then call on different students to read aloud the information in the ads. Answer any questions. Next point out and read aloud the information on the floor plan and in the box beneath it. Answer any questions. If necessary, tell the students how to convert inches into feet (12 inches = 1 foot).

- Tell the students to work with a partner and follow the second set of instructions. You may want to act out a sample conversation with a student in front of the class before the students practice theirs.

- Go around the room and listen in on the conversations, giving help if necessary. Then call on different pairs to act out their conversations for the class.

OPTION

Bring to class (or have the student bring) magazine or newspaper pictures of different household items—for example, furniture and appliances. Distribute the pictures to pairs of students. Tell them to make up measurements for the items unless they're already stated. Then have them act out conversations similar to the one in the exercise, using the pictures and the floor plan in their books. Depending on the kind of household items featured in their pictures, they may have to first expand their floor plans by drawing additional rooms with appropriate dimensions. Go around the room and check the pairs' work.

23. What were they like?

 1 ▶ Listen to people describe some old-fashioned items. Number the items in the order of the conversations you hear.

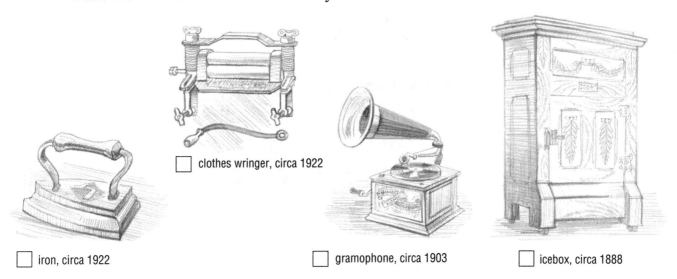

☐ clothes wringer, circa 1922

☐ iron, circa 1922   ☐ gramophone, circa 1903   ☐ icebox, circa 1888

 2 ▶ Listen to the conversation.
▶ Act out similar conversations with a partner. You would like to buy the items in the ad for your house or apartment. Your partner will help you figure out if you can use each one.

A I saw an ad for a beautiful old pine table. I'm thinking of buying it.
B Really? Where would you put it?
A I thought I'd put it in the dining area.
B Well, will it fit? How big is it?
A It's four feet wide and six feet long.
B I think it would be too long. Your dining area is only eight feet by eight feet.

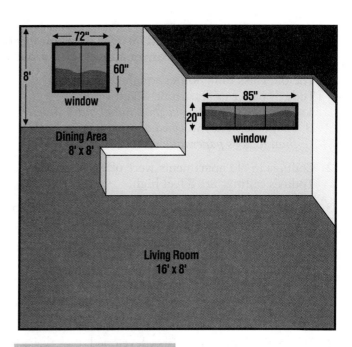

Beautiful old pine table, 4' wide x 6' long. Reasonable price. Call 555-4043.

Pair of floor-length red Japanese curtains. 100% silk. 72" wide x 90" long. $35. Call Marion at 555-9756.

Antique Swiss grandfather clock, 7½ feet tall. 555-7566 after 6 P.M.

Large, sturdy oak bookcase, 7' wide x 8' high x 1' deep. Deep enough for those annoying big books. Must sell. Only $125. Call 555-4321.

4' × 6' = 4 feet by 6 feet
89" = 89 inches

3 ▶ **Study the frames: Dimensions and weight**

How	tall	is Tom?
	high	is the ceiling?
	wide	is the material?
	long	is the trail?
	thick	is the steak?
	deep	is the bookcase?

He's	six feet	tall.
It's	eight feet	high.
	two yards	wide.
	three miles	long.
	an inch	thick.
	one foot	deep.

Singular	Plural
foot	feet

Some opposites

tall	short
high	low
wide	narrow
long	short
thick	thin
deep	shallow
heavy	light

How	big	is your living room?

It's	12 feet by 14 feet.

How	heavy	is the box?
How much		does the box **weigh**?

It's / It **weighs**	ten pounds.

Comparisons of dimensions

The bookcase is	two feet / ten pounds	**higher** / **heavier**	**than**	the desk.
The bookcase weighs	ten pounds	**more**	**than**	the desk.

Always use the word *tall* when talking about a person's height. When talking about an object, generally use the word *high*. *Clock* is one exception.

4 ▶ **Write a question and answer for each item. Then act out the conversations with a partner.**

1. The old glass milk bottles weighed 15 ounces.
   Today's paper milk cartons weigh 1 ounce.
   A *How much did the old glass milk bottles weigh?*
   B *15 ounces. They weighed about 14 ounces more than today's paper milk cartons.*

2. Ceilings in old apartments were often 10 feet high.
   Today's ceilings are 8 feet high.

3. The first pocket calculators weighed about 14 ounces.
   The new ones weigh less than 2 ounces.

4. The average woman in the eighteenth century was under 5 feet tall.
   The average woman today is about 5 feet 5 inches tall.

5. The first television screens were only 10 inches wide.
   Now some television screens are 36 inches wide.

6. When computers were first developed, they were 10 feet high by 10 feet wide.
   Today some laptop computers are only 10 inches tall and less than 1 foot wide.

- Have the students examine the frames as you and different class members read aloud the possible sentences. You can also have the students repeat the sentences after you.

- Point out the information in the boxes and have the students repeat the pairs of words after you. Answer any questions students have about the structures and vocabulary in the frames and boxes.

OPTION

Divide the class into two teams—A and B. Tell the team members to make up ten original questions with *How . . . ?* like the ones in the frame. Tell them to make up questions about persons and things which are probably familiar to their classmates. Then have them compile answers which are as accurate as possible. Next have a member from Team A ask the other team a question. If the other team answers correctly, they score a point. Next have a member from Team B ask a question, etc. The team with the most points wins. For example:

Team A: How tall is (*Team A member's name*)?
Team B: He/She's six feet tall.
Team A: Sorry. She's five feet eleven inches.

- Point out the illustration and ask a student to describe the two items. Then have the students listen to the sample conversation.

- Have the students follow the instructions. Tell them to model their questions and answers on the sample in their books. They can work in pairs on the exercise. Go around the classroom and answer any questions about the questions and answers they're writing.

- Tell the students to act out the conversations with a partner. Go around the room and listen in, giving help if necessary. Finally, call on different pairs to act out the conversations for the class.

ANSWERS

2. **A** How high were ceilings in old apartments?
   B Often 10 feet high. They were about 2 feet higher than today's ceilings.
3. **A** How much did the first pocket calculators weigh?
   B About 14 ounces. They weighed about 12 ounces more than the new ones.
4. **A** How tall was the average woman in the eighteenth century?
   B Under 5 feet tall. The average woman today is at least 5 inches taller.
5. **A** How wide were the first television screens?
   B Only 10 inches wide. Nowadays some screens are 26 inches wider.
6. **A** How big were the first computers?
   B 10 feet high by 10 feet wide. They were much taller and wider than today's laptop computers.

DESCRIBE A HOUSEHOLD PROBLEM • ORDER OF ADJECTIVES

- Point out the first illustration and read the language in it aloud. Then have the students listen to the conversation. Answer any questions.

- Point out the other illustrations and the information in the box and have the students repeat the language after you. Then ask a student to read the instructions aloud. Answer any questions about the procedure.

- Have the students act out similar conversations with a partner. Go around the classroom and listen in, giving help when needed. Finally, call on different pairs to act out their conversations for the class.

CULTURE CLOSE-UP

Americans are known for fixing up and even building things around home during their free time. While in many countries, persons hire skilled laborers to perform such tasks as painting houses, putting down floor tiles, and building furniture, Americans often take on these tasks themselves. (And what often surprises visitors from other countries is that Americans engaged in these activities seem to be enjoying themselves!)

- Have the students examine the frames as you read aloud the contents. Point out how the stress on each of the adjectives is usually of the same degree of intensity unless one of them is being emphasized. (See the Pronunciation Note which follows.) Have the students repeat the phrases after you.

- Read aloud the information beneath the frame. Then provide some examples of the variable order—for example, say "the old ugly black dress." Next read aloud the information in the box. Answer any questions.

OPTION

Have the students copy the headings from the frame onto separate paper. Tell them to create columns under each heading. Then ask them to come up with four appropriate words and write them under the "Noun" column. Next have them exchange papers with a partner. Tell the students to write phrases—modeled on those in the frame in

their books—across the columns of the papers they received from their partners. For example:

Student A writes in the "Noun" column: bicycle

Student B writes:

the   beautiful,   new   red

Have the pairs compare and check their phrases. Go around the room and check their work. Finally, call on different pairs to write their phrases on the board.

PRONUNCIATION NOTE

Note the usual stress pattern:

the fírst twó Japanése movies (equal stress)

However, if the speaker is referring to several pairs of Japanese movies but wants to emphasize the first pair, the stress pattern would be:

the fírst twó Japanése movies (not the second two)

- Tell the students to read over the incomplete letter. Answer any questions. Then read the instructions aloud and have the students complete the letter.

- Tell the students to compare answers with a partner. Then call on different students to read aloud the sentences from the letter and write the answers on the board.

ANSWERS
fascinating old Roman, little Italian, several beautiful turn-of-the-century, hand-painted Italian, small green porcelain, square rosewood

OPTION

Tell the students to answer Mona's letter. Have them pretend they just took a trip to an interesting city and bought several unusual things there. Tell them to use Mona's letter as a model and to include several nouns preceded by adjectives. When they finish, have them compare letters with a partner. Finally, call on different pairs to read their letters aloud and write them on the board.

FOLLOW-UP

Students can write out the conversations they acted out in exercise 5.

5 ► **Listen to the conversation.**
► **Act out similar conversations with a partner, using the information in the box and the solutions suggested by the pictures.**

A I really ought to do something about my kitchen floor. The linoleum looks so dull and worn.
B Why don't you put down some new tiles?
A You know, that's a good idea. Some of these nice yellow vinyl tiles would make a big difference.

Some problems
a dull, worn linoleum floor
peeling paint on the bathroom walls
piles of books cluttering up the floor

6 ► **Study the frame: Order of adjectives**

	Ordinal number	Cardinal number	General	Age	Color	Material	Origin	Noun
the	first	two					Japanese	movies
			ugly,	old	black			dress
			large		blue	cotton		pants
			shiny,	new		leather		boots

▲

This category includes adjectives of opinion, size, shape, cost, and condition. Their order is generally flexible.

Use a comma between adjectives if the comma could be replaced by *and*.
the charming, intelligent professor =
the charming and intelligent professor

7 ► **Rewrite the letter, completing the sentences by putting the adjectives in parentheses in the correct order.**

Dear Charles,

August 14

I'm having a wonderful time sightseeing in Italy. I've especially enjoyed the _____ (fascinating, Roman, old) ruins. You know I've always been interested in history.

I've also done some shopping. I went to a _____ (Italian, little) antique shop over the weekend, and I bought _____ (beautiful, turn-of-the-century, several) things I think you'll like. I bought a _____ (Italian, hand-painted) mandolin and a _____ _____ (green, small, porcelain) vase. I also bought a _____ _____ (rosewood, square) table, which will look great in our apartment.

See you soon.

Love,
Mona

24. Your turn

How does the photo of New York 100 years ago compare
with the photo of New York today? What do you think
will be different about big cities by the year 2500?
Discuss these questions in small groups. Then work
together to design an ideal "city of the future."

New York City 100 years ago

New York City today

24. Your turn

- Point out the photos on p. 48 and read aloud the captions. Ask two students to describe the pictures.

- Ask a student to read aloud the instructions. Answer any questions about the exercise procedure.

- Have the students work in small groups to discuss the questions. When they finish, tell them to design their ideal city. Explain that they should make a sketch of it and write a description on separate paper.

- Go around the classroom and check the groups' work. Then call on different group reporters to show the class their sketches and read aloud the corresponding descriptions.

CULTURE CLOSE-UP

New York City is probably the most famous city in the U.S. The core of the city, Manhattan, was first settled by the Dutch in 1624. During the 19th century, thousands of European immigrants arrived and settled in the city. Today New York is the largest city in the U.S.—the population of its metropolitan area is over eighteen million people. The city is located at the mouth of the Hudson River on a complex assortment of islands and parts of islands. Its most famous island, of course, is Manhattan, the most densely populated part of the city and its economic and cultural center. There are many famous places to visit in New York City. Among them are the Statue of Liberty, Central Park, the United Nations headquarters, the Lincoln Center for the Performing Arts, the Empire State Building, the World Trade Center, Greenwich Village, and several world-famous museums such as the Metropolitan Museum of Art.

Listen in

- Read the boldfaced instructions aloud. Then, so the students know what to listen for, have them read over the exercise items before they listen to the conversation. Next point out the pictures and ask different students to read the captions aloud. Ask other students to briefly describe the pictures.

- Have the students listen to the conversation and answer the questions. When they finish, have the students compare answers with a partner. Then call on different students to read their answers aloud and write them on the board.

TAPESCRIPT

Guide Welcome to our current exhibit on "The Home in History." It is the intention of this exhibit to show how the design of the home reflects the economic, social, and perhaps even the political trends of different periods of history. There is no better place to start, I think, than in that center of family activity—the kitchen. If you will please follow me. . . . The first kitchen in our exhibit is probably a little bigger than your own. You will notice that it is one enormous open room with a high ceiling and large work tables. There is a huge open fireplace to the left where food could be cooked for hundreds of people at one time. It took about twenty-five people to prepare a meal here, and a meal for a special occasion could take several days to prepare. As you can see, this kitchen was not designed for the frozen dinner. This particular kitchen dates back to the early 1700s. It is not an example of the ordinary family's kitchen, but it does represent certain requirements in building a kitchen that were common in homes of that era. Can you point out what some of these necessary design features were? Yes. . . .

Woman 1 Well, the ceiling was probably high so all the smoke and heat from the fireplace could rise. Otherwise, it would be extremely hot and uncomfortable to work in.

Man 1 And the fireplace itself was so large because all the food was prepared at home in those days and many things had to be cooked at the same time. I mean, you didn't have frozen and canned foods in those days to make your life easier.

Guide Good point. Anybody else?

Woman 2 Well, in general, I think kitchens were larger than they are today because people needed more room just to store things and to prepare and cook food. Look at all the things you had to do in the kitchen in those days. You even had to clean and cut up your own animals for meat.

Man 2 And I suppose you needed a lot of room to . . .

ANSWERS

1. An eighteenth-century Italian kitchen
2. 1. a
   2. a
   3. a

- Read aloud the second set of instructions. Tell the students to work in groups. Go around the room and join in the discussions. Finally, call on different students to point out the similarities and differences among the kitchens in the pictures and to tell the class that they think kitchens will be like in the year 2500.

FOLLOW-UP

Students can write down their descriptions of what kitchens will be like in the year 2500.

WORKBOOK Lessons 23-24, pp. 27-29

▣ Listen in

A group of people at a museum are listening to a museum guide. Read the questions below. Then listen to the conversation and answer the questions.

1. Which kitchen in the photos did the guide describe?

2. What explanations did members of the group give for features of this kitchen? Choose *a* or *b*.
   1. The ceiling was high so
      a. smoke and heat from the fireplace could rise.
      b. there could be more space for storage.
   2. A large fireplace was necessary because
      a. all food was prepared at home and many things were cooked at the same time.
      b. families were much larger in those days.
   3. In general, kitchens were larger than they are today because
      a. people needed more space to store supplies and to prepare and cook food.
      b. families spent a lot of their time in the kitchen.

An eighteenth-century Italian kitchen with helpers preparing vegetables, meat, and poultry.

A kitchen in the 1950s.

A modern kitchen, spacious and airy.

Work with a group to discuss the similarities and differences among the kitchens in the photos. Then discuss what you think kitchens will be like in the year 2500.

25. On your own

1. **You've just won the lottery and are planning to do many exciting things. Write a letter to your friend describing exactly what you'll buy and do. Use at least two adjectives in each descriptive sentence. You can continue the letter below or write your own.**

Dear _____,

I've just won the lottery! You've no idea how excited I am. Besides taking a trip to visit you, here are some of the other things I want to do:

- I plan to buy two shiny, new cars—one for city driving and one for the country.
- I want to take my mother on a wonderful, long ocean cruise.
- . . .

2. **Write an essay, choosing one of the options below.**

1. Describe something that really impresses you about contemporary living and compare it to the way it was in the past. Some possible topics are entertainment, clothing, transportation, and appliances.
2. Describe something that people in your country used to do (or an item they used to use) that has changed significantly. You may choose a topic you've discussed in this unit or an idea of your own.

25. On your own

- Have a student read aloud the instructions. Ask another student to read the letter aloud. Answer any questions. Then point out the illustrations and ask a student how they relate to the letter.

- Tell the students to continue the letter or write their own on separate paper. When they finish, have them go over their work with a partner.

- Go around the room and answer any questions students have about their own writing. Finally, call on different students to read their letters aloud and write them on the board. Alternatively, you can collect the letters, mark any errors, and return them to the students so they can rewrite them.

- Read aloud the general instructions for the second exercise. Then have two students read aloud the specific instructions. Answer any questions.

- You can assign the exercise for homework. (See the Option which follows.) After the students hand in their essays, mark any errors and return the papers so the students can make necessary corrections. Collect the essays again and check the corrections.

OPTION

Have the students use magazine or newspaper pictures or photos they have at home to complement their descriptions. Tell them to prepare their homework for presentation and display in class.

WORKBOOK Lesson 25, p. 30. Before assigning the writing task, point out the words and phrases used by Mr. Fautier to describe his apartment. Remind the students to use similar expressions in their letters.

PREVIEW

Before you begin teaching, go over the functions/themes, language, and forms in the chart. This will give you a preview of what you will encounter as you guide the students through the unit.

Preview the reading.

- Point out the illustration. Then read aloud the instructions for the first exercise and have the students work in small groups to discuss birth rank. Go around the room and join in the discussions. Finally, call on different students to tell the class about their birth rank.

- Read aloud the instructions for the second exercise. Answer any questions. Then have the students do the exercise. When they finish, tell them to compare answers with a partner.

FUNCTIONS/THEMES	LANGUAGE	FORMS
Give reasons Talk about consequences	What were your parents like when you were growing up? They were very strict with me since/as they believed children needed a lot of discipline. One of my brothers was near my age, so we played together a lot.	Connectors (conjunctions and prepositions)
Make a proposal Talk about people	Ms. Abrams, on the other hand, is very friendly and easygoing. Therefore, I think she would make a much better impression on clients. I suggest that we have Ms. Martin and Ms. Abrams switch jobs. I don't get along with my older sister. I try to stand up for myself.	Three-word verbs

Preview the reading.

1. Work in small groups. Your birth rank means the order in which you were born among the children in your family. Tell the members of your group your birth rank. Then guess and discuss how your birth rank has affected your life.

2. Substitute *Firstborn children* or *Later children* for the pronoun *They* in each statement below. Try to guess the answers.

1. They may have trouble making close friends.
2. They like creative fields such as music, art, or writing.
3. They are relaxed and sociable.

4. They like professions such as teaching and politics.
5. They are usually very ambitious.
6. They often make good salespeople.
7. They tend to be somewhat conservative.

It was probably no accident that George Orwell used the term Big Brother for the dictator in his novel *1984.* Psychologists have long been aware that birth order generally creates certain personality traits.

Big brothers and sisters usually develop leadership tendencies early in life, mainly because of the responsibilities for younger siblings given to them by their parents. The danger, experts on family and child psychology report, is that if the older sibling takes that role to an extreme, he or she can become an overbearing and tyrannical adult.

Studies of nearly 3,000 people conducted by Walter Toman, former professor of psychology at Brandeis University in Massachusetts, have found that, under normal circumstances, firstborns are usually the most strongly motivated toward achievement. This, he maintains, is mainly a result of parental expectations.

This and other research suggests that firstborn children generally become more conservative than their siblings because they receive most of the parental discipline. Used to caring for others, they are more likely to move toward such leadership professions as teaching and politics. Less social and flexible because they became accustomed in the very early years to acting alone, they may have difficulty making close friends.

By contrast, the researchers say, later children are more likely to be more relaxed and sociable, and less inhibited than the eldest child because their parents were more relaxed. However, the later children are often less ambitious and are uncomfortable making decisions for others, and will seek work that fits such needs. This, according to researchers, may help explain why younger siblings tend to favor the creative fields such as music, art, or writing.

Later children often make good salespeople because persuasion may have been the only tool they had to counteract the power of the eldest. Younger children tend to remain forever "the baby," enjoyable to be around, and inspiring compassion; but they can become overdependent on others.

While birth order is clearly only one of the many factors that affect development, its impact should not be underestimated. When people understand how their birth order causes them to react, they do

26. Birth Rank: Effects on Personality

PROCEDURE

- Point out the illustrations and have two students describe them.

- Have the students read through the article. Follow a procedure similar to that on p. 2 of this book.

Figure it out

1. Read the article.

- After the students have read the article, tell them to check their answers to item 2 on p. 51. Then have them find the reasons in the article.

- Have the students compare answers with a partner. Then call on different students to say the answers aloud.

  ANSWERS
  1. Firstborn children – They are less social and flexible because they became used to doing things alone when they were young.
  2. Later children – They are less ambitious and are uncomfortable making decisions for others, so they look for work that fits these needs.
  3. Later children – Their parents were more relaxed with them than they were with the oldest child.
  4. Firstborn children – They are used to caring for others, so they look for work where they can do this.
  5. Firstborn children – Their parents had very high expectations for them.
  6. Later children – They learned to use persuasion when they were young to protect themselves against their older brothers and sisters.
  7. Firstborn children – Their parents were stricter with them and disciplined them more.

2. Make a list of the personality traits discussed in the article.

- Answer any questions about the procedure. Then have the students do the exercise.

- Have the students compare answers with a partner. Then make four columns on the board for the four categories. Call on different students to write the personality traits in the appropriate column. Next ask them to share with the class their explanations about marrying someone.

  ANSWERS
  1. Firstborn children, advantages:
     They make good leaders and enjoy caring for others. They are high achievers.
  2. Firstborn children, disadvantages:
     They can be overbearing and bossy. They may not be very social and flexible.
  3. Later children, advantages:
     They are relaxed and sociable. They are often creative. They are good at persuading people to do things. They are enjoyable to be around.
  4. Later children, disadvantages:
     They may not be very ambitious. They may feel uncomfortable making decisions for others. They may be overdependent on others.

If two firstborn children marry, they may have a lot of arguments because both people will want to make the decisions, and they won't be flexible or willing to change their minds. If two later children marry, they both may expect the other to take charge and also be ambitious. They may become angry when this doesn't happen. However, if a firstborn child marries a later child, each will be able to play the role he or she is most comfortable with. The later child will be happy that the firstborn child is making the decisions. Even though the firstborn child may not be flexible, the later child will be good at persuading him or her and preventing conflicts.

3. ...Complete the sentences with either *over-* or *under-* plus the word in parentheses.

- Answer any questions about the procedure. Then have the students read over the incomplete sentences. Answer any questions.

- Tell the students to do the exercise and then compare answers with a partner. Then call on different students to read the completed sentences aloud and write the answers on the board.

  ANSWERS
  1. overweight, overeat
  2. underachiever
  3. overprotects
  4. underpaid

OPTION

Tell the students to use the five words in the answers in sentences which show they know the meaning of these words. Tell the students to write their sentences on separate paper. When they finish, have them compare sentences with a partner. Next ask them to write their sentences on the board and read them aloud.

FOLLOW-UP

Students can write down the main idea of the article.

WORKBOOK Lesson 26, p. 31

EFFECTS ON PERSONALITY
by Andrée Brooks

not find change so threatening, says Lucille Forer, a clinical psychologist in Malibu, California, who has written extensively on the subject.

An understanding of birth order can sometimes help a marriage work. Not long ago, Dr. Forer was working with a woman who had become so domineering that her marriage was in trouble. Once she understood her tendencies, Dr. Forer said, she could begin to modify her behavior.

Maida Webster, a family therapist and school consultant in Norwich, Connecticut, recently conducted a workshop called "Birth Order Factor." She told of a husband and wife who complained bitterly about being let down by the other. Neither, it seemed, had taken over the leadership role that each had expected the other to assume. When it was

pointed out that this was probably because each had been a younger sibling, they began to comprehend the problem.

"Is there an ideal combination for marriage?" Mrs. Webster was asked. Both at work and in personal relationships, she said, people seem to get along best when they repeat the patterns of childhood, which means that it helps to marry someone in a complementary position. In contrast, two people who were the eldest children can expect conflict.

"Is there any best position in the birth order?" asked someone else. Mrs. Webster said no, that there were benefits and disadvantages to all. However, she went on, recognizing tendencies can enhance opportunities to make the most of positive traits and minimize negative ones.

Figure it out

1. **Read the article. When you have finished, check your answers to item 2 on page 51. Then, for each statement, find a reason given in the article to explain it.**

2. **Make a list of the personality traits discussed in the article, dividing them, according to the author's opinion, into the four categories listed below. Then, using the information in your lists, explain why it might be best to marry someone whose birth rank is different from your own.**

1. Firstborn children, advantages
2. Firstborn children, disadvantages
3. Later children, advantages
4. Later children, disadvantages

3. **The prefixes *over-* and *under-*, as in *overdependent* and *underestimate*, may be placed before many words to mean "more than normal or desired" and "less than normal or desired," respectively. Complete the sentences below with either *over-* or *under-* plus the word in parentheses.**

1. The reason Marcy's son is so _____ (weight) is that he eats constantly. I don't understand why she lets him _____ (eat) so.
2. My daughter's teacher says she's an _____ (achiever), and that I don't push her enough. That may be, but I want her to enjoy herself.
3. Tony really _____ (protect) his brother. He never lets him out of his sight.
4. I'm really _____ (paid) on my job. If I don't get a good raise, I'm going to leave.

27. Look at the bright side.

1. **Which of the following words best describes the way you were as a child? Explain to your partner why you think you were that way.**

outgoing	friendly
shy	unfriendly
cooperative	self-confident
uncooperative	insecure

 Angela Mendez, a sales representative, is discussing her childhood with a coworker, Nick Andros, at an office party.

Listen to the conversation.

2

Angela Hi, Nick! How's that boring desk job going these days?

Nick Boring? I happen to like working at my desk. As a matter of fact, I don't know how you can put up with being a sales representative, Angela. I mean, don't you ever get tired of trying to convince people all the time?

Angela Actually, that's the part I enjoy most. It reminds me of my childhood.

Nick How's that?

Angela Well, I had an older sister, so I quickly learned to stand up for myself and not give in to everything she wanted.

Nick But what does that have to do with being a sales representative?

Angela Well, in order to get my way, I had to convince her that my way was right. It took a lot of effort, too. Since she was older, she usually thought she knew better.

Nick I've heard that older brothers and sisters can be pretty bossy. I wouldn't know. I was an only child.

Angela My sister was as tough as nails. She never let me get away with anything. She even used to punish me for misbehaving.

Nick She sounds like a real tyrant!

Angela Yes, but look at the bright side. As a result, I learned the skills I use now when I deal with my toughest customers. They almost always have a soft side underneath.

Nick Well, I guess there's always something you can learn from your childhood. . . .

3. **Match.**

1. I was an only child,
2. Since my parents thought discipline was important,
3. I had to stand up for myself
4. My parents always rewarded me
5. My brother was older than I was,

a. in order to get what I wanted.
b. for getting good grades in school.
c. so I didn't have to share things with anyone else.
d. so he always treated me like a baby.
e. I didn't misbehave very often.

27. Look at the bright side.

1. Warm-up Activity

- Have a student read aloud the instructions in the box. Then have the class repeat the words after you. Answer any questions.

- Tell the students to work with a partner on the exercise. Go around the classroom and listen in. Then, have different students tell the class about their childhoods.

2. Conversation

BACKGROUND

Angela Mendez, a sales representative, is discussing her childhood with a coworker, Nick Andros, at an office party. She tells Nick about her relationship with an older sister and how it affects her job.

LANGUAGE

As a matter of fact is used to introduce information to support what the speaker had said previously.

…put up with means *tolerate.*

How's that? is used to ask for an explanation. It's like asking "Why?"

…stand up for (myself) means *defend (myself).*

…give in to means *accommodate.*

…what does that have to do with is another way of saying "how is that related to."

…in order to get my way is another way of saying "for me to do what I wanted."

It took (a lot of effort) is another way of saying "It required (a lot of effort)."

…an only child is the single offspring of a set of parents.

as tough as nails is an idiomatic expression used to describe someone who is very strong-willed.

…get away with is another way of saying "avoid being punished for."

…look at the bright side is an expression of optimism. It's another way of saying "look at the positive aspects."

…deal with here means *do business with.*

…a soft side underneath. is another way of saying "a gentle side." It refers to the sensitive part of someone's personality or character.

PROCEDURE

- As the students examine the illustration, point out the two characters and have a student describe what's happening in the picture.

- Follow a procedure similar to that indicated for the opening conversation in Unit 1.

3. Match.

- Have the students read over the language in the two columns. Answer any questions they have. Then tell the students to do the exercise.

- Have the students compare their answers with a partner. Next call on different students to read the answers aloud as you write the answers on the board.

ANSWERS
1. c
2. e
3. a
4. b
5. d

FOLLOW-UP

Students can write out the sentences in exercise 3.

WORKBOOK Lesson 27, p. 32

28. How did you get along with them?

WARM-UP

Refer the students to the illustrations at the bottom of the page. Then tell them your favorite activity as a child. Next call on different students to tell the class their favorite childhood activities.

GIVE REASONS • TALK ABOUT CONSEQUENCES

- Have the students listen to the conversation as they read it in their books. Then ask a pair of students to act it out for the class.

- Point out the boxes and call on different students to read aloud the possible sentences. Answer any questions.

- Read aloud the second set of instructions. Then have the students work with a partner to act out similar conversations.

- Go around the classroom and listen in on the conversations, giving help as needed. Then call on different pairs to act out their conversations for the class.

- Point out the illustrations and have a student describe them. Then have them read over the possible conversations and listen to them. Next point out the boxes and read aloud the information in them. Answer any questions.

- Tell the students to follow the second set of instructions and work with a partner to act out similar conversations. Go around the classroom and listen in on the conversations, giving help when needed. Then call on different pairs to act out their conversations for the class.

OPTION

.Have the students bring pictures of their family members to class. Tell them to work in small groups to show their pictures and talk about the family members. Encourage them to explain when the picture was taken, how old the persons in it were, etc. Next call on different students to show the entire class their favorite family picture and talk about it.

28. How did you get along with them?

1 ► Listen to the conversation.
► Act out similar conversations with a partner. Describe what your parents were like when you were a child and give reasons for their behavior.

A What were your parents like when you were growing up?

B My parents? Well, they were very strict with me, [since / as] they believed children needed a lot of discipline. That's how they had been brought up. How about yours?

A Well, they weren't very strict, but they used to pressure me a lot. [Since / As] my father loved music, he wanted me to learn to play the piano. He used to get mad at me for not practicing.

My parents . . .	They believed . . .
were strict.	children needed discipline.
were supportive.	children needed encouragement.
were permissive.	children should have fun.
pressured me to study a lot.	education was important.
wanted me to make my own decisions.	children should develop independence.
spent a lot of time with me.	family life was important.

He used to get mad at me *for* not practicing. =
He used to get mad at me because I didn't practice.

2 ► Listen to the two possible conversations.
► Act out similar conversations with a partner. Tell your partner whether you had brothers and/or sisters and discuss the consequences of having (or not having) them.

A Do you come from a large family?

B Yes. I have two brothers and three sisters.

A How did you get along with them when you were growing up?

B Well, one of my brothers was near my age, so we played together a lot. My other brother and my sisters were older, and as a result, they were always ordering us around.

B No. I was an only child.

A Did you ever wish you had brothers and sisters?

B Yes. I was the only one my parents had to worry about. Therefore, they expected an awful lot from me.

Some ways to talk about consequences
One of my brothers was near my age, so we played together a lot.
One of my brothers was near my age. As a result, we competed for things. Thus, he always knew what I was doing. Therefore, we had to learn to share.

So is less formal than *as a result, thus,* and *therefore.*

3 ▶ Study the frames: Connectors (conjunctions and prepositions)

Connectors that show a reason		
She punished me	**because**	I had misbehaved.
	for	misbehaving.
She thought she knew better	**as** **since**	she was older.

Connectors that show a consequence		
My sister was older.	**Thus,** **Therefore,** **As a result,**	she was always giving me advice.
My sister was older,	**so**	

More formal	Less formal
as	since
thus therefore as a result	so
in order to so that	to so

Connectors that show a purpose		
I went to business school	**(in order) to**	study marketing.
	so (that)	I could study marketing.
	for	a degree in marketing.

▲
in order to + base form
so that + sentence

4 ▶ Listen to the conversations. Write *R* if the speaker is giving a reason for a childhood event and *C* if the speaker is talking about the consequences of a childhood event.

5 ▶ Find out about something your partner is doing or a decision he or she has made. Then ask for an explanation.

A *Why are you studying English?*
B *(I'm studying it) in order to get a job with an international company.*

Ask someone why he or she . . .
is studying _____ .
is going back to _____ .
decided to be a(n) _____ .
took a trip to _____ .
moved into his or her own apartment.

Some reasons
(in order) to get a job
(in order) to be closer to my family
so (that) I could work abroad
so (that) I could learn about the culture
for the peace and quiet

1.

2.

3.

4.

- Have the students examine the frames as you read aloud the headings and possible sentences. You can have the students repeat the sentences after you. Answer any questions about the use of the connectors in the sentences.

- Point out the boxes and read aloud the information in them as the students follow along in their books. Then have the students make up additional sentences modeled after the ones in the frame. Call on different students to read their sentences aloud and write them on the board.

- Point out the pictures and ask different students to describe what's happening. Then read the instructions aloud. Answer any questions.

- Have the students listen to the conversations and match each picture with the appropriate conversation as they write *R* or *C* in the boxes. When they finish, call on different students to say the answers.

TAPESCRIPT

1. **Man** You grew up in the city, didn't you?
   Woman Yes, I lived in the city until I went to college. That's the reason for one of the saddest things that happened to me when I was a kid.
   Man What was that?
   Woman Oh, I always wanted a dog, but my parents thought out apartment was too small. Then one day they decided to give in. We got a dog, and I was so happy.
   Man So why did you say "one of the saddest things"?
   Woman I was happy, but the dog wasn't. He used to sit at the door of our apartment and cry to get outside. No matter how much I walked him, it didn't seem to be enough. Finally, we had to give him to a family in the country because he was so miserable.
   Man Wow, that is sad. So you never had another pet when you were a kid?
   Woman Only goldfish.

2. **Woman** Still working, Ben? It's seven o'clock. I think I've seen you work late every night this week.
   Man Oh, I don't mind, Ms. Farina. I like to get things done.
   Woman How did you get to be so hardworking?
   Man I'm not sure. When I was a kid, I decided to get a job delivering newspapers after school. My family really needed the extra money, so I guess I learned to like work. It became something I really wanted to do, and I've been like that ever since.
   Woman Well, we're certainly glad about that. You're the kind of employee a boss can count on.

3. **Man** Hi, Claire, how's it going?
   Woman Oh, not so great. I've got to move out of my apartment. The landlord is raising my rent 20%, and I just can't afford it.
   Man Have you been looking?
   Woman Yes, but everything's so expensive. I just saw a nice two-bedroom near where I work, but it's way out of my price range.
   Man Why don't you get a roommate?
   Woman No, I prefer to live alone. It has to do with my childhood. I had a big family—six brothers and sisters—and I never had a moment alone. I remember trying to read quietly in the living room while my sister was playing the piano and one of my brothers was listening to music and another was talking on the phone. It was chaos. As a result, I guess, I've always liked to have my own place.
   Man Well, let me know if I can do anything to help. I'm sure you'll find something.

4. **Man** It's funny—whenever I hear someone say "Honesty is the best policy" I think about something that happened to me when I was about five years old.
   Woman What?
   Man I was throwing a ball in the house, something my mother had told me not to do a thousand times. I knocked over a lamp in the living room and it broke. I wanted to run and hide, but instead I went right into the kitchen and told my mother.
   Woman And she was angry, right?
   Man She was angry, but you know what? She didn't punish me since I was so honest.

ANSWERS

C	R
C	C

- Read the instructions aloud. Then ask two students to read aloud the sample conversation. Answer any questions.

- Point out the boxes and have different students read aloud the information in them. Tell the students to use the information in their conversations if they wish.

- Have the students work with a partner to act out the conversations. Go around the room and check their work. Finally, call on different pairs to act out their conversations for the class.

- Tell the students to read through the memo. Answer any questions. Then read aloud the instructions and have the students rewrite the memo.

- Tell the students to compare answers with a partner. Then call on different students to read aloud the paragraphs from the memo and write the answers on the board.

ANSWERS
Therefore/As a result, so, As/Since, in order to/to, for, Thus/Therefore, so/so that

- Have the students examine the frames as you and different students read the sentences. Answer any questions about the different meanings of the three-word verbs.

OPTION

Tell the students to use the three-word verbs in sentences which show they know the meaning of these verbs. Tell them to write their sentences on separate paper. When they finish, have them compare sentences with a partner. Next ask them to write their sentences on the board and read them aloud.

- Have the students read through the incomplete conversation. Answer any questions. Then read the instructions aloud and have the students complete the conversation.

- Tell the students to compare answers with a partner. Then call on two students to read aloud the completed conversation. Ask a student to write the answers on the board.

ANSWERS
was up to, get out of, get away with, put up with, end up with, catch up with, was in for, walked in on, run out of

OPTION

Have the students work in pairs to act out the conversation. Then tell them to write their own versions of the conversation and act out the new versions. Tell them to use their imaginations and as many three-word verbs as possible. Go around the classroom and listen in. Finally, call on different pairs to act out their conversations for the class. Give a prize for the most original conversation.

FOLLOW-UP

Students can write down their completed sentences from exercise 8.

6 ▶ Rewrite the memo, completing the sentences with appropriate connectors. Some items have more than one answer.

TO: Caroline MacGregor, President
FROM: Marcel Jacobi, Office Manager
SUBJECT: Personnel reassignment

About a month ago, both our receptionist and our secretary left the company on short notice. _____ , I had to hire their replacements, Andrea Martin and Judy Abrams, rather quickly. Ms. Martin had worked as a receptionist before, _____ I made her the receptionist.

_____ both employees are new, I have been watching their work closely. I am writing this memo _____ give you the results of my observations.

Ms. Martin is a conscientious worker, but she is not very friendly on the job. I have had to call her into my office several times _____ being rude to clients. Ms. Abrams, on the other hand, is very friendly and easygoing. _____ , I think she would make a much better impression on clients. I suggest that we have Ms. Martin and Ms. Abrams switch jobs.

I would appreciate a quick response from you _____ I can make this change as soon as possible.

Thank you.

7 ▶ Study the frames: Three-word verbs

I don't	**get along with**	my older sister.
I'm tired of	**putting up with**	the way she treats me.

I refuse to	**give in to**	her.
I try to	**stand up for**	myself.

Some other three-word verbs

My daughter, Mary, **is up to** no good. She **gets away with** anything she wants. She **looks up to** the wrong people and **goes along with** whatever they do. Last week her teacher **walked in on** her while she was smoking in the girls' room. She told me to **check up on** Mary more closely and **find out about** her activities.

I want her to **keep out of** trouble. I made her **cut down on** parties during the week, but she still **ends up with** bad grades. She doesn't **keep up with** her schoolwork, and she can't **come up with** the answers on tests. She always tries to **get out of** work and **looks down on** kids who study.

I'm starting to **run out of** patience. She's always one step ahead of me, and I just can't seem to **catch up with** her. But someday she'll **be in for** a big surprise.

8 ▶ Rewrite the interview with the famous burglar Eric Sheridan in his prison cell, completing the sentences with appropriate three-word verbs from exercise 7.

Q: What do you suppose led you to a life of crime, Mr. Sheridan?
A: Who knows? As a kid I _____ some kind of mischief twenty-four hours a day. And I was always trying to _____ work. Maybe I'm just lazy.

Q: So your parents let you _____ your bad behavior?
A: Oh, no! My father never _____ anything! That's why I left home.

Q: Did you ever think you'd _____ a twenty-five-year jail sentence?
A: No, I never thought I'd get caught. I thought I was too smart.

Q: How *did* the police finally _____ you?
A: Well, it was late at night and I was in this fancy house—Lady Waverly's house. I was almost sure no one was home, but as it turned out, I _____ a big surprise. Just as I was opening up Lady Waverly's jewelry box, she _____ me. And believe it or not, she had a black belt in karate!

Q: Well, it looks as if you have a long vacation ahead of you, Mr. Sheridan.
A: Oh, no, I haven't _____ tricks yet. I'll be out of prison a lot sooner than you think.

29. Your turn

Look at these pictures of different families. Then, working in groups, describe and compare the home life of the families. Discuss the questions below, and give reasons for your opinions. Say whether your opinions are based on your own childhood experiences or on those of people you know.

1. What are some of the advantages and disadvantages of each family situation?
2. How do you think the children in each family get along with each other and with other people as a result of their family life?
3. How do you think the family life of these children will affect their lives as adults?

the Alvarez family
Ramon
Anita
Luisa
Cecilia

the Patterson family
Shirley
Susan
Sandra
Evan
Maureen
Donald

the Gibson family
Billy
Kathleen
Clare
Colleen
Terry
Heather
Kevin
Gwen

29. Your turn

- Point out the illustrations on pp. 58 and 59 and have the students study them carefully. Then tell them to work in pairs to make observations about each family—for example, "Mr. and Mrs. Alvarez have two daughters, Luisa and Cecilia. Each daughter has a pet rabbit." Tell the pairs also to make assumptions about each family situation—for example, "Mrs. Gibson is divorced; the Gibsons are a single-parent family." (See the Culture Close-Up which follows.)

- Read aloud the boldfaced instructions as the students follow along in their books. Then have the students work in groups to discuss the three questions. Tell the group captains to make sure each group member gets a chance to express his or her opinion. When they finish, call on the students to share their opinions with the class.

OPTION

Divide the class into two teams—A and B. Help the members of one team write descriptive statements about the different families featured in the pictures on pp. 58-59. For example:

This family is planting something.
There are more girls than boys in this family, and there's a pet.

Next have different members of Team A take turns reading aloud the statements. After each statement is read, have a member of Team B say which family the description is about.

CULTURE CLOSE-UP

Single-parent families are very common in the U.S. They may result from divorce or the death of a spouse. Single-parent families also occur when a single mother gives birth to a child and decides to raise the child on her own. Another type of single-parent family which has become more common recently is one in which a single person adopts a child.

Listen in

- Read the boldfaced instructions aloud. Then, so the students know what to listen for, have them read over the statements and questions. Answer any questions. (See the Culture Close-Up which follows.)

- Have the students listen to the conversation as many times as necessary and answer the questions. Then have them compare and discuss answers with a partner. Finally, call on a student to say the answers aloud.

TAPESCRIPT

Host Dr. Dorne, in your recent book, *One to One,* you say that a very important factor in a child's development is the amount of contact he or she has with adults. Can you tell us more about this?

Dr. Dorne Certainly. Studies have shown that attention from adults leads to better schoolwork and higher scores on achievement tests. For this reason, only children and firstborn children generally do better than the youngest child in a family.

Host And, you say in your book, children from smaller families do better than children from very large families.

Dr. Dorne Yes, that's true, since children with many brothers and sisters have less personal contact with their parents. Of course, the oldest child in a very large family is there before any of the others. As a result, he or she has more contact with adults, at least in the early years.

Host Dr. Saporta, I believe you disagree with Dr. Dorne.

Dr. Saporta Yes. I can't go along with the idea that if you have many siblings, you can't be successful. Success in life, even in your career, doesn't depend only on how you do in school. How you get along with other people is just as important, sometimes more important.

Host And getting along with others is something we generally learn as children, isn't it?

Dr. Saporta We generally learn how to get along with others and how to solve problems from our parents. But children from large families can learn these skills from their siblings as well. Therefore, it can be a very good thing to have a lot of siblings. More people, more teachers.

Host Thank you, Dr. Saporta, Dr. Dorne.

CULTURE CLOSE-UP

The media in the U.S.—TV, radio, newspapers, and magazines—often feature interviews or columns by so-called experts in different fields. The most popular fields are those having to do with human behavior and health. One can find out a wide range of opinions on a variety of issues from psychologists, psychiatrists, medical doctors, nutritionists, and fitness trainers.

FOLLOW-UP

Students can write down the opinions they expressed in the **Your turn** exercise.

WORKBOOK Lessons 28-29, pp. 33-35

the Stevens family

Nora

Gordon

Megan

the Ono family

Nobuo

Yoshio

Teruo

Akira

the Simek family

Florence

Roger

Joanna

Dr. Dorne and Dr. Saporta, two child psychologists, are being interviewed on a radio talk show. Read the statements below and the questions that follow them. Then listen to a part of the interview and answer the questions.

a. Only children show higher achievement than children from very large families.
b. The size of a family has nothing to do with the development of the children in it.
c. Children with many brothers and sisters have more people to teach them how to get along with others and how to solve their problems.

1. Which two of the three viewpoints were expressed in the discussion?
2. Who expressed each viewpoint, Dr. Dorne or Dr. Saporta?

30. On your own

1. You write an advice column for young people. Answer the letter.

> I'm having a hard time getting along with my older sister. She's always bossing me around and telling me what to do. I know that most of the time she means well, but the way she treats me bothers me. For example, yesterday she came into my room without knocking and said "Get some air in this place. Open a window or two. And you're not sitting at your desk properly. Don't slouch; sit up!" Then she went over and opened a window and came over and made me sit up at my desk. I could have screamed! What should I do?
>
> *Frustrated*

2. Choose one of the options below.

1. You are a teacher and one of the children in the pictures in Lesson 29 is in your class. The child has a problem with a brother or sister and is doing poorly in school as a result. Write a report to the principal, explaining the problem and its causes. Make a recommendation.
2. You are a family counselor and you have to give a speech on sibling relationships to a group of parents. Write a speech in which you discuss the importance of sibling relationships in personality development, and the consequences of growing up with brothers and/or sisters as opposed to growing up alone.
3. Write a short article on different ways of raising children. Include some different ideas on how to raise children; some opinions on how you personally think children should be raised, and why you think so; and some experiences from your own childhood that support your opinions.

30. On your own

- Point out the illustration and have a student describe it. Then have a student read the letter aloud. Answer any questions. Then have a student read aloud the instructions for the first exercise. (See the Culture Close-Up which follows.)

- Have the students answer the letter on separate paper. Go around the classroom and answer any questions they have about their writing.

- Tell the students to compare their letters with a partner. Then call on different students to read their letters aloud and write them on the board.

- Read aloud the general instructions for the second exercise. Then call on different students to read aloud the options. Answer any questions.

- You may want to assign this exercise as homework. Collect the students' writing, mark any errors, and return the assignments to the students for any necessary corrections.

CULTURE CLOSE-UP

Many U.S. newspapers feature advice columns on a regular basis. Readers are invited to seek answers to questions or problems by writing to an "expert" in a particular field. There are advice columns on everything from behavior problems to pet and plant care. Some newspapers and magazines feature advice columns especially for teenagers. In some cases, teenagers give the advice to other teenagers.

WORKBOOK Lesson 30, p. 36. Before assigning the writing task, ask a student to point out the solutions or remedies mentioned in the memo. Tell the students to write about the corresponding problems in their letters.

Review of units 1-6

1

- Read the instructions aloud. Then have the students try to answer the questions. You can have them discuss their answers with a partner.

- Tell the students to read the article. Answer any questions about the vocabulary and structures. Then have the students make any necessary corrections to their answers.

- Have the students compare their final answers with a partner. Then call on different students to read aloud their answers and write them on the board.

SAMPLE ANSWERS

1. The following can cause a sleepless night: too little daytime activity, too much exercise, taking things too hard, feeling you haven't lived the right kind of life, being nervous and tense, spending too much time relaxing, sleeping late on weekends
2. Try moderate afternoon exercise along with methods such as psychotherapy and biofeedback. Drink milk or eat cheese or tuna. Don't take sleeping pills or exercise strenuously just before bedtime.
3. Answers will vary.

2

- Tell the students to read through the paragraph and the information in the box. Answer any questions they have.

- Ask a student to read the instructions aloud. Then have the students rewrite the paragraph. When they finish, tell them to compare answers with a partner. Next call on different students to read the sentences in the paragraph aloud and write the answers on the board.

ANSWERS
Because/As/Since, because, so (that), for, (in order) to, Thus/Therefore/As a result

Review of units 1-6

1 ▶ Before you read the article on insomnia—difficulty falling or staying asleep—try to answer these questions. When you have finished reading, compare your answers with the information in the article and make any necessary corrections.

1. What are some things that can cause a sleepless night?
2. What should someone with insomnia do about it? What should he or she not do?
3. Have you ever had insomnia or do you know of anyone who has? What did you or that person do about it?

Laying Insomnia to Rest by Susan Gilbert

When the task at hand is to get a good night's sleep, trying hard is not the way to succeed. Twisting and turning in search of a comfortable position in bed makes your body do the opposite of what it's supposed to do at night. Instead of slowing down, your heartbeat races. Instead of relaxing, your leg muscles twitch. You watch the clock and wonder what you're doing wrong.

Over ten million people in the United States alone are seeking medical help for chronic insomnia—difficulty in falling asleep or staying asleep. For years it has been called a symptom of a number of psychological problems, such as depression, that somehow alter the body's sleep pattern. Now sleep specialists are saying that "bad habits" can have the same effect. These include too little daytime activity and, ironically, its opposite, too much exercise.

"Insomniacs usually begin losing sleep over some problem, such as a death in the family," says psychiatrist Robert Watson, director of the Sleep Disorder Center affiliated with Yale University in Connecticut. "But unlike other people," he adds, "they continue to have trouble sleeping—for months, even years." According to Joyce and Anthony Kales, two psychiatrists at Penn State University in Pennsylvania, insomniacs present a consistent personality profile, as outlined in the November American Journal of Psychiatry. They take things hard, feel they haven't lived "the right kind of life," and are nervous and tense.

Insomniacs share another trait, says psychiatrist Thomas Coates of the University of California, San Francisco: They spend an excessive amount of time thinking about sleep. Contrary to the image of bad sleepers as workaholics, Coates's study indicates that insomniacs spend more time relaxing than others do. He thinks their relative inactivity during the day may alter the body's "clock." Instead of signaling the brain to slow down at night, the clock calls for more activity.

Sleeping late on weekends can also disrupt your body's clock. This is the first bad habit Robert Watson makes patients change at the Sleep Disorders Center. He tells them to rise at the same time each day, even after a night of poor sleep. "After a while," he says, "sleep improves."

Even though it tires you out, exercise won't guarantee a sound sleep. If it is too strenuous, especially just before bedtime, it can drive your pulse too high, causing a restless night. Joyce and Anthony Kales use moderate afternoon exercise, along with methods such as psychotherapy and biofeedback, to treat severe insomniacs.

What is the best thing to do on occasional sleepless nights? Forget sleeping pills. They can actually cause insomnia after three days, by altering the brain's chemistry. Watson recommends drinking milk or eating cheese or tuna, because they are rich in natural sleep-producing aids.

There's something to the old-fashioned remedy of drinking warm milk before bedtime, Watson says. Warming it won't make any difference, but it will help you relax.

2 ▶ Rewrite the paragraphs on insomnia, completing the sentences with appropriate connectors from the box. Some items have more than one answer.

To show a consequence	To show a reason	To show a purpose
thus	because	(in order) to
therefore	for	so (that)
as a result	as	for
so	since	

_____ so many people suffer from insomnia, many doctors have begun to study sleep disorders seriously. Their findings show that many insomniacs can't sleep _____ they have one or more "bad habits."

Some people do strenuous exercise before bedtime _____ they can get a good night's sleep. Many others try to spend a lot of time relaxing _____ the same reason. Still others sleep late on weekends _____ catch up on lost sleep. The sleep specialists say that these "bad habits" actually alter the body's normal processes. _____ , they make the problem even worse.

3 ▶ **Rewrite this letter to a doctor who is a sleep specialist, completing the sentences with appropriate connectors from exercise 2. Some items have more than one answer.**

Dear Dr. Mehta,

_____ I'm having so much trouble falling asleep at night, I decided to write to you for your advice. _____ you can get a better idea of my problem, let me tell you a little about myself.

I'm employed full time, but _____ my job as a bookkeeper doesn't pay very well, I'm also studying at night _____ a degree in business. In addition, I have three teenage children to cook, clean, and wash for, _____ I actually have another full-time job at home. _____ , I always get to bed very late, and although I'm exhausted, I can never fall asleep.

A few months ago, I started taking sleeping pills. That was my little secret _____ getting a good night's sleep, but lately the pills haven't been working. Maybe I should take two pills instead of one. I don't know what to do _____ get the rest I need, and I am hoping you can help me.

Sincerely,

Lilly Wolff

Lilly Wolff

4 ▶ **Mrs. Wolff made an appointment with Dr. Mehta. Restate the conversation, combining Dr. Mehta's responses in brackets [ ] into one sentence.**

Mrs. Wolff I'm so tired. What can I do?
Dr. Mehta [You need to get enough rest. It's essential.]

Mrs. Wolff *I'm so tired. What can I do?*
Dr. Mehta *It's essential that you get enough rest.*

Mrs. Wolff That's why I've been taking sleeping pills.
Dr. Mehta [You should stop depending on medication for sleep. I recommend that.]

Mrs. Wolff But . . .
Dr. Mehta [People have to simplify their lives in order to get a good night's sleep. Sometimes it's necessary.]

Mrs. Wolff But there's so much I have to take care of.
Dr. Mehta The solution to your problem is your three children. [They should take over a good part of the housework. I seriously suggest this.] [They must do their fair share. You must insist.] [They need to begin to assume some of the responsibility for their own lives. At their age it is also important.]

Mrs.Wolff Yes, I guess they are old enough to take care of themselves.

5 ▶ **What problems does Ming have? What does Vincent suggest as solutions? Read the statements below. Then listen to the conversation and say *Right* or *Wrong* for each item.**

Ming's problems
1. She is exhausted.
2. She doesn't like her job.
3. She doesn't like her assistant.
4. She has too much work to do.
5. She doesn't think Vincent understands her.

Vincent's solutions
1. He thinks Ming should talk to her boss.
2. He thinks Ming should work overtime more.
3. He thinks Ming should stop working overtime.
4. He thinks Ming should quit her job.
5. He thinks Ming should take better care of herself.

- Tell the students to read over the letter. Answer any questions. Then have a student read the instructions aloud. Answer any questions about the procedure.

- Tell the students to rewrite the letter and then compare answers with a partner. Then call on different students to read aloud the paragraphs from the letter and write the answers on the board.

ANSWERS
Because/As/Since, So (that), because/as/since, for, so, Thus/Therefore/As a result, for, (in order) to

OPTION 1

Tell the students to pretend they are Dr. Mehta and answer Lilly Wolff's letter. When they finish, have them compare and discuss their answers with a partner. Then call on different students to read their letters aloud and write them on the board.

OPTION 2

Have the students write their own letters to Dr. Mehta about a real or imaginary problem. Tell them to try to include as many connectors as possible. Go around the room and answer any questions students have about their work. When they finish, have them give their letters to a partner to answer. Next have the partners read each other's answers. Finally, call on different pairs; have one partner read his or her letter to Dr. Mehta and the have the other read aloud the answer.

- Ask a student to read aloud the instructions. Then have a pair of students read aloud the conversation as it appears in their books. Next have the students restate the sentences in brackets.

- Tell the students to compare answers with a partner. Then call on different students to read aloud the answers and write them on the board.

ANSWERS
It's essential that you get enough rest.
I recommend that you stop depending on medication for sleep.
Sometimes it's necessary that people simplify their lives in order to get a good night's sleep.
I seriously suggest that they take over a good part of the housework.
You must insist that they do their fair share. At their age, it is also important that they begin to assume some of the responsibility for their own lives.

OPTION

Have the students work in pairs to plan and then write down their own lines for a similar conversation. Tell them to try to include expressions used for giving advice such as *I recommend that . . .* , *It's necessary that . . .* , *I seriously suggest that . . .* , *You must insist that . . .* , and *It's important that . . . .* Next tell the pairs to practice acting out their conversations. Finally, call on different pairs to act out their conversations for the class. Give prizes for the most grammatically correct and the most interesting conversations.

- Read the instructions aloud as the students follow along in their books. Answer any questions students have about the procedure.

- Tell the students to read over the statements. Answer any questions. Then have them listen to the conversation and answer *Right* or *Wrong*.

- Tell the students to compare answers with a partner. Then ask a student to say the answers aloud and write them on the board.

TAPESCRIPT
Vincent What's the matter, Ming? You look exhausted.
Ming Oh, hi, Vincent. I am. It seems like I never get caught up on my work. I've been working until 8:00, 9:00 at night and Saturdays, too. But there's always so much to do.
Vincent Well, something's certainly wrong. I suggest you talk to your boss. If you have to work that hard, you need help. I thought you were going to get an assistant.
Ming Well, Mr. Calvin promised he'd hire someone, but now he says the company can't afford it. I like my job, so I don't want to quit, but I don't know what I'm going to do.
Vincent I recommend that you start working normal hours before you get sick. If the work doesn't get done, it isn't your fault. Then maybe Mr. Calvin will see the problem. I mean, why should he hire anybody else if he knows you're going to work overtime for free?
Ming I know but . . .
Vincent No buts! It's important to take care of yourself—and all that work and stress isn't going to get you anywhere.
Ming Maybe you're right. I think I'll take your advice.

ANSWERS

Ming's problems:	Vincent's solutions:
1. Right	1. Right
2. Wrong	2. Wrong
3. Wrong	3. Right
4. Right	4. Wrong
5. Wrong	5. Right

- Have the students read the title and the first paragraph of the article. Then ask different students to guess what the article is about.

- Read the instructions aloud. Then point out the illustrations at the bottom of the article and have the students read the article. You can also have them listen to it as they follow along in their books. Answer any questions about the vocabulary or structures.

- Have the students put the steps in order. Then tell them to compare answers with a partner. Next call on different students to read the steps aloud in the correct order. Ask a student to write the sequence in numbers on the board.

ANSWERS

3
7
2
9
6
5
8
1
10
4

OPTION

If appropriate or practical, bring to class the materials to replace a broken windowpane (or have the students bring them). Have different class members read the steps aloud while others take turns performing the steps.

Alternatively, use materials you have on hand in place of the real things—for example, cut out a piece of heavy cardboard to represent the window frame; use a piece of stiff paper to represent the glass; use cups of water to represent the putty and the paint; etc. Tell the students to pretend these materials are the real things as they perform the steps.

- Call on a student to read the instructions aloud. Answer any questions. Then point out the time markers in the box and have the students repeat them after you.

- Tell the students to read over the incomplete paragraphs. Answer any questions. Then have the students do the exercise.

- Tell the students to compare answers with a partner. Then call on different students to read aloud the completed paragraphs. Ask a student to write the answers on the board.

ANSWERS

before, by then, first, Next/Then, Next/Then, As soon as/After/When/Once, As soon as/After/When/Once, As soon as/After/When/Once

OPTION 1

Practice applying a tourniquet with the students. Bring to class a wide piece of cloth and a stick. Have a pair of students act out applying a tourniquet as a class member reads aloud the instructions in the second paragraph. You can call on other students to practice as well.

OPTION 2

Have the students work in pairs to write instructions for any process they can think of and know about. Tell them to use as many of the time markers from the box as possible. You can suggest some different processes:

How to change a flat tire.
How to make an omelet.

6 ► As you read the article, try to remember in what order the different steps are done. When you have finished the reading, put the steps below in order.

___ Once the broken glass has been removed, clean out the old, dried putty from the frame.

___ When the glass is in place, fasten it with glazing points.

___ Then loosen the broken glass with a hammer.

___ Next paint the putty.

___ Then place the new glass in the frame.

___ Before you place the glass in the frame, apply a thin layer of putty to the inside of the frame.

___ After the glass has been secured, apply putty along the frame edge.

___ First place the window frame on a flat surface.

___ As soon as the paint is dry, clean the glass inside and out.

___ After the old, dried putty has been removed, apply a thin coat of paint to the inside of the frame.

7 ► While he was fixing a broken window, Andy cut his wrist badly and his brother had to apply a tourniquet. Read the instructions on applying a tourniquet and complete the sentences with appropriate time markers from the box. Some items have more than one answer.

first	finally	before
then	once	after
next	as soon as	when
last	by then	

In case of a serious cut, always apply a tourniquet _____ you do anything else. Don't wait for an ambulance because _____ the injured person might have already lost too much blood.

To apply a tourniquet, _____ place a wide cloth close to the wound. _____ , wrap the cloth around the arm or leg and tie a half knot. _____ , place a stick on top of the knot and tie a square knot. _____ you've done that, twist the stick. _____ the bleeding stops, tie the stick in place. _____ you've secured the tourniquet, go to the hospital immediately.

Replacing a Broken Windowpane

When window glass or panes get broken, you can save money and avoid a repair bill if you know how to install the new glass yourself.

MATERIALS
The materials needed for replacing a broken windowpane are putty, glazing points, a small amount of thin paint, and a piece of new glass.

TOOLS
The tools required are a hammer, a pair of pliers, a screwdriver, a putty knife, and a paintbrush.

> **putty:** a thick waterproof mixture used in fitting glass
> **putty knife:** a wide, flat knife used to apply putty
> **glazing points:** small three-cornered pieces of metal used to hold glass in place

REPLACING BROKEN GLASS

1. Place the window frame on a worktable or flat surface with the side showing the old putty facing up.
2. Loosen the broken glass by tapping it lightly with a hammer. Remove the broken pieces from the frame with a pair of pliers. (Wear gloves so you don't cut your hands and goggles to protect your eyes.)
3. Clean out the old, dried putty with a screwdriver or putty knife (Figure 1).
4. Apply a coat of thin paint to the inside of the frame where the glass fits. This will help the putty last longer.
5. Use a putty knife to apply a thin layer of putty to the inside of the frame.
6. Place the glass in the frame. Make sure it's in place properly so it won't break. Press the glass firmly in order to smooth out and seal the putty.
7. To make the glass fit tightly, secure it by driving glazing points into the frame on top of the glass every 5 or 6 inches (Figure 2). Drive these three-cornered points in gently with a screwdriver. Drive them only deep enough to keep the glass in place.
8. Apply putty along the frame edge to cover the glazing points and seal in the glass (Figure 3).
9. Paint the frame after the putty is dry.
10. Clean the glass inside and out with a good window cleaner after the paint is dry.

Figure 1.
Broken glass and old putty are removed from a window frame.

Figure 2.
The new piece of glass is secured with glazing points.

Figure 3.
Putty is applied with a putty knife to seal in the new glass.

8 ▶ **You are at a yard sale with a friend who would like to buy the items discussed below for his or her apartment. Develop a conversation for each item, using the first sentence and the information about dimensions below it.**

1. I'd like to get that stained glass to put in my hall window.
   stained glass = 64 inches high
   hall window = 66 inches high
   A *I'd like to get that stained glass to put in my hall window.*
   B *How high is your hall window?*
   A *It's 66 inches high.*
   B *Then I don't think the glass would fit. It's two inches shorter than your window.*

2. This window box would look nice full of flowers on my kitchen windowsill.
   window box = 4 feet wide
   windowsill = 2½ feet wide

3. I could use that table to put my television on.
   table = 22 inches wide
   television = 26 inches wide

4. I think this rug would look better in the living room than the one we have now.
   rug = 14 feet long
   length of floor = 12 feet long

5. I'd really like to put this mirror up beside the door.
   mirror = 18 inches wide
   space beside the door = 15 inches wide

9 ▶ **Complete the sentences by choosing an appropriate item from the box and putting the adjectives in the correct order.**

1. My mother likes antiques. She'd probably love these _____ .
2. Our kitchen needs fixing up. It could really use some of this _____ .
3. My sofa and chairs are falling apart. I'd like to buy some _____ .
4. Ursula wants to get a pet. I think she'd love this _____ .
5. I have a long, narrow hall in my apartment. I'd like to find a _____ .

kitten: Siamese/white/little
rug: blue/long/Turkish
cooking pots: black/iron/old
living room chairs: brown/leather/new
wallpaper: yellow/washable

10 ▶ **Complete the conversation with the correct forms of the two-word verbs in the box and the direct objects in parentheses.**

call up   think about
look for   run into
take back   worry about

A I want to redecorate my living room.
B Really? Have you decided what colors to use?
A Well, not definitely. I _____ (beige walls and light blue furniture). But I can't decide what kind of rug to get.
B I think you should _____ (rug) that has beige and blue in it.
A I _____ (expensive purchases) like that. I'm afraid I won't be able to _____ (it) if I decide I don't like it.
B Why don't you _____ (a few carpet stores) and ask them what their return policy is?
A That's a good idea. I'm glad I _____ (you) today.

- Make sure the students know what a yard sale is. Then read the instructions aloud. Answer any questions about the procedure.

- Point out the first exercise item and have a pair of students read the sample conversation aloud. Then have the students read over the other exercise items. Answer any questions.

- Tell the students to work with a partner to develop a conversation for each item. Go around the room and listen in, giving help if needed.

- Call on different pairs to act out the conversations for the class. You can ask different students to write the conversations on the board.

ANSWERS
2. **A** How wide is your kitchen windowsill?
   B It's 2½ feet wide.
   A Then I don't think the window box would fit. It's 1½ feet wider than your windowsill.
3. **A** How wide is your television?
   B It's 26 inches wide.
   A Then I don't think it would fit. It's four inches wider than the table.
4. **A** How long is the living room?
   B It's 12 feet long.
   A Then I don't think the rug would fit. It's two feet longer than the floor.
5. **A** How wide is the space beside the door?
   B It's 15 inches wide.
   A Then I don't think the mirror would fit. It's three inches wider than the space.

- Have the students read over the incomplete sentences. Then have the students repeat the items in the box after you. Answer any questions. Next ask a student to read aloud the instructions.

- Tell the students to do the exercise and then compare answers with a partner. Next call on a student to read aloud the sentences. Have another student write the answers on the board.

ANSWERS
1. old black iron cooking pots
2. washable yellow wallpaper
3. new brown leather living room chairs
4. little white Siamese kitten
5. long blue Turkish rug

OPTION

Have the students work in pairs to create alternative exercise items—to make up sentences similar to those in the exercise and adjectives like those in the box to fit the sentences. For example:

1. My mother likes classic cars. She'd probably love that _____.
   Jaguar: old/shiny/1950

When they finish, have the pairs try out their exercise items on other pairs. After that, call on different pairs to write their exercises on the board for the class to do. Finally, call on different students to read the answers aloud.

- Point out the illustration and ask a student to describe what's happening. Then have the students read over the incomplete conversation. Next have them repeat the two-word verbs in the box after you. Answer any questions.

- Have the students complete the conversation and then go over their answers with a partner. Next ask a pair of students to read the conversation aloud.

ANSWERS
A 'm thinking about beige walls and light blue furniture
B look for a rug
A worry about expensive purchases, take it back
B call up a few carpet stores
A ran into you

OPTION

Tell the students to work in pairs to act out the conversation. Encourage them to add some lines of their own. Go around the room and listen in. Give help with pronunciation if necessary. Then call on different pairs to act out their conversations in front of the class.

- Have a student read the instructions aloud. Then have the students read the article. You can ask separate students to read aloud the different paragraphs in the article. Answer any questions.

- Tell the students to choose the correct statement. Then call on a student to read the answer aloud.

ANSWER
1.

OPTION 1

Find out if anyone in the class has ever seen a movie or television program starring Robin Williams. Ask the student(s) to tell the class about the movie or TV performance. Share with the class any of Robin Williams' performances you've watched.

OPTION 2

If possible, rent a video of one of the movies starring Robin Williams and show it to the class. When they've finished seeing the movie, have a class discussion about the characters in it, Robin William's role, and the main theme. You can also have the students write brief summaries of the movie.

- Ask a student to read aloud the instructions. Then have the class repeat after you the words in the columns and the two sentences in the small box. Next have the students read over the incomplete play review. Answer any questions.

- Have the students complete the play review. Then call on different students to read the completed paragraphs aloud. Ask some students to write the answers on the board.

ANSWERS
found . . . extremely funny, called . . . a natural comic, made . . . the lead character, considered . . . a mistake, couldn't imagine . . . playing, saw . . . play, found . . . applauding, make . . . laugh

OPTION 1

Have the students write reviews of a TV program, movie, play, or other performance that they've seen. Go around the room and answer any questions they have about their writing. When they finish, have the students compare and check their reviews with a partner. You can also collect the reviews, mark them, and return them to the students for any needed corrections. Finally, call on different students to read aloud their reviews and write them on the board.

OPTION 2

Tell the students to write a paragraph describing a TV or movie personality they know about. Tell them to use as many of the words from the columns as possible. When they finish, have them compare paragraphs with a partner. Then call on different students to read aloud their paragraphs and write them on the board.

Alternatively, choose a TV or movie character all the students are familiar with and have them do the activity.

11 ▶ **Read the article and decide which of the statements below gives the better description of Robin Williams's career.**

1. Robin Williams became famous for his roles on television and in movies.
2. Robin Williams's fame can best be attributed to his acting studies and his stand-up comedy routines.

by Sylvia P. Bloch

"My childhood was kind of lonely and quiet. My father was away working, my mother was away working, and I was basically raised by the maid. I'd spend most of my time alone in our huge house, playing with my toy soldiers." This is how actor-comedian Robin Williams describes his childhood. Born in 1952 in Chicago, Illinois, Williams grew up in Chicago and Detroit and attended eight different schools in eight years because his father, an automobile executive, was frequently transferred.

When his father retired, the family moved to a town near San Francisco, California. Williams went to college and studied political science, but when he discovered theater, he dropped out to pursue acting. After studying in New York City for two years, he returned to San Francisco and started working on his stand-up comedy routines.

Williams began to get noticed and soon received offers to appear on television. His career took off in

1978 with the TV series "Mork & Mindy," where he played the part of Mork, an alien from another planet. Almost 60 million people would tune in to each episode just to watch Williams ad lib and clown around. The show became a hit, and unable to handle the pressure of instant fame, Williams turned to alcohol and drugs.

In 1983, two things happened that influenced Williams to change his life for the better—his friend John Belushi, a fellow comic and actor, died of a drug overdose, and his wife became pregnant. Williams told a magazine, "I knew I couldn't be a father and live that kind of life." He was able to turn his life around.

Williams went on to star in movies, receiving an Academy Award nomination for his role in the film *Good Morning, Vietnam.* He played the part of a grown-up Peter Pan in *Hook* and the part of a divorced father who disguises himself as an English housekeeper in order to be with his children in *Mrs. Doubtfire.*

When the opportunity came to do the voice of the Genie in the Disney movie *Aladdin*, Williams jumped at the chance. He said he wanted to act in something that his children would enjoy, and was very happy when the movie came out and people told him, "I loved it as much as my kid did."

For Robin Williams, being a father is very important. "My kids are the most sobering, most wonderful things in my life."

12 ▶ **Rewrite the play review, filling in the first blank in each pair with an item from column A and the second blank with an item from column B. Make sure to use the correct tense of the verbs in column A. There is more than one answer for most blanks.**

Column A	Column B
call	act (v)
can't imagine	a mistake
consider	a natural comic
find	applauding
make	do
see	extremely funny
watch	laugh
	play
	playing
	the lead character

Compare:
I'm going to *act in* a play.
I'm going to *play the part of* Hamlet.

Surprise of the Theater Season
by Rosanna Stewart

Everyone _watched_ child actor Eddie Perez _act_ in situation comedies. Audiences _____ him _____ , and critics _____ him _____ .

And so it was a surprise to this critic when the Director of the National Shakespeare Festival Theater _____ Perez _____ in *Hamlet*. I _____ this decision _____ . I _____ this actor _____ a serious part.

However, I went to the opening night, and I _____ Perez _____ the part. And I _____ myself _____ with the rest of the audience. The actor who used to _____ us all _____ has another side to his talent.

13 ▸ **Read these short interviews with performers. Rewrite the responses in brackets [ ], combining the two statements and using *before*, *after*, *when*, or *while*. Some items have more than one answer.**

1. **A** How did you get interested in singing as a career?
   B [I was going to high school. I sang in the school chorus then.] I guess I decided to be a singer at that time.
   A *How did you get interested in singing as a career?*
   B *While going to high school, I sang in the school chorus. I guess I decided to be a singer at that time.*

2. **A** Did you always know you wanted to be an actor?
   B [I didn't take up drama right away. First, I studied accounting.] I'm glad I changed because I enjoy being an actor.

3. **A** When did you decide to become a theater make-up artist?
   B [I was working as a hairdresser. I got interested in make-up at that time.] I really enjoy doing theater make-up.

4. **A** How did you become a composer?
   B [First, I took guitar lessons. Then I started writing songs for fun.] I became a composer more or less by accident.

5. **A** When did you first realize you wanted to be a dancer?
   B [I went to visit my cousin during summer vacation. I saw my first ballet then.] From that time on, the only thing I ever wanted to do was dance.

14 ▸ **Read about the problems of these teenagers. Then say what they hope and wish about the past.**

1. Susan tried our for the school chorus, but she doesn't know if she was chosen. She's worried because she didn't practice her song before the tryouts.
   Susan hopes _____ .
   She wishes _____ .

2. Maria's high school offers only one drama class but two music classes. Maria wanted to take drama, but there wasn't enough room in the class. She took music, even though she's more interested in acting, and now she's afraid she failed the test yesterday.
   Maria hopes _____ .
   She wishes _____ .

3. The Drama Club had auditions for a play yesterday. Peter was nervous when he tried out for the part.
   Peter hopes _____ .
   He wishes _____ .

4. Jason likes Polly, another thirteen-year-old in the school band. He's too shy to talk to her, so he wrote her a love letter and put it in her saxophone case. Polly never said anything about the letter.
   Jason hopes _____ .
   He wishes _____ .

13

- Point out the illustration and ask a student to describe it. Then ask a student to read the instructions aloud. Next have the students read over the exercise items. Answer any questions. After that, have a pair of students read aloud the sample conversation in italics.

- Tell the students to do the exercise and then compare answers with a partner. Then call on different pairs to read aloud the conversations. You can ask some students to write the answers on the board.

POSSIBLE ANSWERS

2. No. Before taking up drama, I studied accounting.
3. While/when working as a hairdresser, I got interested in make-up.
4. After taking guitar lessons, I started writing songs for fun.
5. When/While visiting my cousin during summer vacation, I saw my first ballet.

OPTION

Have the students work in pairs to take turns asking each other questions like those from the exercise. Explain that the partner who replies should make up his or her own answers and should try to use *before, after, when* or *while* in the answers. You can write a sample conversation on the board and act it out with a student before the pairs begin their work. For example:

A When did you first realize you wanted to be a daredevil?

B While attending a circus, I got to see a man feeding an alligator with one hand tied behind his back. From that day on, I always wanted to tempt fate.

Encourage the students to use their imaginations. Go around the room and listen in as you check their work. Finally, call on different pairs to act out their conversations for the class.

14

- Read the instructions aloud. Then have the students read over the exercise items. Answer any questions. It may be a good idea to do the first exercise item with the students.

- Tell the students to do the exercise. Then have them compare answers with a partner. Next call on groups of three students; ask one student to read aloud the first sentence in the exercise and have the other two read aloud the completed sentences with *hopes* and *wishes*. Ask different students to write the answers on the board.

SAMPLE ANSWERS

1. she was chosen for the school chorus
   she'd practiced her song before the tryouts.
2. she passed the test
   there had been room in the drama class
3. he got the part
   he hadn't been nervous
4. Polly got the letter
   she'd reply.

OPTION

Have the students work in groups to come up with a situation similar to those in the exercise items. Tell them to write the situations down along with the two corresponding incomplete statements with *hopes* and *wishes*. Go around the room and answer any questions the pairs have about their work. When they finish, have them exchange their work with other pairs. Tell the pairs to read and complete the sentences they've just received. Next have them go over their work with the other pairs. Finally, call on different pairs to read aloud their sentences for the class. You also can ask them to write the sentences on the board.

- Ask a student to read aloud the instructions and the subtitle. Then tell the students to read over the items in exercise 16.

- Have the students read the article. Answer any questions about the vocabulary and structures. Next have the students write down what the two things are that you can't leave to chance.

- Tell the students to compare answers with a partner. Then call on two students to say what the two things are.

SAMPLE ANSWER

The two things are putting more variety in our lives and accepting ourselves exactly as we are at the present moment.

- Read aloud the instructions as the students follow along in their books. Then have them do the exercise.

- Have the students check their answers with a partner. Then call on different students to read aloud the statements and say *Right* or *Wrong*.

ANSWERS
1. Wrong
2. Right
3. Right
4. Wrong
5. Wrong
6. Right
7. Right
8. Wrong

OPTION 1

Tell the students to correct the "Wrong" statements. When they finish, have them compare answers with a partner. Then call on three students to read aloud their corrections.

POSSIBLE ANSWERS

The article suggests that . . .
1. people find things to do that are different.
4. people find pleasure in the unexpected and the surprising.
5. people find the courage to welcome uncertainty.
8. people realize that life insurance doesn't protect them from uncertainty.

OPTION 2

Have the students write summaries of the article. You can have them begin by looking for the main point in each paragraph. When they finish writing their summaries, have them compare their work with a partner. Then have the partners compare their summaries with other partners. Finally, call on different students to read their summaries aloud and write them on the board.

15 ► Before you read the article, look carefully at the subtitle. When you have finished reading, say what the two things are that you can't leave to chance.

How to Step Up Your Luck
Two Moves You Can't Leave to Chance

by Catherine Lilly, Ph.D. and Daniel Martin, Ph.D.

What does it mean to be lucky? It commonly means someone who gets something valuable without really trying, someone who is in the right place at the right time. The person who discovers a lost painting by a famous painter, or who buys a winning lottery ticket—these are lucky people. They meet up with unexpectedly fortunate events. Since we have no control over the "when" and the "where" of such events, we can't make them happen to us. The only way to make a difference in our luck is to control ourselves.

Variety can increase your luck

The first rule is to look for variety, new experiences. More variety will result in a richer life with more opportunities. The more varied life is, the more likely that unexpected combinations of events will occur, giving us the chance to improve our situation. Researchers say that being able to change is the best way to survive in changing, unpredictable times. Individuals who can change are more adaptable.

When we are searching for something, like a lost pair of eyeglasses, it isn't a good idea to always follow the same pattern of search. If we always start looking in the basement and systematically work our way through the house, we're probably wasting time. Instead we can learn from the past. Whenever we misplace our glasses, we should start our search at the place where we last found them in order to make use of our past successes. Searching for happiness is like that as well. Be flexible. Learn from your mistakes. Try lots of different possibilities.

Variety is necessary for happiness. No matter how rich our lives may seem, if they consist only of expected events and repetition, boredom steps in.

We find pleasure in the unexpected and the surprising. Birthday presents that we expect do not excite us, but we can be strangely affected by unexpected small signs of generosity or affection. Chance makes the difference. Saying yes to uncertainty adds pleasure to life and contributes to our luck. Sometimes it seems easier, however, to use our strength to build walls to try to protect ourselves from uncertainty. We buy life insurance, household insurance, car insurance. We work hard and put money aside. But all this planning can't guarantee safety. We need to find the courage to welcome uncertainty.

Taking the first step is crucial. Each of us should find one action that will increase variety: subscribe to a new magazine, take a different route to work, sign up for a night-school course. Then focus on its positive results. This positive reinforcement, together with the pleasure of sensing the power in doing what we want to, should give us the courage for the next act.

Saying yes to yourself

Accepting ourselves exactly as we are at this present moment provides the courage to move forward. Believing that all our choices in the past were the best we could have made at the time frees us from regret and reinforces our belief that we are as good as we can be at this moment. The best preparation for the future is self-acceptance in the present. Self-acceptance and trust in people are the foundations of confidence and courage.

Self-acceptance, courage, and action don't guarantee good luck, but they do guarantee a richer and fuller life. They lead to more opportunities from unexpected events that can enrich our lives.

16 ► As you read the article, pay attention to the authors' suggestions on how to increase your luck. When you have finished reading, say *Right* or *Wrong* for each item below.

The article suggests that people
1. do the same things every day.
2. add variety to their lives and try out new things.
3. be flexible and learn from mistakes.
4. be cautious of new experiences.
5. try to protect themselves from uncertainty.
6. be willing to change.
7. accept themselves as they are.
8. buy life insurance.

17 ▶ **Tony's friend Marcel is always complaining. Complete Marcel's responses, using an item from box A and a phrase from box B in each of your answers.**

1. **Tony** Let's check out that sale on radios at Radio World.
   Marcel It seems . . .
   Tony *Let's check out that sale on radios at Radio World.*
   Marcel *It seems whenever I buy anything on sale it breaks the next day.*

2. **Tony** There's a dance tonight. Why don't we each ask a date to go with us?
   Marcel I'm sure . . .

3. **Tony** I'm not familiar with Indian food, so will you order for me?
   Marcel I'm sure . . .

4. **Tony** I don't care which movie we see. You pick one out.
   Marcel I'm sure . . .

5. **Tony** Why don't you go get two seats and I'll get the popcorn?
   Marcel I know . . .

6. **Tony** If you'd just study for your tests, you'd do better on them.
   Marcel It seems . . .

Box A	
whatever	however much
whenever	whichever
whoever	wherever

Box B

will say no
will be one you don't want to
  see
it breaks the next day
you'll think is too spicy
will be too close or too far
  from the screen for you
I always fail

18 ▶ **Angela Solera ran into some bad luck. Complete her account of the incident with the correct form of an appropriate three-word verb from the box.**

The other day I _____ file folders, so I went to look for some in Mr. Clemente's desk drawer. Just as I opened the drawer, he _____ and thought I _____ no good. He said I should _____ his files. He thought I was trying to _____ the new job at the company and that I wanted to know who else he was considering for it.

I tried to _____ myself, but he wouldn't listen. He told me to leave his office before he _____ patience. He said he wasn't going to let me _____ such dishonest behavior. I used to _____ Mr. Clemente and I thought he liked me, too. However, I wasn't able to convince him I was innocent, so I guess someone else _____ the new job.

be up to
end up with
find out about
get away with
keep out of
look up to
run out of
stand up for
walk in on

19 ▶ **These people feel they are unlucky. Give each of them advice, using the information in the article on luck on page 67 and one of the expressions in the box below.**

1. I've bought a lottery ticket at the same store every Friday for five years, but, although most of my friends have won at least once, I never have.
2. Everybody else finds money in the street, but I've walked the same way to school for three years without finding a penny.
3. At work I'm afraid to ask for a raise because, with my luck, the boss would probably fire me.
4. I've had four accidents in four years and I drive the same way to work every day. I know the road perfectly. I don't know what's wrong.
5. I haven't had a vacation in over two years. Every time I get ready to go away, something happens. The airplanes don't have any seats. I lose my passport. I forget to buy travelers checks. There's always something.

It's essential that . . .
It's important that . . .
I recommend that . . .
I suggest that . . .

- Have a student read the instructions aloud. Then point out the boxes and have different students read aloud the information in them. Next ask two students to read aloud the sample answer.

- Tell the students to read through the exercise items. Answer any questions. Then have the students do the exercise.

- Have the students compare answers with a partner. Then call on different pairs of students to read aloud the conversations. You can ask other students to write the answers on the board.

ANSWERS

2. whoever we ask will say no.
3. whatever I order you'll think is too spicy.
4. whichever I pick will be one you don't want to see.
5. wherever I want to sit will be too close or too far from the screen for you.
6. however much I study I always fail.

OPTION

Have the students work in pairs to convert the exercise into one which is more optimistic. Tell them to substitute optimistic statements for the pessimistic ones which Marcel says in the original exercise. Provide an example:

1. . . .
   Marcel Great! It seems whenever I buy anything on sale at Radio World I get a good deal.

When they finish, have the pairs compare their conversations with other pairs. Then call on different pairs to act out their conversations for the class.

- Read the instructions aloud as the students follow along in their books. Then have them repeat the three-word verbs in the box after you. Make sure they know the meanings of the verbs.

- Tell the students to read over the incomplete account. Answer any questions. Then have the students do the exercise.

- Tell the students to compare answers with a partner. Then call on different students to read aloud the sentences from the paragraphs. Have other students write the answers on the board.

ANSWERS

'd run out of, walked in on me, was up to, keep out of, find out about, stand up for, ran out of, get away with, look up to, will end up with

OPTION 1

Have the students make up sentences of their own that each contain a different three-word verb from the box. Tell them to make sure their sentences make sense and indicate that the students know the meanings of the verbs. Go around the room and

answer any questions students have about their work. Then have them compare sentences with a partner. Finally, call on different students to read aloud their sentences and write them on the board.

You can continue the practice and make it more communicative by next having the students use their sentences (or write different ones) to form part of a brief conversation. If possible, use a sentence a student has already written to form one line of a sample conversation. Help the class come up the other line(s). For example:

A We just ran out of popcorn and the movie isn't over yet.
B Well, why don't you get up and make some more?
A O.K. I will.

OPTION 2

Have the students work in pairs and make up a continuation of Angela's account. Tell them to use their imaginations to write at least one more paragraph to end Angela's story. Suggest some possible endings. For example:

Angela's best friend gets the new job. OR
Angela gets fired but then finds a much better job on another floor of the same office building.

When they finish, tell the pairs to share their accounts with other pairs. Finally, call on different pairs to read aloud their accounts.

- Read the instructions aloud. Then have different students pretend they are the unlucky people as they read aloud the exercise statements. Answer any questions. Next have the students repeat the expressions in the box after you.

- Have the students work in pairs to take turns reading aloud the statements and giving advice with information from the article on p. 67. Go around the room and check the pairs' work.

- Call on different pairs to act out their exchanges. You can have some students write the statements of advice on the board.

POSSIBLE ANSWERS

1. I suggest (that) you change your routine and go to another store.
2. It's essential that you accept yourself without comparing yourself to other people.
3. I recommend (that) you take a chance and ask for that raise.
4. It's important that we learn from our mistakes. Maybe you should take a different road to work.
5. I suggest (that) you forget about these past problems and take a vacation.

WORKBOOK Review of Units 1–6, pp. 37-40

PREVIEW

Before you begin teaching, go over the functions/themes, language, and forms in the chart. This will give you a preview of what you will encounter as you guide the students through the unit.

Preview the reading.

- Tell the class to look at the illustration as you have a student describe it. Then read aloud the instructions for the first exercise and have the students follow them.

- Go around the room and join in the discussions. Then call on different pairs to share their discussions with the class.

- Have a student read aloud the second set of instructions. Then have the students discuss with a partner what the article is probably about. Next call on different students to share their guesses with the class.

PREVIEW

FUNCTIONS/THEMES	LANGUAGE	FORMS
Identify someone Describe something	Who's the woman (who's) drinking coffee? That's Olga Sandoval. Do you know what *budín de tortilla* is? It's a casserole made with tortillas, chicken, and cheese. I've never seen *Citizen Kane*. What's it about? It's a story modeled on the life of the famous newspaper publisher, William Randolph Hearst.	Relative clauses with pronouns as subjects: Reduced restrictive clauses
Recall something	My teacher used to sit at her desk the whole day, waiting for us to do something wrong.	Placement of adverbs
Describe an activity	He sat in his room all morning playing the guitar. She banged on the wall loudly, making a lot of noise.	

Preview the reading.

1. Do you know what a music video is? Would you rather just listen to music or "see" it as well? Why? Discuss your answers with a partner.

2. Before you read the article on pages 70–71, look at the title and the pictures. What do you think the article is about? Discuss your ideas with a partner.

31. Playing with Music

Ever since music videos became popular in the early 1980s, television viewers have become used to the idea of experiencing music by "seeing" it as well as listening to it. The creation of colorful, artistic music videos allowed millions of viewers to watch visual interpretations of their favorite rock group's songs. Now, thanks to a new technology called CD-ROM (Compact Disc-Read Only Memory), music fans can do more than sit back and listen to music; they can participate in it as well. Imagine directing a music video, recreating your favorite performer's appearance, or composing your own songs— all while sitting at a computer! This new way of experiencing music—called "interactive rock"—is quickly becoming a popular new way for people to enjoy music.

CD-ROM technology allows what was once only possible in your imagination to take place in the comfort of your home. You can listen to, watch, record, and create music, all at the same time.

CD-ROMs look like CDs (compact discs), but unlike ordinary CDs, they store graphics and text in addition to sound. One CD-ROM can store the contents of an entire encyclopedia. A CD-ROM player connects to a computer and supplies it with data. The increased storage capacity of a CD-ROM puts many more choices at the user's disposal than most computer software.

For example, rocker Todd Rundgren's *No World Order*, the first interactive music CD-ROM, allows you to "play" with Rundgren's music. Have you ever thought that a song was too fast or too slow? Interactive rock allows you to make changes. On Rundgren's CD-ROM,

Figure it out

1. **Read the article. If necessary, change your answer to item 2 on page 69.**

2. **A key word in the article is *interactive*. Check (√) the statements that relate to interactive behavior.**

____ 1. Music fans participate in the music.
____ 2. We just sit back and enjoy the song.
____ 3. You can manipulate the graphics on the CD-ROM.
____ 4. The listener can "talk back" to the music.
____ 5. The discs store graphics and text.
____ 6. With the original music videos, you could only listen and watch.
____ 7. You can control the colors and some of the sounds.
____ 8. They never become involved with the music.
____ 9. The audience becomes the performers.

31. Playing with Music

PROCEDURE

- Point out the illustration and the photo and ask different students to describe them.

- Have the students read through the article. Follow a procedure similar to that on p. 2 of this book.

Figure it out

1. Read the article.

- Have the students make any necessary changes to their answers to item 2 on p. 69. Then call on different students to tell the class what the article is about.

OPTION

Have the students scan the article for a sentence (or sentences) that best expresses the main idea. Then tell them to compare answers with a partner. Finally, call on different students to share their answers with the class.

POSSIBLE ANSWER

CD-ROM technology allows what was once only possible in your imagination to take place in the comfort of your home. You can listen to, watch, record, and create music, all at the same time.

2. ...Check (✓) the statements that relate to interactive behavior.

- Make sure the students understand the meaning of the word *interactive*. Then have them read through the exercise items. Answer any questions.

- Tell the students to do the exercise. Then have the students compare answers with a partner. Next call on different students to read aloud the statements that relate to interactive behavior.

ANSWERS

1.
3.
4.
7.
9.

3. Read the questions.

- Tell the students to read through the questions. Then have them scan the article for the answers.

- Tell the students to compare answers with a partner. Then call on different students to say the answers.

POSSIBLE ANSWERS

1. You can listen to, watch, record, and create music.
2. A CD-ROM is a compact disc that stores graphics and text in addition to sound.
3. Todd Rundgren is a rock musician. He produced an interactive music CD-ROM that allows one to "talk back to the music."
4. You can choose where you would like to "travel" and what you would like to do. You can manipulate graphics and view realistic graphics and sound.
5. People will become increasingly interested in "playing" with music. As interactive rock gains popularity, it is likely that more artists will create exciting CD-ROMs, allowing fans to become more involved in the music than ever.

4. ...Say whether the words in italics are nouns or verbs.

- Have the students repeat the four exercise sentences after you. Then have them do the exercise.

- Tell the students to compare answers with a partner. Next call on different students to say the answers and write them on the board.

ANSWERS

1. *Récord* – noun (used as an adjective here), *prodúce* – verb
2. *suspéct* – verb
3. *recórd* – verb
4. *rébel* – noun

OPTION

Tell the students to use the words in italics from the exercise as both nouns and verbs in sentences of their own. Explain that their sentences should show that the writers know the meaning of the words. When they finish, tell them to compare sentences with a partner. Then call on different students to read aloud their sentences and write them on the board.

FOLLOW-UP

Students can write down the answers to the questions in exercise 3.

WORKBOOK Lesson 31, p. 41

you can select a new tempo with the push of a button. At the same time, you can decide to write new lyrics for his songs, or hear the songs in a different order. Rundgren calls this "your opportunity to talk back to the music."

Using the CD-ROM *Xplora I: Peter Gabriel's Secret World* is a lot like exploring a foreign country. You can choose where you would like to "travel" and what you would like to do. You can manipulate graphics in order to put together parts of rock star Peter Gabriel's face on your computer screen. Or, if you prefer, you can experience the thrill of going backstage with Gabriel at the music industry's annual Grammy award show by viewing realistic graphics and sound. With *Jump: David Bowie Interactive*, you create your own videos of Bowie's songs, and if you press "rewind," you see your video played as many times as you like.

Unlike the experience of listening to music, using interactive CD-ROMs let you control the music. Interactive rock has become so popular that multimedia expert Marc Canter has established the Media Band, the first "software rock and roll band." The Media Band is a collection of images, sounds, and text that the user controls. For example, guitar performances, vocals, and visual effects can all be created by the user. The group exists entirely within the world of "interactive rock" and individual users become the band's managers, producers, and technicians. Media Band lets the audience become the performers.

What is the future of CD-ROM and interactive rock? Singer Lou Reed says that "at a certain point, we'll all

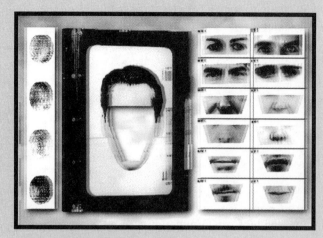

Using the CD-ROM *Xplora I: Peter Gabriel's Secret World*, music fans can construct Gabriel's face on the computer screen.

be dealing with our albums on CD-ROM." Industry analysts agree that people will become increasingly interested in "playing" with music. As interactive rock gains popularity, it is likely that more artists will create exciting CD-ROMs, allowing fans to become more involved in the music than ever.

For now, interactive CD-ROMs offer a choice. As Peter Gabriel explains, "There will be times when you just want to listen to music as a one-sense operation, and there will be other times when you want to sit down and get your hands dirty and play with it."

---

3. Read the following questions. Then scan the article for the answers.

1. What are four ways of experiencing music through "interactive rock"?
2. What is a good definition of a CD-ROM?
3. Who is Todd Rundgren and what has he contributed to interactive rock?
4. How can you use the CD-ROM *Xplora I: Peter Gabriel's Secret World*?
5. What does the article say about the future of CD-ROM and interactive rock?

4. Many words in English stress the first syllable if they are nouns and the second if they are verbs, as in *record* [rékərd], a noun, and *record* [rikɔ́rd], a verb. Say whether the words in italics are nouns or verbs, and place a stress mark (´) over the correct syllable.

1. *Record* companies now *produce* CDs.
2. Experts *suspect* that CD-ROM will greatly change the music industry.
3. I'm going to *record* my own version of that song on my computer.
4. My sister is a rock singer. My parents say she's the *rebel* in our family.

32. Do you call *that* singing?

1. Tell your partner who one of your favorite movie stars, singers, or singing groups is. Then describe one of the films or recordings that this person or group has made.

Paul Cooper is watching music videos on TV when his grandmother comes in.

Listen to the conversation.

2

Mrs. Cooper Are you watching TV again, Paul? Isn't that the same show that was on yesterday?

Paul It's not just one show, Grandma. It's actually a lot of different shows. They're music videos.

Mrs. Cooper Oh, really.

Paul Why don't you sit down and watch a couple? They're really good.

Mrs. Cooper Well, I guess it won't hurt. . . . What's that woman with the tambourine supposed to be doing?

Paul She's singing.

Mrs. Cooper Do you call *that* singing?

Paul Sure.

Mrs. Cooper Hmmm. Music was very different when I was young. It was . . . pleasant. It made you feel happy. It wasn't just a lot of angry noise.

Paul Music today isn't just angry noise, Grandma. Times are different now.

Mrs. Cooper I suppose so. . . . What's this, another video?

Paul Yeah. This one's really cool.

Mrs. Cooper Who's that guy?

Paul Which guy?

Mrs. Cooper The one wearing the crazy hat.

Paul He's the leader of the band. In the video he plays a normal kid who stands on the corner all day, playing the guitar. Then this big, shiny car comes along . . .

Mrs. Cooper Oh, let me guess! This "normal kid" stands on a street corner all day waiting for a big, shiny car to come along so he can get his big chance to be a star?

Paul How did you know?

Mrs. Cooper I saw it in the movies about 40 years ago. If you don't mind, I think I'll put on my headphones and listen to Julio Iglesias singing *real* music. . . .

3. Combine these sentences. Then shorten them as in the second example sentence.

1. The boy is Paul. The boy is watching music videos.
   The boy who is watching music videos is Paul.
   The boy watching music videos is Paul.

2. The woman is his grandmother. The woman is talking to Paul.

3. The video was on yesterday. The video is on TV now.

4. That guy is the leader of the band. That guy is wearing a crazy hat.

5. The music was quite different. The music was played when Paul's grandmother was young.

32. Do you call *that* singing?

1. Warm-up Activity

- Have a student read aloud the sentences in the box. Then have the students follow the instructions and talk to a partner.

- Go around the classroom and listen in. Then have different students tell the class about their favorite movie star, singer, or singing group.

2. Conversation

BACKGROUND

Paul Cooper is watching music videos on TV when his grandmother comes in. They watch together and have a discussion about music.

LANGUAGE

...(show that was) on is another way of saying "(show that was) playing."

...just (one show) means *only (one show)*.

...Grandma. is the short, informal form of *Grandmother.*

...a couple is short for *a couple of music videos.*

...I guess it won't hurt. is another way of saying "I suppose it's all right."

*Do you call **that** (singing)?* is a somewhat cynical way of expressing disbelief.

I suppose so... means the same thing as *I guess so.* It's used to more-or-less agree with what the previous speaker has just said.

...really cool. is used to express approval. It's a slang expression meaning *really good.*

...stands on the corner all day doesn't necessarily mean to stand in one spot all day. Instead it means to be in the general vicinity (on a street) all day.

...comes along... means *passes by.*

...get (his) big chance means *have a tremendous opportunity.*

If you don't mind is used to excuse one's self. It's like saying "If it's O.K. with you."

PROCEDURE

- As the students examine the illustration, point out the two characters from the conversation. Ask a student to describe what's probably going on in the picture. (See the Culture Close-Up which follows.)

- Follow a procedure similar to that indicated for the opening conversation in Unit 1.

3. Combine the sentences. Then shorten them as in the second example sentence.

- Have a student read aloud the first exercise item and the sample answer. Answer any questions. If necessary, review clauses and participles. Then tell the students to do the exercise.

- Have the students compare answers with a partner. Next call on different pairs; have one partner read aloud the exercise sentences in their books and the other the answers. Ask other students to write the answers on the board.

ANSWERS

2. The woman who is talking to Paul is his grandmother. The woman talking to Paul is his grandmother.
3. The video that is on TV now was on yesterday. The video on TV now was on yesterday.
4. That buy who is wearing a crazy hat is the leader of the band. That guy wearing a crazy hat is the leader of the band.
5. The music that was played when Paul's grandmother was young was quite different. The music played when Paul's grandmother was young was quite different.

CULTURE CLOSE-UP

MTV (Music Television) is a cable-television channel in the U.S. that viewers can purchase for a small monthly cost. It was started in 1981 at a time when the record business was in trouble. MTV shows mainly short video clips, running about three minutes—the usual length of a song. The clips consist of scenes that are brief blends of rock music and visual images. MTV shows hundreds of videos every day and reaches more than 12 million homes. Its target audience is between the ages of 12 and 34.

FOLLOW-UP

Students can write down their descriptions from exercise 1.

WORKBOOK Lesson 32, p. 42

33. Who's the woman drinking coffee?

WARM-UP

Play a recording of a favorite song in English. (Alternatively, you can sing or say the words.) Have the students copy down the words. Answer any questions about the vocabulary or structures used in the song. Then sing the song with the entire class.

IDENTIFY SOMEONE • DESCRIBE SOMETHING

- Point out the woman drinking coffee in the illustration. Then tell the students to read over the conversation. Answer any questions. Next have the students listen to the conversation. You can ask a pair of students to act it out for the class. Remind them to use appropriate stress and intonation.

- Point out the characters in the illustration and the box on the right. Have three students read aloud the sentences in the box.

- Read aloud the second set of instructions. Then have the students act out similar conversations with a partner, using the information in the box.

- Go around the classroom and listen in on the conversations, giving help if needed. Finally, call on different pairs to act out their conversations for the class.

2

- Have the students read over the two possible conversations. Answer any questions. Then have the class listen to the conversations. You can also ask a pair of students to act them out for the class.

- Point out the box and have different students read aloud the contents. Answer any questions. Then have the students work with a partner to follow the second set of instructions.

- Go around the room and listen in on the conversations and check the pairs' work. When the partners have finished, call on different pairs to act out their conversations for the class.

OPTION

Find out if any students have the recipes for the foods described in the exercise. If they do, tell them to bring the recipes to class to share with their classmates (in English, of course). If possible, have the students prepare the dishes in class as they describe the different steps involved. If that's not possible, ask the students to bring samples of the foods to class to share with their classmates.

Alternatively, have the students bring their favorite recipes to class and have them translate them into English. Then call on different students to read the recipes aloud and write them on the board.

33. Who's the woman drinking coffee?

 1 ▶ **Listen to the conversation.**
▶ **Act out similar conversations. Tell your partner who each person in the illustration is, using the information in the box.**

A Who's the woman (who's) drinking coffee?

B That's Olga Sandoval. She's a dancer and she teaches ballet. She's writing a book about dance in Argentina.

> **The people in the illustration**
>
> 1. Olga Sandoval is a dancer. She also teaches ballet. She's writing a book about dance in Argentina.
> 2. Julio Mata is a singer. He has a very good voice and sometimes does opera.
> 3. Dolores Calderon is a musician. She's very talented and also composes music.

 2 ▶ **Listen to the two possible conversations.**
▶ **Act out similar conversations with a partner, using the descriptions in the box.**

A Do you know what *budín de tortilla* is?

B Yes. It's a casserole made with tortillas, chicken, and cheese. It's served with chili sauce.

A That sounds delicious. I like anything made with cheese.　　**A** I don't really care for things made with cheese.

> *I don't care for* is more polite than *I don't like* when commenting on another person's preferences.

Some foods	Some descriptions
budín de tortilla (Mexico) tempura (Japan) feijoada (Brazil) keftedakia (Greece)	*Budín de tortilla* is a casserole (that is) made with layers of tortillas, chicken, and cheese. It's served with chili sauce. *Tempura* consists of fish, shrimp, and vegetables (that are) dipped in a light batter and fried in oil. *Feijoada* is a stew (that is) made with black beans, beef, pork, and sausage. *Keftedakia* is meatballs (that are) seasoned with mint.

3 ► Study the frames: Relative clauses with pronouns as subjects:
Reduced restrictive clauses

4 ► Rewrite the description
of each movie in the box,
reducing the relative
clauses.
► Act out similar
conversations with
a partner.

A *I've never seen* Citizen Kane.
What's it about?
B *It's a story modeled on the life of*
the famous newspaper publisher,
William Randolph Hearst.

Some classic films

Citizen Kane is a story that is modeled on the life of the famous U.S. newspaper
publisher, William Randolph Hearst.
Rashomon is a Japanese movie about a crime that is committed in eleventh-century
Japan. It's a story that is told from four different points of view.
Das Boot is a German film about some sailors who are trapped in a submarine. The men
that are in the submarine eventually get out alive, but the fate that is awaiting them is
just as bad.
La Dolce Vita is a famous Italian film about a journalist who is enjoying the "sweet life"
of Rome's high society. At the same time, the journalist is a man who is deeply
disturbed by the "sweet life."

RECALL SOMETHING

5 ► Listen to the speakers recall people or experiences they think of when
they hear one of the words in the box. For each speaker, write the
appropriate word.

1. _____
2. _____
3. _____
4. _____
5. _____

obnoxious	sad
mean	kind
funny	lonely
strict	

- Have the students examine the frames as you and some students read aloud the headings and possible sentences. Then you can have the students repeat the sentences after you.

- Answer any questions about the structures in the frames. You can have students come up with additional sentences of their own.

OPTION

Dictate to the class some sentences with relative clauses like those in the frames on the left. Then have the students compare what they wrote down with a partner. Next write the sentences on the board so the students can check their work. After that, tell the students to write down the reduced versions of the sentences. When they finish, have them compare their work with a partner. Finally, call on different students to write the reduced versions on the board.

- Point out the box and ask different students to read aloud the information in it. Then go over any unfamiliar vocabulary with the students. Next read aloud the instructions and then act out the sample conversation with a student.

- Have the students work with a partner to act out similar conversations. Go around the room and check the pairs' work. Finally, call on different students to act out the conversations with a partner.

POSSIBLE ANSWERS

Rashomon is a story told from four different points of view about a crime committed in eleventh-century Japan.
Das Boot is a movie about some German sailors trapped in a submarine. The men in the submarine eventually get out alive, but the fate awaiting them is just as bad.
La Dolce Vita is a famous Italian film about a journalist enjoying the "sweet life" of Rome's high society. At the same time, the journalist is a man deeply disturbed by the "sweet life."

RECALL SOMETHING

- Read the instructions aloud. Answer any questions students have about the procedure. Then point out the words in the box. Ask

different students to tell the class the meanings. If necessary, help them with the definitions.

- Have the students listen to the speakers' accounts and write down the appropriate words. When they finish, call on different students to say the answers aloud.

TAPESCRIPT

1. I'll never forget one teacher I had in high school. She used to sit at her desk the whole day, waiting for us to do something wrong or make a mistake. She wouldn't put up with anything. We were all scared to death of her. But looking back on it, I think she really just wanted us to learn. She wasn't so bad.
2. When I was little, there was an older boy in my neighborhood who I tried to stay away from. But he was in front of my house at least twice a week, trying to cause trouble. He used to call me names and hit me. I would yell to my mother, hoping he would run away. But he never did. I still don't know why he was like that.
3. When I got out of college, I didn't know what I wanted to do. I had a degree in English, but I didn't want to teach. I looked at the employment advertisements desperately every week, hoping I would see something interesting. Finally, I took a job as an assistant in a law office. There was an attorney there, Maureen Davies. She constantly went out of her way to be nice to me, telling me I had a lot of potential. She's the one who encouraged me to go to law school. Today I'm a lawyer, and I have Maureen Davies to thank.
4. I'll always remember Steve Harris, a guy I used to work with. He wasn't a very good engineer, but he sure thought he was a good comedian. At office parties, he used to stand on his desk and sing, I mean, try to sing . . . loudly. It was almost impossible to carry on a conversation! Then he would get in the middle of a group of people and tell jokes, laughing hysterically. The problem was, no one else was laughing. Even during the work day, no one could get anything done when Steve was around. He came into my office at least three times a day, wanting to chat. He was the most difficult person I've ever had to work with.
5. We lived in the same house until I was eleven. My best friend's name was Lisa, and we played with each other every day. As soon as we got home from school, I would run to her house or she would run to mine. We had so much fun all the time, playing basketball, walking to the store, or just talking. When my family moved to a different city, I cried and cried. I met new friends, but I missed Lisa for a long time.

ANSWERS
1. strict
2. mean
3. kind
4. obnoxious
5. lonely

- Have the students examine the frame as you point out the different types of adverbs and read aloud the sentences. You can have the students repeat the sentences after you. Answer any questions students have.

- Ask different students to read aloud the information in the boxes. Answer any questions.

OPTION

Have the students work in pairs to come up with additional sentences of their own, similar to those in the frame and in the boxes. Go around the room and answer any questions the pairs have about their work. Then have the pairs compare their sentences with other pairs. Finally, call on different pairs to read aloud their sentences and write them on the board.

- Point out the illustration and ask a student to describe it. Then have two students read aloud the sample conversation.

- Read the instructions aloud. Answer any questions about the procedure. Then have the students do the exercise.

- Tell the students to compare answers with a partner. Then call on different pairs to read aloud the restated conversations. If necessary, have different students write the answers on the board. Finally, have the pairs act out the restated conversations.

ANSWERS

2. **B** They caught him secretly looking through his boss's files.
3. **A** He sits in his room all day, listening to loud music.
   B He spends hours talking to his friends on a street corner/on a street corner talking to his friends.
4. **A** Last night I was at home, quietly playing the piano/playing the piano quietly.

FOLLOW-UP

Students can write out the conversations they acted out in exercise 1.

6 ▶ **Study the frame: Placement of adverbs**

Adverbs of place, manner, and time

	Place	Manner	Time			Manner	Place	Time
He sat	at his desk	quietly	all day.		He sat	quietly	at his desk	all day.

Sentences with participial phrases

Adverbs modifying the main verb

	Adverbs	Participial phrases
He sat	in his room all morning,	playing the guitar.
She banged	on the wall loudly,	making a lot of noise.

Adverbs modifying the verb in the participial phrase

	Participial phrases	Adverbs
She caught the thief,	shooting him	in the leg.
He stood there,	listening	quietly for ten minutes.

> An adverb of manner ending in *-ly* may also precede the participial phrase.
> He stood there, *quietly* listening.

Sentences with two meanings

The position of the comma (,) shows which verb an adverb modifies.
  He stood there, quietly listening to his friends. (He listened quietly.)
  He stood there quietly, listening to his friends. (He stood quietly.)

The use of a comma shows which noun is the subject of the verb in the participial phrase.
  She caught the thief, shooting him in the leg. (She shot the thief.)
  She caught the thief shooting him in the leg. (The thief shot somebody.)

7 ▶ **Restate the conversations, combining the sentences in brackets [ ] into one sentence and putting the adverbs followed by a slash (/) in their correct positions. Check to make sure you have used commas correctly, when they are needed.**

1. **A** Wasn't yesterday a beautiful day?
   B It sure was. [for hours/outside/I just sat. I was reading a book.]
   A *Wasn't yesterday a beautiful day?*
   B *It sure was. I just sat outside for hours, reading a book.*

2. **A** Did you hear John was fired last week?
   B Yes, Sally told me. [They caught him. secretly/He was looking through his boss's files.]

3. **A** I don't know what I'm going to do with my son. [all day/in his room/He sits. He listens to loud music.]
   B Mine isn't any better. [on a street corner/He spends hours. He talks to his friends.]

4. **A** I think there's something wrong with my neighbor.
   B Why do you say that?
   A [Last night I was at home. quietly/I was playing the piano.] It wasn't even 8:30 and he started knocking on my wall.

34. Your turn

1. Work with your classmates. Talk about each of the different types of music pictured here. What do you know about each one? Which singers and musicians do you know who perform the different types of music?

2. Choose one type of music that you like best. Work with a partner who also likes this kind of music and share your impressions. What are some of your favorite songs? Who are your favorite performers? Have you ever seen this music performed live? What do you like most about this type of music? Can you remember the words to any songs? Can you sing a song? Report your ideas to the class.

country western

classical

rock 'n' roll

salsa

34. Your turn

- Read aloud the instructions for the first exercise as the students follow along in their books. Answer any questions. (See the Culture Close-Up which follows.)

- Point out the photos on pp. 76 and 77. Call on different students to read aloud the captions and tell the class what they know about the different kinds of music.

- Have the students work in groups to do the exercise. Go around the room and join in the discussions as you check the groups' work. Then talk about the different types of music and discuss the questions with the entire class.

CULTURE CLOSE-UP

One of the most popular kinds of music in the U.S. is country western music. Country western music originates from two other kinds of music—from the traditional music of the people who lived in the Appalachian Mountains in the eastern U.S. and from cowboy music from the West. Country western singers usually play guitars. In the 1920s, they started using electric guitars. Today about 1,200 radio stations broadcast country western music 24 hours a day in the U.S. and Canada. It's also become popular in England, and people in other countries sing it in their languages.

Jazz is the only music form started in the U.S. that has had an influence on musical development throughout the Western world. It originated with obscure African-American musicians in the South in the late 19th century. Jazz is a combination of Western harmonic forms and rhythms and melodic inflections of black Africa. Jazz is characterized by improvisation, syncopation, and by a kind of intonation that sometimes seems "out of tune." Jazz has had a tremendous influence, not only on other forms of American music, but on music in many different parts of the world

Rock 'n' roll because popular in the U.S. in the 1950s. The history of rock 'n' roll is tied to American history. It was derived from a whole range of types of music over a period of time—jazz, blues, boogie-woogie, soul, country western, and gospel music. The most famous rock 'n' roll performer or all time was Elvis Presley.

Rap was first created by black urban disc jockeys in the mid-1970s. These disc jockeys manipulated the records they were playing in dance clubs by making scratching rhythms and other sounds resulting in a staccato or chant-like beat of its own. A "rapper" speaks over the music in street-language rhymes, often with themes of anger and protest. Rap became popular in the early 1980s and by 1986 had reached mainstream audiences. Break-dancing, which includes acrobatics such as flips and headspins, often accompanies rap. Recent rap lyrics deal with murder, drug dealing, and political and sexual issues.

Listen in

- Read the instructions aloud. Then have the students listen to the interview. When they finish, tell them to talk to a partner about the kind of music the musician in the interview performs. Finally, call on a student to say the answer.

TAPESCRIPT

Russ Parker Welcome back to "Close Up" on WKHZ radio—the show that lets you call in and talk to all your favorite musicians and performers. I'm Russ Parker. We've been taking with legendary musician Emma Katon. Thanks again for being with us, Emma.

Emma Katon Well, I'm happy to be here.

Russ Parker Let's take our next caller. Hello? Welcome to "Close Up."

Caller Hello?

Russ Parker Yes, go ahead.

Caller Oh . . . I'm so excited to get to talk to you, Emma. I've been a fan of yours ever since I was a little girl. And I don't want to tell you how long ago that was!

Emma Katon You don't have to tell me—I *know* how long ago that was.

Caller (*laughs*) O.K. Here's my question, Emma. Your career has lasted over fifty years, from your early work in the 1940s up to your most recent work today. What do you think the key to your lasting appeal is?

Emma Katon I've been lucky. I started my career when this style of music was at its height—I just got carried along by the wave. But if I have to be specific, I guess I'd say it's because of two things. The first is consistency. I've never tried to be any other kind of musician than what I am. I am a singer, but I know that I can't sing classical music or country western . . . and rap and rock n' roll came along a little too late for me. I've always known that my strength was singing one specific kind of music, and that's what I stick to. *I think I can play a little saxophone too,* but some of my friends might disagree with that. (*laughs*) The second thing that has made my career last is variety. Within my specific focus, I've tried to find every opportunity to explore. I've worked with many other types of performers—from reggae to salsa to classical musicians. And every time I do, it brings a little more "variety" to my music.

Caller Well, I think you're just wonderful. I can't wait to hear your next CD.

Emma Katon Well, it should be out in about a month.

Russ Parker Thank you for calling. Hello, next caller. You're on "Close Up."

ANSWER
Jazz

OPTION

Have the students work in pairs to conduct their own interviews. Tell the partners to pretend they are either the caller or a famous musician. Encourage them to use their imaginations. Go around the room and listen in on the interviews. When they finish, call on different pairs to act out their interviews for the class.

FOLLOW-UP

Students can write out their answer to the questions in the first exercise in **Your turn**.

WORKBOOK Lessons 33–34, pp. 43–45

rap

jazz

📼 Listen in

A musician is being interviewed on WKHZ radio. Listen to the interview and then say what type of music the musician performs.

reggae

35. On your own

1. Imagine that you went to one of the performances in the photos. Write a review for a local magazine or newspaper.

opera

Broadway musical

Kabuki theater

ballet

mime

Ballet Fólklorico

2. Write a short biography of a performer whose music you enjoy. Include important facts about his or her life and interesting information about his or her music. Tell what makes this performer so popular.

35. On your own

PROCEDURE

- Point out the photos and ask different students to describe them. Ask students if they've ever been to any of the performances featured in the photos. Have them tell the class about the performances.

- Have a student read aloud the instructions for the first exercise. Then tell the students to write their reviews on separate paper.

- Have the students compare their reviews with a partner. Then call on different students to read aloud their reviews and write them on the board. Alternatively, assign the exercise for homework, collect the reviews, mark any errors, and return the homework to the students for any needed corrections. Collect the homework again and check the corrections.

- Read aloud the second set of instructions. Assign the exercise for homework. Remind the students that they may have to use the library or other sources of information to gather the biographical facts.

- Collect the biographies, mark any errors, and return the homework to the students for any needed corrections. Collect the homework again and check the corrections.

OPTION

Tell the students to add appropriate pictures to their reviews and biographies. Then collect their work and display it for all the class members to enjoy. Alternatively, call on different students to show their pictures to the class and read aloud their work.

CULTURE CLOSE-UP

Broadway is a street in New York City which has become synonymous with important dramatic plays and musicals in the U.S. Some famous Broadway musicals include *Oklahoma*, *West Side Story*, and *A Chorus Line*.

WORKBOOK Lesson 35, p. 46. Before assigning the writing task, review some of the rules for capitalization and punctuation by pointing out the use of capital letters, commas, and periods in the newspaper review. Remind the students to use appropriate capital letters and punctuation in their reviews.

PREVIEW

Before you begin teaching, go over the functions/themes, language, and forms in the chart. This will give you a preview of what you will encounter as you guide the students through the unit.

Preview the reading.

- Tell the class to look at the illustration as you have a student guess what's probably just happened. Have the students work in pairs. Ask a pair to read aloud the instructions for the exercise. Answer any questions.

- Tell the pairs to play the two roles. Go around the room and check the pairs' work. Finally, call on different pairs to act out their role plays for the class. Encourage class discussion of the different approaches to solving the problem.

UNIT 8 • LESSONS 36-40

79 Unit 8

FUNCTIONS/THEMES	LANGUAGE	FORMS
Convince someone	There's a computer technology conference that I would like to attend. It's a very important meeting and I think it's essential that I go. It's very important for me to keep up to date on what's going on.	Subjunctive clauses vs. infinitive clauses
Inform someone	It is essential for us to fill the vacancy left by Mr. Franco.	
Make judgments	Karen just bought a new television and a stereo and now she wants a personal computer. You know what they say: The more you get, the more you want.	Double comparatives
Give advice	Speed limits have a purpose, and the sooner you start paying attention to them, the better for everyone.	
Ask someone to do something	Oh, Larry, could you help me for a minute, please? Excuse me, Dr. Bellini. I wonder if you could help me for just a minute, please. Melissa, I'd like you to help me for a minute, please.	

Preview the reading.

Student A
You are the office manager at a large accounting firm. Student B is your employee and has just arrived at the office, late for the third time this week. Student B does excellent work, but the chronic lateness has become a topic of discussion among the other employees. Talk to this employee and try to resolve the problem.

Student B
You are an employee at a large accounting firm. You just haven't felt like going to work the past few days so you've been arriving fifteen or twenty minutes late. Although you like your work, you feel a need to be more independent and creative at your job.

36. How Do Real Managers

You're irresponsible and lazy. Be here at 9:00 A.M. from now on!

Wrong

by
Kermit Moore

An employee comes to you with a suggestion about changing the budgeting process. You think it's wildly impractical. Do you tell the employee that the budget really isn't his or her area and that someone else will take care of it? Not if you want an involved, motivated employee. When you take a negative approach toward your workers, you merely send them the underlying message that they are stupid not to know their places and even stupider not to stay in them. The result: defensive and alienated employees. Yet too many managers simply aren't sensitive to the message behind their words. Here are some reminders about how to communicate to get results:

● **Realize that communication involves risks.** "Every time you open your mouth, you are taking a risk," says Dr. Gay Lumsden, a professor at Kean College in Union, New Jersey, and a management consultant. "You are risking rejection—of yourself, your ideas, your values, your opinions. And when your employees talk to you, they are not only taking these risks, they are risking their jobs and their careers as well."

Most of us take rejection of our ideas personally, so effective managers are careful to show appreciation and sensitivity, says Lumsden. Managers should never feel that they must agree with an employee, of course, but by acknowledging a worker's idea before they dismiss it, they create an atmosphere that invites participation, cooperation, innovation, and creativity.

● **When criticizing someone, describe, don't judge.** "Always focus on, and confine criticism to, observable behavior," advises Dr. Linda Eagle, a manager at Arthur Andersen and Company's Management Information Consulting Division. For instance, telling someone who's consistently late, "You've been coming in late, and we need you here on time," is more likely to

encourage promptness than snapping. "You're irresponsible and lazy. Be here at 9:00 A.M. from now on." The time for determining that a person is irresponsible is in a formal performance evaluation, says Eagle.

● **Focus on goals rather than image.** Take the example of a manager who drops a report on the desk of an assistant and says, "Photocopy this for me." If photocopying is the secretary's responsibility, not the assistant's, the manager is obviously going out of his or her way to remind the assistant who's boss. The manager may get the copy, but he or she may also get a defensive assistant along with it. What's more, since defensiveness often leads to more defensiveness, the manager and the assistant will now be locked in a bitter power struggle, with both trying to protect their self-esteem and defend their positions. Therefore, the manager would do better to request, rather than demand, a copy from an assistant.

● **Remember to show recognition, acknowledgment, and appreciation.** Surveys suggest that workers want, above all, to be acknowledged for a job well done, says Dr. Barry Eisenberg, director of employee education at the Memorial Sloan-Kettering Cancer Research Center in New York. Lumsden adds that "one of the best ways to acknowledge workers is to bring them into the day-to-day processes of the business: Listen to their ideas, share information, encourage creativity, let them know you value their input."

Above all, be consistent with praise and punishment. People feel more self-confident and more willing to take chances about being innovative when they know what to expect from their bosses.

36. How Do Real Managers Communicate?

PROCEDURE

- Point out the illustrations on pp. 80-81 and ask different students to describe them and read aloud the lines in the speech balloons.

- Have the students read through the article. Follow a procedure similar to that on p. 2 of this book.

Figure it out

1. As you read the article, pay careful attention to the suggestions given for effective communication between managers and employees.

- Have the students read over the instructions and the statements. Answer any questions. Then have them do the exercise. When they finish, tell the students to compare and discuss their answers with a partner.

- Call on different pairs; have one partner read aloud the exercise statement and say "Effective" or "Ineffective" and have the other read the supporting statement. You can also have different students write the answers on the board.

  ANSWERS
  1. Ineffective – "When you take a negative approach to your workers, you merely send them the underlying message that they are stupid not to know their places and even stupider not to stay in them."
  2. Effective – "Always focus on and confine criticism to observable behavior."
  3. Effective – ". . . workers want, above all, to be acknowledged for a job well done."
  4. Ineffective – "Always . . . confine criticism to observable behavior."
  5. Effective – "Focus on goals rather than image."

2. Imagine that you write a weekly advice column on business.

- Read the complete instructions aloud and answer any questions students have. Then have them write the answer for the advice column.

- Have the students compare answers with a partner. Then call on different students to read aloud their answers and write them on the board. You can have them compare their answers with the sample which follows.

SAMPLE ANSWER
Dear Frustrated:
    You should speak to "Sick Every Monday" as soon as possible, but when you do, it is very important that you describe and not judge his or her behavior. Since you cannot know for sure that that person has not been sick, be careful not to accuse your employee of lying. Instead, try to find out if something is wrong and encourage the worker to be honest with you. Emphasize that there is a lot to do at the office, and you are counting on your employee. You and your staff depend on his or her efforts and you know he or she can do the job. If the problem continues after this conversation, you may have to be more forceful. But in the beginning, give the person a chance to change his or her behavior.
    I hope this advice has been helpful to you, and I wish you good luck.
              Sincerely,

3. ...Complete each sentence with one of the words.

- Have the students repeat the four words with *self-* after you. Then have them read over the incomplete sentences. Answer any questions.

- Have the students do the exercise and then compare answers with a partner. Finally, call on different students to read aloud the completed sentences. Write the answers on the board.

  ANSWERS
  1. self-sufficient
  2. self-confidence
  3. self-destructive
  4. self-control

OPTION

Tell the students to use the *self-* words in original sentences which show that they know the meaning of the words. They can write their original sentences on separate paper and then compare their work with a partner. Finally, call on different students to say their sentences aloud and write them on the board.

FOLLOW-UP

Students can write down the main ideas from the article.

WORKBOOK Lesson 36, p. 47

Communicate?

> You've been coming in late, and we need you here on time.

Right

Figure it out

1. As you read the article, pay careful attention to the suggestions given for effective communication between managers and employees. When you have finished, say *Effective* or *Ineffective* for each of the manager's comments below. For each comment, identify a statement in the article that supports your answer.

   1. You don't have time to think of ideas for the new project. Your job is to finish the old one.
   2. It's very important that you be on time for your appointments. I've noticed that you've kept a few clients waiting more than 15 minutes.
   3. This letter is excellent, and I can see you've put a lot of thought into it. There are only a few small changes I'd like you to make.
   4. Your coworkers tell me you're uncooperative. I suggest you change your attitude.
   5. I know this isn't part of your job, but I'd really appreciate it if you could file these papers.

2. Imagine that you write a weekly advice column on business. A frustrated manager writes to you complaining that an employee has been taking long weekends by calling in sick every Monday. Based on what you have learned from the article, write a short letter to "Frustrated," giving advice on what to say to the employee.

3. The prefix *self-* may be placed before many words, as in *self-esteem* and *self-confident*. Complete each sentence with one of the words below, using your dictionary if necessary.

self-confidence	self-destructive
self-control	self-sufficient

   1. Tony is very _____ for a ten-year-old. He even cooks his own meals.
   2. Lola does excellent work, but she lacks _____ . She finds something wrong with everything she does.
   3. Louis stays out late every night, comes to work late every morning, and even insults his boss. I think he's really _____ .
   4. Nancy has no _____ . She's always losing her temper over nothing.

37. Maybe you'd better stay here after all!

1. You want to do one of the following things with your partner who isn't interested. Try to persuade your partner to change his or her mind.

1. Skip class tomorrow and go to a movie.
2. Take a weekend bike trip.
3. Invite the class to one of your houses for a party.
4. Sign up for a self-defense class like karate.

Linda Rueda and her boss, Sam Greene, work for an architectural firm. They are in Guadalajara on business.

Listen to the conversation.

2

Sam Listen, Linda . . . I'm afraid you're going to have to cut your trip short. Bill had to go into the hospital suddenly, so there's no one back home supervising things.

Linda The hospital! What happened to him?

Sam Well, it seems he had an appendicitis attack. The doctor told him it was essential that he be operated on right away.

Linda Oh, well, I suppose we should be glad it wasn't anything more serious. Is it really necessary for me to go home, though? I would think everyone could manage without us for a week.

Sam Well, I'm worried about the new project. I can't emphasize enough how important it is for us to get that contract.

Linda Do you mean the shopping center? I'm sure Ray and Nancy can handle it. You know they're very capable, Sam, and the more responsibility we give them, the less work we'll have in the long run.

Sam In principle, I agree with you. But in this particular case I'd feel more comfortable if you were there. I think the sooner you get back, the better.

Linda Well, I'll change my plans then. Still, there's one point I think I should mention. The people we're scheduled to meet with here on Monday don't speak any English.

Sam Oh! Well, uh . . . hmm . . . it looks as if maybe you'd better stay here after all!

3. Check (√) the statements that are stated or implied in the conversation.

_____ 1. Linda wasn't planning to leave Guadalajara so soon.
_____ 2. Bill got appendicitis in Guadalajara.
_____ 3. Linda thinks there are more serious illnesses than appendicitis.
_____ 4. Bill needed to have surgery immediately.
_____ 5. Bill was handling the shopping center contract when he became ill.

_____ 6. Linda wants to go back home right away.
_____ 7. Sam thinks Ray and Nancy can handle the shopping center contract by themselves.
_____ 8. Linda thinks Ray and Nancy should be given more responsibility.
_____ 9. Sam speaks Spanish.
_____ 10. Linda speaks Spanish.

37. Maybe you'd better stay here after all!

1. Warm-up Activity

- Have different students read aloud the sentences in the box. Answer any questions about the vocabulary and structures.

- Tell the students to work with a partner on the activity. Go around the classroom and check the pairs' work. Then have different pairs act out their conversations for the class.

2. Conversation

BACKGROUND

Linda Rueda and her boss, Sam Greene, work for an architectural firm. They are in Guadalajara, Mexico on business when Mr. Greene decides Linda should go back home to supervise a new project. A co-worker, Bill, who had been supervising things at home, had to be hospitalized.

LANGUAGE

I'm afraid as it's used here has nothing to do with fear. It's just another way of saying "unfortunately."

…cut (your trip) short. is another way of saying "interrupt (your trip) and return (home)."

…back home is used here to refer to the place Linda and Sam came from—the city where they usually work.

right away. is another way of saying "immediately."

…manage (without us) means *get along (without us).*

…handle (it). means *cope with (it).*

…in the long run. means *ultimately.* It's another way of saying "over a (long) period of time."

In principle is another way of saying "Basically."

Still is another way of saying "However."

…after all. means *ultimately* or *despite* (certain circumstances).

PROCEDURE

- As the students examine the illustration, point out the characters from the conversation. Ask a student to describe what's going on in the picture. Explain that the two characters are in Guadalajara, Mexico. Ask a student to point out Guadalajara on a globe or world map.

- Follow a procedure similar to that indicated for the opening conversation in Unit 1.

3. Check (✓) the statements that are stated or implied in the conversation.

- Have the students read over the statements. Answer any questions. Then have them scan the conversation to find the statements that are stated or implied.

- Have the students compare their answers with a partner. Next call on different students to read aloud the correct statements.

ANSWERS
1.
3.
4.
5.
7.
8.
10.

CULTURE CLOSE-UP

Since the women's movement took hold in the U.S. in the 1960s, more and more women have taken over management positions at small and large companies. Although men still hold the majority of top management positions in the U.S., the number of women being placed in such positions has been increasing each year.

FOLLOW-UP

Students can write sentences explaining why they want or don't want to do the things listed in exercise 1.

WORKBOOK Lesson 37, p. 48

38. It's very important that I keep up to date . . .

WARM-UP

Tell the students to work with a partner. Have them pretend they are their partner's boss. Tell them to try to convince their partner to take on an extra assignment. Begin by having a sample conversation with a student in front of the class:

T: (*Student's name*), I'm afraid you're going to have to work this weekend. I need this report finished.
S: Oh, no! I've made plans to go camping.
T: Well, we *are* planning to pay you double time . . . .
S: Oh, well, in that case . . . .

CONVINCE SOMEONE • SUBJUNCTIVE CLAUSES VS. INFINITIVE CLAUSES

- Tell the students to read over the conversation. Answer any questions. Then have them listen to the conversation. You can act it out with a student.

- Point out the notebook pages and have different students read aloud the information. Answer any questions students have about the contents. Then read aloud the second set of instructions. Explain to the students that they can use the information on the notebook pages or their own information in their conversations.

- Have the students work with a partner to act out similar conversations. Go around the classroom and listen in, giving help if needed. Finally, call on different pairs to act out their conversations for the class.

OPTION

Tell the pairs to continue the conversation. Provide two possible scenarios:

Mr. Harwood thinks Sylvia should go to the conference, but he wants her to explain exactly what she can learn there that will benefit the company.

Mr. Harwood tells Sylvia she can't go to the conference, and Sylvia threatens to quit her job.

Encourage the pairs to use their imaginations. Then go around the room and listen in. Finally, call on different pairs to act out their conversations for the class. Give a prize for the most original continuation.

- Have the students examine the frames as you read aloud the headings and ask different students to read aloud the possible sentences. Answer any questions. If necessary, review the subjunctive.

OPTION

On the board, write the main clauses from the frames—*It's important that/for . . .* , etc. Tell the students to work in pairs to come up with their own subjunctive clauses and infinitive clauses to go with the clauses on the board. Ask them to try to write sentences about people and things in their own environment. For example:

It's important that we speak English fluently when we finish this course.
It's essential for (*student's name*) to be here on time tomorrow.

When they finish, have the pairs compare sentences with other pairs. Go around the room and answer any questions students have about their work. Finally, call on different pairs to read aloud their sentences and write them on the board.

38. It's very important that I keep up to date...

1
- ▶ Listen to the conversation.
- ▶ Act out similar conversations. You would like to attend a conference, take a course, or give a speech at a meeting. Using your notes, try to convince your boss that the activity is important.

A Excuse me, Mr. Harwood. Could I speak to you for a minute?

B Yes, of course, Sylvia. What is it?

A I'll get right to the point. There's a computer technology conference that I would like to attend in Houston next month.

B Oh?

A Yes. It's a very important meeting and I think

it's essential [that I / for me to] go.

B I'm not sure it's really necessary. And, anyway, I'm not sure the company can afford it.

A Well, sir, it happens to be my field, and I think

it's very important [that I / for me to] keep up to date

on what's going on—for the company's sake.

B Well, maybe you have a point. I'll give it some thought.

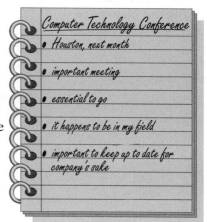

Computer Technology Conference
- *Houston, next month*
- *important meeting*
- *essential to go*
- *it happens to be in my field*
- *important to keep up to date for company's sake*

Course in English Conversation
- begins in two weeks
- interesting course
- important to enroll
- I happen to know some English
- crucial to learn English for international meetings

MEETING OF THE NATIONAL ORGANIZATION
- I'VE BEEN INVITED TO SPEAK ON FRIDAY
- THE LARGEST ORGANIZATION OF _____
- IMPORTANT TO ATTEND
- THERE WILL BE MANY WELL-KNOWN PEOPLE THERE
- IMPORTANT TO REPRESENT THE COMPANY

2 ▶ Study the frames: Subjunctive clauses vs. infinitive clauses

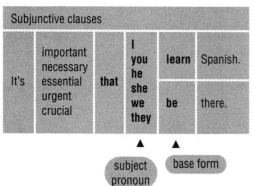

Subjunctive clauses				
It's	important necessary essential urgent crucial	that	I you he she we they	learn	Spanish.
				be	there.

subject pronoun — base form

Infinitive clauses				
It's	important necessary essential urgent crucial	for	me you him her us them	to learn	Spanish.
				to be	there.

object pronoun — infinitive

Unit 8 **83**

3 ▶ **Rewrite this memo about the warehouse of a publishing company. Change the subjunctive clauses to infinitive clauses and the infinitive clauses to subjunctive clauses.**

Start like this:
It is essential for us to fill the vacancy. . . .

> # INTEROFFICE MEMORANDUM
>
> **TO:** Clifford Olsen, Personnel
> **FROM:** Paula Davis
> **SUBJECT:** Vacancy left by Mr. Franco
>
> It is essential that we fill the vacancy left by Mr. Franco. Because of our current workload, it is urgent for us to do this immediately. As for qualifications, it is crucial that the candidate have previous warehouse experience, and since we have many Spanish-speaking customers, it is also important that he or she have a knowledge of that language.
>
> I am confident that I can leave the matter of finding a replacement in your hands. Please bear in mind that it is crucial for the warehouse to have a full staff. The sooner this is accomplished, the better.
>
> Thank you for your help in this matter.

 4 ▶ **Listen and match each conversation with the picture it describes.**

5 ▶ **Study the frame: Double comparatives**

The	**more work**	we give her,	the	**less work**	we'll have.		of nouns
	angrier	she became,		**more depressed**	I got.		of adjectives
	louder	he yelled,		**more quietly**	I spoke.	◀	of adverbs
	more	she talked,		**less**	I listened.		of verbs

> One kind of comparative may appear in a sentence with any other kind. The *faster* he drove, the *more nervous* I got. (comparative of adverb and comparative of adjective)

INFORM SOMEONE • SUBJUNCTIVE CLAUSES VS. INFINITIVE CLAUSES

- Tell the students to read over the memo. Answer any questions about the vocabulary and the structures. Then you can ask different students to read aloud the contents of the memo. Next it may be helpful if you have the students underline or write on separate paper all the subjunctive and infinitive clauses.

- Have a student read the instructions aloud. Answer any questions. Then have the students do the exercise.

- Tell the students to compare answers with a partner. Then call on different pairs; have one partner read the original clause from the letter and have the other read the change. You can ask different students to write the changes on the board.

ANSWERS

. . . it is urgent that we do this immediately. . . . it is crucial for the candidate to have previous warehouse experience

. . . it is also important for him or her to have a knowledge of that language.

. . . it is crucial that the warehouse have a full staff.

MAKE JUDGMENTS • DOUBLE COMPARATIVES

- Have the students look at the illustrations. Call on different students to tell the class what's going on in the illustrations.

- Read aloud the instructions and have the students listen to the conversations and match them with the appropriate pictures. Then call on a student to say the answers aloud and write them on the board.

TAPESCRIPT

1. **Woman** Well, I'm heading home. Eleven hours of work is about all I can take in one day. How about you, Dave?
   Man No, I think I'll stay a little longer. If I work until nine, I can probably finish this report a day early.
   Woman Terrific! Marilyn will be happy with that. You know what she always says: The sooner, the better.
2. **Woman** Hi, Michael? This is Andrea.
   Man Hi, Andrea. I hope you're still planning to come to the party Friday night.
   Woman I sure am. In fact, that's why I'm calling. Would it be all right if I brought a friend with me to your party?
   Man Sure, no problem. The more, the merrier.

3. **Man** Have you heard the news?
   Woman What news?
   Man About the vice-president. He was fired, and he's making a lot of trouble.
   Woman Hmmm. Well, the bigger they are, the harder they fall, as the saying goes.
4. **Man** I'm thinking of buying a computer. I wonder what kind I should get.
   Woman You should ask Karen. She's going to buy one.
   Man Really? She's been spending a lot of money lately. Didn't she just buy a new television and CD player?
   Woman Yes, I can't believe it either. But I guess the more you get, the more you want.

ANSWERS

4	2	1	3

OPTION

Point out the double comparative constructions in the frame that follows. Then have the students listen to the conversations again. This time tell them to write down the double comparatives they hear. When they finish, call on different students to write the double comparatives on the board. Explain that these comparatives are called "adages" or "sayings." Make sure the students understand what each adage means. Then you can have the students talk about adages in their native languages.

- Have the students examine the frame as you call on different students to read aloud the sentences. Then have the class repeat the sentences after you.

- Point out the box and read aloud the information in it. Then answer any questions about double comparatives and the meanings of the sentences in the frame.

OPTION

Have the students work in pairs. Tell one partner to write down a comparative construction like those on the left side of the frame. Have the other partner write down a comparative like the ones on the right side of the frame. Then have the partners exchange papers and complete the sentences. When they finish, call on different students to read aloud the sentences they just completed and write them on the board.

GIVE ADVICE • DOUBLE COMPARATIVES

- Point out the illustration and ask a student to describe what's happening. (See the Culture Close-Up which follows.) Then have the students read over the conversation. Answer any questions they have.

- Have the class listen to the conversation. You can also ask a pair of students to act it out for the class. Remind them to use appropriate pronunciation, intonation, and body language.

- Point out the box and have different students read aloud the contents. Answer any questions the students have about the contents.

- Have the students work with a partner to follow the second set of instructions. Remind them to use the information in the boxes.

- Go around the room and listen in on the conversations to check the pairs' work. When the partners have finished, call on different pairs to act out their conversations for the class.

OPTION

Have the pairs come up with similar but original conversation of their own. Tell them to use their imaginations. Suggest that the police officer give the other person a ticket, arrest him or her, etc. Tell the pairs to write down their original conversations. Go around the room and answer any questions the pairs have about their work. Then have the pairs practice acting out their conversations. Go around and listen in. Finally, call on different pairs to act out their conversations for the class. Give prizes for the most original and the most grammatically correct conversations.

CULTURE CLOSE-UP

In the U.S., state and city police officers trained in traffic surveillance can stop any motorist they think is breaking the law. Offenses range from going through a red light to causing an accident. If the offense is very minor and the driver does not have a record of previous offenses, the officer may only issue a warning. However, in most cases, a traffic ticket is issued. This means the driver can either plead guilty by paying a fine or go to court and try to convince a judge that he or she is innocent. In most cases, ticketed drivers end up paying severe fines. In cases of drunken driving or accidents caused by reckless driving, guilty drivers often lose their licenses and spend time in jail.

- Have the students read over the sample conversation as you and a student read it aloud. Then read the instructions aloud. Answer any questions.

- Tell the students to work with a partner and follow the instructions. Go around the room and listen in on the conversations.

- Call on different pairs to act out their conversations for the class. You can have the pairs write the double comparatives they used in their conversations on the board.

ASK SOMEONE TO DO SOMETHING

- Read the instructions aloud as the students follow along in their books. Then point out the phrases in italics and the beginning sentences in each conversation and read them aloud. Ask different students to comment on how the sentences differ and why. Point out the use of first names in the first and third conversations. (See the Culture Close-Up which follows.)

- Tell the students to work with a partner to practice the conversations. Go around the room and check the pairs' pronunciation and intonation. Then call on three pairs of students to read the conversations aloud.

- Point out the box and have the students follow along in their books as you have different class members read aloud the contents. Next answer any questions about the exercise procedure. After that, have the pairs act out the role plays.

- Go around the room and listen in on the role plays, giving help when needed. Then call on different pairs to act out their role plays for the class. Make sure all the situations in the box are acted out.

CULTURE CLOSE-UP

In the U.S., it is common for co-workers to address each other on a first-name basis. Employees usually address employers and supervisors by their titles and last names unless the person specifically asks to be addressed by his or her first name. Employers and supervisors usually address employees by their first names.

FOLLOW-UP

Students can write out the conversations they acted out in exercise 7.

6 ▶ **Listen to the conversation.**
  ▶ **Act out similar conversations. You are a police officer who has stopped your partner for one of the offenses in the box. Tell him or her to be more cautious.**

A I'm sorry, Officer. I wasn't paying attention.
B Listen, I'm going to give you some advice. Slow down! When you're speeding, you're taking your life, and very possibly someone else's, in your hands.
A Yes, I realize that. I'm sorry. I just wasn't thinking.
B Well, you'd better start thinking. You have to remember that you aren't the only one on the road. Speed limits have a purpose, and the sooner you start paying attention to them, the better for everybody!
A Yes. You're right. Thanks for the advice.

Some offenses
speeding (not paying attention to speed limits) crossing the street against the light (ignoring traffic lights) turning without signaling (not using turn signals)

7 ▶ **Work with a partner. Student A: Tell your partner about a problem you have and ask for advice. Student B: Give advice to Student A, using double comparatives.**

A *I can't find an apartment that I can afford.*
B *I think you should keep looking. The more you look, the better chance you have of finding something.*

8 ▶ **The way you ask someone to do something for you depends on who you are speaking to. First, practice the conversations below. Then play the role of one of the people in the box and ask for help or ask a favor appropriately.**

To an equal: a doctor to another doctor
A Oh, Larry, *could you help me for a minute, please?* I can't seem to find the file on Joyce Rollins.
B Sure, Rita.

To a boss: a nurse to a doctor
A Excuse me, Dr. Bellini. *I wonder if you could help me for just a minute, please.* I can't seem to find the vaccine you said was in the refrigerator.
B Sure, Amanda.

To an employee: a doctor to a receptionist
A Melissa, *I'd like you to help me for a minute, please.* I lost the list of this afternoon's patients that you gave me.
B Certainly, Dr. Engel.

Some situations at a doctor's office
Amanda Vega, a nurse, has dropped a contact lens and asks Larry Bellini, a doctor, to help her find it. Rita Engel, a doctor, usually locks up the office at night. Today she has to leave early because of an emergency at the hospital, so she asks Dr. Bellini to lock up. Dr. Engel asks Melissa Dale, a receptionist, to call two patients, Mrs. Chen and Mr. Adamski, to reschedule their appointments.

39. Your turn

1. Work with a group. You are a member of a planning team whose goal it is to decide where to hold a big international conference of travel agents next year. Look at the photos and read the descriptions to decide which city should host the conference. Talk about each city and discuss the advantages and disadvantages of holding the conference there.

Kyoto, Japan   Founded in 794, in the beautiful setting of a river valley surrounded by mountains, Kyoto was Japan's capital until 1600. It remains the center of traditional Japanese culture today. Kyoto has several hundred Buddhist temples and Shinto shrines, many parks and gardens, several architecturally outstanding palaces—each with its own impressive gardens—and over thirty colleges and universities. Kyoto is also a modern city, as important for its large industries as for its silks, ceramics, and other crafts.

Salvador de Bahia, Brazil   Salvador de Bahia, the first Portuguese settlement in Brazil, was founded in 1549. Located on All Saints Bay, it is divided into an Upper City, on cliffs overlooking the bay, and a Lower City; the two are connected by elevators as well as by roads. Salvador is known for its colonial architecture—especially its elaborate churches—for its beautiful beaches, and as a center for African culture, brought over to Brazil by slaves long ago. Salvador is also one of Brazil's main ports and a center of industry.

Taxco, Mexico   Located in southwestern Mexico, Taxco was founded by Spaniards in 1529 and soon became important for its silver mines. Since modern architecture is prohibited, Taxco preserves much of its colonial character—its steep cobblestone streets are lined with white stucco houses, which have red tile roofs and wrought-iron balconies filled with colorful flowers. In addition to its beauty, Taxco is known for its many silver shops, which produce and sell the finest jewelry and other silverwork in Mexico.

Volendam, the Netherlands   Volendam is located in Ijsselmeer, a freshwater lake separated from the North Sea by a dike. It is famous as a fishing village, as well as for the traditional costumes of the women, especially their winged lace caps. Volendam is only 11 miles from Amsterdam, one of Europe's most exciting cities.

39. Your turn

- Read aloud the instructions for the first exercise as the students follow along in their books. Answer any questions about the procedure. Then call on different students to read aloud the descriptions. Answer any questions. Next ask different students to point out the cities featured in the photos on a world map or globe. (See the Option which follows.)

- Tell the students to work in groups to discuss the advantages and disadvantages of holding the conference at the various cities. Remind the group captains to make sure each group member has a chance to express an opinion. Go around the room and join in the discussions.

- Call on the different group reporters to summarize the opinions of their group members for the class. You can also take a vote to see how many students favor the various cities.

OPTION

See if there are students who come from or have visited or lived in any of the four cities. If so, ask them to expand on the descriptions by telling the class additional information about the cities. Encourage the class members to ask questions as well.

- Read aloud the general instructions. Then ask two students to read aloud the specific instructions for Student A and Student B. Next point out the memo, the conference information, and the graph. Have different students read the information aloud. Answer any questions.

- Tell the students to work with a partner to play the different roles. Go around the room and check the pairs' work, giving help if needed. Finally, call on different pairs to act out their conversations for the class. You can have the class decide which students' arguments were the most convincing.

Listen in

- Read the boldfaced instructions aloud as the students follow along in their books. Then have the students read over the exercise items so they know what to listen for.

- Have the students listen to the conversation and do the exercise. Have them listen as many times as necessary.

- Tell the students to compare answers with a partner. Then call on a student to read aloud the answers.

TAPESCRIPT

1. **Amy Britt** I'd like you to go down to the twentieth floor and pick up the brochures I need for the meeting with the managers of the local offices.

   Jennifer Sahfi Oh, I can't go right now, Ms. Britt. Mr. Gilbert told me to finish this letter as soon as possible.

   Amy Britt Oh, I see.

2. **Amy Britt** Hey, Craig, would you mind doing me a favor? Could you go down to the twentieth floor and pick up the brochures for the meeting? I'm waiting for a call, so I can't leave the office, and the meeting starts in ten minutes.

   Craig Pabon Sorry, but I'm sending some files by e-mail right now, and I'll be busy for the next ten minutes.

   Amy Britt O.K.

3. **Walt Gilbert** Come in.

   Amy Britt Excuse me, Mr. Gilbert, but I have to leave the office for a minute, and I'm expecting a call from the Southwest office. I wonder if I could ask you to take the call for me if it comes in while I'm out.

   Walt Gilbert No problem. I need to talk to them, anyhow.

ANSWERS
1. c
2. b
3. a

Amy Britt ends up picking up the brochures.

FOLLOW-UP

Students can write sentences comparing the different cities featured in the photos on p. 86.

WORKBOOK Lessons 38-39, pp. 49-51

2. Work with a partner. Play these roles.

Student A You are the head of the management committee of Worldwide Travel, Inc., a large travel organization with branch offices in many different cities. Because sales have gone down over the last three years, you have decided that it is impossible for you to send travel agents from the different offices to a big international conference of travel agents. Tomorrow you will meet with Student B, the head of a group of managers from different offices. Student B will try to convince you to change your mind. Look at the memo, a page from the conference brochure, and the graph. Then reply to Student B's arguments.

Student B You work for Worldwide Travel, Inc., a large travel organization with branch offices in many different cities. You are the head of a group of managers from the different offices. Student A, the head of the main office, has decided that there is no money in the budget to send travel agents from the branch offices to the conference. Tomorrow you will meet with Student A to discuss this issue. Look at the memo, a page from the conference brochure, and the graph. Then try to convince Student A to change his or her mind.

MEMO

TO: Management Committee
FROM: Joanne Wagner,
            Manager—Southwest Office
DATE: May 14
RE: International Conference

You may be interested in knowing that travel agents in our office feel that it is essential that they attend the international conference in

The Conference will include workshops on:

- promoting off-season tourism
- increasing peak-season travel
- sales personnel effectiveness
- advances in computer technology

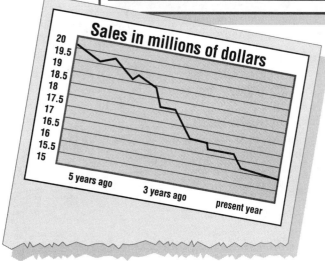

Sales in millions of dollars

20
19.5
19
18.5
18
17.5
17
16.5
16
15.5
15

5 years ago   3 years ago   present year

🔊 Listen in

Amy Britt works at Worldwide Travel, Inc. She has conversations with three different people in her office. Read the questions below. Then listen to the conversations and answer the questions.

1. In each conversation, who is Ms. Britt talking to? Choose *a*, *b*, or *c*.
   a. her boss
   b. a coworker
   c. an employee who works for her

2. Who ends up picking up the brochures?

40. On your own

1. Write a memo to your boss explaining why you think he or she should send you to one of the conferences featured in the posters.

MANAGEMENT SEMINAR & RETREAT
at "The Mountainside Resort" in Seattle, Washington

Audience: Mid-level management personnel from any size company

° Overview of advances in computer technology
° Dealing with "High Tech Stress"
° The diplomacy of effective management
° Handling employee complaints
° "Letting go" without losing control

For information and reservations, call The Management Consortium 1-800-555-2121

LEARN HOW TO REALLY INTERACT!
Attend the Annual "Information Highway" Conference in Aspen, Colorado

• TV, modems, & networking
• Communicating via electronic bulletin boards
• The latest about virtual reality
• Video conferences

Package includes:
– Excellent hotel accommodations next to the Conference Center
– International gourmet dinner evening
– Optional ski package

For more information, call Internetworks, Inc.
1-800-555-2000

2. Choose one of the options below.

1. Write a memo to your employee explaining why you think he or she should attend one of the conferences featured in the posters.
2. Write a memo to your real boss. Try to convince him or her to make a change you think is necessary in your company.

40. On your own

PROCEDURE

- Read aloud the instructions for the first exercise. Then ask two students to read aloud the information on the posters. Answer any questions.

- Tell the students to write their memos on separate paper. When they finish, have them go over their memos with a partner. Go around the room and answer any questions students have about their work.

- Call on different students to read their memos aloud and write them on the board. You can also collect the memos, mark any errors, and return them to the students so they can rewrite them. You can give a prize for the most convincing memo.

OPTION

Have the students exchange memos with a partner. Tell them to answer their partner's memo. Then have the partners exchange memos and read the answers. Finally, call on different pairs to read their memos aloud.

- Read aloud the general instructions for the second exercise. Then have two students read the specific instructions aloud. Answer any questions.

- Have the students write their memos and then compare their work with a partner. Go around the room and answer any questions students have about their writing. Finally, call on different students to read aloud their memos and write them on the board for you to check.

CULTURE CLOSE-UP

The so-called "information highway" is expected to transform the world of communications in the U.S. by the 21st century. Already in place are telephone and computer connections which allow the user to access libraries for data, do banking transactions, go shopping from the comfort of home, and use e-mail and electronic bulletin boards to send and receive information from other users. The information highway also allows students to interact with teachers, employers with employees, employees with other employees, etc.—all via computers and telephone modems. Virtual reality on computer will allow users to experience the sights, sounds, and feel of imaginary worlds.

WORKBOOK Lesson 40, p. 52. Before assigning the writing task, point out the double comparative in Mr. Zenga's memo. Also indicate to the students that the expressions *It is essential* and *It is crucial* are used to convince someone about something. Tell the students to try to use similar expressions in their memos.

Before you begin teaching, go over the functions/themes, language, and forms in the chart. This will give you a preview of what you will encounter as you guide the students through the unit.

Preview the reading.

- Tell the class to look at the illustration. Ask a student to describe it. Then read aloud the instructions and the questions for the first exercise.

- Have the students work with a partner to discuss the questions. Go around the room and listen in. Then call on different students to share their answers with the class.

- Have a student read aloud the second set of instructions. Then have the students work with a partner to follow the instructions and answer the question. Next call on different students to share their answers with the class.

PREVIEW

FUNCTIONS/THEMES	LANGUAGE	FORMS
Talk about plans Give reasons	What are your plans for the future? After I graduate, I'll get a job and work for five or ten years. By then, I will have gotten some experience. I've decided to quit my job. You're kidding! I'm surprised to hear that. By the end of this year, I will have been working for the company for four years, and I haven't even had a promotion yet.	The future perfect and the future perfect continuous
Make predictions	Futurist Ronald Herd feels that dwellings will have changed significantly by the year 2025.	
Imagine something Give explanations	What do you suppose your life would be like if you hadn't finished high school? Well, I suppose I'd be working in a boring job somewhere, and I probably wouldn't speak a word of English. Whenever I talk to Chris, he laughs, even when we're talking about something serious. I'm sure if he weren't so nervous, he wouldn't laugh all the time.	Mixed contrary-to-fact conditional sentences: Present and past

Preview the reading.

1. Discuss these questions with a partner.
   a. What is the illustration below about?
   b. Have you ever had your fortune told? If so, what was it?
   c. What kinds of fortunetelling or prediction do people use in your country? Do you believe in any of them? Why or why not?

2. Before you read the article on pages 90–91, look at the title and the photos. What kinds of fortunetelling do you think the article discusses?

The ANCIENT ART OF PREDICTION

by Leanna Skarnulis

After winning the Nobel Prize in 1957, two physicists from the United States, Chen Ning Yang and Tsung-Dao Lee, faced the question of whether or not to continue their research. They consulted the *I Ching,* the ancient Chinese book of prophecy. It assured them that a breakthrough in particle physics would be achieved in the next two years. The two scientists continued their work.

Today, many people who have been influenced by the modern scientific age rarely use fortunetelling for anything other than amusement, but it wasn't always so. Before the arrival of the scientific method, with its demand for proof, most people believed that the future could be foretold, and they had countless ways of doing it.

Fortunetellers had to be inventive because the art of prophecy was a risky business. When a prophecy failed, fortunetellers would deal with their predicament by coming up with an explanation and then proposing a new, improved method. Here are some of the more creative methods that have been used to forecast the future.

Both ordinary and unusual objects may contain prophetic signs. If someone gives you a black pearl, a sapphire, or a weapon, beware of bad luck. On the other hand, you should be glad to get a white rat or white mouse, for they bring good luck.

Onomancy is prophecy from first names. Aurelia will be intelligent and likely to remain single. Armand will let

success with women go to his head, miss an opportunity, and finally marry just anyone.

Dominoes laid face down and then turned over have prophetic meaning; but don't consult them on Monday or Friday because bad luck will follow. Each domino in the set has meaning. The double blank is the worst to draw for it indicates great disappointment in love, school, or business; however, for dishonest people, it predicts success in their dishonest activities.

Coffee grounds can be read by pouring grounds and water onto a white plate and draining off the water after the grounds settle. The figures are then interpreted. Several broken lines mean money troubles, an elephant means success, and thick and rounded blots foretell a lawsuit.

Even shoes have been used in prophecy. Young women wanting to know if they will marry can throw a shoe downstairs. If the shoe lands with the toe propped up, no marriage will take place. If the heel end is up, the marriage will occur in as many days, months, or years as the number of steps the shoe falls down.

Other familiar objects, such as paper and playing cards, also figure in prophecy. Tarot cards, a set of twenty-two playing cards, contain special pictures that depict vices and virtues. The hanged-man card, for instance, frequently indicates spiritual growth.

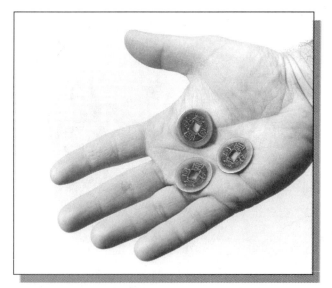

I Ching coins. For their meaning, consult the *I Ching*, a Chinese book of prophecy.

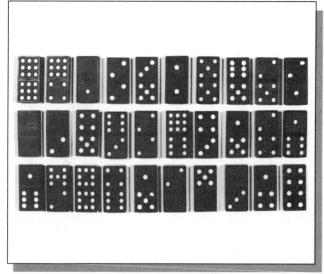

Notice the double blank in this set of dominoes (second row, far left).

41. The Ancient Art of Prediction

PROCEDURE

- Point out the photos and ask different students to describe them.

- Have the students read through the article. Follow a procedure similar to that on p. 2 of this book. When the students have finished reading the article, have them review their answers from the second exercise on p. 89.

Figure it out

1. Choose *a, b,* or *c.*

- Have the students read over the exercise item and do the exercise. Then tell the students to compare their answer with a partner.

- Call on a student to read the correct sentence aloud.

ANSWER
b

2. As you read, try to remember which prophetic signs bring good luck and which bad luck.

- Have the students read over the exercise instructions and the items. (See the Option which follows.) Then have them follow the instructions and read over the article again and say *Good luck* or *Bad luck.*

- Have the students compare answers with a partner. Then call on a pair of students to say the answers. Next call on different students to tell the class why they chose their answers.

ANSWERS
1. Good luck
2. Bad luck
3. Bad luck
4. Bad luck
5. Bad luck
6. Good luck

OPTION

Have the students guess the answers to the exercise items before they look through the article for the actual answers. Call on different students to share their guesses with the class and explain why they chose their answers.

3. Do you feel that the author personally believes in the prophecies she discusses?

- Have the students answer the questions. Then have them compare and discuss their answers in small groups.

- Call on different students to discuss their answers with the class. Ask some students to write on the board what the author says to support their answer to the first question.

SAMPLE ANSWER
The author probably doesn't personally believe in these practices. She mentions that when a prophecy failed, the fortunetellers had to invent an explanation and then propose a new, improved method. She also ends the article by mentioning that the breakthrough in particle physics took place later than predicted and that two other physicists made the breakthrough.

4. ...Give the correct words.

- Have different students read aloud the exercise items. Answer any questions. Then have the students follow the instructions and do the exercise.

- Have the students compare answers with a partner. Finally, call on different students to read aloud the answers and write them on the board.

ANSWERS
1. physicist
2. chemist
3. scientist
4. novelist
5. cellist
6. capitalist
7. communist
8. socialist

OPTION

Tell the students they are going to play a memory game. Give them five minutes to read over the article. Tell them to try to remember as many facts as possible. Don't allow them to copy down any information. Next have them close their books and write down as many ways of predicting the future as they can remember from the article. When they finish, ask for a show of hands to determine who wrote down the most ways. Call on different students to read their lists aloud and write them on the board.

FOLLOW-UP

In their own words, students can write down a description of one way of predicting the future.

WORKBOOK Lesson 41, p. 53

Curiously, though, with the exception of some fortunetelling computers in shopping centers and carnivals, few prophetic methods involve modern objects. Perhaps the fortunetellers have not been able to keep up with the pace of change. But one day the results of our technology just might include prophecy by clothes dryer, where people study the arrangement of shorts and towels at the end of a cycle, or prophecy by laser price codes, where people study the order and number of wide and narrow stripes on canned tuna. Perhaps these methods sound far-fetched, but it is probably safe to say that modern disillusionment with science and renewed interest in fortunetelling will lead to innovations.

And what finally happened to the physicists who consulted the *I Ching*? Remember that they were assured that a breakthrough in particle physics would occur very soon. It actually came in 1963 and involved application of their earlier principles, but it was two other physicists—Val L. Fitch and James W. Cronin—who made the breakthrough. They received the 1980 Nobel Prize in physics.

Tarot cards from Spain, in a traditional fortunetelling pattern.

Figure it out

1. Choose *a*, *b*, or *c*.

The main purpose of this article is to
  a. explain why fortunetelling was popular.
  b. describe methods of fortunetelling and comment on its future.
  c. make a judgment on whether fortunetelling is reliable.

2. As you read, try to remember which prophetic signs bring good luck and which bad luck. When you have finished, say *Good luck* or *Bad luck* for each of the items below. Then skim the article again to check your answers, and make any necessary corrections.

  1. receiving a white rat or white mouse
  2. naming a child Armand
  3. the double-blank domino (for honest people)
  4. broken lines or rounded blots in the figures formed by coffee grounds
  5. a shoe that lands with the toe pointing up when it is thrown down a flight of stairs by a young woman who wants to know if she will marry
  6. the hanged-man Tarot card

3. Do you feel that the author personally believes in the prophecies she discusses? What does she say in the article to support your answer?

4. The suffix *-ist* refers to people and has several different meanings. Give the correct words for the following, using your dictionary if necessary.

Someone who specializes in . . .
  1. physics   2. chemistry   3. science

Someone who . . .
  4. writes novels   5. plays the cello

Someone who believes in . . .
  6. capitalism   7. communism   8. socialism

42. You'll have a lucky break.

1. Tell your partner what you think you'll be doing in the future. Mention topics such as where you plan to live, what kind of job you think you'll have, and whether you'll be married and have a family.

June Sanders, a young veterinarian, is visiting a fortuneteller.

Listen to the conversation.

2

Fortuneteller	Let's begin by seeing what's in your cards. *(Shuffles and lays out the cards)* Hmm . . . I see a big change in your life . . . not immediately, perhaps, but five or six years from now. Yes, by then you will have been married for a couple of years.
June	What? Me, married?
Fortuneteller	Yes. To a musician—a musician with green eyes and black hair.
June	Not my friend Anton? You must be kidding! Why, the thought never crossed my mind.
Fortuneteller	Well, it's certainly crossed his.
June	What about the big change in my life? The first thing you mentioned?
Fortuneteller	Ah, yes. You'll have a lucky break in five or six years. Your financial worries will be a thing of the past.
June	That's nice to hear! If I hadn't opened that animal hospital, I'd have a lot more money right now. It's used up all of my savings.
Fortuneteller	*(Flips cards)* In the meantime, you must be very careful, though. Someone has a grudge against you.
June	Oh, no! Against me? Who could it be?
Fortuneteller	It's someone who knows your future husband. Apparently, you've offended him. If he weren't so shy, he would have confronted you already. But he still wants to get even with you.
June	What do you mean "get even with me"?
Fortuneteller	I don't know. But don't get too alarmed. You're not in any physical danger. I'm only telling you about this because by this time next week, you will have received a letter from him.
June	Are you serious?
Fortuneteller	Yes, and it's essential that you answer it *very* carefully.

3. A prediction is a statement someone makes about what he or she thinks will happen in the future. Based on the dialogue, say *Prediction* or *Fact* for each sentence below.

1. In five or six years, June will have been married for a couple of years.
2. June has a friend named Anton who is a musician with green eyes and black hair.
3. June used up all of her savings to open an animal hospital.
4. By this time next week, June will have received a letter from someone who knows her future husband.
5. June is visiting a fortuneteller in order to find out about her future.

42. You'll have a lucky break.

1. Warm-up Activity

- Have a student read aloud the sentences in the box. Then have the students tell their partners the things mentioned in the box.

- Go around the classroom and share your personal information with the pairs. Then call on different students to tell the class their personal information.

2. Conversation

BACKGROUND

June Sanders, a young veterinarian, is visiting a fortuneteller. The fortuneteller surprises June with two predictions.

LANGUAGE

...*lays out* means to place or arrange in a particular order.

...*six years from now* is another way of saying "in six years."

...*by then* means *at that time.*

...*crossed my mind* means *occurred to me.*

...*have a lucky break* is another way of saying "be lucky for a change."

...*a thing of the past* is another way of saying "over."

...*has a grudge against* is another way of saying "is angry at."

...*get even with* is another way of saying "get revenge against."

PROCEDURE

- As the students examine the illustrations, point out the characters from the conversation. Ask a student to describe what's probably going on in the picture. Be sure to point out Anton in June's thought bubble.

- Follow a procedure similar to that indicated for the opening conversation in Unit 1.

3. ...say *Prediction* or *Fact* for each sentence.

- Have the students read over the exercise sentences. Answer any questions.

- Tell the students to follow the instructions and do the exercise. Then have them compare answers with a partner. Next call on different pairs; have one partner read aloud the exercise sentence and have the other say "Prediction" or "Fact."

ANSWERS

1. Prediction
2. Fact
3. Fact
4. Prediction
5. Fact

OPTION

Have the students work in pairs to "play fortuneteller" with each other. Tell them to use whatever materials or methods they want—for example, having their partner turn some coins up a certain way or choosing a certain sequence of numbered slips of paper. Of course, remind them that this is just a game and that they should freely use their imaginations and senses of humor in forming their predictions. Go around the room and join in the fun. Then call on different pairs to act out their role plays for the class.

FOLLOW-UP

Students can write out the information requested in exercise 1.

WORKBOOK Lesson 42, p. 54

43. What are your plans for the future?

To review and practice the future tense with the students, ask different class members what life will be like in the future. Begin by expressing your own opinion. For example:

In the future, we'll travel in "robot cars." It won't be necessary to actually drive ourselves.

Remind the students to use *will ('ll)* or *won't* in their comments.

TALK ABOUT PLANS • GIVE REASONS • THE FUTURE PERFECT AND FUTURE PERFECT CONTINUOUS

- Point out the illustration and ask a student to guess what the two characters are probably discussing. Then tell the students to read over the conversation. Answer any questions. Then have them listen to the conversation. You can also act it out with a student.

- Point out the boxes and have different students complete and read aloud the possible sentences. You can also have the class repeat the sentences after you. Answer any questions students have.

- Have the students work with a partner to follow the second set of instructions. Remind them to use appropriate stress, intonation, and body language as they act out similar conversations.

- Go around the classroom and listen in, giving help if needed. Finally, call on different pairs to act out their conversations for the class.

CULTURE CLOSE-UP

A person who wants to start his or her own business in the U.S. can get help from a federal government agency called the Small Business Administration (SBA). The headquarters of the SBA are located in Washington, D.C. The agency helps small businesses get started by loaning them money, by providing information about licensing and federal regulations, and by making it possible for qualified businesses to do business with the government itself.

- Tell the students to read over the conversation. Answer any questions. Then have the students listen to the conversation. You can ask two students to act it out.

- Point out the box and have different students read aloud the possible sentences. Answer any questions.

- Have the students work with a partner to follow the second set of instructions. Tell them to use the information in the box or their own information.

- Go around the classroom and listen in, giving help if needed. Finally, call on different pairs to act out their conversations for the class.

- Have the students examine the frames as you and some class members read aloud the possible sentences.

- Point out the box and read aloud the information in it. Answer any questions students have about the future perfect and the future perfect continuous.

OPTION

Have the students work in pairs to come up with pairs of sentences of their own—one sentence in the future perfect and the other in the future perfect continuous. Tell them to use the frames as a guide but to write sentences about their own class or surroundings if possible. You can write an example on the board:

By next week, we will have completed Unit 9.
By next week, (*teacher's name*) will have been teaching us for three months.

When they finish, have the pairs show their sentences to other pairs. Finally, call on different pairs to read their sentences aloud and write them on the board.

43. What are your plans for the future?

 1 ▶ Listen to the conversation.
▶ Act out similar conversations. Tell your partner what you would like to do in the future. Use your own ideas or the information in the boxes below.

A What are your plans for the future?
B My dream is to open my own business someday. After I graduate, I'll get a job and work for five or ten years. By then, I will have gotten some experience and I can go off on my own.
A What kind of business would you like to start?
B I think a clothing store might be nice. I've always been interested in fashion.

I'd like to . . .
open my own business.
get a job as a _____ .
move to _____ .
have children.
spend a year in an English-speaking country.

By then I will have . . .
gotten some experience.
finished school.
lived here for _____ years.
saved more money.
been studying English for _____ years.

 2 ▶ Listen to the conversation.
▶ Act out similar conversations. Tell your partner about a decision you have made and explain your reasons for it.

A I've decided to quit my job.
B You're kidding! I'm surprised to hear that.
A Well, by the end of this year, I will have been working for the company for four years, and I haven't even had a promotion yet. I feel that . . .

You've decided to . . .
quit your job because you've been working for the company for almost four years and haven't had a promotion.
stop studying English because you've been studying it for almost six years and are getting bored.
go back to your country/hometown because you've been away for almost five years and are getting homesick.

3 ▶ Study the frames: The future perfect and the future perfect continuous

The future perfect

By then	he	will	have	mailed	it.
	June	won't		spoken	to him.

The future perfect continuous

By then	I	will	have	been	working	for years.
	she	won't			teaching	very long.

The future perfect

Use the future perfect to talk about an event in the future that will take place before another event.
    By the time you get here, I will have eaten. (I'll eat dinner before you arrive.)

Use the future perfect to talk about a state that will already be in progress when an event takes place.
    By the time my wife stops working, I *will have been* retired for two years.

The future perfect continuous

Use the future perfect continuous to talk about an activity that will already be in progress when an event takes place.
    By the time you come to Spain, I *will have been living* there for almost a year.

Do not use the future perfect continuous with verbs such as *be, have, want*, or *like* that describe states.

4 ▶ **Rewrite this book review of *Modern Living*, completing the sentences with the future perfect or the future perfect continuous forms of the verbs in parentheses.**

MODERN LIVING *by Ronald Herd*
208 pp New York Bookworld, Inc.
$18.95
by Gabriela Alvarez

    Imagine that the year is 2025 and that you are looking for a place to live. What will your house or apartment be like? Futurist Ronald Herd feels that dwellings _____ (change) significantly by then. In his new book, *Modern Living*, Herd says that architects _____ (stop) building single-family homes because of lack of space, and most people _____ (move) into apartment buildings.
    According to Mr. Herd, apartments themselves will be much smaller and will not have living rooms. In fact, by then architects _____ (design) apartments without living rooms for some time, so most people _____ (get) used to them. However, Mr. Herd warns us that housing certainly _____ (not become) any less expensive. So start saving your money now!

---

 5 ▶ **Listen to the two possible conversations**
    ▶ **Act out similar conversations, using your own information or the information in the box below. Imagine that something in your past had been different. Tell your partner what you think your life would be like today.**

A Did you finish high school?

B Yes. Fortunately.

A What do you suppose your life would be like if you hadn't finished?

B Well, I suppose I'd be working in a boring job somewhere and I probably wouldn't speak a word of English.

B Oh, things probably wouldn't be much different.

Suppose you had(n't) . . .

finished high school.
gone to college.
been the only child in your family.
left home when you finished school.
lived abroad.

---

6 ▶ **Study the frame: Mixed contrary-to-fact conditional sentences with past condition and present result**

Past condition		Present result	
If	**I had (I'd) been** more practical,	**I would (I'd) have** more money now.	▶
	I hadn't moved here,	**I would (I'd) be living** in Italy now.	▶

▲ past perfect form of verb   ▲ present conditional

If I had been more practical means "I wasn't more practical."

If I hadn't moved here means "I did move here."

MAKE PREDICTIONS • THE FUTURE PERFECT AND THE FUTURE PERFECT CONTINUOUS

- Have the students read over the book review. Answer any questions.

- Ask a student to read aloud the instructions. Then have the students do the exercise.

- Tell the students to compare answers with a partner. Finally, call on different students to read aloud the sentences from the book review and write the answers on the board.

ANSWERS

will have changed, will have stopped, will have moved, will have been designing, will have gotten, won't have become

IMAGINE SOMETHING • MIXED CONTRARY-TO-FACT CONDITIONAL SENTENCES: PRESENT AND PAST

- Tell the students to read over the conversation. Answer any questions. Then have them listen to the conversation. You can ask two students to act it out.

- Point out the box and have different students read aloud the possible sentences. Answer any questions. (See the Language Note which follows.)

- Have the students work with a partner to follow the second set of instructions. Tell them to use the information in the box or their own information.

- Go around the classroom and listen in, giving help if needed. Finally, call on different pairs to act out their conversations for the class.

- Have the students examine the frame as you read aloud the possible sentences. You can have them repeat the sentences after you. Answer any questions.

OPTION 1

Have the students work in pairs. Tell one partner to write down a past condition like the ones in the frame. Tell the other partner to write down a present result like those in the frame. Then have them exchange papers and complete each other's sentences. Next have them compare their sentences. Call on different pairs to read aloud their sentences and write them on the board.

OPTION 2

Divide the class into teams A and B. Tell the members of Team A to make up five past conditional clauses like those in the frame. Have the members of Team B make up five present result clauses. When they finish, call on a student from Team A to read aloud and then write on the board one of the past conditional clauses. Go over the clause to make sure it's correct. Then ask someone from Team B to go to the board and complete the sentence with a present result clause. Give Team B a point if someone correctly completes the sentence. Next continue the game by calling on a Team B member to write a present result clause on the board for Team A to complete. The Team that receives the most points wins.

LANGUAGE NOTE

The past conditional *if* clause can be placed either at the beginning or the end of a sentence. Note that no comma is used when it's placed at the end. For example:

I'd have more money now if I'd been more practical.

- Have the students examine the frame as you ask a class member to read aloud the possible sentences. You can have the students repeat the sentences after you. Answer any questions.

OPTION

Have the students play the games described in the two Options for exercise 6, except this time have them pattern their clauses after the frame in this exercise. Tell them to use their imaginations as they write the different clauses. You can also suggest that they write clauses about the class or the surrounding environment. For example:

If (*student's name*) weren't so serious all the time, our teacher wouldn't have given us an exam yesterday.

- Have the students look at the illustrations as you ask different class members to describe what's happening in each one.

- Ask a student to read the instructions aloud. Then have the students listen to the conversation and check the appropriate pictures.

- Tell the students to compare answers with a partner. Then call on a student to tell the class which pictures should be checked.

TAPESCRIPT

Mark Jonathan! How are you? I haven't seen you since we graduated from college.

Jonathan It's great to see you too, Mark. What have you been doing since college?

Mark I'm working as an account executive at an advertising agency. And I'm going to get married in July. How about you?

Jonathan Well, you know I started out as a business major in college, but then I switched to theater. If I had gotten my degree in business, I'd be working in advertising too. Right now, though, I'm working in a restaurant. If I weren't working nights, I wouldn't have been able to go on so many auditions over the past couple of months.

Mark Have you been working there since college?

Jonathan No. After I graduated, I wanted to travel, so I went to Europe for a few years.

Mark That sounds great! I wish I had done that.

Jonathan It was a lot of fun. While I was in Italy, I met a wonderful woman, Isabelle, and we fell in love. When I came back, she came with me. If she hadn't, I'd probably be living in Italy right now.

Mark What do you do on weekends?

Jonathan I try to relax as much as I can. I used to volunteer as a coach with a kids' baseball team, but I had to give it up. If my weeks weren't so busy, I would have continued doing it.

Mark Well, let's get together soon. Maybe the four of us can have dinner some night.

ANSWERS

✓	✓

- Explain what an archeologist does or have a student so it. Then have the students read over the conversation. Answer any questions.

- Point out the boxes and have different students read aloud the contents. Answer any questions the students have.

- Ask a student to read the instructions aloud. Then have the students complete the conversation. Next have them compare answers with a partner.

- Call on a pair of students to act out the conversation for the class. Then have the other pairs practice the conversation as you go around the room and check their pronunciation and intonation.

ANSWERS
'd allowed, 'd feel, wouldn't have disappointed, weren't, would have asked, spoke, would have hired

- Tell the students to read over the conversation. Answer any questions. Then have the students listen to the conversation. You can ask two students to act it out.

- Point out the box and have different students read aloud the sentences. Answer any questions.

- Have the students work with a partner to follow the second set of instructions. Tell them to use the information in the box. You may want to act out a sample conversation with a student before the pairs begin.

- Go around the classroom and listen in, giving help if needed. Finally, call on different pairs to act out their conversations for the class.

FOLLOW-UP

Students can write sentences to describe what's going on in each of the pictures in exercise 8.

7 ► **Study the frame: Mixed contrary-to-fact conditional sentences with present condition and past result**

Present condition		Past result
If	he **weren't** so shy,	he **would have called** you.
	she **liked** him,	she **wouldn't have been rude** to him.

▲ past form of verb   ▲ past conditional

► *If he weren't so shy* means "He is shy."

► *If she liked him* means "She doesn't like him."

8 ► **Listen to the conversation. Check (√) the pictures that show what Jonathan's life is like now.**

9 ► **The director of an archeology expedition to South America has just hired six field assistants to go with him. Complete his conversation with another archeologist. Use the correct forms of the verbs in parentheses.**

A Well, how did you make out?

B I hired six excellent students, but I wish I could have hired more. If they _____ (allow) me to hire more than six students, I _____ (feel) a lot happier right now.

A Why is that?

B I _____ (not disappoint) so many people. There were a lot of other good candidates, and they were all so interested and eager.

A Anyone I know?

B Alex Dua. He knows a lot about archeology, but I thought he'd have a lot of difficulty getting along in a foreign country. He's not very outgoing, unfortunately. If he _____ (not be) such a shy person, I _____ (ask) him to join the expedition. Then there's Nancy Ryder. She's very qualified, but her Spanish is quite poor. If she _____ (speak) better Spanish, I think I definitely _____ (hire) her, too.

10 ► **Listen to the conversation.**
► **Act out similar conversations with a partner. You are puzzled by the behavior of the people described in the box. Your partner will try to explain why they act as they do.**

A You know Chris better than I do. Maybe you can explain something.

B Maybe. What is it?

A Well, whenever I talk to him, he laughs, even when we're talking about something serious.

B Oh, don't let it bother you. Chris is just a very nervous person. Why don't you talk to him about it? I'm sure if he weren't so nervous, he wouldn't laugh all the time.

Some people who behave strangely	Some reasons for their behavior
Whenever you talk to Chris he laughs, even when the topic is serious.	Chris is a very nervous person.
Helene keeps borrowing money from you, but she never pays it back. She still owes you twenty dollars from two weeks ago.	Helene is a very absent-minded person.
You invited Raul and three of your friends to dinner last week. Raul seemed very uncomfortable and hardly said a word the whole evening.	Raul is an awfully shy person.
You're always very open with Lillian, but she never seems to want to talk about herself. You can't understand why not.	Lillian has had a lot of health problems in the past year.

44. Your turn

Look at the pictures and read the information about Blake Hudson and Sofia Estrada. Working in groups, discuss the choices open to Blake and Sofia that are given in the box below, and try to predict what the consequences of each choice would be. Then, as a group, decide what you think Blake and Sofia should do.

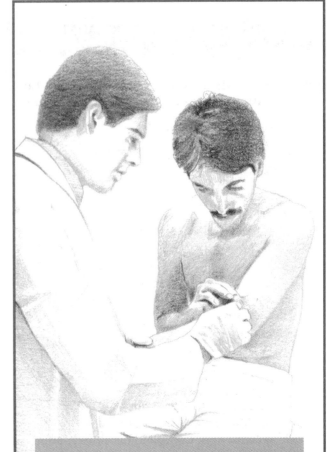

Blake and Sofia's choices

1. Blake and Sofia can forget each other, get married now, or separate and plan to get married at some future date.
2. Blake can return to the United States and take the job there, give up that job and try to get a job in Ecuador, or stay in Ecuador and do something else.
3. Sofia can finish medical school in Ecuador, try to continue her studies in the United States, postpone finishing her studies, or give up medical school completely.

Blake Hudson is a specialist in infectious diseases from the United States. He's in Ecuador on a special one-year research program. He's supposed to leave in March to take an important job at Jackson Memorial Hospital in Miami. Blake is extremely good at his work. He's also very lucky to have been offered the job in Miami.

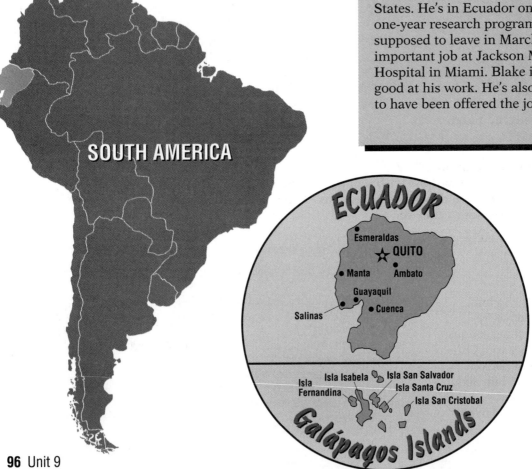

SOUTH AMERICA

ECUADOR

• Esmeraldas
☆ QUITO
• Manta   • Ambato
Guayaquil
Salinas   • Cuenca

Isla Isabela   Isla San Salvador
Isla   Isla Santa Cruz
Fernandina   Isla San Cristobal

Galápagos Islands

44. Your turn

- Read aloud the instructions as the students follow along in their books. Then point out Ecuador on the map. Tell the class that the Galápagos Islands belong to Ecuador. If anyone in class comes from or has visited Ecuador, ask the person to tell the class about the country.

- Have the students look at the pictures on pp. 96 and 97 as you have different class members read aloud the captions. Answer any questions. Then read aloud Blake and Sofia's choices as the students follow along in their books. Answer any questions.

- Have the students work in groups to follow the instructions. Go around the classroom and join in the discussions. Finally, call on different groups to share their ideas with the class.

OPTION

Find out if any of the students have ever been in a dilemma similar to the one Blake and Sofia are in. If so, ask the student(s) to tell the class about the situation and how or if it was finally resolved.

Listen in

- Have the students read over the first set of instructions and the question. Then have them listen to the conversation and answer the question.

- Tell the students to compare answers with a partner. Then call on a student to say the answer.

TAPESCRIPT

Blake Look, Sofia. I know you don't want to interrupt your studies at this point. I don't blame you. You shouldn't.

Sofia If only I hadn't had to work my way through school, I'd be finished by now, and I'd be able to work in the States.

Blake I've been thinking that I could always stay here and work. I could turn down that job.

Sofia You could, but if you do, you will have turned down one of the greatest opportunities in your life. That just doesn't make sense.

Blake I know. But the thing is . . .

Sofia Yes?

Blake Well . . . it's just that if I go back to the States, I won't see you for a long time and . . . well, I'm afraid that you'll forget me.

Sofia That's just what I've been worrying about! Every time I think about those two years I have to complete, I worry that in two years you will have met someone else.

Blake I guess the only thing to do is . . .

ANSWER

They're afraid that they'll meet other people and forget each other.

- Read aloud the second set of instructions. Then have the students work in groups to discuss the questions.

- Go around the room and join in the discussions as you check the groups' work. Then call on different group members to discuss the questions with the class.

<table>
<tr><td>CULTURE CLOSE-UP</td></tr>
</table>

Jackson Memorial Hospital in Miami, Florida is one of the leading teaching and research hospitals in the U.S. It opened in 1918 and today conducts clinical residency programs for doctors in 47 different medical specialties. There are over 1,100 physicians on its teaching, research, and treatment staff. Jackson Memorial Hospital is affiliated with the University of Miami.

FOLLOW-UP

Students can write down sentences which briefly describe each picture on pp. 96 and 97.

WORKBOOK Lessons 43-44, pp. 55-57

Sofia Estrada is a medical student from Ecuador. She still has one more year of medical school to complete and then a year of residency. Sofia has had to work her way through medical school, and she has made a lot of sacrifices to do so.

Blake and Sofia met at the hospital where she's studying, and they fell in love. They've talked about getting married, and the time has come to make some choices.

📼 Listen in

Read the question below. Then listen to the conversation between Blake and Sofia and answer the question.

What are both Blake and Sofia afraid of?

Would you have a similar fear if you were Blake or Sofia? Do you think what they are afraid of will happen? Why or why not? Discuss these questions in groups.

45. On your own

1. Imagine that you are a close friend of Blake and Sofia's. You have just received this letter from Sofia. Suggest a solution and explain why you think your solution will have a favorable outcome.

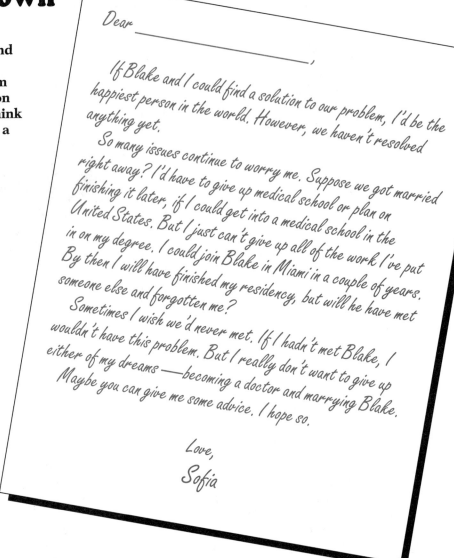

Dear _____,

If Blake and I could find a solution to our problem, I'd be the happiest person in the world. However, we haven't resolved anything yet.

So many issues continue to worry me. Suppose we got married right away? I'd have to give up medical school or plan on finishing it later, if I could get into a medical school in the United States. But I just can't give up all of the work I've put in on my degree. I could join Blake in Miami in a couple of years. By then I will have finished my residency, but will he have met someone else and forgotten me?

Sometimes I wish we'd never met. If I hadn't met Blake, I wouldn't have this problem. But I really don't want to give up either of my dreams —becoming a doctor and marrying Blake. Maybe you can give me some advice. I hope so.

Love,
Sofia

2. Write an essay about a personal situation in which you are, or were, faced with a variety of choices.

45. On your own

- Read aloud the instructions for the first exercise. Then ask a student to read Sofia's letter aloud.

- Tell the students to pretend they are Sofia's and Blake's friend and answer Sofia's letter. Go around the room and answer any questions students have about their work.

- Have the students compare their letters with different classmates. Then call on different students to read their letters aloud and write them on the board.

- Point out the illustrations. Ask a student to describe the different choices the man in the picture is faced with. Then read aloud the second set of instructions.

- Tell the students to write their essays. Go around the classroom and answer any questions students have about their writing. When they finish, ask different students to read their essays aloud and write them on the board.

- Alternatively, assign exercise 2 for homework. Collect the essays, mark any errors, and return them to the students for any needed corrections. Collect the essays again, check the corrections, and return them to the students.

CULTURE CLOSE-UP

It is not unusual among friends in the U.S. to talk or write to each other about very personal problems. In fact, Americans are known for being "very open" about themselves, so even people meeting for the first time may talk about their personal situations or problems.

WORKBOOK Lesson 45, p. 58. Before assigning the writing task, have the students read over Al's letter. Then have them think of ways to convince Al to change his mind.

Before you begin teaching, go over the functions/themes, language, and forms in the chart. This will give you a preview of what you will encounter as you guide the students through the unit.

Preview the reading.

- Tell the class to look at the illustration as you have a student describe it. Then read aloud the instructions for the first exercise and have the students discuss the questions with a partner.

- Go around the room and listen in on the discussions. Then call on different students to share their answers with the class.

- Have a student read aloud the instructions for the second exercise. Then have the students work with a partner to follow the instructions. Next call on different pairs to share their descriptions with the class.

FUNCTIONS/THEMES	LANGUAGE	FORMS
Talk about feelings	What do you think of Leslie? I think she's nice, and I appreciate her always being so frank. But I'm getting tired of her teasing me about my diet.	Infinitives with subjects vs. gerunds with subjects
Complain about someone Talk about likes and dislikes	I just can't stand being talked about behind my back. I don't like to be talked about either.	
Complain to someone Give an evaluation	Not only don't you help me around the house, but you also don't help me with the kids. I'm tired of your assuming that I'll do everything. The Wakefield Little Theater either wants to lose money, or it has the worst luck in the history of local theater groups.	*Either . . . or, neither . . . nor,* and *not only . . . but (also)*

Preview the reading.

1. Work with a partner. Would you like to be a famous actor or singer? How do you think your life would be different?

2. Before you read the article on pages 100–101, look at the photos. What words would you use to describe Julio Iglesias? Discuss your ideas with a partner.

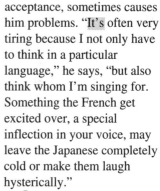

Julio Iglesias: Spanish Prince of Song

1 He is the most popular singer in the world today, and the most popular Spanish singer in history. Since 1968, when he began his professional career, he has sold more than 180 million albums. His face is recognized everywhere, from Moscow to Buenos Aires, and he sings and records in seven languages. He is Julio Iglesias, and in any language his melodic, romantic ballads and warm style appeal to people of all ages and cultures, from Japanese teenagers to Cuban grandmothers.

2 His fans know him as the "Spanish prince of song," but in interviews Iglesias seems relaxed and unassuming. Underneath his natural humility, however, is a driving ambition and an obsession with meeting new challenges. "Let me tell you a story," he says. He is sitting next to one of three swimming pools at his Florida mansion. "You see my house—the swimming pools, the manicured lawn, the Rolls Royce, my success as you put it. When I was finishing this house, I was very happy. But when the house was done, I suddenly got very depressed. And now I know why. It was simply that everything had been finished. What makes my life meaningful is the feeling that I'm actively doing something, that I'm being challenged and my work is never complete."

Julio Iglesias in concert.

3 The challenges have not always been in the arena of music. Before he became a singer, Iglesias was living in Spain and playing for a Madrid soccer team. Then, at age 23, he was nearly killed in a car crash that left him paralyzed from the waist down. Doctors predicted he would never walk again, but during three years of intensive rehabilitation he went from wiggling his toes to crawling to walking with crutches, and finally to walking unaided.

4 Iglesias talks of that experience as a turning point in his life. "It's all about making a disadvantage an advantage. I couldn't move, so I opened my eyes more, I listened more, I was more alert for signs, smells, thoughts, and motivations. I discovered I could play a little guitar, I could write something, how to put the songs and the words together."

5 After his recovery, Iglesias went to a local Spanish music festival, submitted a song, and won an award. Almost overnight, he went from being an unknown to being a star.

6 Today, Iglesias is often on tour, traveling from country to country. His proficiency with different languages, while an essential part of his worldwide acceptance, sometimes causes him problems. "It's often very tiring because I not only have to think in a particular language," he says, "but also think whom I'm singing for. Something the French get excited over, a special inflection in your voice, may leave the Japanese completely cold or make them laugh hysterically."

7 But the fact remains that Iglesias is fundamentally Spanish. "I know what I represent for the Spanish world," he says with pride and absolute assurance. "As a singer, I am a leader."

8 In his songwriting, too, he is completely Spanish. "I write only in Spanish. My lyrics are stories that are very simple, common, even naive. These songs come out like a conversation you might have with someone on the street. It's musical talk. I sing the little stories between couples in the world. That is, perhaps, my success in my own language—capturing the intimate *historias*."

9 Until the early 1980s, most North Americans had never heard of Julio Iglesias, but since then he has put out a number of albums in English, all of them highly successful. After his second all-English album was released, his concert schedule included appearances with Placido Domingo, Charles Aznavour, and Zubin Mehta at Lincoln Center in

46. Julio Iglesias: Spanish Prince of Song

PROCEDURE

- Point out the photos and have a student read the captions aloud.

- Have the students read through the article. Follow a procedure similar to that on p. 2 of this book.

OPTION

Find out if any students have heard any of Julio Iglesias' songs. Ask them what they think of his music. If possible, have a student (or students) bring recordings of Iglesias' music to class to play for the class members. Choose one of his songs in English and have the students write down the lyrics as they listen to the song. (It may be necessary to have them listen several times.) Then ask different students to copy the lines of the song on the board.

Figure it out

1. Read the article.

- If necessary, have the students change their descriptions from item 2 on p. 99. Then call on different students to tell the class how their descriptions changed.

2. ...Say *Right* or *Wrong*.

- Have the students read over the five statements and then scan the article for the answers.

- Tell the students to compare answers with a partner. Then call on different pairs of students to say the answers. If necessary, have other students write the answers on the board.

ANSWERS
1. Wrong
2. Right   "Underneath his natural humility, however, is a driving ambition and an obsession with meeting new challenges."
3. Right   "His proficiency with different languages, while an essential part of his worldwide acceptance, sometimes causes him problems."
4. Wrong
5. Right   "'I know what I represent for the Spanish world,' he says with pride and absolute assurance. 'As a singer, I am a leader.'"

3. Explain what you think each highlighted use of *it* refers to.

- Read the instructions aloud as the students follow along in their books. Then have them scan the article for the highlighted words and surrounding context. You can have the students write what the words refer to on separate paper.

- Tell the students to compare answers with a partner. Then call on different students to read the answers aloud and write them on the board.

POSSIBLE ANSWERS
1. a statement about his success, made by someone else
   the reason Iglesias got depressed
2. life, especially the challenges involved in life
3. using different languages
4. Iglesias' songwriting

4. ...Say *Right* or *Wrong* and correct the wrong statements.

- Tell the students to read through the exercise items. Answer any questions. Then have the students follow the instructions and do the exercise.

- Have the students compare answers with a partner. Finally, call on different students to share their answers with the class.

ANSWERS
1. Wrong – It's about his world-wide popularity.
2. Right
3. Right
4. Wrong – It describes his work for UNICEF.

5. ...Form nouns from the adjectives.

- Read the instructions aloud. Then read aloud the words from the list and have the students repeat them after you.

- Have the students do the exercise. Then have them compare answers with a partner. Finally, call on different students to read aloud the answers and write them on the board.

ANSWERS
1. proficiency
2. privacy
3. accuracy
4. illiteracy
5. vacancy
6. urgency

OPTION

Tell the students to use the adjectives and the corresponding nouns in separate sentences to show they know the meanings of the words. You can write an example on the board as a model:

Julio Iglesias is proficient in several languages. His proficiency in speaking several languages is remarkable.

When they finish, have the students compare their sentences with a partner. Then call on different students to read aloud their sentences and write them on the board.

FOLLOW-UP

Students can choose a paragraph from the article and write a short summary of it.

WORKBOOK Lesson 46, p. 59.

Iglesias playing soccer.

New York City. At one point he had six albums—English and Spanish—on the charts in the United States.

⑩ His international triumphs have been even greater, as a single example will show: His album *Momentos*, released in Spanish, French, and Italian versions, became the number-one album in ninety countries!

⑪ As special representative for the performing arts for UNICEF, Iglesias has traveled around the world to perform in fund-raising concerts and to meet with underprivileged children. This aspect of his career holds deep meaning for him. "The world has given me so much," he says. "I am able to live my life in song, and my work with UNICEF is, in a small way, my way of repaying my debt."

⑫ When asked whether his astounding success makes it hard for him to separate Julio Iglesias the public person from Julio Iglesias the human being, he answers: "I can't separate my life from what I represent or what I do. When I go on stage, of course I get dressed and put on a tie, but the blood runs in my body—I don't fake anything. I'm a natural. And I'm a natural because I don't know how to do any other thing. I know I have talent enough to make people believe I am something else. And I have the talent to sing. I am a singer for sure."

Iglesias signing autographs.

Figure it out

1. **Read the article. Was your description of Julio Iglesias in item 2 on page 99 correct? If necessary, change your description.**

2. **When you have finished reading, decide which of the sentences below describe Julio Iglesias as he is presented in the article. Say *Right* or *Wrong* for each one. If your answer is *Right* find at least one statement in the article that supports it.**

1. His music appeals only to older people.
2. He is hardworking and enjoys a challenge.
3. He speaks more than one language.
4. He is nervous and impatient.
5. He is self-confident about his music.

3. **Iglesias uses the pronoun *it* in a number of his quotes in a way that implies, rather than states, what the pronoun refers to. Explain what you think each highlighted use of *it* listed below refers to.**

1. paragraph 2
2. paragraph 4
3. paragraph 6
4. paragraph 8

4. **Do the statements below accurately state the main purpose of the paragraphs? Say *Right* or *Wrong* for each one, and correct the wrong statements.**

1. Paragraph 1 is about Iglesias's involvement in sports.
2. Paragraphs 3 and 4 are about a non-musical challenge in Iglesias's life.
3. Paragraph 6 is about problems Iglesias sometimes encounters when singing for audiences from different countries.
4. Paragraph 11 describes Iglesias's home.

5. **The suffix -*y* may be added to many words to form nouns. When forming nouns from adjectives, a final *t* or *te* often changes to *c* when the -*y* suffix is added. Form nouns from the adjectives below.**

1. proficient
2. private
3. accurate
4. illiterate
5. vacant
6. urgent

47. I'm sick and tired of his snapping at me.

1. Tell your partner about something you are sick and tired of, and say what you are going to do about it.

Michelle, an aspiring singer, is talking to the band leader, Ray, after a run-in with Kyle, the band's drummer.

Listen to the conversation.

2

Ray What's wrong, Michelle? You look as if you're going to either cry or scream.

Michelle It's Kyle. He really infuriates me. Either he starts acting differently or I'm going to quit. I'm sick and tired of his snapping at me.

Ray What happened this time?

Michelle Well, just now, I couldn't help thinking he was misinterpreting the music. So I made a suggestion, politely, of course.

Ray And?

Michelle Well, not only didn't he take my suggestion, but he interrupted me in the middle of a sentence. He told me to stop complaining and mind my own business. I was only trying to be helpful, and I didn't appreciate being talked to that way.

Ray It sounds to me as if he has trouble accepting criticism.

Michelle Well, nobody likes to be criticized, but I still expect to be treated with some respect.

Ray Maybe it's none of my business, but I'd suggest that you take it up with Kyle directly.

Michelle You're absolutely right. There's no point in my wasting time complaining behind Kyle's back.

Ray I agree. But at the same time, I don't think you should worry about it too much. You need to focus all your energy on our next concert. You know how important that concert is to us. And it's a big opportunity for you.

Michelle You're right. I guess I just have to learn not to take these things so seriously.

3. Check (√) the statements that are stated or implied in the conversation.

____ 1. Michelle and Kyle have had problems before.

____ 2. Kyle is very easygoing.

____ 3. Kyle criticized the way Michelle was singing.

____ 4. Kyle doesn't like to be criticized.

____ 5. Michelle and Ray get along well.

____ 6. Ray gives Michelle advice on how to handle the situation.

____ 7. Ray offers to help by talking to Kyle.

____ 8. Michelle isn't really upset at all.

47. I'm sick and tired of his snapping at me.

1. Warm-up Activity

- Read aloud the instructions in the box. Then have the students follow the instructions and talk to a partner.

- Call on different students to tell the class what they told their partners. You can share similar information about yourself with the class.

2. Conversation

BACKGROUND

Michelle, an aspiring singer, is talking to the band leader, Ray, after a run-in with Kyle, the band's drummer. Michelle complains about Kyle's behavior, and Ray gives her some advice.

LANGUAGE

…as if means the same thing as *like*.

…snapping at means *speaking abruptly or sharply at*.

…just now means *at the moment that just passed*.

…I couldn't help thinking is another way of saying "It occurred to me."

…made a suggestion means the same thing as *suggested something*.

…mind my own business is another way of saying "pay attention to my own affairs."

…that way. is another way of saying "in that manner."

Maybe it's none of my business is another way of saying "maybe I shouldn't give my opinion."

…take it up means *discuss it*.

There's no point in my wasting time is another way of saying "There no reason for me to waste my time."

…behind (Kyle's) back. means *without (Kyle's) knowledge*.

…at the same time here means *in addition*.

…take these things so seriously. is another way of saying "become so upset about these things."

PROCEDURE

- As the students examine the illustration, point out the characters from the conversation. Ask a student to describe the setting of the picture.

- Follow a procedure similar to that indicated for the opening conversation in Unit 1.

3. Check (✓) the statements that are stated or implied in the conversation.

- Have the students read over the statements. Answer any questions they have.

- Have the students do the exercise. When they finish, tell them to compare answers with a partner. Then call on different students to read aloud the statements that are stated or implied.

ANSWERS
1.
4.
5.
6.

FOLLOW-UP

Students can correct the false statements in exercise 3 and write down the correct versions.

WORKBOOK Lesson 47, p. 60

48. I have to learn not to take things so seriously.

WARM-UP

Go around the room and ask different students what traits in other people they particularly like or dislike. Begin by mentioning your own likes and dislikes about personal traits. For example:

I like people who are easygoing.
I dislike people who criticize others all the time.

TALK ABOUT FEELINGS • INFINITIVES WITH SUBJECTS VS. GERUNDS WITH SUBJECTS

- Tell the students to read over the conversation. Answer any questions they have. Then have them listen to the conversation. You can also act out the conversation with a student.

- Point out the box at the top and ask different students to read aloud the information in it. Then read aloud the information in the other boxes. Answer any questions students have.

- Have the students work with a partner to follow the second set of instructions. Go around the classroom and listen in, giving help if needed. Finally, call on different pairs to act out their conversations for the class.

- Read the instructions aloud. Then have the students read over the behaviors. Answer any questions.

- Have the students listen to the conversation and check the appropriate behaviors. Then call on a student to say the answers.

TAPESCRIPT
David Aaargh!
Janet David! What's wrong?
David I've had it with this place! These people are driving me crazy!
Janet Who? What are they doing?
David Well, since you asked—Vicki, for example. I don't like her talking about me behind my back. Sarah told me all about what she said about me to Mr. Foster. Oh, and Sarah's another one—always teasing me about my car. O.K., so I don't have the newest car in the world, but does she have to mention it every time she sees me?

Janet David, you've got to calm down. Why don't you tell Vicki and Sarah how you feel and see if you can work it out with them?
David Maybe you're right. But it's not just them. I'm tired of being ignored at meetings and I'm sick of being yelled at for being late. I work hard, and it's not that important if I get in a little late.
Janet You sound really stressed out. Maybe you should take a vacation. If not, your work is going to suffer.
David Well, actually, that's what's been happening lately. I can't stand Jennifer criticizing my work, and she's done it every day this week. A vacation isn't a bad idea. Thanks for listening, Janet. I'll think about what you said.

ANSWERS
X
Vicki
Jennifer
Sarah
X

- Have the students examine the frames as you and some class members read aloud the contents. Answer any questions about the structures.

- Point out the boxes and read aloud each rule. Ask a student to read aloud the sentence examples after you read aloud the first rule. Answer any questions students have.

OPTION

Have the students work in pairs to come up with pairs of sentences of their own—one sentence in the active mood and another corresponding sentence in the passive. Tell them to use the sentences in the frames as models but, if possible, to write about persons and situations familiar to the class. When they finish, have the pairs compare their sentences with other pairs. Finally, call on different pairs to read their sentences aloud and write them on the board.

48. I have to learn not to take things so seriously.

1 ▸ **Listen to the conversation.**
  ▸ **Act out similar conversations. Tell your partner what you like and don't like about the people in the box.**

A What do you think of Leslie?
B Well, I think she's nice and I appreciate her always being so frank. But I'm getting tired of her teasing me about my diet.
A Maybe you should say something to her.
B Hmm . . . I doubt it would do any good. I guess I just have to learn not to take things so seriously.

Some people

Leslie is nice, but she is extremely frank. Also, she often teases people about personal things.
Arturo is very smart and he knows something about every subject. However, he dominates every conversation.
Patricia works hard and she is always busy trying to get ahead. However, she's never on time for anything.
Jeff is a nice guy and he tries to be a good friend. However, he's always telling everyone what to do.

---

2 ▸ **Listen to David talk about some people where he works. For each behavior listed below, write the name of the person David talks about. If David doesn't mention a name, write X.**

_____ ignores him at meetings.
_____ talks about him behind his back.
_____ criticizes his work.
_____ teases him about his car.
_____ yells at him for being late.

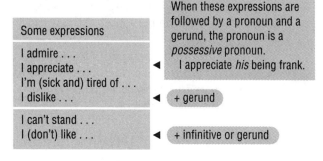

When these expressions are followed by a pronoun and a gerund, the pronoun is a *possessive* pronoun.
  I appreciate *his* being frank.

Some expressions

I admire . . .
I appreciate . . .   ◂
I'm (sick and) tired of . . .
I dislike . . .   ◂ + gerund

I can't stand . . .
I (don't) like . . .   ◂ + infinitive or gerund

---

3 ▸ **Study the frames: Infinitives with subjects vs. gerunds with subjects**

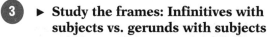

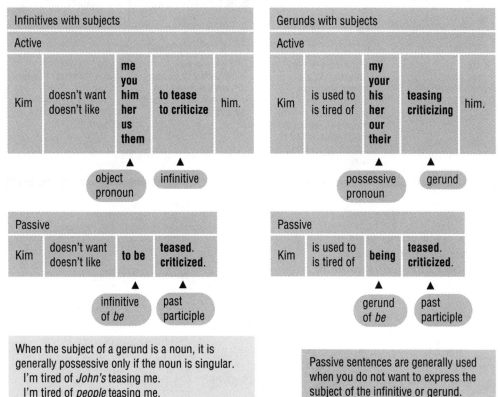

Infinitives with subjects				
Active				
Kim	doesn't want doesn't like	me you him her us them	to tease to criticize	him.
		▲ object pronoun	▲ infinitive	
Passive				
Kim	doesn't want doesn't like	to be	teased. criticized.	
		▲ infinitive of *be*	▲ past participle	

Gerunds with subjects				
Active				
Kim	is used to is tired of	my your his her our their	teasing criticizing	him.
		▲ possessive pronoun	▲ gerund	
Passive				
Kim	is used to is tired of	being	teased. criticized.	
		▲ gerund of *be*	▲ past participle	

When the subject of a gerund is a noun, it is generally possessive only if the noun is singular.
  I'm tired of *John's* teasing me.
  I'm tired of *people* teasing me.

Passive sentences are generally used when you do not want to express the subject of the infinitive or gerund.

4 ▶ Listen to the conversation.
  ▶ Act out similar conversations with a partner. Imagine that you are upset because someone has done one of the things in the box to you. Tell your partner what's wrong.

A What's wrong?
B Oh, nothing. I just can't stand being talked about behind my back.
A I don't like to be talked about, either, but I think it's worse if you don't do anything about it.
B What do you mean?
A Maybe it's none of my business, but I'd suggest that you take it up with the person directly.

Has someone . . .
talked about you behind your back?
insulted you to your face?
asked you personal questions about your finances?
yelled at you for no reason?
ignored you?
laughed at you?

5 ▶ Rewrite what these performers said about their work, combining the sentences in brackets [ ] into one sentence that contains an infinitive or gerund with a subject.

We asked some performers what they love and hate about their work.

1. Directors can be very impatient and very sensitive. [They yell at me in front of everyone else. I especially don't like that.]

2. Writers often seem indecisive. [They change our lines. I get tired of that.]

3. Our music is very different. It's a completely new sound. [People sometimes criticize our music when they don't understand it. I don't appreciate that.]

4. It's nice to be recognized in public. [People ask me for my autograph. I really like that.]

5. I used to work on stage, but now I'm in television. [The audience applauds after a performance. I miss that.]

6 ▶ Work with a partner. Talk about your situation at work, home, or school. Say what you like and don't like, using some of the expressions in the box.

I really like	being . . . to be . . .
I don't like	being . . . to be . . .
I get tired of	people . . . my boss's . . . my classmates/coworkers . . .
I appreciate	my teacher's . . . my relatives . . . people . . .

COMPLAIN ABOUT SOMEONE • TALK ABOUT LIKES AND DISLIKES • INFINITIVES WITH SUBJECTS VS. GERUNDS WITH SUBJECTS

- Have the students read over the conversation. Answer any questions they have. Next have the class listen to the conversation. You can also ask a pair of students to act it out for the class.

- Point out the box and have different students read aloud the possible questions in it. Answer any questions. Then read aloud the second set of instructions.

- Tell the students to act out similar conversations with a partner. Go around the room and listen in, giving help if needed. Finally, call on different pairs to act out their conversations for the class.

- Point out the photos and read aloud the heading. Make sure the students understand what the word *performers* means. Then ask different students to read aloud what the performers said about their work. Next read the instructions aloud. Answer any questions.

- Tell the students to do the exercise. Then have them compare answers with a partner. Then call on different students to read aloud the answers and write them on the board.

ANSWERS
1. I especially don't like them to yell at me in front of everyone else.
2. I get tired of them changing our lines.
3. I don't appreciate people criticizing our music when they don't understand it.
4. I really like people to ask me for my autograph.
5. I miss the audience applauding after a performance.

OPTION

Tell the students to use their imaginations and write different sentences to replace the ones that occur first in the brackets. Give them an example for the first item:

[They push me to memorize new lines in only a few minutes.]

When they finish, tell the students to exchange papers with a partner. Then have them follow the instructions for the exercise, combining the new sentences with the second ones in brackets. For example:

I especially don't like them to push me to memorize new lines in only a few minutes.

Next have the students go over the combined sentences with their partners. Finally, call on different students to read aloud the combined sentences and write them on the board.

- Point out the expressions in the box and have different students read them aloud. Answer any questions.

- Read the instructions aloud and have the students follow them. Go around the room and join in the conversations as you check the students' work.

- Call on different students to tell the class what they like and don't like. Write some of their sentences on the board.

- Have the students read over the conversation. Answer any questions they have. Next have the class listen to the conversation. You can also ask a pair of students to act it out for the class.

- Point out the box on the right and have different students read aloud the situations. Then read aloud the information in the box to the left. Answer any questions. Next you can help the students come up with additional sentences beginning with *Not only . . . .*

- Read aloud the second set of instructions. Tell the students to act out similar conversations with a partner. Go around the room and listen in, giving help if needed. Finally, call on different pairs to act out their conversations for the class.

- Have the students examine the frames as you have two students read aloud the contents. Then have the class repeat the sentences in the frame after you. (See the Pronunciation note which follows.)

- Read aloud the information in the boxes. Answer any questions.

OPTION

Have the students write original sentences modeled after those in the frame on the left. Then tell them to exchange papers with a partner and convert their partner's sentences to ones like those in the frame on the right. Next have the students go over their work with their partners. Finally, call on different students to read their sentences aloud and write them on the board.

Tell the students to rewrite the sentences they converted so that the conjunctions connect two complete sentences like those in the box on the right. Then have them go over their work with their partners. Finally, call on different students to read aloud their sentences and write them on the board.

PRONUNCIATION NOTE

A slight pause with sustained intonation occurs just before the second conjunction. Note:

Jim's either tired or angry.

Jane neither called nor did she come to work.

- Have the students read over the play review. You can also have two students read the different paragraphs aloud. Answer any questions. (See the Culture Close-Up which follows.)

- Tell the students to follow the instructions and rewrite the review. When they finish, have them compare their answers with a partner. Then call on different students to read aloud the combined sentences and write them on the board.

ANSWERS

Either the Wakefield Little Theater wants to lose money or it has the worst luck in the history of local theater groups.
Not only was its last production terrible, but its current one, *Out Back,* is just as bad.
. . . it's neither a musical nor a comedy.
Either a lot of the actors are amateurish or they're badly cast . . .
It is not only run-down but also uncomfortable.
Either shape up immediately or close down.

CULTURE CLOSE-UP

Local community theaters, sometimes known as "little theaters," can be found in many U.S. cities and in some towns. The actors and actresses in such theaters are usually ordinary, local residents who usually haven't had any formal training in acting. However, sometimes these theaters become famous for the excellent performances they put on and, as a result, the performers go on to act in professional theater productions. For example, some famous actors and actresses on Broadway and in Hollywood started out in little theaters.

FOLLOW-UP

Students can write out the sentences they used to express their likes and dislikes in exercise 6.

7 ▶ Listen to the conversation.
▶ Act out similar conversations. You are unhappy about one of the situations in the box. Complain to your partner, who will play the role of the person you're angry with.

A Oscar, can I talk to you for a second?
B Sure. What is it?
A Well, not only don't you help me around the house, but you also don't help me with the kids. It really infuriates me. I'm tired of your assuming that I'll do everything.
B I'm sorry. Why didn't you say so before? I didn't realize you wanted help.

> **Some situations**
>
> Your spouse doesn't help you around the house. What's more, he or she doesn't help you with the kids. Your spouse assumes you will do everything and you're tired of it.
> An employee of yours is always late for work. What's more, the employee never apologizes when he or she finally arrives. You don't like the fact that the employee treats the job so casually.
> A coworker always comes back from lunch late. What's more, he or she always leaves work early. You think it's unfair that you always have to make excuses for your coworker and finish his or her work.
> Your brother or sister is always listening to your phone conversations. What's more, he or she is always opening your mail. You really don't appreciate it.

> Compare the order of the words in italics.
> Not only *don't you* help around the house, but *you don't* help with the kids.

8 ▶ Study the frames:
Either . . . or, neither . . . nor, and *not only . . . but (also)*

| Jim must be tired. *If not, then* he's angry. |
| Jane didn't call, *and* she didn't come to work. |
| Tim is a snob. *What's more,* he's a bore. |

▶

Jim's	**either**	tired	**or**	angry.
Jane	**neither**	called	**nor**	came to work.
Tim's	**not only**	a snob	**but (also)**	a bore.

> **Emphatic word order**
>
> Jane neither called nor *did she come* to work.
> Not only *is Tim* a snob, but he's also a bore.

> When these conjunctions connect two subjects or two complete sentences, a conjunction starts the sentence.
> *Neither* Jim *nor* Jane called him.
> *Either* the director apologizes *or* I'm going to quit.

 9 ▶ Rewrite the play review, combining the sentences in brackets [ ] into one sentence using *either . . . or, neither . . . nor,* or *not only . . . but (also)*.

> ## A DISGRACE FROM BEGINNING TO END
>
> **by Kent Brownridge**
>
> [The Wakefield Little Theater must want to lose money. If not, then it has the worst luck in the history of local theater groups.] [Its last production was terrible. What's more, its current one, *Out Back*, is just as bad.] Although *Out Back* is billed as a "hilarious new musical," [it's not a musical and it's not a comedy.] [A lot of the actors are amateurish. If not, then they're badly cast,] and the few songs they sing out of tune are far from humorous.
>
> Moreover, the play is not the only disgrace. The theater itself is a disgrace. [It is run-down. What's more, it is uncomfortable.] I have only one piece of advice for this theater: [Shape up immediately. If not, then close down.] There is no reason for a theater to have one bad production after another, and I would not be at all surprised if the theater is half empty at its next performance.

49. Your turn

1. Read the descriptions of the three men and three women. Then, working in groups, decide which people would be happiest together as married couples. Match each person with a partner.

2. Now work with a partner and discuss two of the people who you did not think would make a happily married couple. Imagine that they are married and discuss the problems they are having living together. Try to find a solution to their disagreements.

Edmund is an engineer who is independent and climbing rapidly in his field. He wants to marry and start a family. He spends more time at work than anywhere else.

📼 Listen in

One of the people in the pictures is complaining to a friend about his wife. Read the questions below. Then listen to the conversation and answer the questions.

1. Who do you think the husband and wife are? Why?
2. The friend started to offer some advice. What do you think she was going to suggest?

Ellen is a secretary who is easygoing and not ambitious. She doesn't expect to work after having children, and she isn't interested in material things. She's very sensitive.

49. Your turn

- Point out the illustrations on pp. 106 and 107. Then have different students read aloud the captions. Next ask different students to describe the people in the pictures.

- Have the students work in groups to follow the first set of instructions. Tell each group's secretary to write down the group members' decisions. Then call on the group reporters to share the decisions and the reasons for them with the class. Encourage class discussion of the different decisions.

- Have the students work with a partner to follow the second set of instructions. Go around the classroom and listen in on the discussions as you check the pairs' work. Finally, call on different pairs to share their discussions with the class.

CULTURE CLOSE-UP

What the students are asked to do in the first exercise is similar to what special computers can do for single persons looking for partners. Sometimes referred to as a "computerized dating service," this kind of business asks its clients to describe themselves and feeds their descriptions into a computer which then matches the clients with suitable partners. Computerized dating services are advertised on TV and radio and in newspapers and magazines throughout the U.S.

Listen in

- Read the instructions aloud as the students follow along in their books. Then have the students read the questions.

- Have the students listen to the conversation. Then tell them to do the exercise. Next have them compare answers with a partner. Finally, call on different students to read aloud their answers.

TAPESCRIPT

Man I'm getting tired of her not doing the housework. I get home and I can't relax and read the newspaper or watch the news because the place is such a mess. And dinner isn't ready. My mother always had dinner on the table at six o'clock. Not only is it not ready, but sometimes she doesn't want to cook at all!

Woman Isn't she working full-time?

Man Yeah, sure. And she travels on business a lot, too. But I knew that when we got married. If she wants to work, O.K., but either she does the housework or I'm going to do something about it . . . I don't know what . . . but something!

Woman You know, this is really none of my business, but I think maybe you should . . .

POSSIBLE ANSWERS

1. Derek and Hilda. I think the man is Derek because he expresses traditional views on male-female roles in marriage. The description of the wife matches Hilda, who strongly wants to pursue her career.

2. She was going to suggest that Derek either take his wife's job as seriously as his own job or quit his job so that *he* can get dinner on the table at six o'clock.

FOLLOW-UP

Students can write down their answers to the questions in the **Listen in** exercise.

WORKBOOK Lessons 48-49, pp. 61-63

Derek is an accountant who likes to take charge of things. He has traditional views on male–female roles in marriage. He's very critical and ambitious.

Victor is an actor who is a pleasant, likeable person with a strong wish to help others. Unfortunately, he's often out of work and doesn't make much money.

Hilda is a lawyer who is independent and intellectual. She's not sure if she wants to get married, and she strongly wants to pursue her career. She is a tolerant person, but not outgoing.

Natalie is a professor who is conservative, ambitious, materialistic, critical, and family-oriented. She admires hard work.

50. On your own

1. **Read the following advertisements. Then write an advertisement of your own, explaining your requirements for a roommate, traveling companion, or partner for some activity you enjoy.**

Share my spacious two-bedroom, two-bathroom apartment. I'm looking for a new roommate. I'd appreciate your being neat and quiet and having a 9–5 job. Nonsmokers only. Call Rafael after 6 P.M. at 555-6009.

I got tired of my boss's criticizing me all the time . . . so yesterday I quit! Now I'm going to travel around the world and see the sights. I'm not used to traveling alone, so I'm seeking someone to share travel expenses with me. You're either an experienced traveler or ready for a new adventure. Call anytime before May 31—555-4582.

I love to go to art museums . . . but my friends don't! Not only do I love to look at beautiful art, but I enjoy talking about it. If you feel the same way, call Sandra at 555-2373.

2. **Write about a problem or disagreement that you either had in the past or have now with someone—for example, a boss, a spouse, or a friend. First, describe the problem and your feelings about it. Then, explain what you did or are going to do about the situation and why.**

50. On your own

- Read the instructions aloud. Then ask three students to read aloud the ads. Answer any questions.

- Tell the students to write their ads and then show them to a partner. Go around the room and answer any questions students have about their work. Then call on different students to read their ads aloud. You can also ask them to write their ads on the board.

- Ask a student to read aloud the instructions for the second exercise. Then have the students write about their problems. Go around the classroom and answer any questions students have about their work.

- Tell the students to compare their work with a partner. Then call on different students to read aloud their compositions and write them on the board for you to check.

OPTION

Assign the second exercise for homework. Collect the compositions, mark them, and then return them to the students for any needed corrections. Next collect them again to check the corrections.

CULTURE CLOSE-UP

Many newspapers and some magazines in the U.S. feature ads similar to the ones in the first exercise. These ads are called "personals" and are read not only by persons searching for a partner but by the curious as well. Part of what attracts the general public's attention to these ads is their raw, personal nature as well as their occasional humor.

WORKBOOK Lesson 50, p. 64. Before assigning the writing task, point out the different features of a formal letter—the inside address, the greeting followed by a colon, and the closing. Remind the students to include these features in their letters.

PREVIEW

Before you begin teaching, go over the functions/themes, language, and forms in the chart. This will give you a preview of what you will encounter as you guide the students through the unit.

Preview the reading.

- Tell the class to look at the illustration as you have a student describe the person in it. Then read aloud the questions for the first exercise and have the students discuss them with a partner.

- Go around the room and listen in. Next call on different partners to share their answers with the class.

  ANSWERS
  The person is Sherlock Holmes, one of the most famous detectives in literature. He is a fictional character created by the world-famous English mystery writer Sir Arthur Conan Doyle (1859-1930). (See the Culture Close-Up which follows.)

- Have a student read aloud the instructions for the second exercise. Then have the students work with a partner to follow the instructions. Next call on different pairs to share their ideas with the class.

CULTURE CLOSE-UP

The closest American counterpart to Sir Arthur Conan Doyle was Rex Stout (1886-1975). Stout wrote a series of detective novels featuring a Sherlock Holmes-type character, Nero Wolfe. Wolfe became a famous character in U.S. detective fiction because of his eccentric behavior. Some readers of Stout's novels have organized a fan club called "The Wolfe Pack."

PREVIEW

FUNCTIONS/THEMES	LANGUAGE	FORMS
Speculate about possibilities	You know, I tried to get hold of Mike all weekend, but the phone was always busy. He couldn't have been talking that whole time. Maybe the phone was off the hook. I suppose it might have been.	Short answers with modal auxiliaries
Give a description	We're looking for a red-haired woman who stole a white Toyota. Did you happen to see her? I don't believe so. But I did see a gray-haired woman riding a bike and holding a cat under her arm, which I thought was odd. The woman we're looking for, who we think had on a black skirt, was very tall and she was wearing glasses.	Nonrestrictive vs. restrictive relative clauses
Tell a story React to a story Speculate about possibilities	The Freeman Gallery, which is located in London, sells paintings and other art objects. It seems to me that they must have climbed in through the window.	

Preview the reading.

1. What is the person in the picture below doing? Do you know his name and what he's famous for? Discuss your answers with a partner.

2. Before you read the article on pages 110–111, look at the title and the diagram. What do you think the article is about? Discuss your ideas with a partner.

The Science of Murder

① Painful as it is to think about, murder has become a grim fact of modern society, and solving one involves more than the contributions of the police and witnesses. It also involves the detailed work of people in the fields of forensic science and medicine: scientists and doctors who analyze evidence to help solve murders.

② Forensic science has a colorful history. An early case was the 1849 murder by a chemistry professor of a man who had contributed large sums of money to Harvard University. In that case, pieces of bone and teeth found in the ashes of the professor's laboratory furnace were used in the courtroom as evidence. In 1892, the first murder case that was solved through fingerprint evidence occurred in Argentina, and in 1910, a doctor was found guilty of murdering his wife based on a small piece of skin found in his basement. A scar on that skin was identified as a surgical scar the victim had on her stomach. The doctor was hanged.

③ Today the evidence of forensic scientists ranges from footprints to blood samples, from hair analyses to identification of bite marks. Their work begins at the scene of the crime, and their first piece of evidence is a body—a dead body.

④ Before the body is removed to the morgue, the location of every item in the scene is diagrammed, and then the search is begun for physical evidence that could identify the killer. The killer could have left saliva on a cigarette butt, a good set of fingerprints on a glass, hairs on a hat, or blood from a cut. Once the possible sources of evidence are identified, investigators must be careful to protect them, as all too easily, evidence may be destroyed. If the murderer was smoking a cigarette and threw it in a toilet, the evidence will be gone if someone flushes the toilet. Likewise, if a police officer picks up the telephone at the scene of the crime, the fingerprint evidence may disappear.

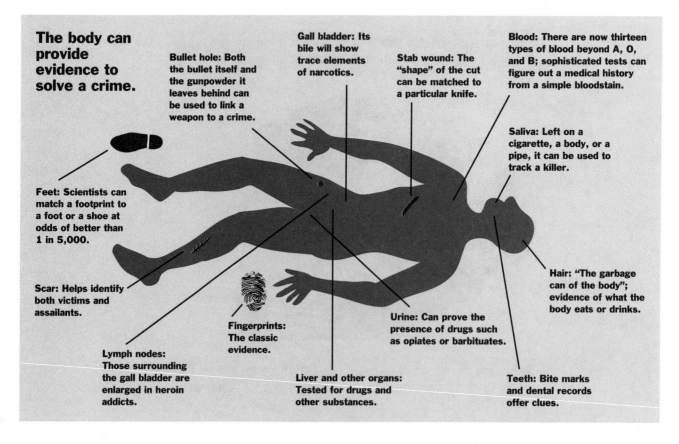

The body can provide evidence to solve a crime.

Bullet hole: Both the bullet itself and the gunpowder it leaves behind can be used to link a weapon to a crime.

Gall bladder: Its bile will show trace elements of narcotics.

Stab wound: The "shape" of the cut can be matched to a particular knife.

Blood: There are now thirteen types of blood beyond A, O, and B; sophisticated tests can figure out a medical history from a simple bloodstain.

Saliva: Left on a cigarette, a body, or a pipe, it can be used to track a killer.

Feet: Scientists can match a footprint to a foot or a shoe at odds of better than 1 in 5,000.

Scar: Helps identify both victims and assailants.

Hair: "The garbage can of the body"; evidence of what the body eats or drinks.

Fingerprints: The classic evidence.

Urine: Can prove the presence of drugs such as opiates or barbituates.

Teeth: Bite marks and dental records offer clues.

Lymph nodes: Those surrounding the gall bladder are enlarged in heroin addicts.

Liver and other organs: Tested for drugs and other substances.

51. The Science of Murder

PROCEDURE

- Point out the diagram and ask different students to read aloud the information in it. Answer any questions.

- Have the students read through the article. Follow a procedure similar to that on p. 2 of this book. When the students have finished reading the article, ask them if they guessed correctly when they did exercise 2 on the previous page.

Figure it out

1. Read the first paragraph of the article.

■ Have the students read the first paragraph of the article and then explain to a partner what forensic science is. When they finish, call on a student to tell the class the appropriate definition.

POSSIBLE ANSWER

Forensic science is the study of evidence left after a murder. The evidence is studied in order to solve the crime.

2. ...find the paragraph...

■ Have the students follow the instructions and do the exercise.

■ Tell the students to compare answers with a partner. Then call on different students to say the answers and write them on the board.

ANSWERS
1. 5
2. 4
3. 8
4. 2
5. 6
6. 9

3. Try to answer the questions from memory.

■ Have the students read over the questions. Then have them try to answer without looking at the article. You can have them write their answers on separate paper.

■ Tell the students to compare answers with a partner. Then have them scan the article and make any necessary corrections to their original answers. Finally, call on different students to read aloud their answers and write them on the board.

SAMPLE ANSWERS
1. Fingerprint evidence left on a telephone may be destroyed if a police officer used the telephone.
2. A bullet could be found in the body, or evidence that the victim took drugs could be discovered.
3. They will try to match bullets taken from the scene with any bullet holes found, and they will try to identify the gun.
4. It can show exactly what the victim ate and when.
5. It can show a person's medical history.

4. ...Complete the paragraph, using words from the list.

■ Have the students repeat the list of words after you. Answer any questions about their meanings. Then have the students read over the paragraph. Answer any questions.

■ Have the students follow the instructions and do the exercise. When they finish, tell them to compare answers with a partner. Then call on a student to read aloud the completed paragraph as another student writes the answers on the board.

ANSWERS
painful, useless, fearful, careful

OPTION

Have the students write sentences of their own to show they know the meaning of the words in the list. When they finish, have them compare their sentences with a partner. Then call on different students to read their sentences aloud and write them on the board.

CULTURE CLOSE-UP

DNA stands for deoxyribonucleic acid. In 1944, an American bacteriologist, Maclyn McCarty, a Canadian-born American, Colin MacLeod, and a Canadian, Oswald Avery, were the first scientists to show that DNA is the basic genetic component of chromosomes.

FOLLOW-UP

Students can write down a definition of "DNA fingerprinting."

WORKBOOK Lesson 51, p. 65

⑤ The next step is the medical examination, and an examiner will arrive at the scene to confirm the death and check the body for injuries. The body will then be shipped to the morgue, where a forensic autopsy will be performed. This involves close examination of both the outside and inside of the body. The specialist will study the hands and face for signs that a fight took place and will remove any evidence, such as a bullet, that is in the body. He or she will also send samples of body organs to the laboratory to see if the victim took any drugs.

⑥ Besides testing the body for evidence, forensic technicians must also analyze all evidence the police have provided from the scene. If the murder involved a shooting, ballistics experts—specialists in firearms and ammunition—will also be involved in the investigation. Using a microscope, they will try to match bullets taken from the scene with any bullet holes found, and they will also try to identify the gun. A gun leaves unique marks on bullets fired from it; in fact, marks on two bullets from the same gun are as alike as two prints from the same finger. In addition, experts will examine any gunpowder found around a bullet hole to see how far away the gun was when it was fired. By examining the gunpowder, they will also try to identify where the gun came from and on what day it was sold.

⑦ It is common knowledge that fingerprints can be traced to an individual person; likewise, footprints can be used. "There are 46 points of measurement and 120 points to examine for shape," says anthropologist Louise Robbins. Footprints can also be found in people's shoes, and scientists like Robbins help the police match a shoe to its wearer.

⑧ Hair, too, can be matched with increasing accuracy. People's hair can differ in color, texture, thickness, and twenty other characteristics. "The hair is the garbage can of the body," says forensic scientist, Dr. Robert Shaler. "Everything you eat shows up there." Since hair grows one millimeter a day, an analysis can tell "if you took aspirin yesterday and drank beer from an aluminum can a week ago."

⑨ Blood type has long been used as evidence. Since 1988 a new kind of evidence, known as DNA fingerprinting, can also be used in court. This method involves matching the genetic material (DNA) of a suspect to genetic material found at the scene of the crime. DNA can be obtained from blood, skin, or hair left by the murderer. This DNA matching has tied hundreds of individuals to their crimes—and has established the innocence of others who were wrongly found guilty before DNA tests were available. DNA matching does not completely eliminate the possibility of mistakes, but it is extremely accurate.

⑩ Murder is a dreadful business indeed, but let the murderer beware. The findings that come out of a forensic scientist's work may be very dramatic and revealing.

Figure it out

1. **Read the first paragraph of the article. Then explain what forensic science is.**

2. **As you read the article, pay attention to the purpose of each paragraph. When you have finished, find the paragraph that . . .**

1. describes the forensic autopsy.
2. describes the initial investigation and discusses the importance of protecting evidence.
3. discusses why hair is useful in solving a murder.
4. gives the history of forensic science.
5. describes what ballistic experts do.
6. explains the importance of DNA tests.

3. **Try to answer the questions below from memory. Then scan the article and make any necessary corrections**

1. What is one way evidence could be destroyed by accident?
2. What is one type of evidence that could be found during the forensic autopsy?
3. What is one thing ballistic experts will try to do?
4. What can an analysis of hair show?
5. What can an analysis of blood show?

4. **The suffixes -ful and -less, which are opposites, are used to form many adjectives, as in careful (with care) and careless (without care). Complete the paragraph below, using words from the list.**

careful   fearful   painful   useful
careless   fearless   painless   useless

Crime is spreading to the far reaches of our society, and the _____ fact is that we are doing very little to stop it. It is _____ to simply talk about violence, while people are becoming more and more _____ and suspicious of each other. Unless we are very _____ , the problem is likely to get out of control.

52. This isn't "Murder in Madrid"!

1. You and your partner were supposed to meet your friend Sheila at a restaurant at 8:00. It is now 9:30 and you have just finished eating. Sheila never showed up. What do you think happened to her? Discuss all of the possibilities.

 Jeanette and Tony Huber are looking forward to watching the final episode of "Murder in Madrid" on television.

Listen to the conversation.

2

Tony Hey, it's 9:00. Time for "Murder in Madrid."

Jeanette Oh, that's right. Tonight's the final episode. Let me change the channel.

Tony Look, this isn't "Murder in Madrid"!

Jeanette Do you suppose they canceled it?

Tony They couldn't have. Not my favorite program.

Jeanette Well, it must not be on tonight, which is odd.

Tony It has to be. Let me check the TV listings. (*Opens newspaper*) Oh, no, look at this! "Due to special programming, the final episode of 'Murder in Madrid' will be shown next week at this time." It seems the Academy of Music awards are on instead.

Jeanette I can't believe it! Now we'll have to wait a week to find out who the murderer was.

Tony Listen, don't worry. Look what I bought.

Jeanette *Murder in Madrid?* You bought the book?

Tony I hear it's even better than the series, which is why I wanted to read it. But now I can look at the end and find out what happens.

Jeanette Oh, Tony, you wouldn't!

Tony Why not? I'm dying to know who killed Ackerman . . . and that woman in the nightclub, who I thought was the best one in the series.

Jeanette As long as you don't tell *me* who did it. I can wait until next week.

Tony Well, I can't. But don't worry. My lips are sealed.

Jeanette They'd better be.

Tony (*Opens book and starts to read*) Oh, no . . . she couldn't have. She was only . . . Jeanette, you won't believe this. . . .

Jeanette Tony! Come on! I don't want to hear it.

Tony What's wrong with reading the book before you see the end? You're so conventional.

Jeanette Maybe I am. In any case, I *don't* want to know what happened!

3. Match.

1. They're showing the Academy of Music awards instead of "Murder in Madrid."
2. Do you suppose they canceled the show?
3. It must not be on tonight.
4. Don't tell me who did it.
5. I can wait until next week.
6. You're so conventional.

a. It has to be.
b. Maybe I am.
c. They can't be.
d. Well, I can't.
e. They couldn't have. Not my favorite program.
f. Don't worry. I won't.

52. This isn't "Murder in Madrid"!

1. Warm-up Activity

- Have a student read aloud the instructions in the box. Then have the students work in pairs to discuss what could have happened to Sheila.

- Go around the classroom and join in the discussions. Then call on different students to share their thoughts with the class.

2. Conversation

BACKGROUND

Jeanette and Tony Huber are looking forward to watching the final episode of "Murder in Madrid" on television. They especially want to know who the murderer was. Then they find out the program has been postponed for a week.

LANGUAGE

Time for "Murder in Madrid." is short for *Nine o'clock is the time when "Murder in Madrid" is on TV.*

Let me is used here to indicate that the speaker is about to do something. It's like saying "I'm going to."

I can't believe it! is used to express surprise or disbelief.

…you wouldn't! is another way of saying "I can't believe you would (find out what happens)."

I'm dying to (know) is an idiomatic way of saying "I'm eager to (know)."

As long as means *under the condition that.*

Come on! is used here to plead with the other speaker. It's like saying "Please (don't tell me)!"

…so (conventional) means *very (conventional).*

In any case is another way of saying "That may be true but… ."

PROCEDURE

- As the students examine the illustration, point out the characters from the conversation. Ask a student to describe what's going on in the picture.

- Follow a procedure similar to that indicated for the opening conversation in unit 1.

3. Match.

- Have the students read over the sentences in the two columns. Answer any questions. Then tell them to do the exercise. Suggest that they try to match the sentences without looking back at the conversation.

- Tell the students to compare answers with a partner. Then call on different pairs to read aloud the matched sentences. Ask a student to write the answers on the board.

ANSWERS
1. c
2. e
3. a
4. f
5. d
6. b

CULTURE CLOSE-UP

Probably the most popular murder mystery program on U.S. TV has been "Murder, She Wrote." The series started in 1984 and continues into the 1990s. It stars Angela Landsbury as Jessica Fletcher. Fletcher is a widowed mystery writer who lives in Cabot Cove, a town in Maine. On the series, Mrs. Fletcher gets involved in solving crimes.

FOLLOW-UP

Students can write down what they think happened to Sheila in exercise 1.

WORKBOOK Lesson 52, p. 66

53. Maybe the phone was off the hook.

WARM-UP

Tell the students about an experience you had waiting for someone or something. For example:

I was expecting a call from my mother at 9 P.M. By 10 P.M. she still hadn't called, so I called her, but there was no answer. I was really worried, so I drove to her house only to find out that she was at the neighbors watching TV and had forgotten to call.

Ask students to tell the class about similar experiences they had.

SPECULATE ABOUT POSSIBILITIES • SHORT ANSWERS WITH MODAL AUXILIARIES

- Ask the students if they know what it means to "speculate about possibilities." Then point out the illustrations and ask different students to describe what's happening in them. Then read aloud the instructions.

- Have the students listen to the conversation and check the appropriate picture. Then call on a student to tell the class the answer.

TAPESCRIPT
Man Looks like a routine burglary, doesn't it, Joan?
Woman Sure does, Phil. The woman next door says she saw a man walking around the outside of the house. She didn't see anyone else, so he must have been alone.
Man No, he can't have been. Look, here are two sets of footprints. He must have had someone with him.
Woman You're right, he must have. A woman, judging by the size of those footprints. What do the owners say is missing?
Man A TV, a VCR, and quite a bit of cash. Mr. Burke says he kept a lot of cash at home because he needed it for his business.
Woman Well, he shouldn't have. Why do people do foolish things like that? Even if we find the TV and VCR, the cash will probably be gone. Any signs of forced entry?
Man No broken windows. Maybe they forced the front door?
Woman They might have, but I don't think so. It doesn't look forced. They must have had a key.

ANSWERS
	✓	

OPTION

Have the students work in small groups to speculate who robbed Mr. Burke. You can make up some clues and write them on the board. For example:

employee   neighbor   relative

Go around the room and join in the discussions as you check the students' work. Then call on different group reporters to share their group's speculations with the class. Have the students vote on which speculation sounds the most realistic.

- Tell the students to read over the conversation. Answer any questions. Next have the students listen to the conversation. You can also act the conversation out with a student.

- Point out the box and ask different students to read aloud the sentences. Answer any questions. Then have the students work with a partner to follow the second set of instructions.

- Go around the classroom and listen in, giving help if needed. Finally, call on different pairs to act out their conversations for the class.

- Have the students examine the frames as you and some class members read aloud the exchanges. Answer any questions.

- Review what short answers are. Then read aloud the information in the box at the bottom. Answer any questions.

OPTION

Tell the students to work in pairs. Tell them to write down sentences like those on the left side of the frames. Then have them exchange papers and write short answers for their partners' sentences. When they finish, have the pairs compare their sentences with other pairs. Finally, call on different pairs to read their sentences aloud and write them on the board.

- Tell the students to read over the incomplete conversation. Answer any questions they have. Then tell them to read the instructions and do the exercise.

- Tell the students to compare answers with a partner. Then have two students act out the completed conversation as the others check their own work. Ask a student to write the answers on the board.

ANSWERS
Hiro can't
Hiro must have been
Hiro should have been
Yoko might not be
Yoko will

53. Maybe the phone was off the hook.

SPECULATE ABOUT POSSIBILITIES • SHORT ANSWERS WITH MODAL AUXILIARIES

 1 ► Listen to two police officers talk about a crime. Check (√) the picture that shows what they think happened.

 2 ► Listen to the conversation.
   ► Act out similar conversations with a partner. You are puzzled about one of the situations in the box. Your partner will help you come up with a possible explanation.

A You know, I tried to get hold of Mike all weekend, but the phone was always busy. He couldn't have been talking that whole time.
B Maybe the phone was off the hook.
A I suppose it might have been. Either that or it was out of order.

> Compare these short answers.
> *It might have been* (off the hook).
> *He might have* (taken it off the hook).

Some situations

You tried to get hold of Mike all weekend, but the phone was always busy. You know he couldn't have been talking that whole time.
Maria had promised to call you tonight, but she didn't. You were going to get together. You wonder what happened.
You got a vase in the mail today, but you don't know who it was from. You didn't buy it, and there was no name or address on the package.
You went over to Glen's after work, but no one was home. He knew you were coming, and you can't imagine why he wasn't there.

3 ► Study the frames: Short answers with modal auxiliaries

With forms of *be*		Without forms of *be*	
Maybe Eva's still at work.	**She can't be.**	Try to remember the robber.	**I can't.**
Do you think she's sleeping?	**She might be.**	I hope the police find him.	**They might not.**
Was Eva at home?	**She must not have been.**	Has Lee called the police?	**He must have.**
Was she expecting us?	**She should have been.**	Did he change the door lock?	**He should have.**

> When the complete sentence contains a form of *be*, the form of *be* is part of the short answer.
> She might *be* sleeping. → She might *be*.
> She must not have *been* at home. → She might not have *been*.

4 ► It's closing time and Hiro and Yoko Otani, who own a small stationery store, have just noticed that their cash box is missing. Complete their conversation, choosing the correct modal auxiliaries in parentheses.

Yoko Try to think of someplace we haven't looked.
Hiro I _____ (can't/couldn't/can't be). We've looked everywhere.
Yoko Well, I guess it was stolen then.
Hiro It _____ (will have been/must have been/must be). But I can't figure out how.
Yoko There were lots of people in here today. Do you remember if it was locked up?

Hiro It _____ (couldn't have been/should have/should have been), but perhaps Linda or Ken left it out by mistake. Do you think they're home yet? It's 5:45.
Yoko They _____ (will be/might not be/might not), but I could try calling them.
Hiro O.K. Maybe you'd better call the police, too.
Yoko I _____ (will/shouldn't/should have), but first I want to speak to Linda and Ken.

5 ► **Listen to the conversation.**

► **Act out similar conversations with a partner. Imagine you are a police officer who is questioning bystanders about several incidents. Your partner will play the role of the bystander and describe what he or she saw.**

A Excuse me, sir. We're looking for a red-haired woman who stole a white Toyota from Dan's Parking Lot a few minutes ago. Did you happen to see her?

B I don't believe so. But I did see a gray-haired woman riding a bike and holding a cat under her arm, which I thought was odd.

A The woman we're looking for, who we think had on a black skirt, was very tall and she was wearing glasses. . . .

Compare:
This woman, *who* . . .
This dog, *which* . . .

The police officer is looking for . . .	The bystander saw . . .
a red-haired woman who stole a white Toyota from Dan's Parking Lot. She was very tall and she was wearing glasses. She probably had on a black skirt.	a gray-haired woman riding a bike and holding a cat under her arm. It was an odd sight.
a little boy with a baseball bat who broke the window at Sims' bakery. He was wearing shorts and he had on a baseball hat. He probably had blond hair.	a little girl wearing a football uniform and carrying a tennis racket. It was an unusual sight.
a large dog that bit a man on the ankle. It was black and it had a white spot on its tail. It probably was wearing a leather collar.	a striped cat chasing a butterfly down the street. It was a funny sight.
a young man who walked out of Friendly Appliance Store with an electric iron under his raincoat. He was very heavy and he had a mustache. He was probably in his early twenties.	a young woman walk into Friendly Appliance Store with four toasters in her arms. It was a strange sight.

6 ► **Study the frames: Nonrestrictive vs. restrictive relative clauses**

Nonrestrictive relative clauses					
Relative pronouns as subjects			Relative pronouns as objects		
Amy Bing,	**who**	**looks so nice**,	stole a car.	That's Mr. Smith,	**who(m)**	**I told you about.**
That dog,	**which**	**is very mean**,	once bit me.	I miss my old car,	**which**	**I sold.**

Sometimes a relative pronoun may take the place of a subject or an object that is a whole clause or sentence.
    "Murder in Madrid" must not be on tonight, which is really odd.
    (Which = the fact that "Murder in Madrid" must not be on.)
	Whom is used when the relative pronoun is an object.
	    I told you about *him* (Mr. Smith).
	    That's Mr. Smith, *whom* I told you about.
	In everyday speech, *who* can also be used in these cases.

Nonrestrictive vs. restrictive relative clauses

Nonrestrictive clauses	Restrictive clauses

A nonrestrictive clause gives information that is *not* essential in order to identify the subject or object it refers to. Therefore, the clause is set off by commas.
    That dog, which is very mean, once bit me.
    That's Mr. Smith, who(m) you once met.
	A restrictive clause gives information that *is* essential in order to identify the subject or object it refers to. Therefore, the clause is not set off by commas.
	    The dog that bit me belongs to my neighbor.
	    The man who(m) you met at my house is my boss.

The pronouns *who* and *whom* are used to refer to people, and the pronoun *which* is used to refer to things.	The pronouns *who, whom*, and *that* are used to refer to people, and the pronoun *that* is used to refer to things.

GIVE A DESCRIPTION • NONRESTRICTIVE VS. RESTRICTIVE RELATIVE CLAUSES

- Have the students read over the conversation. Answer any questions. Then call on different students to read aloud the possible sentences in the boxes. Next point out the small box on the right and have two students read the contents aloud and complete the sentences.

- Have the students follow along in their books as you read aloud the second set of instructions. Then have the students work with a partner to act out similar conversations, using the information in the boxes.

- Go around the classroom and listen in as you check the students' work. Then call on different pairs to act out their conversations for the class.

- Have the students examine the frames as you read aloud the possible sentences and have the students repeat them after you. (See the Pronunciation Note which follows.)

- Read aloud the information in the boxes. Answer any questions students have about nonrestrictive and restrictive clauses.

PRONUNCIATION NOTE

Note and compare the intonation patterns of sentences with relative pronouns as subjects vs. those with relative pronouns as objects:

Nonrestrictive relative clauses

Amy/Bing, who looks so nice, stole a car.

That's Mr./Smith, who(m) I told you about.

Restrictive relative clauses

The dog that bit me belongs to my neighbor.

The man who(m) you met at my house is my boss.

OPTION

Tell the students to work in pairs. Have them write sentences like those in the frames but without the clauses. Then tell them to exchange papers and include clauses like those in the frames in their partners' sentences. Next have the students go over their sentences with their partners. Finally, call on different students to read their sentences aloud and write them on the board.

TELL A STORY • REACT TO A STORY • SPECULATE ABOUT POSSIBILITIES • NONRESTRICTIVE VS. RESTRICTIVE RELATIVE CLAUSES

- Have the students read over Millicent Berger's notes. Answer any questions they have about the vocabulary and structures.

- Ask a student to read aloud the instructions and the sample answer. Then tell the students to do the exercise.

- Have the students compare answers with a partner. Then call on different students to read aloud the rewritten sentences and write them on the board.

ANSWERS
Mr. Baldwin, who is the manager, has two assistants . . .
Upstairs is Mr. Baldwin's office, where the money is kept.
Sally Dupont, whom Mr. Baldwin dislikes, came . . .
Mr. Baldwin, who usually walks home for lunch, left . . .
Mr. Kumar offered to take Sally Dupont to a gallery that would probably agree to exhibit her work.
Miss Farkas said she was going to put away the money that the gallery had made that morning.
Mr. Baldwin, who usually returns at 1:00, came back unexpectedly at 12:40.
Mr. Kumar returned at 1:00 and couldn't open the door, which was locked.

- Read the instructions aloud. Answer any questions about the procedure. Then have the students work with a partner and follow the instructions.

- Call on different pairs to share their discussions with the class. You can take a vote to see how many students think the police arrested the right person. Then find if any students think the police should have arrested someone other than Sally Dupont.

OPTION

Have the students work in pairs to write their own versions of the end of the plot. Encourage them to use their imaginations. Tell them to begin their versions after the sentence *Before she left for lunch, she locked up the gallery.* Go around the room and answer any questions the pairs have about their writing. When they finish, have the pairs compare their versions with other pairs. Finally, call on different pairs to read aloud their versions.

- Read aloud the sample conversation with two students. Answer any questions. Work with the students to come up with possible ways to finish the sample conversation. Then have a student read aloud the instructions.

- Ask different students to read aloud the information in the boxes. Answer any questions. Then have the students work in groups of three to follow the instructions.

- Go around the room and listen in on the conversations, giving help if needed. Finally, call on different groups to act out their conversations for the class.

OPTION

Have the groups write their own situations. Then have them exchange papers with other groups. Next have the groups follow the exercise instructions; tell them to act out conversations based on the situations they received. Go around the room and listen in on the conversations. Finally, call on different groups to act out their conversations for the class. Give a prize for the most original conversation.

FOLLOW-UP

Students can write out the conversations they acted out in exercise 2.

7 ▶ **Millicent Berger, a famous mystery writer, is working out the plot for her latest book, *A Matter of Murder*. Rewrite her notes, combining each pair of sentences in brackets [ ] into one sentence with either a nonrestrictive or a restrictive relative clause.**

Start like this:

The Freeman Gallery, which is located in London, sells paintings and other art objects. . . .

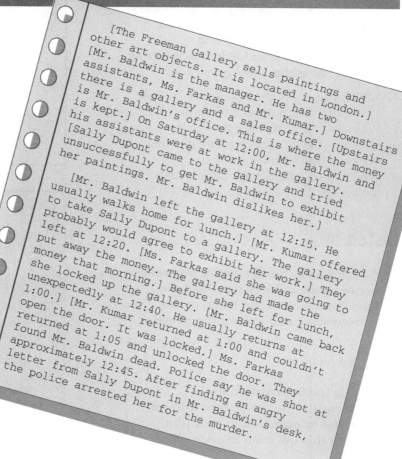

[The Freeman Gallery sells paintings and other art objects. It is located in London.] [Mr. Baldwin is the manager. He has two assistants, Ms. Farkas and Mr. Kumar.] Downstairs there is a gallery and a sales office. [Upstairs is Mr. Baldwin's office. This is where the money is kept.] On Saturday at 12:00, Mr. Baldwin and his assistants were at work in the gallery. [Sally Dupont came to the gallery and tried unsuccessfully to get Mr. Baldwin to exhibit her paintings. Mr. Baldwin dislikes her.] [Mr. Baldwin left the gallery at 12:15. He usually walks home for lunch.] [Mr. Kumar offered to take Sally Dupont to a gallery. The gallery probably would agree to exhibit her work.] They left at 12:20. [Ms. Farkas said she was going to put away the money. The gallery had made the money that morning.] Before she left for lunch, she locked up the gallery. [Mr. Baldwin came back unexpectedly at 12:40. He usually returns at 1:00.] [Mr. Kumar returned at 1:00 and couldn't open the door. It was locked.] Ms. Farkas returned at 1:05 and unlocked the door. They found Mr. Baldwin dead. Police say he was shot at approximately 12:45. After finding an angry letter from Sally Dupont in Mr. Baldwin's desk, the police arrested her for the murder.

8 ▶ **Now discuss Millicent Berger's notes with a partner. Do you think the police arrested the right person? Why or why not? Who do *you* think killed Mr. Baldwin? What do you think happened?**

9 ▶ **Imagine that one of the items mentioned in the box was stolen from you. Work in small groups and try to figure out what happened to it.**

A *All they took is the Picasso, which I think is pretty strange. What's more, I can't figure out how they got in here.*

B *It seems to me they must have climbed in through the window. After all, it was open.*

A *They couldn't have. Someone definitely would have seen them.*

C *Well, it had to be someone who knew you had the painting. Is there any possibility that . . . ?*

Some situations

You came home and found that a window was open. Your valuable Picasso painting was missing, but nothing else was taken. Your apartment faces the street, and it was still light out.

You are a history professor. Two days before final exams, one copy of the exam disappeared from your desk. You always lock your office door, but not your desk drawer, when you leave the office.

You are a lawyer attending a conference with the president of your company. While you were taking a shower, your briefcase, which contained confidential papers concerning your company's finances, was taken from your room. Your wallet and watch were not taken.

Some expressions

It seems to me (that) . . .
(Who) do you suppose . . . ?
Is there any possibility (that) . . . ?
It seems unlikely (that) . . . ?
It couldn't have been . . .

54. Your turn

Study the pictures carefully, and then work in groups to develop a plot for *Murder at the Villa*, a new murder mystery. Give each character a name and make notes about the personality and background of each one. When developing your story, consider these questions.

1. Which one of the characters was killed? Was more than one person murdered?
2. What was the motive for the murder?
3. How was the murder committed? What evidence was found at the scene?
4. Which of the characters committed the crime?

 Listen in

1. **A police officer and a police sergeant are discussing the crime. Read the question below. Then listen to the conversation and answer the question.**

   What evidence did the police officer find, and where did he find it?

2. **How is the information in the conversation you just heard different from the information in your plot? Discuss this question in your group.**

54. Your turn

- Read aloud the instructions as the students follow along in their books. Then call on different students to read aloud the exercise questions. Answer any questions students have. Make sure they know what a plot is.

- Point out the illustrations on pp. 116 and 117. Read aloud the captions on p. 117. Then ask different students to describe the illustrations.

- Have the students work in groups on the exercise. Encourage them to use their imaginations. Go around the room and listen in on the stories. Ask the group captains the names their groups gave the different characters pictured on p. 116.

- Call on different group members to tell the class their stories. Have them answer the exercise questions.

ANSWERS
Answers will vary.

Listen in

- Read aloud the instructions for the first exercise. Then ask a student to read aloud the question. Answer any questions.

- Have the students listen to the conversation as many times as necessary. Then tell them to answer the question on separate paper.

- Tell the students to compare answers with a partner. Then call on a student to read aloud the answer and write it on the board.

TAPESCRIPT

Police Officer It can't be . . . well, would you look at this . . . and of all places. I'd better call the sergeant right away.

Sergeant Sgt. Clemente here.

Police Officer Sergeant, this is Officer Peters.

Sergeant Yeah? Have you got anything new for me?

Police Officer Yes. We found something. And you'll never guess where . . . in a potted plant. Do you believe that? I don't know what made me look there, but . . . .

Sergeant All right, Peters, don't waste my time congratulating yourself. Just give me the facts. What is it?

Police Officer Oh, yeah . . . sorry, sir. It's a needle. A hypodermic needle.

Sergeant Hmmm. That *is* interesting.

Police Officer Yeah, it is. It's empty, but you can tell it's been used.

Sergeant Anything else?

Police Officer No, that's all, sir. What should I do with this needle?

Sergeant Send it on over to the lab, and let's see what was in it. Oh, and good work, Peters.

Police Officer Thanks, Sergeant. I . . . (*Click*)

ANSWER
The police officer found a hypodermic needle in a potted plant.

- Ask a student to read aloud the second set of instructions. Then have the students discuss the question in groups. Go around the classroom and listen in. Finally, call on different students to share their answers with the class.

FOLLOW-UP

Students can write down their answers to the
questions in the **Your turn** exercise.

WORKBOOK Lessons 53-54, pp. 67-69

a bottle of poison

a plant

a hypodermic needle

a bottle of wine

55. On your own

1. Choose one of the options below.

1. Write an account of your group's version of *Murder at the Villa*.
2. Write a short summary of a real mystery, such as a book you read or a movie you saw recently. Include what happened, how it happened, who did it, and why.

2. Think about a well-known crime that happened recently. Write a newspaper account, including as many details as possible.

FAMOUS PAINTING STOLEN

The modern art masterpiece "Exile," which was painted by Venezuelan artist Mariluz Calderón in 1973, has disappeared from the Patton Museum. Police speculate that it was stolen sometime early Saturday morning.

Investigators are looking for clues throughout the international art world. When asked if the motive for the theft was money, Police Chief Edward Singer said, "It must have been. We think the thieves will try to sell the painting, which our experts tell us is worth over one million dollars."

Police search the scene of the crime for clues after discovering the theft of the modern art masterpiece "Exile" Saturday morning.

55. On your own

- Have the students read over the different instructions for the first exercise. Answer any questions.

- Tell the students to write their accounts or summaries on separate paper. When they finish, have them compare their work with a partner. Finally, call on different students to read aloud their work and write it on the board. Alternatively, you can assign the exercise as homework.

- Read aloud the instructions for the second exercise. Then point out the newspaper article and tell the students they can use it as a model as they write their own newspaper accounts. Next ask two students to read the article aloud. Answer any questions.

- Have the students write their accounts in class or as homework. Go around the room and answer any questions they have about their work. Then have them compare accounts with a partner. Finally, call on different students to read their accounts aloud and write them on the board.

OPTION

Have the students work in small groups to solve the crime featured in the newspaper account on p. 118. Tell them to use their imaginations. After they've had time to discuss the imaginary solution, have them write a newspaper article about it. Go around the room and give help as needed. Finally, call on different group secretaries to read aloud their group's account.

WORKBOOK Lesson 55, p. 70. Before assigning the writing task, have two students read aloud the conversation. Then write a sample sentence on the board to show students how to report on Sergeant Blaine's investigation.

PREVIEW

Before you begin teaching, go over the functions/themes, language, and forms in the chart. This will give you a preview of what you will encounter as you guide the students through the unit.

Preview the reading.

- Read aloud the instructions for the first exercise. Then ask different students to describe the pictures. Next have the students work with a partner and follow the instructions.

- Go around the room and join in the discussions. Next call on different partners to share their answers with the class.

- Have a student read aloud the instructions for the second exercise. Then have the students work with a partner to follow the instructions. Next call on different pairs to share their guesses with the class.

CULTURE CLOSE-UP

Apart from numerous Native American dances, the first social dance explosion in the U.S. occurred with the introduction of the two-step in 1891. This dance was quickly followed by the cakewalk and ragtime dances of the late 19th and early 20th centuries. The early part of the 20th century also saw the adoption of the Argentine tango and the Brazilian maxixe, but Americans also created such dances as the castle walk, the fox-trot, and the jitterbug. The 1920s saw the arrival of jazz—people danced to Dixieland rhythms, the Charleston, and the Lindy hop. In the 1930s the Latin American rumba, conga, and samba became very popular. The American dance evolution was interrupted in the 1940s because of World War II, but the 1950s saw the arrival of the Latin American cha-cha and the merengue. The face of American dancing took on its most dramatic change in the mid-1950s with the introduction of rock 'n' roll and all its associated dance rhythms. With the 1960s came the bossa nova from Brazil and discotheque dancing, which produced many individualized, free-moving dances such as the twist, in which couples often danced without touching. By the 1970s, disco dancing had brought couples back together in carefully choreographed and often complex dance moves. Break dancing—street dancing that combines martial-arts movements and acrobatics—became popular in the 1980s, and the Brazilian lambada made a brief appearance in the 1990s. The 1990s also saw a new interest in country western dancing, which suddenly moved from its rural southern and western roots to urban America to compete in popularity with rock. Country western dancing takes the form of both coupled dances and the popular individual or "line" dancing, sometimes specially choreographed for a specific song.

UNIT 12 • LESSONS 56–60

FUNCTIONS/THEMES	LANGUAGE	FORMS
Talk about preferences Respond tactfully	Do you like modern dance? Actually, I'm not all that crazy about it. What I really like is folk dancing. There's a new exhibit of fifteenth-century Italian paintings at the museum. Maybe we ought to go there sometime. That might be interesting, but modern art is what I really like.	Special word order for emphasis
Give opinions	That sounds good, but what I'd really like to see sometime is an opera.	
Respond tactfully	There's nothing wrong with innovative styles, yet I'm personally more comfortable with a conservative look. Well, you might like it once you get used to it.	
Give a reaction	I love opera, whereas/while my husband can't stand it. He said he'd rather listen to a cat fight. How did you react when he said that? I just laughed it off.	Connectors *in spite of* and *despite; yet; nevertheless* and *nonetheless; whereas* and *while;* and *however* and *on the other hand*

Preview the reading.

1. Work with a partner. Discuss the different kinds of dances in the pictures below. Talk about the kinds of dances you like to watch and the kinds you like to do.

2. Before you read the article on pages 120–121, look at the title and the photos. Discuss with your partner what you think the article will tell you about Martha Graham.

56.

Martha Graham:
A SYNONYM FOR MODERN DANCE

by Anna Kisselgoff

The name Martha Graham is practically a synonym for the art form known as modern dance, which dates from her pioneering days as a dancer and a choreographer in the late 1920s. Often seen as a rebellion against the 350-year-old tradition of classical ballet, modern dance is the world's

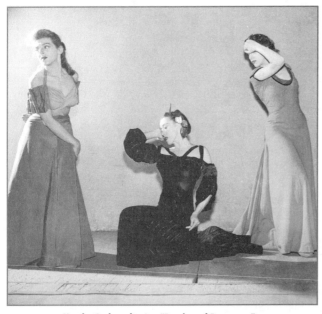

Martha Graham dancing "Primitive Mysteries."

Martha Graham dancing "Deaths and Entrances."

first lasting alternative to that tradition. Graham has rightly been called a genius and one of the greatest artists the United States has ever produced. When she died in 1991, at age 96, of heart failure following pneumonia, the dance world went into mourning.

Change was a major factor throughout Graham's career. In the early 1920s, Graham came to feel that the radical changes brought by World War I required a new and different style of dance. After attending a famous dance school in California called Denishawn, she and two other dancers made a dramatic break from the Denishawn dance company. In 1927, a reporter for the *New York Times* coined the term "Modern Dance" to describe their new and innovative style.

Graham's early dances of the 1930s were stark and simple; these contrast with the poetic theater pieces of the 1940s and even more sharply with the complex dance-dramas based on Greek mythology that characterized the 1950s and 1960s. In these, several performers would each portray different aspects of the same character's personality. Often, scenes from the past, present, and future would occur at the same time, making it impossible to distinguish clearly one period of time from another. Graham's later work, on the other hand, tended to be less complex. "The absolute thing is now," she said once. "Change is the only constant."

Yet, despite these changes, Graham always remained true to a basic belief that dance expresses emotion we often try to hide and cannot express in words. "I don't want to be understandable," she declared. "I want to be felt." Indeed, people who saw her dances often spoke of feeling enormously moved by what they didn't truly understand. As a child in Allegheny, Pennsylvania, Graham made a discovery that she later saw as related to her belief in the importance of expressing hidden emotion. One day her father invited her to look through a microscope. "My father," she recalled, "asked, 'What does it look like?' 'Water,' I said, 'clear water.' 'Yes, but what kind?' he asked. I said, 'There are wriggles in it.' And he said, 'Yes, it's impure. You must look for truth below the surface.'" Graham's dances are open to many interpretations, and like abstract painters, she invites the viewer to bring his or her emotions to the work, to complete the picture. She remembers being influenced by Wassily Kandinsky when, as as a young woman, she happened to see a painting of his—a slash of red against a field of blue—and decided, "I will dance like that."

Graham also focused throughout her career on certain themes. The theme of rebirth, for example, was a central one for her. This theme is evident in the dramatic series of

56. Martha Graham: A Synonym for Modern Dance

PROCEDURE

- Point out the photos and ask different students to read aloud the captions and describe what's happening.

- Have the students read through the article. Follow a procedure similar to that on p. 2 of this book. When the students have finished reading the article, ask them if they guessed correctly when they did exercise 2 on the previous page.

Figure it out

1. As you read the article, pay attention to the examples the author uses to support what she feels are Martha Graham's main ideas on dance.

- Have the students read the instructions and the exercise statements. Answer any questions students have. Then tell them to do the exercise.

- Tell the students to compare answers with a partner. Then call on different students to read aloud the example statements and the corresponding main ideas. Ask a student to write the answers on the board.

ANSWERS
1. b
2. c
3. a
4. b

2. Now look at a few of Martha Graham's quotes from the article.

- Read the instructions aloud. Then ask a student to read the quotes. Answer any questions. Then have the students do the exercise.

- Tell the students to compare answers with a partner. Then call on a student to say the answers and write them on the board.

ANSWERS
1. b
2. b
3. a

3. ...Complete the sentences by changing the verbs in parentheses to adjectives.

- Have the students follow the instructions and do the exercise.

- Tell the students to compare answers with a partner. Then call on different students to read aloud the completed sentences.

ANSWERS
1. preferable
2. creative
3. enjoyable
4. overprotective, active

OPTION

Tell the students to use the words in their answers in original sentences that show they know the meanings of the words. Have them write their sentences on separate paper. When they finish, tell them to compare sentences with a partner. Finally, call on different students to read aloud their sentences and write them on the board.

FOLLOW-UP

Students can write brief summaries of the article.

WORKBOOK Lesson 56, p. 71

falls to the floor that Graham invented, in which the dancer seems to sink backward. Graham described the fall as "a spring up to life." Another theme is that of defiance and conformity, as expressed in the early dance, "Heretic," in which a group of dancers in gray reject and punish a single dancer in white because she is different. Graham was also interested in themes of ritual, sexuality, and death. All her themes related ultimately to her desire to explore the human spirit.

Will Martha Graham's influence survive her? The answer is almost certainly yes. First of all, there is her repertoire of over 180 dances; second, the Martha Graham Dance Company continues to tour the United States and the world under the successors she picked; third, many of today's leading choreographers were once members of her dance company and acknowledge their debt to Martha Graham. But perhaps the most important reason her work will last is that she so successfully mixed her themes with her individuality and with self-discovery. Although her message is universal, her work is distinctive because, as she said, "It has to come from one person's experience. I have never been able to divorce the dancing from life."

Martha Graham, rehearsing a dancer to perform "Heretic" with the Martha Graham Dance Company.

Figure it out

1. **As you read the article, pay attention to the examples the author uses to support what she feels are Martha Graham's main ideas on dance. When you have finished, say which of the main ideas (*a, b,* or *c*) the author has tried to illustrate with each of the examples below.**

   a. Change is essential. Everything cannot always remain the same.
   b. Dance appeals to the viewer's hidden emotions, which are hard to express in words, and is open to more than one interpretation.
   c. Dance, like life with its rises and falls, is a continuous cycle of rebirth.

   1. Graham's early dance "Heretic."
   2. Graham's dramatic series of falls.
   3. The differences in the style of Graham's work over the years.
   4. Wassily Kandinsky's painting and her father's lesson.

2. **Now look at a few of Martha Graham's quotes from the article, and say which main idea listed in exercise 1 you think each quote expresses most closely.**

   1. "I don't want to be understandable. I want to be felt."
   2. "You must look for the truth below the surface."
   3. "The absolute thing is now. Change is the only constant."

3. **The suffixes *-able,* as in *understandable,* and *-ive,* as in *innovative,* are used to form many adjectives. Complete the sentences below by changing the verbs in parentheses to adjectives ending in either *-able* or *-ive.* Use your dictionary if necessary.**

   1. There are still many people who find classical ballet _____ (prefer) to modern dance.
   2. Juana is extremely _____ (create). She's written three novels.
   3. Nothing is more _____ (enjoy) than a relaxing day at the beach.
   4. The Stones are too _____ (overprotect) of their children. They should let them be more _____ (act).

57. What I really like is...

1. Praise something that you like very much, such as a kind of music, a musical group, an artist, a book, or a kind of food, and ask your partner how he or she likes it. Your partner should answer honestly. If your partner's preferences are different, he or she should try to respond without hurting your feelings.

 Rita has two tickets to see the Pilobolus Dance Theater, and she invites her friend Rick to go with her.

Listen to the conversation.

2

Rita I have two tickets to see the Pilobolus Dance Theater on Saturday. Would you like to go with me?

Rick Is that a ballet company? I love ballet.

Rita Well, this is more innovative. It combines mime, dance, and acrobatics.

Rick That sounds interesting, but do you think I'd enjoy it? What I really like is classical ballet.

Rita Well, as I said, this isn't ballet, yet it's so entertaining that I think you would like it.

Rick You're right. I don't want to sound like my brother Fred did at a ballet once.

Rita Why, what happened?

Rick Oh, it's just that I sat there spellbound, whereas *he* fell asleep. All he had to say afterwards was, "They looked like a bunch of frogs hopping around in nightgowns."

Rita Weren't you insulted?

Rick No, I just laughed it off. Fred's always been tactless. But I'll be glad to go with you to see this other group.

Rita Good. And we can have dinner at that new Tex-Mex place.

Rick What's that?

Rita It's the kind of Mexican food they make in southern Texas. It's pretty spicy, because they use lots of chile peppers.

Rick Hmm . . . Well, I guess it wouldn't hurt to give it a try. Traditional American food is what I prefer—you know, hamburgers and french fries—but I suppose it's good to try new things every once in a while.

3. Say *Tactful* or *Tactless*.

1. The Pilobolus Dance Theater sounds interesting, but what I really like is classical ballet.
2. I really can't stand Tex-Mex food.
3. Ballet dancers look like a bunch of frogs hopping around in nightgowns.
4. I guess it wouldn't hurt to give it a try.
5. Actually, ballet isn't my favorite kind of dance. Flamenco dancing is what I really love.

57. What I really like is . . .

1. Warm-up Activity

- Read aloud the instructions in the box. Then have the students work with a partner and follow the instructions.

- Go around the classroom and listen in to check the pairs' work. Then call on different pairs to act out their conversations for the class.

2. Conversation

BACKGROUND

Rita has two tickets to see the Pilobolus Dance Theater, and she invites her friend Rick to go with her. Rick accepts and tells Rita about a bad experience he had with his brother Fred.

LANGUAGE

...this is more innovative. is short for *the Pilobolus Dance Theater is more innovative.*

...yet (it's so entertaining) means *but (it's so entertaining).*

All (he had to say) means *The only thing (he had to say).*

...laughed it off is an idiomatic expression meaning *ignored it.*

...lots of is another way of saying "a lot of."

...give it a try is another way of saying "try it out."

...you know is used to confirm or establish something as fact.

...once in a while. means *occasionally.*

PROCEDURE

- As the students examine the illustration, point out the characters from the conversation. Ask a student to describe what's going on in the thought bubble.

- Follow a procedure similar to that indicated for the opening conversation in Unit 1.

3. Say *Tactful* or *Tactless*.

- Read the instructions aloud. Answer any questions about the procedure. Make sure the students know the meaning of the words *Tactful* and *Tactless*. Then have them read over the exercise items. Answer any questions.

- Have the students do the exercise. When they finish, tell them to compare answers with a partner. Then call on a student to say the answers.

ANSWERS
1. Tactful
2. Tactless
3. Tactless
4. Tactful
5. Tactful

FOLLOW-UP

Students can write down their own opinions about ballet.

WORKBOOK Lesson 57, p. 72

58. That might be interesting, but . . .

Tell the students about your favorite entertainment preferences. Then call on different students to tell the class about their entertainment likes and dislikes. For example:

I just love to attend jazz concerts, but I really don't like rock concerts at all.

> TALK ABOUT PREFERENCES • RESPOND TACTFULLY • SPECIAL WORD ORDER FOR EMPHASIS

- Have the students read over the conversation. Next have two students act out the conversation for the class. Then point out the box and have the students repeat the possible questions after you.

- Ask a student read aloud the second set of instructions. Then have the students work with a partner to act out similar conversations, using the information in the box. Remind the students to give their true opinions.

- Go around the room and listen in to check the pairs' work. Then call on different pairs to act out their conversations for the class.

- Read the instructions aloud. Then have the students listen and check the appropriate column.

- Have the students compare answers. Then you can have them listen again to check their answers. Finally, ask a student to say the answers and write them on the board.

TAPESCRIPT

1. **Man** Guess what! I have free passes for the sneak preview of a new Roger Valenti movie this Friday night. How would you like to go with me?

    Woman Roger Valenti, hmm? To tell you the truth, I really haven't enjoyed his last few movies. But Helen loves Roger Valenti. Why don't you ask her, and I'll meet you both for dinner afterwards?

2. **A** My daughter's second grade class is performing a play tonight. Would you like to come? It should be adorable!

    B Are you kidding? Why would I want to watch a bunch of kids trying to put on a play? It sounds really boring.

3. **Woman** Do you like folk music?

    Man No, I can't stand it. Why?

    Woman Oh . . . I just thought . . . I mean, there's a great folk guitarist performing at the coffee shop this weekend. I thought you might like to go with me.

    Man Not me. I only like classical music.

4. **A** I've been dying to hear this lecture on colonial days in the United States, and now Marie can't go with me this afternoon. Want to join me?

    B That might be interesting, but I had planned to go to the baseball game this afternoon, and you know what I really love is sports. Let me think. . . . O.K., how about if I go to the lecture with you, and you come to the night game with me tonight?

    A Sounds great. We'd better hurry if we don't want to be late.

5. **Man** There's an exhibit of modern abstract paintings at the museum. Want to go sometime?

    Woman I wouldn't mind seeing it, but you know folk art is what I really like.

    Man Then you're in luck. There's also an exhibit of handcarved American dolls from the nineteenth century. We can see both.

    Woman Wonderful! It's a date.

ANSWERS

	TACTFULLY	TACTLESSLY
1.	✓	
2.		✓
3.		✓
4.	✓	
5.	✓	

- Tell the students to read over the conversation. Answer any questions. Next have the students listen to the conversation. You can also read it aloud with a student.

- Point out the top part of the box and ask different students to read aloud the possible sentences. Then have the students read over the lower part of the box. Answer any questions.

- Read aloud the second set of instructions. Answer any questions about the procedure. Then tell the students to work with a partner to act out similar conversations.

- Go around the room and check the pairs' conversations. Then call on different pairs to act out their conversations in front of the class.

- Have the students examine the frames as you and some class members read aloud the headings and sentences. You can read aloud the sentences on the left and have different students read aloud the corresponding sentences on the right. Answer any questions about the structures.

- Have the students work with a partner to make up their own sentences to match those in the frame. (See the Option which follows.)

OPTION

Tell the students to work in pairs. Have one partner write down a sentence modeled after one on the left side of the frames. Tell the other partner to read the sentence and write a corresponding version like those on the right side of the frames. Next have the partners switch roles. After that, tell the partners to check one another's sentences. Finally, call on different pairs to read aloud their sentences and write them on the board.

58. That might be interesting, but...

1 ► Listen to the two possible conversations.
► Act out similar conversations with a partner. Give your true opinions.

A Do you like modern dance?

B Yes, I do. In fact, the dance group I like best is Pilobolus.

B Actually, I'm not all that crazy about it. What I really like is folk dancing.

Do you like . . .	
modern dance?	science fiction?
ballet?	rock music?
murder mysteries?	jazz?
music videos?	opera?

2 ► Listen to the conversations. Does the second speaker respond *tactfully* or *tactlessly*? Check (√) the correct column.

TACTFULLY   TACTLESSLY

1. _____   _____
2. _____   _____
3. _____   _____
4. _____   _____
5. _____   _____

3 ► Listen to the conversation.
► Act out similar conversations. Your partner will suggest an activity from the box. Respond tactfully. If the activity does not appeal to you, be sure not to hurt your partner's feelings.

A There's a new exhibit of fifteenth-century Italian paintings at the museum. Maybe we ought to go there sometime.
B That might be interesting, but modern art is what I really like.
A Oh, really? I guess I'm rather traditional. Modern art doesn't appeal to me too much.

You've heard that . . .
there's a new exhibit of fifteenth-century Italian paintings at the museum.
the Pilobolus Dance Theater is going to be at the Cultural Center for a week.
Julio Iglesias is going to perform at the Bijou Theater.
there's a terrific seven-day tour of Great Britain advertised in the newspaper.

Some tactful responses
That might be interesting, but _____ is what I really like.
Actually, I don't really care for _____ too much. _____ is what I really like.
I wouldn't mind seeing _____ , but _____ is who I actually prefer.
To tell you the truth, _____ doesn't really appeal to me. _____ is where I'd rather go.

4 ► Study the frames:
Special word order for emphasis

Noun clauses as subjects			
I'd like to hear	jazz.	What I'd like to hear	**is jazz.**
I want to go	to Greece.	Where I want to go	**is Greece.**
I want to see	Julio Iglesias.	Who I want to see	**is Julio Iglesias.**

subject

Noun clauses as subject complements			
I'd like to hear	jazz.	**Jazz is**	what I'd like to hear.
I want to go	to Greece.	**Greece is**	where I want to go.
I want to see	Julio Iglesias.	**Julio Iglesias is**	who I want to see.

subject complement

Unit 12 **123**

5 ▶ **Restate the conversation, changing the sentences in brackets [ ] to give them more emphasis. Each sentence may be restated in two different ways.**

A A new play is opening at the National Theater. It's a musical. We'll have to see it.
B That sounds good, but [I'd really like to see an opera sometime.]
A I don't know. In musicals, [you hear lively music.] Music you can remember and sing. I think opera is kind of dull.
B How do you know? You've never been to one!

A Well, that may be, but [I'd still rather go to that new musical.] The problem with opera is that you can't understand any of the words.
B [You need a translation.]
A Well, maybe, but . . .
B Listen, I can't stand the fact that we never do anything different. Maybe *we're* dull.
A Well, O.K. But if I have to go, [I'd really like to hear Placido Domingo.]

A *A new play . . .*
B *That sounds good, but what I'd really like to see sometime is an opera.* or
That sounds good, but an opera is what I'd really like to see sometime.

RESPOND TACTFULLY

6 ▶ **Listen to the conversation.**
▶ **Act out similar conversations with a partner. You are enthusiastic about modern things, but your partner is more conservative. Respond tactfully to his or her opinions.**

A Would you ever consider getting a tattoo?
B Me? Never. There's nothing wrong with innovative styles, yet I'm personally more comfortable with a conservative look.
A Well, you might like it once you get used to it. I wasn't sure about it myself at first, but now I think it's a great look.

Some questions

Would you ever consider getting a tattoo?
What do you think of ultramodern architecture?
Isn't abstract painting just great?
Why don't we take a Thai cooking class?

Some opinions

You like conservative styles.
You think Notre Dame is the most beautiful building in the world.
You think Renaissance painting is much more appealing.
You prefer other styles of cooking.

Some tactful responses

You might like it once you get used to it.
I wasn't sure about it myself at first, but now I think it's a great look.
Try it, you'll like it.
It's not for everyone.
It's not your cup of tea, I guess.
It takes time getting used to.

GIVE OPINIONS • SPECIAL WORD ORDER FOR EMPHASIS

- Have the students read over the conversation. Answer any questions about the vocabulary and structures.

- Read the instructions aloud. Then point out the sample answer in italics and ask two students to read aloud A's complete line and B's line.

- Tell the students to do the exercise. When they finish, have them compare answers with a partner. Then call on different pairs to read aloud the exchanges and write the answers on the board.

ANSWERS

A . . . what you hear is lively music./ . . . lively music is what you hear.

A . . . what I'd still rather go to is that new musical./ . . . that new musical is what I'd still rather go to.

B What you need is a translation./A translation is what you need.

A . . . who I'd really like to hear is Placido Domingo./Placido Domingo is who I'd really like to hear.

OPTION

Tell the pairs to make up conversations of their own modeled after the one in the exercise. Remind them to use special word order for emphasis. Tell the pairs to write their conversations down and then practice them. Finally, call on different pairs to act out their conversations for the class. Give a prize to the pair that presents the most grammatically correct conversation.

RESPOND TACTFULLY

- Point out the illustration and the man's tattoo. Then tell the students to read through the conversation. Next have them listen to it. Answer any questions.

- Point out the boxes and have the students read the headings and different sentences. You can also have the students repeat the sentences after you or call on different students to read the sentences aloud.

- Have the students follow the second set of instructions and act out similar conversations with a partner. Remind them to use the information in the boxes or their own information.

- Go around the room and listen in on the conversations, giving help when needed. Then call on different pairs to act out their conversations for the class.

- Have the students read over the conversation. Answer any questions. Next have the students listen to the conversation.

- Point out the boxes and have different students read aloud the headings and sentences. Answer any questions.

- Read aloud the second set of instructions. Then tell the students to work with a partner to act out similar conversations. Remind them to refer to the sentences in the boxes when making up their conversations.

- Go around the classroom and listen in on the conversations, giving help as necessary. Then call on different pairs to act out their conversations for the class.

- Have the students examine the frames as you and some class members read aloud the possible sentences. Answer any questions about the vocabulary and the connectors.

OPTION

Write the sentence parts from the left side of the frames on separate slips of paper. Then write the remaining parts of the sentences from the right side on other slips of paper. For example:

On one slip, write:
I really didn't like that movie

On another slip, write:
in spite of the good reviews.

Mix up the slips and hand them to different pairs or small groups of students to match. Refer the students to the frames to check their work.

- Tell the students to read over Christie's letter. Answer any questions.

- Have the students follow the instructions and rewrite Christie's letter. When they finish, tell the students to compare answers with a partner. Then call on different students to read aloud the sentences from the letter and write the answers on the board.

ANSWERS

whereas/while, yet, Nevertheless/Nonetheless, however/on the other hand, in spite of/despite, in spite of/despite

OPTION

Tell the students to write letters to a partner about some place they've visited. Tell them to include as many of the connectors from exercise 8 in their letters as possible. Go around the room and answer any questions students have about their work. When they finish writing, have them give their letters to their partners to read. Next you can call on different students to read the letters they received and write them on the board.

FOLLOW-UP

Students can write personal answers to the questions in the box in exercise 1. Tell them to write down reasons for their answers.

7 ▶ **Listen to the conversation.**
▶ **Act out similar conversations with a partner. You don't agree with the opinions in the box. Discuss your reactions to these people's blunt remarks with your partner.**

A I love opera, | whereas / while | my husband can't stand it.

He said he'd rather listen to a cat fight.
B How did you react when he said that?
A Well, I just laughed it off. People have a right to their opinions.

B | Nevertheless, / Nonetheless, | I think they should be more

open-minded.

Some opinions
Your husband said he'd rather listen to a cat fight than an opera.
Your wife says she can't stand abstract painting. She thinks any five year old could do better.
Your friend thinks modern architecture is horrible. He/She said new buildings all look like cereal boxes.

Some reactions to blunt remarks
I found it offensive/rude.
I considered it an insult/insulting.
I found it amusing.
I just laughed it off.

8 ▶ **Study the frames: Connectors *in spite of* and *despite; yet; nevertheless* and *nonetheless; whereas* and *while;* and *however* and *on the other hand***

I really didn't like that movie	**in spite of** / **despite**	the good reviews.
The acting was excellent,	**yet**	I was still disappointed.
I wouldn't recommend the movie.	**Nevertheless, Nonetheless,**	I'm not sorry I went.
The heroine was perfect for her role,	**whereas** / **while**	the hero was completely miscast.
The acting was excellent. The subject,	**however, on the other hand,**	was boring.

9 ▶ **Christie, an American teenager, is visiting relatives in Germany during her summer vacation. Rewrite her letter to her parents, completing the sentences with appropriate connectors from exercise 8. All items but one have two answers.**

July 23

Dear Mom and Dad,

Wait till I tell you where I've been. You know how Uncle Karl and Aunt Marlene love opera, _____ I have never been able to stand it. Well, they decided to take me to the Wagner Festival in Bayreuth! I really didn't want to go, _____ I didn't want to say anything to hurt their feelings. I wasn't looking forward to sitting through days and days of opera. _____ , I actually enjoyed the whole trip.

The city is full of fantastic eighteenth-century buildings, and the festival theater is beautiful. The singers were really good and some of the music wasn't bad, either. The operas, _____ , were too long for me. I don't think I'd want to go again _____ the good time I had. I'll take a rock concert any day!

All our relatives here send you their love. I miss you both a lot _____ the fact that I'm having such a great time.

Love,
Christie

59. Your turn

1. Look at the posters advertising the different events, and look at the pictures of the people and the information about them. Then, working in groups, discuss these questions.

1. Which event would each of these people probably prefer to attend the most? Why?
2. Suppose each of these people asked your group to go to the event with him or her. Which events would you want to go to and why? Which ones would you not want to go to and why not?

2. Work with a partner and discuss the event or events you would never go to. What would you say if someone invited you to one of them?

🔈 Listen in

Bart is talking to a friend about one of the events in the posters. Listen to the conversation and then say which event Bart is talking about.

Great Rivers of the World
LECTURE

Thursday, October 9, 8:00 P.M.
Public Library, Main Branch

Illustrated with color slides from five continents

Ancient Instruments

An Exhibition at the University School of Music

Including instruments from the Roman Empire through medieval times. On display will be a sistrum, a lyre, a viola da gamba, a cithara, a harpsichord, and many more.

Starts Tuesday, Noon to 7:00 P.M.

Rosa is a retired legal secretary who spends her time playing music on a variety of instruments. She composes the music herself.

Martin is a scholar who is interested in geography and history and would like to be a professor someday.

59. Your turn

- Read aloud the boldfaced instructions as the students follow along in their books. Then call on different students to read aloud the information on the posters and the captions under the pictures of the people. Answer any questions.

- Read aloud the two exercise items as the students follow along in their books. Answer any questions about the procedure. Then have the students work in groups to discuss the questions. (See the Option which follows.)

- Go around the room and listen in on the discussions as you check the students' work. Finally, call on different group members to share their answers with the class.

OPTION

Have different group members take turns playing the role of the various characters featured in the pictures. For example, tell a female group member to pretend she is Rosa. Have her try to convince the group to go with her to the exhibition of ancient instruments.

- Have the students follow the second set of instructions. You can tell them to invite their partner to some of the events and to refuse their partner's invitation. Remind them to refuse tactfully.

- Go around the room and listen in. Then call on different pairs to act out their discussions or conversations for the class.

POSSIBLE ANSWERS

1. Rosa: The exhibition of ancient instruments because she plays a variety of instruments herself.

   Martin: The film preview of a new documentary on the Spanish Civil War because he is interested in history.
   The lecture on "Great Rivers of the World" because he's interested in geography.

   Janice: The Midnight Musical Cruise and possibly the rock opera because she likes to dance.

   Juan: The lecture on "Great Rivers of the World" because the lecture will feature color slides.
   The new documentary on the Spanish Civil War because it contains rare historical photographs.

2. Answer will vary.

Listen in

- Read the instructions aloud as the students follow along in their books. Then have them listen to the conversation as many times as necessary.

- Call on a student to tell the class which event Bart is talking about. You can ask different students why the correct answer is *the rock opera*.

TAPESCRIPT

Friend So, did you have a good time at your cousin's?

Bart Yeah, on the whole I had a very nice visit, in spite of the fact that we like such different things—but then, Tony is younger than I am.

Friend Not much.

Bart Well, maybe not *much* younger, but I'm just more . . . I don't know . . . conservative than he is.

Friend Yeah, you are pretty conservative.

Bart Well, anyway, he took me to this . . . this show—I don't know how to describe it. It was really weird. I never did figure out what was happening. It wasn't really boring; there was too much going on. But there was a lot of loud music, and half the time you couldn't understand what anybody was saying. There were a lot of weird people in the audience, too. But you know Tony.

Friend Did Tony enjoy himself?

Bart Oh, yeah. He thought it was great. Actually, I told him I thought it was very interesting, too. I knew he'd be disappointed if I said I didn't like it.

Friend Well, that was nice of you, at least.

Bart Yeah, I know.

Friend So, what was this show about? . . .

ANSWER
The rock opera.

CULTURE CLOSE-UP

Dixieland jazz was the first type of jazz to become popular throughout the U.S. It became the music craze of dance halls and theaters in the 1920s and is still popular today. Its original star musicians were African Americans such as King Oliver and his Creole Jazz Band and the famous trumpet player and singer Louis Armstrong. Dixieland is characterized by its unwritten forms—improvised rhythms which are a complex interweaving of melodic lines featuring the trumpet or coronet, clarinet, trombone, and a steady chomp-chomp beat from the rhythm instruments—piano, bass, and drums. The texture of the music is polyphonic.

FOLLOW-UP

Students can write down their own answers to the item 2 questions in the first **Your turn** exercise.

WORKBOOK Lessons 58-59, pp. 73-75

MIDNIGHT MUSICAL CRUISE

Live Dixieland Jazz Band

Departs from Seaside Wharf for a cruise of the upper and lower bay

Breakfast provided at sunrise

**Saturday night, October 11
Call 555-4198 for reservations.**

Rock Opera
LIVE PERFORMANCE OF A NEW ROCK OPERA

Featuring Local Performers

Municipal Auditorium
People in costume
admitted free

Oct. 10–17, 8:00 P.M.
No advance reservations.
Tickets on sale
from 6:00 P.M. on

FILM PREVIEW
NEW DOCUMENTARY ON THE SPANISH CIVIL WAR

Featuring rare film clips and stills
Sponsored by the Discovery History Club
Soundtrack features Spanish folk songs of the era

Tuesday night, October 7 • One performance only

Call 555-8062
Tickets are limited.

Janice works very hard at an import-export business. What little spare time she has she likes to spend fishing. She also likes to dance.

Juan is a photographer who has traveled around the world on assignments. He also has a large collection of historical photographs.

60. On your own

1. **Answer the letter. Respond tactfully as you tell your friends your preferences.**

> Dear _____,
>
>   It was great talking to you on the phone the other evening. We're really happy you can spend the weekend with us. We plan to have a lot of fun—just like we used to have when we all lived in the same city. Here are some of the things we think you might be interested in doing with us:
>
> • Attend the Classic Film Festival sponsored by the Film Club at our local community college. We can see four films in one day!
> • Watch the annual Kitty Beauty Pageant at the downtown mall. They give prizes to the best groomed and most originally dressed cats.
> • Go camping in Moorland Forest, about twenty miles north of us. Although it might get a little cold at night, we can build a nice big fire and take warm clothes with us.
> • Watch the annual fireworks display as we listen to the city band play. That's in Central Park. We can take a picnic supper and sit on a blanket and eat as we enjoy the show.
> • Stay home one night so you can watch the slides of our vacation to Lazy Lake. We must have taken a hundred of them!
>
>   How's that sound to you? Write and let us know your preferences.
>
>   See you soon,
>
>   Sally & Chris

2. **Sometimes we accept invitations to do things or to go places, just to be polite, so we don't hurt other people's feelings. Write about an experience you didn't enjoy, but which you felt obligated to participate in.**

60. On your own

PROCEDURE

- Have the students read through the letter. Answer any questions about the vocabulary and structures.

- Read the instructions aloud and have the students answer the letter. Go around the room and answer any questions they have about their work.

- Tell the students to compare their letters with a partner. Then call on different students to read their letters aloud and write them on the board.

CULTURE CLOSE-UP

Pet dogs and cats in the U.S. probably outnumber children. Americans can become very attached to their pets even to the point of enrolling them in "beauty contests" or shows. Throughout the U.S., there are pet shows where dogs or cats are specially groomed and sometimes even dressed up to be paraded in front of judges who pick the winners.

- Ask a student to read the instructions for the second exercise aloud as the class members follow along in their books. Then point out the illustration and ask a student to describe what's happening.

- Tell the students to write about their experiences on separate paper. When they finish, have them compare their work with a partner.

- Go round the room and answer any questions students have about their work. Finally, call on different students to read aloud their accounts. If appropriate, have them write their accounts on the board.

OPTION

Assign the second exercise for homework. Tell the students to use appropriate drawings or pictures to accompany their accounts. After you've marked their papers and had them make any needed corrections, display the students' work for the entire class to enjoy.

WORKBOOK Lesson 60, p. 76. Before assigning the writing task, ask different students to point out the ways in which Karen's letter is tactful. Remind the students to be tactful in their letters.

Review of units 7-12

■ Read the instructions aloud. Then ask different students to read the exercise items aloud. Answer any questions.

■ Tell the students to read the article. You can also have them listen to is as they read. Answer any questions about the vocabulary and structures.

■ Have the students do the exercise. Then tell them to compare and discuss their answers with a partner. Next call on a student to read the answers aloud.

ANSWERS
1. North American
2. Brazilian
3. North American
4. Brazilian
5. North American

OPTION 1

If there are any Brazilian students in the class or if any students have visited Brazil for an extended period of time, have them discuss the article with the class. Encourage them to express their opinions and point out any information in the article which they strongly agree or disagree with.

OPTION 2

Have the students discuss the attitudes toward time which exist in their countries. Go around the room and listen in on the discussions. Then call on different students to discuss the different attitudes with the class.

Review of units 7-12

1 ▶ As you read the article, pay attention to the differences between Brazilian and North American students in their attitudes toward time. Then, based on the information in the article, decide whether the speaker in each of these items is Brazilian or North American.

1. "I'd like to help you, but I can't or I'll be late for class."

2. "I can probably meet you around 1:00. It depends on what time my class ends today."

3. "I don't think Marisa will have much success as a lawyer. She's never on time for anything."

4. "I'm supposed to be at Sylvia's for dinner in five minutes. I guess I'd better start getting dressed."

5. "Marvin used to always keep me waiting—in front of the theater or restaurant, or wherever we went—so I stopped going out with him."

SOCIAL TIME: The Heartbeat of Culture

BY ROBERT LEVINE WITH ELLEN WOLFF

"If a man does not keep pace with his companions, perhaps it is because he hears a different drummer." This thought by Thoreau strikes a chord in so many people that it has become part of our language. We use the phrase "the beat of a different drummer" to explain any pace of life unlike our own. Such colorful vagueness reveals how informal our rules of time really are. The world over, children simply "pick up" their society's time concepts as they mature. No dictionary clearly defines the meaning of "early" or "late" for them or for strangers who stumble over the maddening differences between the time sense they bring with them and the one they face in a new land.

I learned this firsthand, a few years ago, when I accepted an appointment as visiting professor of psychology at the federal university in Niterói, Brazil. On my first day of class I arrived to find an empty room. The class was scheduled from 10:00 until noon. Many students came late, some very late. Several arrived after 10:30. A few showed up closer to 11:00. Two came after that. All of the latecomers wore the relaxed smiles that I came, later, to enjoy. Each one said hello, and although a few apologized briefly, none seemed terribly concerned about lateness. They assumed that I understood.

The real surprise, however, came at noon that first day, when the end of class arrived. Back home in California, I never need to look at a clock to know when the class hour is ending. The shuffling of books is accompanied by strained expressions that say plaintively, "I'm going to die if you keep us one more second." When noon arrived in my first Brazilian class, only a few students left immediately. Others slowly drifted out during the next 15 minutes, and some continued asking me questions long after that.

Are Brazilians simply more flexible in their concepts of time and punctuality? With the assistance of colleagues Laurie West and Harry Reis, I compared the time sense of 91 male and female students in Niterói with that of 107 similar students at California State University in Fresno. When we asked students to give typical reasons for lateness, the Brazilians were less likely to say it was caused by not caring than the North Americans were. Instead, they pointed to unpredictable events that the person couldn't control. Because they seemed less likely to feel personally responsible for being late, they also expressed less regret for their own lateness and blamed others less when they were late.

We found similar differences in how students from the two countries talked about people who were late for appointments. Unlike their North American counterparts, the Brazilian students believed that a person who is consistently late is probably more successful than one who is consistently on time. They seemed to accept the idea that someone of importance is expected to arrive late, and they saw lack of punctuality as a sign of success.

Formal "clock time" may be a standard on which the world agrees, but "social time," the heartbeat of culture, is something else again. How a country paces its social life is a mystery to most outsiders. When we realize we are out of step, we often blame the people around us to make ourselves feel better.

Appreciating cultural differences in people's sense of time becomes increasingly important as modern technology puts more and more people in daily contact. If we are to avoid misunderstandings that involve time perceptions, we need to understand better our own cultural biases and those of others.

2 ▶ Rewrite the paragraphs, completing the sentences with the connectors in the box. Some items have two answers.

> despite
> however
> in spite of
> nevertheless
> nonetheless
> on the other hand
> whereas
> while
> yet

_____ the fact that both Brazilians and North Americans use the standard twelve-hour clock, they have a very different sense of social time. Both Brazilian and North American university students have fixed class schedules, _____ the words "early" and "late" do not have the same meaning in both countries. For example, Brazilian students are casual about arriving exactly on time for class, _____ North American students are very punctual. North Americans see being late for appointments as a sign of a disorganized, unsuccessful person. Brazilians, _____, are likely to consider being late a sign of a busy, successful person.

Robert Levine, the author of an article on social time, was surprised at first by his students' lateness; _____ , he later came to appreciate their relaxed attitudes. Understanding cultural differences makes it possible for people to understand each other and work together _____ cultural biases.

3 ▶ John gives Mike a ride to class every morning, but Mike is always late. Restate their conversation, combining the sentences in brackets [ ] into one sentence that contains an infinitive or gerund with a subject.

John Come on, Mike. [You're late every morning. I'm tired of it.]
Come on, Mike. I'm tired of your being late every morning.

Mike I wish you wouldn't keep telling me that. [People always nag me. I don't like it.]

John Well, [you keep me waiting every day. I don't like that.]

Mike I know, but [people hurry me so much. I'm not used to it.] And [classes start right on time. I'm not accustomed to that,] either.

John I realize that. And [you're getting mad at me. I don't want that,] but we really have to be on time for class here.

4 ▶ Comment on each of the situations below, starting your sentences with *By then* . . . or *By the time* . . . and using the clues in parentheses. Use a future perfect or future perfect continuous form of each verb.

1. Your aunt, who is going overseas for three years, won't be able to see your new apartment before she leaves. (I/live/for three years)
By the time my aunt sees my new apartment, I will have been living in it for three years.

2. You're going to a lecture from 8:00 to 9:30. Your friend Tony wants to go but he has a class until 8:30. (he/miss/more than a half hour)

3. You and your friends are taking part in a clean-up day in your neighborhood from noon until 6:00 P.M. Your friend Susana can't make it until 4:00. (we/work/for four hours)

4. There are two soccer games on Saturday, the first one at 1:00 and the second one at 3:00. You're going to both games, but your friend Hector doesn't get off work until 2:30. (the first game/end)

- Have the students repeat the connectors in the box after you. Then have them read the paragraphs. Answer any questions.

- Tell the students to follow the instructions and complete the paragraph. When they finish. have them compare answers with a partner. Then call on different students to read aloud the sentences from the paragraph and write the answers on the board.

ANSWERS

Despite/in spite of, yet, whereas/while, on the other hand/however, nevertheless/nonetheless, despite/ in spite of

OPTION

Have the students write sentences of their own containing the different connectors from the box. Encourage them to write about the class or their surrounding environment. When they finish, tell them to compare sentences with a partner. Finally, call on different students to read aloud their sentences and write them on the board.

- Have the students read over the conversation. Then read aloud the sample answer. Answer any questions.

- Tell the students to follow the instructions and restate the conversation. When they finish, have them compare answers with a partner.

- Call on a pair of students to read aloud the restated conversation. Ask other students to write the answers on the board. Then you can have all the pairs act out the restated conversation.

ANSWERS

I don't like people to nag me.
. . . I don't like your keeping me waiting every day.
. . . I'm not used to people hurrying me so much.
. . . I'm not accustomed to classes starting right on time.
. . . I don't want you to get mad at me.

OPTION

Tell the pairs to continue the conversation with their own lines. Encourage them to role play the situation to include a longer discussion of the problem of Mike's always being late and a possible solution. Suggest that they write the additional lines down on paper and then practice them. When they finish, call on different pairs to act out their conversations for the class. Give a prize for the most original continuation.

- Have the students read over the situations. Then read aloud the sample answer. Answer any questions.

- Tell the students to follow the instructions and comment to a partner on each of the situations. Go around the room and listen in, giving help if needed.

- Call on different pairs; have one partner read aloud the situation and the other the comment. Ask different students to write the answers on the board.

ANSWERS

2. By the time he gets there, he will have missed more than a half hour.
3. By then we will have been working for four hours.
4. By the time he gets there, the first game will have ended.

OPTION

Have the students work in pairs to come up with an additional exercise item modeled after the ones in their books. Go around the room and answer any questions they have about their work. When they finish, have the pairs exchange items with other pairs and write comments for the items they receive. Finally, call on different pairs to read aloud their additional items.

5

- Read the instructions aloud as the students follow along in their books. Then ask different students to read the four questions aloud. Answer any questions.

- Tell the students to read the story. You can also have them listen to it as they read it. You might suggest that they write down or underline any vocabulary items or structures which they don't understand. When they finish reading, answer any questions about the vocabulary or structures.

- Have the students follow the instructions and answer the questions. Then have them compare and discuss their answers with a partner. Go around the room and join in the discussions. Finally, call on different students to share their answers with the class.

SAMPLE ANSWERS
1. Todd is probably serious and hardworking.
2. He has a lot of loans to pay back to his family and friends.
3. The ending is a surprise if Todd intended to keep the money because the story implies that he's an honest person. It's also a surprise because Todd seemed too nervous to pull out the gun and try to take the money.
4. These lines give possible clues to the ending: "Todd thought of the trouble he and Jess had raising the money for the gas station. . . . " and "He put the gun in his pocket."

OPTION

Do some prereading activities with the students before they actually read the short story. For example, explain what a short story is and what an ending is that "leaves the reader hanging." See if anyone can explain what the title means. Read aloud the first paragraph and have the students describe in their own words the main character—Todd—and the setting of the story. Talk about possible surprising things that could happen to Todd at the gas station during the night shift.

6

- Read the instructions aloud. Then have the students read over the expressions in the box. Answer any questions. Then have the students write their own endings.

- Go around the room and answer any questions students have about their work. When they finish, tell the students to compare and discuss their endings with a partner. Finally, call on different students to read aloud their endings. If appropriate, have them write the endings on the board. Give a prize for the most interesting ending. Point out the illustration of Todd on p. 132.

5

► As you read the story, think ahead to how it might end. When you have finished reading, give your interpretations of Todd's decision, considering these questions.

1. What kind of person do you think Todd is?
2. What problems does Todd have?
3. Is the ending surprising? Why or why not?
4. Are there any lines earlier in the story that give a clue to the ending?

6

► Now write your own ending to the story. When you have finished, share it with a group of classmates. Talk about Todd's motives and decide which of the different possible endings seems most likely. You may wish to use the expressions in the box.

He must have (been) . . .
He couldn't have (been) . . .
He wouldn't have (been) . . .
Despite . . .
Therefore . . .
And so . . .
If he . . . , then . . .
. . . , which seems strange.
What convinces me that . . . is when he says . . .

Night Shift
by Gloria Rosenthal

Todd blew on his fingers as he ran back to the comforting shelter of the gas station office. The car he had just serviced pulled away in a smoke screen of warm air hitting the cold night. Todd was alone.

Three A.M., he thought. Four more hours before Jess would be in to take over. He closed his eyes and listened to the voices coming at him from a beat-up radio. "Wait a minute. Hold it a minute," Todd heard the announcer's voice say. "I've got a news flash, folks." The announcer cleared his throat and changed his tone of voice. "The Country National Bank of Long Island was broken into tonight. Two armed men killed the night guard and a police officer who responded to the alarm. A second police officer was critically injured, but not before he fatally wounded one of the men. The other man got away and was possibly heading for the Southern State Parkway."

Todd stood up and walked around the small office trying to see out into the cold night, but all he could see were his own station lights throwing out a dim circle of light. He couldn't see the Southern State Parkway. But he knew it was out there.

The next news flash came about 20 minutes later. The gunman had abandoned his car on the side of the highway just after Exit 19 in Hempstead. The police did not know how he was traveling but thought that he might have been picked up by another motorist.

"Hey," the talk-show host added, "with his hundred and fifty grand, he could have taken a cab."

Todd whistled, "One hundred and fifty thousand!" Here's this guy who just walks into a bank and helps himself to $150,000. Todd thought of the trouble he and Jess had raising the money for the gas station. So many small loans from family and friends. So many papers to sign. So much money to pay back.

When a horn—sounding too loud in the still night—broke into his thoughts, Todd jumped. He didn't realize how nervous he had become. Even more surprising was finding his hand reaching into the desk drawer. When he finally found the gun beneath some papers, it felt cold in his hand, maybe because his hand had suddenly begun to sweat. He put the gun in his pocket.

He heard, rather than saw, the car door open. Then he saw a short woman in a ski jacket running toward him, "Ladies' room?" she questioned. Todd smiled, a flood of relief actually warming him.

Another news flash: The armed robber had gotten a ride along Sunrise Highway and somewhere near Wantagh Parkway had pushed out the driver. So now they knew the gunman was in a white Cutlass with a red roof. License plate number LJR1939.

"I'm glad I'm in this nice safe studio," came the voice of the announcer. "Watch out, out there. Be careful of white cars. Don't pick up any strangers. And all you guys in gas stations better not service a white Cutlass with a red roof."

Todd saw the headlights coming at him as the car swung into the station and pulled up slowly at the pump. There it was. A white car with a red roof. He saw the license number in the pale light. LJR1939.

What should he do? Todd had to make a quick decision.

"Yes, sir?"

"Fill 'er up—premium," the man said, sounding like a hundred other motorists on a hundred other nights.

The tank was full, and as he replaced the hose, Todd kept his eye on the man.

"Check your oil, sir?" Todd asked while making up his mind for sure. He had to be careful.

"No, thanks," was all the man said, but it was all the time Todd needed. He had the gun in his hand and at the man's head in one smooth motion.

"Freeze!" Todd said, and the man froze. "Keep one hand on the wheel and hand me that briefcase."

7 ▸ **Rewrite the paragraph about the robbery, combining each pair of sentences in brackets [ ] into one sentence using *either . . . or, neither . . . nor,* or *not only . . . but (also).***

Police are completely confused over the robbery at the Country National Bank of Long Island. [They haven't found the robber. What's more, they don't have a clue to his whereabouts.] [The robber must have found a very secure hiding place. If not, then he's vanished into thin air.] After stealing a white Cutlass with a red roof and a nearly empty gas tank, [the robber would have had to get gas. If not, he would have had to find another car.] However, [the police have not found the Cutlass, and they have not received any reports of other stolen cars.] Kevin Daly, the owner of the stolen car, said that [the robber didn't look suspicious, and he didn't seem nervous.] While police are without a clue, they won't give up easily on this crime. [The robber stole $150,000 from the bank. What's more, he killed one police officer and critically injured another.]

8 ▸ **Here is one possible explanation of what happens to the money. Read the statements below. Then listen to the conversation between Todd and Jess, and choose *a* or *b.***

1. Todd decided to _____ .
   a. keep the money
   b. give the money back

2. Jess thinks Todd should have _____ .
   a. kept the money
   b. given the money back

3. Todd is probably _____ honest than Jess.
   a. more
   b. less

4. Jess probably _____ if his kids led a life of crime.
   a. wouldn't care
   b. would be upset

9 ▸ **It is now several days after the robbery. What are the different people thinking now? Complete each statement with the correct form of the verbs in parentheses.**

1. Todd: If I *weren't* (not be) always so honest, I *would have kept* (keep) that $150,000 instead of giving it back to the police.

2. Jess: If Todd _____ (not give back) that money, our troubles _____ (be) over."

3. Jess: If Todd and I really _____ (like) working at the gas station, I _____ (not feel) this way.

4. Night guard's widow: If he _____ (retire) last month like he said he was going to, he _____ (be) alive today.

5. Police captain: They were good cops, but if they _____ (be) a little more careful, Jack _____ (be) alive and Bill _____ (not have) a bullet in his chest.

6. Wounded police officer: If I _____ (not kill) that one guy, I _____ (be) dead now.

7. Radio announcer: If that guy _____ (not be) so dumb, he _____ (not steal) a car without any gas in it.

7

- Ask a student to read the instructions aloud. If necessary, combine the first pair of sentences with the students. Then have the students do the exercise.

- Tell the students to compare answers with a partner. Then call on different students to read aloud the sentences in the paragraph and write the answers on the board.

ANSWERS

Not only haven't they found the robber, but they don't have a clue to his whereabouts.
Either the robber must have found a very secure hiding place, or he's vanished into thin air.
. . . either the robber would have had to get gas or he would have had to find another car.
. . . the police have neither found the Cutlass nor received any reports of other stolen cars.
. . . the robber neither looked suspicious nor seemed nervous.
The robber not only stole $150,000 from the bank, but he also killed one police officer and critically injured another.

8

- Read the instructions aloud. Then have the students read the statements and listen to the conversation. Allow them to listen as many times as necessary.

- Tell the students to compare answers with a partner. Next call on different students to read their answers aloud and write them on the board.

TAPESCRIPT

Todd Oh, come on, Jess. What was I supposed to do? Just keep it?

Jess Yeah, man, I guess you're right. But if we weren't such honest citizens, we'd be rich right now. And we could pay back all the money we owe on this gas station.

Todd Yeah, and not only would we have to live with ourselves, but we'd also feel as if we were being hunted for the rest of our lives. I mean, somebody got killed for that money, Jess.

Jess I hear what you're saying. But I just can't help thinking . . . boy, would my wife kill me if she heard me talking this way . . . her good, old, honest hardworking husband.

Todd Honest pays, Jess. Think about your wife *and* your kids. How would you like it if they grew up and robbed someone . . . or killed a guy?

Jess Hey, look, man. I know the arguments. Can't blame a guy for dreamin', can you?

ANSWERS

1. b
2. a
3. a
4. b

9

- Ask a student to read aloud the instructions and the sample answer as the class members follow along in their books. Then have the students read over the incomplete statements. Answer any questions.

- You can have the students work on the exercise in pairs. When they finish, have them compare answers with other pairs. Finally, call on different students to read aloud the completed statements.

ANSWERS

2. hadn't given back, would be
3. liked, wouldn't feel
4. 'd retired, would be
5. 'd been, would be, wouldn't have
6. hadn't killed, 'd be
7. hadn't been, wouldn't have stolen

- Ask a student to read the instructions aloud. Then call on two students to read the two questions aloud. Answer any questions.

- Tell the students to read the article. You can also have them listen to it as they read. When they finish, answer any questions about the vocabulary and structures. Then tell the students to answer the questions.

- Have the students compare answers with a partner. Then call on two students to read aloud the answers and write them on the board.

SAMPLE ANSWERS
1. People have started eating foreign foods.
2. Restaurants are appealing to people who travel abroad and dine out a lot. Immigrants have brought their foods with them. Many foreign foods are part of a healthier diet. Increased foreign trade has made new foods and ingredients more available in the U.S.

OPTION

Ask the students if they recognize any of the foreign foods mentioned in the article. If so, see if they can tell the class how they are prepared. Ask other students to describe a favorite dish in their country and, if possible, tell the class how it's prepared.

- Have a student read aloud the instructions. Answer any questions about the procedure. Then ask a student to read aloud the sample answer in italics.

- Tell the students to read through the paragraphs. Answer any questions. Then have them do the exercise.

- Tell the students to compare answers with a partner. Then call on different students to read the paragraphs aloud and write the answers on the board.

ANSWERS
The more cheese they added the worse it got.
The more I think about it the more convinced I become that the pizza is prepared in advance and then frozen.
The sooner the place closes the better off we'll be.

10 ► **As you read the article, look for answers to the questions below. When you have finished reading, answer the questions briefly.**

1. How have the eating habits of people in the United States changed over the past several years?

2. What are four reasons for the change?

ETHNIC EATERIES ADD SPICE TO DINING

BY JOHN MARIANI

Former meat-and-potatoes eaters, people across the United States are developing a great appetite for foods they had never heard of.

They are ordering Greek *taramosalata* made of mashed cod roe and olive oil and Japanese sea urchins with green *wasabi* horseradish. They can grasp slippery snow peas with chopsticks, digest red-hot Indian curries, and expertly twirl strands of fettuccine on their forks.

In response, restaurants are serving more authentic ethnic foods. For example, Chinese restaurants are replacing chow mein and egg rolls with shark's fin soup, sea cucumber, and sweet bean-paste buns.

The reasons for this enormous enthusiasm for ethnic food: increased interest in authentic dishes, more dining out, the impact of immigrants, an emphasis on nutrition, and improved trade.

Working men and women who have traveled abroad and who have the money are dining out more often. The restaurant industry is trying hard to appeal to this group.

"People want things made correctly, authentically, and the way they remember them from their travels abroad," says *Food and Wine* magazine columnist Stanley Dry.

Ethnic groups new to the United States have brought their cuisines with them. Immigrant Hoang Ming, who opened one of the first Vietnamese restaurants in Washington, D.C., says that most of the authentic Asian restaurants in Washington have opened in the last few years, primarily in low-rent districts.

Ming admits that the food at his first restaurants, although authentic, was adapted for American tastes. He feels that customers have become more educated. "Now I can serve exotic dishes and know my clientele will love them. They're fascinated."

The popularity of fresh, exotic foods is also due to a demand by diners for healthier, less-fatty foods. Says Chicago cardiologist Dr. Anthony Chan: "The [Asian] diet is not centered on red meat, and they use almost no butter, milk, cream, or cheese. It contains about half the fat of the American diet, and the Chinese eat small portions of non-fatty meats and fish and a lot of fiber like rice."

Most authentic ethnic foods are based on small portions, fresh seasonal vegetables, and quick cooking. True Italian food is not heavily layered with sauces and cheese, but depends on cholesterol-free olive oil, lots of vegetables, and grilled fish.

Asian stir-frying and steaming techniques retain nutrients far better than deep frying or boiling. Mexican food is high in carbohydrates such as beans and rice, and Japanese food centers on fish.

Heavier ethnic cuisines—such as German, Polish, and Hungarian, all high in fat and cholesterol—have not shown any increased popularity.

More than anything else, interest in ethnic cuisines has grown because increased trade has brought in many foods and ingredients never before seen in the United States. One delicacy shop in New York carries 40 different kinds of olive oil and 300 cheeses, as well as a wide array of other foods that couldn't be found at any price ten years ago.

11 ► **Rewrite the paragraphs below about a new restaurant, changing the sentences in brackets [ ] into sentences containing double comparatives.**

Mama Rosa's Authentic Italian Pizzeria doesn't live up to its name. My family and I visited Mama Rosa's several times in the last two weeks, and [each time we ate there, we liked it less.] My children tried to improve the taste of the pizza by adding cheese. But [when they added more cheese, it only got worse.] [Each time I think about it, I become more convinced that the pizza is prepared in advance and then frozen.]

Mama Rosa's pizza is neither authentic nor Italian. [The place should close as soon as possible, and we'll be better off.]

Start like this:
. . . My family and I visited Mama Rosa's several times in the last two weeks, and the more we ate there, the less we liked it.

12 ► Restate the conversations, changing the sentences in brackets [ ]
to give them more emphasis. Each sentence may be restated in two
different ways.

1. **A** These rolls from Stella's Bakery are pretty
good.
   B They're not bad, but [I'd rather have a real
French croissant.]
   A *These rolls from Stella's Bakery are pretty
good.*
   B *They're not too bad, but what I'd rather have
is a real French croissant. or
They're not too bad, but a real French
croissant is what I'd rather have.*

2. **A** I'd like dessert, but I don't want anything
fattening.
   B I can't help you there. [I always order one of
those delicious, rich pastries.]

3. **A** There aren't very many Japanese restaurants
in this city.
   B I've noticed that. [I'd like to find a Japanese
grocery store around here, too.]

4. **A** Are you sure I can't convince you to have
another piece of coconut cream pie?
   B No, thanks. When it comes to my diet, [I
have to listen to my doctor.]

5. **A** When I was in Mexico, I was surprised at
what real Mexican food is like. It's so
different from the Mexican food in
restaurants here.
   B I know what you mean. When I was in Italy,
[real Italian pizza surprised me.]

13 ► Using the information in the article, add more information to each of
these sentences by including a nonrestrictive relative clause.

1. I really like a chili seasoning
called *berbere*.
*I really like a chili seasoning
called* berbere, *which is used in
Ethiopian cooking.*
2. Vietnamese food uses a fish
sauce of fermented anchovies.
3. Korean dishes often have
hot seasoning.
4. Southern Italian cuisine
features dry pasta and seafood.
5. Cooks in northern Italy roast
or braise lamb and veal, and
grill fish.
6. The main seasonings in
Thai food include coriander
and garlic.
7. The Moroccan dish called
couscous is made from
steamed millet grain.

THE FLAVORS OF INTERNATIONAL FOODS

Here are some basic differences in ethnic foods:
KOREAN *Similar to Chinese and specializing in barbecuing and
noodle dishes, often with hot seasoning.*
THAI *Maybe the hottest food in the world, with plenty of chili
peppers. Main seasonings include coriander, garlic, tamarind, lemon
grass, and coconut milk.*
VIETNAMESE *Fragant, with a colonial link to French food. This is
not highly peppered food; the predominant flavoring is a fish sauce
of fermented anchovies.*
ETHIOPIAN *Based on stewed meats and vegetables and eaten on
a thin pancake called* injera. *It can be extremely hot when* berbere, *a
chili seasoning, is added.*
MOROCCAN *A rich, diverse cookery whose national dish is
couscous, made from steamed millet grain topped with chicken,
lamb, and other meats. There is often a sweet-salty balance.*
NORTHERN ITALIAN *Specializes in fresh pasta, vegetables,
cream sauces, mushrooms, and cornmeal polenta. Lamb and veal
are roasted or braised, and fish is grilled.*
SOUTHERN ITALIAN *Lots of tomato, onion, garlic, and basil,
with dry pasta and such seafood as shellfish, squid, or salted cod
called* baccala.

14 ► Nick and George, two waiters at a Greek restaurant, came to work early
to help their boss open the restaurant. When they arrived, they found a
note from their boss. Rewrite
the note, reducing the relative
clauses as in the example.

Start like this:
*The tables in the back room
need to be set. . . .*

The tables that are in the back room need
to be set. The glasses that are in the sink have
to be washed and dried. The pastries that are in
the kitchen have to be displayed in the dessert
case. The woman who is wearing a red shirt and
jeans is Jennifer, the new waitress. Give her the
uniform that is in the storage closet.

- Ask a student to read aloud the instructions. Then act out the sample conversation with a student. Answer any questions.

- You can have the students work in pairs to do the exercise. When they finish, call on different pairs to act out the restated conversations for the class. You can have other students write the answers on the board.

ANSWERS

2. What I always order is one of those delicious, rich pastries. OR One of those delicious, rich pastries is what I always order.
3. What I'd like to find around here is a Japanese grocery store, too. OR A Japanese grocery store is what I'd like to find around here, too.
4. . . . who I have to listen to is my doctor. OR . . . my doctor is who I have to listen to.
5. . . . what surprised me was real Italian pizza OR . . . real Italian pizza is what surprised me.

- Read the instructions aloud. Then have the students read the article. You can also have them listen to it. If there are students in the class from any of the countries featured in the article, have them read the paragraphs about their ethnic foods aloud. (See the Option which follows.) Answer any questions students have.

- Tell the students to do the exercise. Then have them compare answers with a partner. Finally, call on different students to read aloud the answers and write them on the board.

POSSIBLE ANSWERS

2. Vietnamese food, which is not highly peppered, uses a fish sauce of fermented anchovies.
3. Korean dishes, which are similar to Chinese, often have hot seasoning.
4. Southern Italian cuisine, in which lots of tomato, onion, garlic, and basil are used, features dry pasta and seafood.
5. Cooks in northern Italy, who specialize in fresh pasta, vegetables, cream sauces, mushrooms, and cornmeal *polenta*, roast or braise lamb and veal, and grill fish.
6. The main seasonings in Thai food, which may be the hottest food in the world, include coriander and garlic.
7. The moroccan dish called *couscous* is made from steamed millet grain, which is topped with chicken, lamb, and other meats.

OPTION

If there are students in class from the countries represented in the article, ask them to further describe the different foods of their countries. Encourage the other students to ask them questions. You can ask a sample question. For example:

Can I buy the vegetable you use in that soup in this country?

- Read aloud the instructions and the sample answer as the students follow along in their books. Answer any questions. Then have the students do the exercise.

- Tell the students to compare answers with a partner. Then call on different students to read aloud the answers and write them on the board.

ANSWERS

The glasses in the sink have to be washed and dried. The pastries in the kitchen have to be displayed in the dessert case. The woman wearing a red shirt and jeans is Jennifer, the new waitress. Give her the uniform in the storage closet.

OPTION 1

Tell the students to write additional sentences with relative clauses to continue the note. Then have them exchange papers with a partner and reduce the relative clauses in their partner's note. Next have the pairs compare notes. Go around the room and check their work. Finally, call on different students to read aloud the notes they reduced and write them on the board.

OPTION 2

Have the students work in pairs to write notes of their own for another pair to reduce. Tell them to pretend they are owners of some kind of store and need different things done by their employees while they're away. You can give them an example:

For employees of a pet store:
   The cases of dog food that are by the door need to be unpacked and put on the shelves that are against the wall.

When the pairs finish writing their notes, tell them to exchange notes with another pair and reduce the notes they received. Go around the room and check their work. Finally, call on different pairs to read aloud the two versions of their notes and write them on the board.

- Ask a student to read aloud the instructions and the sample answer as the class members follow along in their books. Answer any questions. Make sure the students understand the meanings of *hard, soft,* and *rational* in this context. Then have the students read the article on p. 135. Answer any questions about the vocabulary and structures.

- Have the students read over the exercise sentences on p. 136. Answer any questions. Then tell them to do the exercise. When they finish, have them compare answers with a partner. Then call on different students to read aloud the exercise sentences and write the answers on the board.

ANSWERS
2. Soft
3. Rational
4. Hard
5. Soft
6. Rational

OPTION

Tell the students to write sentences of their own similar to the ones in the exercise on p. 136. Remind them to include the information in parentheses. When they finish, have them exchange papers with a partner and identify the strategies of persuasion used by the speakers in their partner's sentences. Next have them compare their answers with their partner. Finally, call on different students to read aloud their sentences and answers and write them on the board.

THE LANGUAGE OF PERSUASION

BY DAVID KIPNIS AND STUART SCHMIDT

Rational, insistent, and emotional statements all have one thing in common. They show people trying to persuade others, a skill we all treasure. Books about power and influence are read by young executives eager for a promotion, by politicians anxious to influence the voters, by lonely people looking to win and hold a mate, and by upset parents trying to make their children see the light.

Despite this interest in persuasion, most people are not really aware of how they go about it. They spend more time choosing their clothes than choosing their influence styles. Even fewer are aware of how their styles affect others or themselves. Although shouts and demands may make people dance to our tune, we will probably lose their good will. People's opinions of us may change for the worse when we use hard or abusive tactics.

We conducted studies of dating couples and business managers in which the couples described how they attempted to influence their

> **"I had all the facts and figures ready before I made my suggestions to my boss." (Manager)**
> —*Rational Statement*
>
> **"I kept insisting that we do it my way. She finally caved in." (Husband)**
> —*Insistent Statement*
>
> **"I think it's about time that you stop thinking these negative things about yourself." (Psychotherapist)**
> —*Rational Statement*
>
> **"Send out more horses, skirr the country round. Hang those that talk of fear. Give me mine armour." (Macbeth, Act 5)**
> —*Emotional Statement*

partners, and the managers told how they attempted to influence their subordinates, peers, and superiors at work. We then used these descriptions as the basis for separate questionnaires in which we asked other couples and managers how frequently they employed each tactic. We found that the tactics could be classified into three basic strategies—hard, soft, and rational, as shown in the charts below.

People sometimes ask, "Which tactic works best?" The answer is that they all work if they are used at the right time with the right person. But both hard and soft tactics involve costs to the user even when they succeed. Hard tactics often alienate the people being influenced and create a climate of hostility and resistance. Soft tactics—acting nice, being humble—may lessen self-respect and self-esteem. In contrast, we found that people who rely chiefly on logic, reason, and compromise to get their way are the most satisfied both with their business lives and with their personal relationships.

INFLUENCE STRATEGIES

Strategy	Couples	Managers
HARD	I get angry and demand that he/she give in.	I simply order the person to do what I want.
	As the first step I make him/her feel stupid and worthless.	I threaten to give an unsatisfactory performance evaluation.
	I say I'll leave him/her if my spouse does not agree.	I get higher management to back up my request.
SOFT	I act warm and charming before bringing up the subject.	I act very humble while making my request.
	I am so nice that he/she cannot refuse.	I make the person feel important by saying that she/he has the brains and experience to do what I want.
RATIONAL	I offer to compromise; I'll give up a little if he/she gives up a little.	I offer to exchange favors: You do this for me, and I'll do something for you.
	We talk, discussing our views objectively without arguments.	I explain the reason for my request.

WHY PEOPLE CHOOSE EACH STRATEGY

Hard tactics are normally used when:

Influencer has the advantage.
Resistance is anticipated.
Behavior of the other person goes against social or organizational standards.

Soft tactics are normally used when:

Influencer is at a disadvantage.
Resistance is anticipated.
The goal is to get benefits for one's self.

Rational tactics are normally used when:

Neither party has a real power advantage.
Resistance is not anticipated.
The goal is to get benefits for one's self and one's organization.

15 ▶ **As you read the article on page 135, pay attention to the differences among the three basic strategies of persuasion—hard, soft, and rational. Then identify which strategy each of these speakers is using.**

1. (Parent to child) Get upstairs and clean your room! Now. *Hard.*

2. (Employer to employee) I'm awfully sorry to ask you to stay late, but I know I can't solve this problem without your help.

3. (Wife to husband) If you'll do the shopping while I do the laundry, I'll be free to go to the game with you this afternoon.

4. (Employer to employee*)* I strongly suggest that you work this problem out. If not, I will have to write a negative report about you.

5. (Husband to wife) That was the best spaghetti I ever had. Why don't we invite my mother over on Sunday, so you can cook some for her?

6. (Employer to employee) If you can make this trip to Los Angeles over the weekend, I'll see that you get two days off next week.

16 ▶ **Complete each of the conversations below by supplying an appropriate request for the first speaker.**

1. **A** (Bart Conti, a bank branch manager, has lost his copy of the plan for new accounts. He asks Marlene Lundberg, the manager of another branch, to send him a copy.)
   B Sure, Bart, I'll send one right over.

   A *Marlene, I seem to have lost my copy of the plan for new accounts. Could you send me a copy?*
   B *Sure, Bart. I'll send one right over.*

2. **A** (Teresa Colon, the head teller, asks Gilbert Kohler, a teller, to find the records of the Hoffman account for her.)
   B Of course, Ms. Colon.

3. **A** (Jung Kim, a teller, asks Bart Conti if he can change his work schedule the following week, to work late on Friday instead of Tuesday.)
   B I suppose that's all right.

4. **A** (Jung Kim asks Gilbert Kohler, who was planning to work late on Friday but not on Tuesday, to change late days with him.)
   B Yeah, that's O.K., Jung.

17 ▶ **Sophia is a very talented but rather lazy young piano student. Restate her music teacher's advice by changing the subjunctive clauses to infinitive clauses and the infinitive clauses to subjunctive clauses. Then decide if the music teacher's strategy is hard, soft, or rational.**

"I guess there's nothing more I can say or do to persuade you to try harder, Sophia. At this point, it's crucial that *you* decide what you really want to do. In order to be a great pianist, it's important for a person to start early. You're very talented, but it's still essential that you practice on a daily basis. It's also very important for you to come to class regularly and bring your music. No one can do these things for you—and no one should. It's necessary that you decide yourself whether to make these changes in your attitude or to give up your future as a pianist."

- Read the instructions aloud. Then have the students read over the exercise items. Answer any questions. Next tell the students to do the exercise.

- Tell the students to compare answers with a partner. Then call on different pairs to read the conversations aloud and write the answers on the board.

SAMPLE ANSWERS
2. Gilbert, I'd like you to find the records of the Hoffman account for me.
3. Excuse me, Mr. Conti, but I was wondering if I could change my work schedule this week. I'd like to work late on Friday instead of Tuesday.
4. Say, Gil, would you change late days with me this week? I'd like to take Friday instead of Tuesday.

OPTION

Tell the students to identify the strategy of persuasion used by the first speaker in the conversations. Call on a student to tell the class the answer.

ANSWER
Soft.

- Tell the students to look at the illustration as you ask a class member to describe it. Then ask different students to read aloud the music teacher's advice. Answer any questions.

- Read the instructions aloud. Next have the students do the exercise.

- Tell the students to compare answers with a partner. Then call on different students to read aloud the answers and write them on the board.

ANSWERS
. . . it's crucial for *you* to decide what you really want to do. . . . it's important that a person start early. . . . it's essential for you to practice on a daily basis. It's also very important that you come to class regularly and bring your music. It's necessary for you to decide yourself whether to make these changes in your attitude or to give up your future as a pianist.

Rational.

OPTION

Tell the students to work in pairs. Have one partner write five sentences of advice using subjunctive clauses. Tell the other partner to write five sentences of advice using infinitive clauses. When they finish, have the pairs exchange papers with each other and restate their partner's advice. Next have the students compare their work with their partners. Finally, call on different pairs to read aloud the two versions of their sentences and write them on the board.

WORKBOOK Review of units 7–12, pp. 77-80

WORKBOOK TAPESCRIPT

UNIT 1

Lesson 2 (p. 2)

1

Woman I don't see how we can add any employees now. We took on four new ones just last month. No one has left or retired. Furthermore, sales and profits are down. We can't afford more staff.

Man Nevertheless, we need someone in shipping right now. Two people can't handle it all. Moreover, Scott Marino is being transferred to the plant in Kingston.

Woman Really? I wish I'd know that. I hope he had sufficient notice. His wife has a good job here; she may not want to go to Kingston. Scott's leaving doesn't change my mind about the central issue, however. Even with him off the payroll, I still say that we can't afford to add anyone now.

2

Father I wish you wouldn't play that so loud. I can't hear myself think. Furthermore, it's bad for your ears. I've read that people's hearing has been permanently damaged by loud music.

Son Oh, come on, Dad. It's not that loud. Besides, you have to have it kind of loud to get the full effect. It's supposed to sound as though you're right in the middle of the band.

Father Even so, you're not in the middle of the band, you're in the house. What's more, are you sure you even like that kind of music?

Son Of course. I listen to it, don't I?

Father But is that because you like it or because it's what all the other kids are listening to?

Son I wouldn't listen to it if I didn't like it.

Father I hope you're not just following the crowd. Anyway, right now I'm more concerned about the volume. You really could hurt your ears. So you will keep it down?

Son I'll try, Dad.

3

Husband I'd really like to buy that stereo.

Wife So would I. But it's almost $200, and we don't have $200 to spend. And what's more, we're not likely to have an extra $200 very soon. We need every penny for food and rent and clothes and insurance and . . .

Husband But we could use our credit card. That way, we wouldn't have to pay it off for a year or eighteen months. Besides, we deserve to get some enjoyment out of life. It isn't all necessities and paying bills.

Wife True, but with the interest we'd have to pay by buying on credit, the stereo would end up costing a lot more in the long run. If we can't afford $200 now, we won't be able to afford $250 a year or eighteen months from now.

Husband I know you're right. So let's try this. Let's save all we can for the next six months and see where we are then.

Wife Sounds good to me.

UNIT 2

Lesson 7 (p. 8)

1

First interview

Mrs. Reilly Good morning.

David Good morning. I'm David Mitchell.

Mrs. Reilly Yes, David. I've looked over your application, and I have some additional questions for you. First, why are you interested in this particular job?

David Well, I'm interested in a job because I have to help out at home. And I'm interested in this job because I enjoy working with people. I seem to get along with almost everybody wherever I am. I also know where a lot of things are in the store because I come in here pretty often. And besides, it's close to home; I could walk to work.

Mrs. Reilly I see. What kind of person do you consider yourself to be? Besides someone who gets along well with other people, as you have said.

David Well, I'm reliable and I enjoy responsibility. I finish whatever I start. Also, I'm a fairly patient person; I handle pressure well. Oh, and I'm always on time.

Mrs. Reilly Those are all good characteristics for this kind of work. Are there any other reasons why you think we should hire you?

David Well, I'm honest—you could trust me at the cash register. And I'd keep busy; I'd always find something to do.

Mrs. Reilly Thank you very much, David. I'll give you a call in a day or two and let you know my decision.

David Thank you for seeing me, Mrs. Reilly.

Second interview

Mrs. Reilly Good morning.

Mark Hi.

Mrs. Reilly You're, uh, Mark Robinson?

Mark Uh-huh.

Mrs. Reilly Well, Mark, I've looked over your application, and I have some additional questions for you. First, why are you interested in this particular job?

Mark Uhh . . . I don't know. I just thought this would be kind of a cool place to work. You know, talking to whoever comes in and everything. I also need the money.

Mrs. Reilly I see. What kind of person do you consider yourself to be?

Mark I'm easygoing. Not much bothers me. And I have a pretty good sense of humor. That's about all. I can't think of anything else.

Mrs. Reilly Hmm. Would you say you're hardworking and honest?

Mark Yeah, I guess.

Mrs. Reilly Do you think you're creative?

Mark Creative? Yeah, sure. I can imagine myself, uh, making things.

Mrs. Reilly O.K., Mark. Thank you for coming in. I'll call you with my decision in a day or two.

Mark Sure. So Long!

U N I T   3

Lesson 12 (p. 14)

 1 & **2**

First conversation

Mother All right, you can go out tonight, but I want you to be home by 11:00.

Daughter Why so early? All the other kids can stay out later than that on Friday night.

Mother You're not "all the other kids." You're my daughter, and you'll abide by my rules.

Daughter What if something happens so I can't be home right at 11:00?

Second conversation

Man 1 You don't look very cheerful. Are you worried about something?

Man 2 No, I'm O.K.

Man 1 Are you sure? Come on, we've been friends for a long time. You can tell me. It would do you good.

Third conversation

Teacher I asked to see you because I've been worried about Jamie. He's been missing a lot of homework lately.

Father When I was in school, I never did much homework, and I turned out O.K. Is it really so important?

Fourth conversation

Husband You know that bookcase we've been looking at at Baker's? According to an ad in this morning's paper, it's on sale, 20 percent off.

Wife Even at that, I'm not sure we can afford it yet.

Husband But we've been needing one for a long time. We've got books piled up in practically every room of the house.

Wife When does the sale end?

Husband I think it goes for another week.

Fifth conversation

Doctor Well, I'm glad to tell you that all your tests came out O.K. You get a clean bill of health.

Patient That's great. . . . Uh, Doctor?

Doctor Yes?

Patient I've been worried about my wife. She has a persistent cough, but she doesn't have any other symptoms of a cold or flu or anything. Do you think anything's wrong?

Sixth conversation

Salesperson Now, these 19-inch ones are our best bargain.

Customer I'm not sure that I need one that big. My living room is pretty small, and I don't watch TV that much, anyway.

Salesperson You'll get a wonderful picture with this. More for your money.

Customer I don't know. . . . I only wanted a 13-inch. Could I bring it back if I didn't like it?

Seventh conversation

Woman 1 Look, I know you're new here, but would you mind a little friendly advice?

Woman 2 I guess not.

Woman 1 Don't you think you should try harder to get here on time in the morning?

Woman 2 I do try, but traffic is always so heavy that I seem to get here late.

Woman 1 Then maybe you should plan for it and leave home earlier.

Woman 2 Well, the boss has never said anything to me about being late.

U N I T   4

Lesson 17 (p. 20)

1 & **2**

First Aid

Instructor Choking is one of the most unusual medical emergencies for two reasons. First, it generally occurs in happy, lighthearted circumstances. Choking accidents often take place at parties, where there are lots of people laughing and having a good time. Second, choking can happen to anyone—young or old, sick or well, alone or with other people—at any time.

One Sunday evening in 1956, a man ate a heavy meal, then went to bed because he wasn't feeling well. During the night, some food came up from his stomach and choked him. No one else was around, he couldn't help himself, and he died. That man was Tommy Dorsey, a famous trombone player and orchestra leader.

One man was luckier than Tommy Dorsey. He was a politician, flying from one city to another during a political campaign, when he swallowed a whole peanut and began choking. However, an assistant knew what to do to rescue the man: Ronald Reagan, former president of the United States.

There are four common causes of choking on food: large, poorly chewed pieces of meat; laughing or otherwise not paying attention while eating; drinking alcohol while eating; and false teeth.

In the United States, choking ranks sixth as a cause of accidental death; perhaps as many as 5,000 people die from it each year.

Many of these lives could be saved if more people knew the "Heimlich maneuver," named for Dr. Harry J. Heimlich, who invented the technique for rescuing victims of choking. Anyone can use it. Dr. Heimlich himself knows of two eight-year-olds who have saved younger children, and twenty-six people who have saved themselves.

If you are with someone who is choking, follow these steps:

First, find out whether the victim is conscious and able to speak. Shout "Can you speak? Can you cough it up?" If the victim can speak, leave her alone. If she can't, go on to the next step.

Next, if the victim is conscious and is standing up, stand behind her. Place your arms around the victim's waist and look for the soft area below the breastbone.

Then, make a fist with one hand and hold it with the other hand. After that, push hard four times with a quick upward thrust. The object is to force air up through the throat to get rid of the obstruction.

If the victim is sitting down and unable to stand, follow the same steps.

Last, if the victim is lying down, kneel and place one hand over the other and press on the person's abdomen with quick upward thrusts.

You can even use the last part of this technique on yourself if you're alone and choking. Bend over something hard, such as a chair or the edge of a sink, and give yourself the four quick thrusts to the abdomen. According to

scientific experiments, the procedure works 97 percent of the time.

UNIT 5

Lesson 22 (p. 26)

1

Jim Let's begin with the sofa, since that's the biggest piece of living room furniture we have. Where shall we put it?

Carol The logical place is between the windows. How wide is that wall?

Jim Let me look at the figures I wrote down when we were there yesterday and measured everything. No, it won't fit. It's 5 feet 1 inch between the windows.

Carol And how wide is the sofa? It must be wider than that. Uh-oh. It's 6 feet 2 inches wide. We can forget that idea. How about putting the sofa along the wall by the closet? Will it fit there?

Jim Let's see. . . . It'll fit, but then no one could get through the door to the hall, especially with the coffee table in front of the sofa. The same is true of the opposite wall. It's wide enough—7 feet 10 inches—but with the sofa and coffee table there, we wouldn't be able to use the kitchen door, either.

Carol What about between the doors? That's the only place left.

Jim Great. It's just right. 6 feet 6 inches. That's settled then. Now for the piano.

Carol That's easy. The piano is 4 feet 8 inches wide. It'll just fit between the windows.

Jim How deep is the piano? Will it stick out into the room too far? Don't forget to include the bench.

Carol It's O.K. The sofa and the coffee table add up to 3 feet 7 inches, and the piano and the bench add up to 4 feet. That's 7 feet 7 inches, and we have 7 feet 10 inches.

Jim You're forgetting one little thing: We have to walk between them. Three inches won't give us much room.

Carol You're right. Do we have to start all over again?

Jim No, I think I've got it. We'll put the piano and bench along the wall on the left, with the right end near the window. One lamp can go to the left of the piano. Then—and here's my inspiration—we'll put the sofa and coffee table parallel to the piano and facing it, over here, as a kind of room divider. The left end of the sofa can go up against the wall between the doors, next to the door to the hall—with the easy chair next to the door to the kitchen. The other floor lamp can go between the easy chair and the sofa, so we can use it for reading.

Carol And I can either lie down on the sofa or sit in the chair to watch TV while I read. The TV! We were forgetting that!

Jim We'll put it between the windows.

Carol Perfect!

Lesson 27 (p. 32)

2 1. **Woman** My father and mother had a great influence on me, of course. Neither of them had finished eighth grade, so they felt strongly about the need for getting an education. They insisted that I do homework every night—even when my teachers hadn't given me any!

2. **Man** I'm three years younger than my sister, so she had already fought all the battles with our parents before I had to—about things like doing jobs around the house, practicing the piano, and going out on school nights. I always admired her because she was always on my side when I had arguments with my parents.

3. **Woman** I'm both glad and sorry to say that my parents let me do almost anything I wanted to, since I was an only child. I'm glad because I had so much freedom, but I'm also sorry because I'm not sure it was good for me. Now I find it hard to give in to anyone else; I'm awfully stubborn.

4. **Man** I'm one of three children, and we're all artists of one kind or another. My brother writes, my sister is a musician, and I paint. Our parents get the credit for this. They felt that television was a bad influence because it's so passive— you don't even have to think. Thus, they wouldn't allow it in the house. When we were children, they didn't give us many things to play with, either; they wanted us to make up our own games.

5. **Woman** I have two older sisters and an older brother. They're all much older; in fact, the youngest is twelve years older than I am. As a result, they all looked after me and took care of me as though I were their child instead of their younger sister.

6. **Man** Both my brother and my sister seem able to do everything they put their minds to. They're intelligent, athletic, and talented in music. They can fix anything around the house, and they get along great with everyone they meet. I was determined to work as hard as I could, so that I could show them that anything they could do, I could do.

7. **Woman** People were always asking me, "And how many sisters and brothers do you have?" When I answered "None," they always looked at me with pity and shook their heads and said, "Poor thing, you must be lonely." Well, I wasn't. I had plenty of friends, including my parents.

8. **Man** My brother was six years old when I was born. Friends of the family have told me that he was so used to being an only child that he was extremely jealous of me when we were young— and I think he still is. He puts up with me because I'm his brother, but I don't think he's ever really liked me.

Lesson 32 (p. 42)

1 **Benito** Are these your parents?
Amanda Uh-huh.
Benito And who's the little girl standing between them? Don't tell me that's you!
Amanda No, that's my sister Arlene. She can't be more than two there, so it must have been taken about 25 years ago.
Benito And who are those two? The man sitting in a chair and the woman standing next to him?
Amanda My grandparents on my mother's side. I've told you about them. That's my grandmother who worked for the newspaper and my grandfather who had a little grocery store around the corner from where I grew up.
Benito Are they both still living?
Amanda My grandmother is. She'll be—let's see, 86 on her next birthday. Of course she doesn't work for the newspaper anymore, but she has a terrific memory, and she can tell great stories about people living in my hometown. . . . These are my other grandparents, the ones on my father's side. That was typical of them. Once he got home from the factory, he didn't want to do anything else, so my grandmother did all of the gardening and the rest of the work around the house. He just watched.
Benito Who's the funny-looking kid eating an ice cream cone?
Amanda Thanks a lot. That's me.
Benito I knew it was. I was just kidding. Is that your sister Arlene, holding the puppy?
Amanda No, that's my other sister, Brenda. And the girl on my left is my cousin.
Benito You all look quite a bit alike.
Amanda Yeah, there's a definite family resemblance. We all take after my father's mother.

Benito Wow! Who's that, the woman all dressed up and looking like a fashion model?

Amanda That's my Aunt Fay, and she was a fashion model—certainly the most glamorous person in our family. . . . These three guys are my brother, my uncle, and his son, George. My brother's the one wearing the baseball uniform and covered with dirt. I guess he'd just come from a Little League game.

Benito These are all interesting photographs, but I don't think I'll recognize any of these people when I meet them. Don't you have any more up-to-date pictures?

Amanda Hang on. We're coming to those. Now this one is . . .

U N I T 8

Lesson 37 (p. 48)

❶ & ❷

Conversation 1
Man Excuse me, I know that you're busy, but could I talk to you for a minute? Something's come up in shipping.

Woman Of course, come on in. I'm never too busy to listen.

Conversation 2
Woman I had a great idea this morning for rearranging the office. I thought that if we—

Man It isn't your job to rearrange the office; it's your job to work on the budget.

Conversation 3
Man 1 I'm expecting an important call. Take this down to the mail room. It's crucial for it to go out immediately.

Man 2 Yes, sir.

Conversation 4
Woman I'm sorry I got back from lunch so late, but I met—

Man You're just not responsible, are you? Don't you realize how important it is for you to be back on time?

Conversation 5
Woman I've read your report, and I want to tell you that it's excellent work.

Man Thank you.

Woman There's just one section, on the fourth page, that I'd like to go over with you.

Conversation 6
Man I know you have other things to do, and this isn't really part of your job, but we're short-handed in the secretarial pool. I'd like you to fill in there this afternoon.

Woman Certainly. I'd be glad to.

Conversation 7
Man 1 I know you didn't hire me for advertising ideas, but one came to me this morning that I'd like to tell you about some time.

Man 2 Why not right now? I'd like to hear it. I welcome everybody's input.

Conversation 8
Woman 1 But yesterday you said that—

Woman 2 Never mind what I said yesterday. Today's today. Furthermore, I'm the boss here, and the sooner you learn that, the happier you'll be.

❸ #### Conversation 1
Woman I noticed that you kept Mrs. LePage waiting for ten minutes.

Man Yeah, sorry about that.

Conversation 2
Man Could I speak to you for a moment, Ms. Welsh?

Woman Certainly, Jack.

Man They're giving a course on business management at the community college this fall. I'd really like to take it. The problem is that it meets at 4:00 Wednesday afternoons.

Woman Are you sure it would be worth missing an hour of work?

Conversation 3
Woman 1 You know that raise I got a couple of months ago?

Woman 2 Uh-huh.

Woman 1 Well, I can't understand it. I have just as much trouble paying my bills as I did before. I could use another raise!

Conversation 4
Man 1 Yes, sir. You wanted to see me?

Man 2 Yes, I did. Have you put together the order for Famco yet?

Man 1 Well, no, it isn't quite ready.

Conversation 5
Man I'd like to send Habib to that conference in Perth next month.

Woman I'm not sure that he'll be finished with the Viking contract by then.

Man That's true. I'd forgotten about that.

U N I T 9

Lesson 42 (p. 54)

❷ #### Conversation 1
Vito How long have you been working here?

Man Almost ten years.

Vito And you still enjoy it?

Man I do now. I didn't for the first couple of years. I had trouble getting used to the job and getting along with my coworkers.

Vito But you must have gotten over that. You're content now, aren't you?

Conversation 2

Vito You say that you remember when the company was started?

Woman Yes, I do. Oh, I go way back.

Vito Excuse me for asking, but how long have you been here?

Conversation 3

Vito Did you apply for the opening in personnel?

Woman No, I didn't.

Vito How come? You'd be good at it. Weren't you interested?

Conversation 4

Vito I've heard that you're already talking about retiring. You can't be old enough yet.

Man (*Laughing*) No, I'm only fifty. But I'd like to retire in five years.

Vito It really isn't my business, but can you manage that, financially, I mean?

Conversation 5

Vito You've been here for what, five or six years now?

Woman Almost seven.

Vito Are you happy here? Have you ever thought about changing jobs?

3 **Conversation 1**

Interviewer Excuse me. Could I ask you a question?

Lorna Sure.

Interviewer You're . . . ?

Lorna Lorna Genzel.

Interviewer O.K., Lorna, would you tell me what your plans are for the next several years? What do you want to accomplish in, say, five years?

Lorna Well, first, I want to finish school. I'll be a senior at Bingham High this year.

Interviewer Do you want to go to college after that?

Lorna Not really. I'm a swimmer, and I'd like to train full-time for a year or two. Then I'd like to swim in the Olympics.

Interviewer That sounds terrific. I wish you lots of success.

Lorna Thank you.

Conversation 2

Interviewer Excuse me. Would you answer a question for me?

Harry Sure, I guess so.

Interviewer What's your name?

Harry Harry Lockwood.

Interviewer I'm writing an article for the Morning Tribune about teenagers and their plans. What do you hope to accomplish during the next five years?

Harry First, I hope to get a better job. In fact, I'm on my way to an interview now.

Interviewer Well, good luck on your interview. Then what, if you get a better job?

Harry Then if I can save enough money, I want to get married. I have a girlfriend, and we've talked about getting married, but not until we have a little more security. Then I hope to have at least two kids. I'm really anxious to start having a family.

Interviewer Well, good luck, Harry. On that, and on your interview!

Harry Thanks, I'll need it.

UNIT 10

Lesson 47 (p. 60)

2 **First secretary**

Interviewer What do you like or dislike most about your job?

Woman Well, the first thing that comes to mind is either a like or a dislike, depending on how you look at it. You see, I think I'm smarter than my boss. In a way, I like feeling that way, but on the other hand, it seems that the boss ought to be smarter. Mine will give you a quick answer, but it isn't always likely to be right.

Interviewer How do you think things would change at the office if you quit your job?

Woman Things would be pretty hectic for a while. I've been doing the work of at least two people.

Interviewer What would you have your secretary do if you had one?

Woman That's easy. Make *my* dentist's and lawyer's and doctor's appointments for *me*.

Second secretary

Interviewer What would you like to see changed about your job?

Man I have no problem answering that. Higher pay and more benefits. I don't like being paid less than I'm worth.

Interviewer Anything else?

Man Yes. Not only do I think I should be making more money, but I also dislike being called a secretary. I'd change my title to administrative assistant.

Interviewer If you had a secretary of your own, what would you have him or her do?

Man You mean for me, right?

Interviewer Right.

Man I'd like having done for me all the things I don't like doing myself.

Third secretary

Interviewer What do you enjoy about your job?

Man Not much. Frankly, I would have left a long time ago if the job weren't so convenient. It's only a block from where I live, and there isn't much else available in the area. I can't see riding a bus for half an hour every morning and evening.

Interviewer How do you think life at the office would change if you did leave?

Man I don't think they'd even notice I'd left. Not that I don't do my job and more—I do—but no one there seems to appreciate me. Especially my boss. I suppose he's so used to my doing my work that he doesn't think it's necessary to thank me once in a while.

Fourth secretary

Interviewer Do you sometimes feel smarter than your boss?

Woman Well, I'm sure I know more than she does about being a secretary, but other than that, no. She's the most brilliant woman I've ever met; she must know everything there is to know about the law.

Interviewer What kind of person do you think makes a good boss?

Woman One just like mine. She's wonderful. She never complains when I make a mistake, and she's always ready to listen when I have a problem. I admire her for that, especially since her practice is such an active one. She's both a boss and a good friend to me.

 U N I T 1 1

Lesson 52 (p. 66)

1. There are five houses on Maple Street.
2. The person who lives in the middle house is an artist.
3. Mr. and Mrs. Goren, who are both scientists and who live in the brown house, own a dog. They're the only couple who live in the neighborhood.
4. The person living in the green house, which is the one on the right, drinks milk.
5. Alma, who is a waitress, drinks soda. She lives in the blue house.
6. The blue house is between the yellow house and the red house. The red house is the middle house on the street.
7. The person whose hobby is photography and whose pet is a bird is an anthropologist.
8. The anthropologist lives in the yellow house.
9. The people whose hobby is making furniture drink tea.
10. The artist, who drinks coffee, enjoys jogging.

11. The police officer likes to swim.
12. The person who has a snake for a pet likes reading mysteries and lives next to the person whose pet is a cat.

 U N I T 1 2

Lesson 57 (p. 72)

1 **Conversation 1**

Man Did you enjoy the performance as much as you expected to?

Woman Yes, I did. Their work is certainly distinctive. Sometimes it's like living sculpture, yet other times it's almost classical. What did you think?

Man Actually, I wasn't all that crazy about it. What I really like is folk dancing.

Conversation 2

Man Wasn't that terrific?

Woman Well, the music was enjoyable enough. The story, on the other hand, didn't make much sense to me. What I'd like to see is a good old-fashioned drama with strong characters and an exciting plot. A murder mystery, maybe. Nevertheless, I'm not sorry I went; everybody's been talking about it—and almost any Broadway performance is exciting.

Conversation 3

Woman To tell you the truth, that didn't really appeal to me. I'd rather not have spent an evening listening to jazz. Classical music is what I really prefer. I'll stick to the three B's: Bach, Beethoven, and Brahms.

Man But Bach was a great influence on this kind of music, you know. Maybe it just has to grow on you. You might like it once you've gotten used to it.

Woman Maybe so. I'm willing to try again, anyway.

Conversation 4

Woman Did you like the exhibit?

Man Yes and no. Ten Eyck's work was O.K., whereas the stuff out in the garden—it seems to me anybody could put together a bunch of tin cans, paint them different colors, and call it art. What I really like is realistic art, something I can recognize for what it is.

Woman Well, I liked it all. I guess abstract isn't for everyone, though.

Conversation 5

Man I'll bet I've seen that ten or twelve times, and I still find it moving. It's such a universal love story; anybody can relate to it, especially anyone who's had a tragic love affair.

Woman I wouldn't mind seeing another one in the series. However, do you think it could be one of his comedies next time? What I'd enjoy is a good laugh.

Conversation 6

Woman I never expected Marshfield to win, did you?

Man No, not until about two minutes from the end. Did you enjoy yourself? I couldn't really tell.

Woman To be honest with you, I don't really care for the roughness and the fights. What I'd like to see is something a little more civilized, a tennis match, for instance.

Man I find tennis incredibly dull myself.

Woman I guess you have a right to your opinion, too.

3 **Conversation 1**

Woman How did you like the play?

Man Actually, I don't really care that much for straight drama. Musical comedies are what I really like.

Conversation 2

Man Do you like science fiction?

Woman To tell you the truth, it doesn't appeal to me. What I really enjoy reading are autobiographies.

Conversation 3

Man What do you think of opera?

Woman It's the stupidest, most overrated art form there is. I don't want to listen to somebody screeching, "Oh, I've lost my left shoe" for ten minutes.

Conversation 4

Woman I really like abstract art, don't you?

Man Are you serious? How can anybody like that stuff? I haven't seen any that my three-year-old couldn't do, with his eyes closed. I may not know anything about art, but I know what I like, and that isn't it.

WORKBOOK ANSWER KEY

Lesson 1

1 2. against 4. for 6. for 8. for
3. against 5. for 7. against

2 2. share 5. circle 8. regard
3. Experience 6. Panic 9. tape
4. supply 7. base 10. sense

Lesson 2

1 2. a 3. a 4. a 5. a

2 POSSIBLE ANSWERS
The father said that the music was too loud. He said that loud music was bad for people's ears. He said he wasn't sure whether his son really liked that kind of music, or whether his son listened to it because all the other kids did.

The son said that the music was supposed to be loud so people would think they were right in the middle of the band. He said he really liked the music; he wasn't just following the crowd.

3 POSSIBLE ANSWERS
The wife said that the stereo costs almost $200, and they didn't have $200 to spend. They weren't likely to have it soon. If they used the credit card, the stereo would cost even more, because of the interest.

The husband said that they could use their credit card. Then they wouldn't have to pay for the stereo immediately. He said they deserved some enjoyment in life. He said they would try to save money for the next six months and then see where they were.

Lessons 3–4

1 2. b 4. a 6. a 8. c 10. a
3. b 5. b 7. b 9. c

2 1. but, even so, so, what's more
2. furthermore, however, moreover, nevertheless, therefore

3 POSSIBLE ANSWERS
2. What's more, they're often more dedicated to the company.
They don't necessarily have to be paid more than younger workers because they have worked longer; moreover, they're often more dedicated to the company.
3. They may have some health problems, but young people can also have health problems.
They may have some health problems; however, young people can also have health problems.

4. Even so, many still are.
Some workers are not that vigorous in their seventies and eighties; nevertheless, many still are.

4 POSSIBLE ANSWER
I think a company should offer on-site child care. People should not be prevented from working because they have small children; furthermore, they are likely to work better if they know their children are safe and nearby. However, I don't think there should be work-at-home arrangements so people can take care of their children there. The parents are likely to do and think about other things if they stay home; therefore, they won't pay attention to their work. Nevertheless, I think it is a good thing that more companies are finding ways to help employees with small children.

5 POSSIBLE ANSWERS
1. She wishes she hadn't taken chemistry.
2. Emmanual hopes he dressed appropriately. He wishes he'd worn a suit.
3. Elliott hopes the call wasn't from his brother. He wishes he hadn't gone out.

6 Answers will vary.

Lesson 5

Answers will vary.

Lesson 6

1 There should be an *X* next to 1, 4, 6, and 7.

2 basic/historic, nonprofessional, critical, historic/basic, cultural/national, national/cultural

Lesson 7

1 2. a 4. a 6. a 8. a
3. b 5. a 7. b

2 POSSIBLE ANSWERS
If I were Mrs. Reilly, I'd hire David because he seems interested in the job and he needs it to help out at home. He knows where things are in the store. He considers himself reliable, responsible, patient, and honest. He says that he handles pressure well and is always on time. Those are all good characteristics for the job. David is also polite during the interview.

I wouldn't hire Mark because he doesn't seem very interested in the job. He just likes talking to people. He doesn't tell Mrs. Reilly why he needs the money. He says he's easy going and has a good sense of humor, but those aren't important characteristics for the job. Mark doesn't seem sure that he's hardworking, honest, or creative.

Lessons 8–9

①
1. lazy
2. unimaginative
3. conceited
4. outgoing
5. irresponsible; insecure

②
A Who do you think they're going to appoint department head?
B I don't know, but I hope it isn't Lisa. I can't imagine her running the department.
A Why Not? I find her very hardworking and responsible.
B Maybe so, but somehow she makes me feel uncomfortable. She's insincere. Have you ever watched her deal with clients and then heard her talk about them afterward? She's like two different people.
A No, I've never seen her act like that. I still think she'd do a great job.

③

Verb	Noun	Adjective	Base form of verb	Progressive form of verb
appoint	✓			
call	✓	✓		
consider	✓	✓		
elect	✓			
find	✓			✓
hear			✓	✓
imagine				✓
keep	✓			✓
make	✓	✓	✓	
see			✓	✓
watch			✓	✓

④ Whoever, Whichever, Whenever, wherever; whatever

⑤
1. Pisces
2. Sagittarius, Leo
3. Gemini, Aquarius

Lesson 10

Answers will vary.

U N I T 3

Lesson 11

①
2. a verb
3. a noun
4. a noun
5. a noun
6. a verb
7. an adjective
8. an adjective
9. a noun
10. a verb

②
2. complexity
3. creative
4. electricity
5. flexible
6. informality
7. nationality
8. responsibility
9. special
10. uncertainty

Lesson 12

①
2. f
3. d
4. e
5. b
6. c
7. g

②
Second conversation: Thanks, but I really don't want to talk about it.
Third conversation: It's essential that he do it, and I'd also like you to go over it with him.
Fourth conversation: Then I propose that we think it over for a few more days.
Fifth conversation: In a case like that, it's crucial that she see me as soon as possible.
Sixth conversation: Of course. I suggest that you try it out and see what you think.
Seventh conversation: Nevertheless, I recommend that you be more careful in the future. Just a friendly warning.

Lessons 13–14

① get; take; drink, to eat; go; to take, be; go

② POSSIBLE ANSWERS
2. I'd suggest that she use a shoelace or a piece of string if no cord is available.
3. I'd insist that she tie it around the arm or leg as fast as she could.
4. It's important that she tie the cord above the wound.
5. It's essential that she keep the cord loose.
6. It's crucial that she avoid major nerves and blood vessels when cutting the skin.

③ POSSIBLE ANSWERS
2. . . . dress appropriately and ask questions
3. . . . ask less money, clean up the room, and paint it

④
1. talk about it
2. bring it back, filled it out
3. take it back, ask for a refund
4. run into Pam, heard from her

⑤
2. take it back; turned it on
3. go over them; asked (her) for them, filled them in/out, was looking for them

⑥ POSSIBLE ANSWERS
2. it's essential that you fill it in/out
3. I recommend that you think it over
4. I propose that we go over
5. It's crucial that you be, talk over

Lesson 15

Answers will vary.

U N I T 4

Lesson 16

①
2. That's wrong.
3. That's wrong.
4. That's wrong.
5. That's right.
6. That's right.
7. That's wrong.

2 2. takeoff (g) 5. risk (a) 8. deflates (c)
3. clinging (b) 6. descent (h)
4. inland (e) 7. raid (d)

Lesson 17

1 a. 5 b. 2 c. 4 d. 6 f. 3

2 2. b 4. b 6. a
3. a 5. a 7. b

Lessons 18–19

1 Then; Next; As soon as; Once

2 First, form a circle and put one person in the center. Then, the person in the center throws a ball to anyone in the circle, calling out one of these words: "earth," "air," "fire," "water." Next, the person who catches the ball has to give an appropriate response: for "earth," the name of an animal that walks; for "air," one that flies; for "water," one that swims; and no response for "fire." An animal may not be used more than once. As soon as a player makes a wrong response, he or she trades places with the person in the center and a new round begins.

3 POSSIBLE ANSWERS
Next
As soon as
Finally
By the time

4 2. When driving, check your mirror and speedometer frequently.
3. When driving in heavy traffic, keep a safe distance.
4. Before making a turn, always signal.
5. When making a long trip, drive for a couple of hours and then stop and rest.

5 B Before reading the article, I'd heard of graphology, but I didn't know very much about it. So then after thinking about it for a while, I decided to take some courses. After finishing those, I got a job right away analyzing the handwriting of job applicants at Mayco.
A And while working there you met Joe, right?

6 POSSIBLE ANSWERS
2. When dieting, you should get a lot of exercise.
3. While trying to lose weight, you shouldn't eat fattening deserts.
4. After losing weight, you should buy new clothes.

Lesson 20

Answers will vary.

U N I T 5

Lesson 21

1 2. Same 3. Different. 4. Same.

2 I am fortunate to live in this much-loved house. Unusual in this part of the world, it is an eight-sided house. It was built over a century ago by my great-grandfather, from handmade bricks. Looking out of my tree-shaded front windows, I can see well-kept gardens; sun-warmed, just-cut fields of wheat; and green-covered hills.

Lesson 22

1

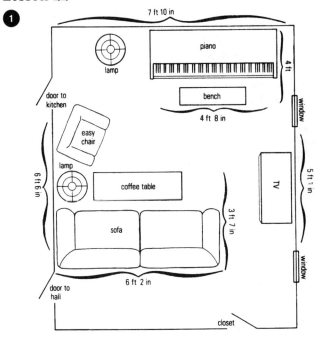

Lesson 23–24

1 2. A TV. 4. A bicycle.
3. Cigarettes. 5. A refrigerator/An icebox.

2 2. b 3. d 4. e 5. c

3 POSSIBLE ANSWERS
A I thought I'd put it in the bedroom.
B In the bedroom! Why would you put it there?
A Because it's the only place it'll fit, under the windows.
B How wide is the desk?
A Sixty inches.
B How high and how deep is it?
A Thirty inches high and thirty-four inches deep.
B Whew! That's pretty big! What's it like?
A It's in pretty bad shape—I guess it's about fifty years old—but it's solid walnut.

4 POSSIBLE ANSWERS
2. A How long are the biggest coral snakes?
B They're 48 inches long. The biggest rattlesnakes are 48 inches longer than the biggest coral snakes.
B They're 48 inches long. The biggest coral snakes are 48 inches shorter than the biggest rattlesnakes.

3. **A** How much do adult African bull elephants weigh?
   B They weigh about 8 tons. Adult blue whales weigh about 142 tons more than/are about 142 tons heavier than adult African bull elephants.
   B They weigh about 8 tons. Adult African bull elephants weigh about 142 tons less than/are about 142 tons lighter than adult blue whales.

⑤ 2. You aren't going to wear your new brown leather jacket out in the rain, are you?
3. If I could afford it, I'd buy an air-conditioned white Mercedes.
4. Have you heard the exciting new Italian opera singer yet?
5. These colorful handmade clay tiles come from Mexico.

⑥ Answers will vary.

⑦ Answers will vary.

Lesson 25

Answers will vary.

UNIT 6

Lesson 26

① Answers will vary.

② 1. underripe
2. overestimated, overcooked
3. overslept, overtime
4. oversupply, undersell

Lesson 27

① 2. e   4. b   6. d   8. g
3. a   5. f   7. h

② 2. . . . his older sister always stood up for him, so he looked up to her a lot.
3. . . . she didn't have any brothers and sisters. As a result, she got away with a lot with her parents.
4. . . . his parents wanted them (him, his brother, and his sister) to develop their creativity; therefore, they had very few toys—and no TV.
5. . . . she was the youngest of four children, so she had five "parents."
6. . . . he had to be very competitive in order to keep up with his siblings.
7. . . . everyone expected her to be lonely because she was an only child.
8. . . . he doesn't think his brother ever forgave him for being born.

Lessons 28–29

① Answers will vary.

② Answers will vary.

③ *First letter:*   for; so; Therefore/Thus/As a result; In order to/To; so (that)
Second letter: as/since, for; Therefore/Thus/As a result

④ POSSIBLE ANSWERS
1. Susan had to work and borrow (in order) to pay her college expenses.
2. Susan had to work and borrow so (that) she could pay her college expenses.
3. Susan had to work and borrow for her college expenses.
4. As/Since Susan's parents couldn't pay her college expenses, she had to work and borrow.
5. Susan's parents couldn't pay her college expenses, so she had to work and borrow.
6. Susan's parents couldn't pay her college expenses; therefore/thus/as a result, she had to work and borrow.

⑤ Answers will vary.

⑥ I'd run out of cigarettes, so I went out to get some. Up ahead of me on the street, I saw my friend Scott, so I hurried to catch up with him. He asked me what I was up to, and when I told him, he said, "I used to smoke, too, because a lot of older kids I looked up to did, and I wanted to get along with them. Then I developed a cough. When I went to the doctor for a checkup, he asked me why I smoked. Of course, I couldn't come up with any good reason. He told me that the other kids wouldn't look down on me if I didn't smoke, and that I shouldn't be afraid to stand up for my own ideas if I didn't really want to smoke. He also said that if I didn't quit, I could end up with all kinds of problems and be in for some real trouble. Well, I was scared, but not scared enough to quit; I'd always give in to the urge to smoke. At first, I tried to cut down on my smoking and put up with the cough, the smell, the expense, and the danger to my health. Finally, I realized that you can't get away with it and keep out of trouble, so I quit, cold. You'd better quit, too!"

Lesson 30

Answers will vary.

Review of units 1–6

① In order to, as/because; As a result/Therefore/Thus; So that, for

② **B** I recommend that it be someone with at least some experience in advertising.
A I agree. Unfortunately, there aren't any people in the company with the right experience. Luis Aragon would have been suitable if he'd taken more courses. I've suggested that he do so, but he hasn't.
B Then I recommend that we go to an employment agency.

③ 2. The curtains are four inches lower (shorter) than the windows./The windows are four inches higher (longer) than the curtains.
3. The clock is four inches higher than the ceiling./The ceiling is four inches lower than the clock.

4 A I think these shiny red plastic plates and those white cotton Mexican napkins would look great together.

B So do I. Should we put these three hand-painted Italian bowls in the same picture? Or would that be too much in one shot?

A Let's save the bowls for the picture with the set of four grass Philippine placemats. They go together better.

5 B enjoyable, consider
A make, mad
B call
A keep, working
B see, making, appoint, president

6 2. Mrs. Brandt hopes she didn't hurt her friend's feelings. She wishes she hadn't had to go home.
3. Mrs. Brandt hopes she bought everything they need. She wishes she'd taken a list.
4. Mr. Brandt hopes Mrs. Brandt didn't spend too much money. He wishes all the more that she hadn't gone to the store alone.

7 1. Nevertheless/ However
2. Therefore
3. Moreover/Furthermore
4. Moreover/Furthermore
5. However

8 Wherever; Whenever, whoever; However; whatever, whichever

9 2. got along with
3. keep up with; looked up to
4. keep out of; is up to
5. got away with; come up with

10 POSSIBLE ANSWERS
1. I suggest that you set aside some of your clothes that you don't mind her borrowing. Don't give in to her when she wants to borrow the "wrong" ones.
2. I recommend that you let your younger son know about his good points. Don't ever compare the two. It's necessary that your younger son learn how to deal with his jealousy, and that your older son be patient with his brother. His younger brother will outgrow his jealousy when he recognizes his own value.

U N I T   7

Lesson 31

1 b. paragraph 5   f. paragraph 8
c. paragraph 7   g. paragraph 1
d. paragraph 4   h. paragraph 6
e. paragraph 3

2 cóntract; Résearch, condúct, súrvey; óbject, résearch, recórd; súrvey, prótests, ínsult; decréase, íncrease; objéct, protést

Lesson 32

3 1. her mother, her sister Arlene, her father
2. her grandfather, her grandmother (on her mother's side)
3. her grandmother, her grandfather (on her father's side)
4. her sister Brenda, herself, her cousin
5. her aunt
6. her brother, her uncle, her cousin

Lessons 33–34

1 POSSIBLE ANSWER
The man sitting in a chair is her grandfather.
The woman standing behind him is her grandmother.
The woman working in the garden is her grandmother.
The man watching her grandmother is her grandfather.
The girl holding a puppy is her sister.
The girl eating an ice cream cone is Amanda.
The girl standing on Amanda's left is her cousin.
The woman all dressed up and looking like a fashion model is her aunt.
The boy wearing a baseball uniform and covered with dirt is her brother.
The man standing between the boys is her uncle.

2 2. a. It's a movie that was produced by Steven Spielberg that's about an extraterrestrial creature who's left behind on Earth by his companions.
b. It's a movie produced by Steven Spielberg about an extraterrestrial creature left behind on Earth by his companions. It's *E.T.*
3. a. It's a famous structure that's in Paris that's made of iron and that was built in 1889.
b. It's a famous structure in Paris made of iron and built in 1889. It's the Eiffel Tower.

3 2. Somebody robbed a store around the corner from where I live.
5. The money stolen from the store was the day's receipts.
6. The police think it was an "inside job" done by someone working at the store.
7. The woman suspected and being sought by the police didn't show up at work today.
8. A man passing the store saw her come out of it at 11:00, long after she should have left.
10. She's someone completely trusted by the owner and respected by the community.

4 Answers will vary.

5 2. I stayed in the house all morning, waiting for their call.
3. He's supposed to be here any minute, bringing our dinner.
4. I worked hard on it all last night, desperately wishing I weren't taking English.

6 2. She sang happily.
3. She approached her destination fast.
4. Julien gave advice.

7 One stone. (Take one stone from the box marked BW. If it's black, the other stone must also be black. [If not, the label would be correct, and we know that all of the labels are wrong.] Therefore, that box should be labeled BB. There are only two boxes left, so their labels should be reversed. The same is true if the one stone you take from the box marked BW is white. The other stone must also be white, so that box should be labeled WW. The labels on the other two boxes should, again, be reversed.)

Lesson 35

Answers will vary.

UNIT 8

Lesson 36

1 2. No.   4. No.   6. Yes.
      3. Yes.   5. Yes.   7. Yes.

2 2. self-conscious   5. self-employed
      3. self-centered   6. self-taught
      4. self-image
Students mark *X* according to their own opinions.

Lesson 37

1 2. No.   4. No.   6. Yes.   8. No.
      3. No.   5. Yes. 7. Yes.

2
	Employee	Employer
Conversation 2	✓	
Conversation 3		✓
Conversation 4	✓	
Conversation 5		✓
Conversation 6		✓
Conversation 7	✓	
Conversation 8	✓	

3 Conversation 1: c
      Conversation 2: a
      Conversation 3: d
      Conversation 4: b
      Conversation 5: e

Lessons 38–39

1 2. a. It's essential that my son stop watching so much TV, so he can develop his own imagination.
         b. It's essential for my son to stop watching so much TV, so he can develop his own imagination.
      3. a. It's necessary that my daughter take a computer course that they're presenting on TV, for college credit.
         b. It's necessary for my daughter to take a computer course that they're presenting on TV, for college credit.
      4. a. It's crucial that we all keep up with world events, in order to understand other people.
         b. It's crucial for us all to keep up with world events, in order to understand other people.

2 Answers will vary.

3 POSSIBLE ANSWERS
      2. The more (things) I have to do, the more efficient I get.
      3. The angrier I get, the quieter my voice gets/the more softly I speak.
      4. The less you have, the less you can lose.
      5. The less you talk, the more people will respect your opinion.
      6. The more you practice, the more you'll improve your playing/the better your playing will be.

4 Answers will vary.

5 POSSIBLE ANSWERS
      1. Could you help me for a moment, please, _____? (I can't seem to work the copying machine.)
      2. Excuse me, sir/ma'am. I wonder if you could help me for just a minute, please. (I can't seem to work the copying machine.)
      3. _____, I'd like you to help me for a minute, please. (I can't seem to work the copying machine.)

6 2. Abraham Lincoln   4. John Dewey
      3. Benjamin Disraeli   5. John Ruskin

7 POSSIBLE ANSWERS
      I think I should leave school because the sooner I start working, the sooner I can start earning money/the longer I stay in school, the further behind I'll be/it isn't crucial that I graduate.

      I think you should stay in school because it's essential that you finish/the more education you have, the better job you can get/the more you know, the happier you'll be/it's important for you to know about other people, their ideas, and their experiences.

Lesson 40

Answers will vary.

UNIT 9

Lesson 41

1 2. That's wrong.   5. That's right.
      3. That's right.   6. That's wrong.
      4. That's wrong.   7. That's wrong.

2 2. a geologist   6. a motorcyclist
      3. a psychiatrist   7. an individualist
      4. a violinist   8. a nationalist
      5. a machinist   9. an internationalist

Lesson 42

1 2. a   3. b   4. e   5. d

2 Conversation 2: I will have been working here for forty years next September 1.
      Conversation 3: If I were interested in the job, I would have applied for it.

Conversation 4: If all goes well, by then I will have saved enough money to retire.

Conversation 5: If I didn't like the job, I wouldn't have stayed here this long.

3 Conversation 1: b. train full-time (as a swimmer) for a year or two
c. swim in the Olympics

Conversation 2: a. get a better job
b. save money
c. get married and have at least two kids

Lessons 43–44

1 POSSIBLE ANSWERS
1. b. she will have trained full-time for a year or two
c. she will have swum in the Olympics
2. a. he will have gotten a better job
b. he will have saved money
c. he will have gotten married and had at least two kids

2 2. By 2005, an automobile company will have produced a 100-mile-per-gallon car.
3. By 2006, an electronics firm will have introduced 3-D TV.
4. By 2007, doctors will have discovered a cancer vaccine.
5. By 2010, robots will have outnumbered human workers.

3 2. will have known his (future) wife for five years
3. will have been driving for five years
4. won't have smoked for five years
5. will have been an amateur radio operator for five years
6. will have studied/been studying Spanish for five years
7. won't have seen a movie for five years

4 2. b   3. a   4. a   5. b

5 2. a   3. a   4. b

6 B 'd gotten; were, would have been, would be
A didn't think, wouldn't have gone ahead, finished; would have suggested
A wouldn't have, hadn't brought up

7 Answers will vary.

Lesson 45

Answers will vary.

UNIT 10

Lesson 46

1 2. Different.   4. Same.   6. Same.
3. Different.   5. Different.

2 frequency, hesitancy, inaccuracy, leniency, secrecy
A adequacy
B leniency
A inaccuracy; frequency
B hesitancy

Lesson 47

1 2. e, h   3. f, l   4. a, g, j   5. d   6. b, k

2 First secretary: f, k
Second secretary: a, g, l
Third secretary: b, d, j
Fourth secretary: e, h, i

Lessons 48–49

1 B Caroline is a great boss in other ways, but I'm sick and tired of her letting Laverne talk all the time.
A I talked with Caroline about that once. She said she appreciated my telling her. However, I don't notice any change.
B I told her the same thing. Maybe she resents our interfering in her business.
A She should be grateful for your wanting to help things run smoothly around here.
B You know what? I think so, too!

2 A criticizing
B being, criticized
A to be, told
B being, told
A us, to tell
B our, embarrassing

3 A to do
B being, given
A being, told
B our, giving
A to be, bossed

4 Answers will vary.

5 B I agree. I've been wanting to talk to you, but I've been either afraid or embarrassed. Do you want to go first?
A Sure. Here's what bothers me most. I'm not only tired of paying more than my share of the rent, but (also) I can't afford to keep it up.
B You're right. I'm sorry. But lately I've either been out of work or just had part-time jobs.
A I know. You're neither stupid nor lazy. What seems to be the problem?
B I seem to be either overqualified for everything or underqualified.
A Well, I not only hope you find work soon, but (also) hope you're able to pay what you owe.

6 POSSIBLE ANSWERS
Your reaction to criticism can be either destructive or constructive.
If you're criticized, don't feel that you failed not only in your action but also as a person.
You should neither react emotionally to setbacks nor confuse your *self* with your *work*.
Don't only take time to cool down, but ask whether the criticism was fair from the other person's point of view.
The problem may be a simple misunderstanding of either what you did or your reasons for doing it.
You can not only try to be objective but take time to cool down and then take positive action.

Maybe neither what you say nor what you do will change the situation.

You may either simply explain your point of view or decide that the battle isn't worth fighting.

Neither be afraid to admit your mistake nor overdo self-criticism.

You may want not only to explain what you're doing to correct the situation but also to ask for any other suggestions.

Criticizing yourself first not only is destructive but also prevents learning from your mistakes.

There are constructive ways of not only receiving but giving criticism.

Lesson 50

Answers will vary.

UNIT 11

Lesson 51

1 2. a   4. g   6. f   8. c
3. b   5. h   7. d

2 cheerful, tearless, painless, thoughtful, harmless, doubtful, hopeful

Lesson 52

1 2. middle, artist
3. scientists, brown
4. green, right
5. waitress, blue
6. between; red
7. photography, anthropologist
8. anthropologist, yellow
9. furniture, tea
10. artist, coffee, jogging
11. police officer, swim
12. reading mysteries

2

color of house	yellow	blue	red	brown	green
occupation	anthropologist	waitress	artist	scientists	police officer
hobby	photography	reading mysteries	jogging	making furniture	swimming
pet	a bird	a snake	a cat	a dog	
drink		soda	coffee	tea	milk

What's the hobby of the person who drinks water? Photography.

What color is the house of the person whose pet is a fish? Green.

Lessons 53–54

1 2. a   4. b   6. e
3. f   5. d   7. c

2 A shouldn't have
B could, can't
A could have had
B would have, must have
A might have
B shouldn't

3 POSSIBLE ANSWERS
1. **B** Maybe you ordered it and forgot about it.
   A I couldn't have!
2. **B** Do you think she made a mistake?
   A She must have.

4 The solutions follow exercise 6 in the workbook.

5 Randall Ming owns a factory that produces auto parts that are shipped all over the country/which produces auto parts which are shipped all over the country. One of his employees is a man named Henry Porter, who has worked for Mr. Ming for many years. Porter, who is a night security guard, works every weeknight from 11:00 p.m. to 7:00 a.m. He also acts as Mr. Ming's chauffeur. One Thursday morning at 7:30, Porter arrives at Mr. Ming's house, which is just outside the city in which his factory is located. Porter is to drive Mr. Ming, who is taking a business trip, to the train station.

"I wish you wouldn't take this trip," Porter tells Mr. Ming. "Last night, just after midnight, I had a dream, which was very realistic, in which you got killed in a train wreck."

Mr. Ming, who immediately becomes very angry, doesn't thank Porter for the warning that/which he has given him. Instead he says, "You, a man whom I trusted! You're fired!"

Why does Mr. Ming fire Porter?
The solution follows exercise 6 in the workbook.

6 Sherlock Holmes, who was created by Sir Arthur Conan Doyle, is probably the most famous detective in literature. Doyle, who lived from 1859 to 1930, wrote sixty novels and short stories about Holmes.

A Study in Scarlet, which was Doyle's first novel about Holmes, also introduced Holmes's faithful friend, Dr. Watson. The book begins with Watson's being wounded in a war that was being fought in Asia. Watson is sent home to London with a small pension, which is hardly enough to pay his bills at the inexpensive hotel where he takes a room. By chance he meets Stamford, who is an old friend, and Watson tells him about his difficulties. Stamford tells Watson about Sherlock Holmes, who is an amateur detective. Holmes, who lives at 221B Baker Street, is looking for someone to share his rooms. The two men meet, and Watson decides to move in with Holmes, whom he likes immediately.

Watson found Holmes to be amazingly contradictory man who knew nothing about literature and philosophy, but who knew everything about chemistry, anatomy, and crime. Holmes found Watson to be a person of average intelligence who nevertheless helped him solve the long series of crimes in which the two became involved. In spite of their differences, the two men formed a friendship and a partnership that lasted for 43 years, until the death of Arthur Conan Doyle, their creator, in 1930.

Lesson 55

Answers will vary.

UNIT 12

Lesson 56

1
2. Fact.   5. Fact.   8. Fact.
3. Fact.   6. Opinion.   9. Opinion.
4. Fact.   7. Opinion.   10. Opinion.

2
2. applicable   7. distinctive
3. breakable   8. admirable
4. informative   9. memorable
5. illustrative   10. inventive
6. unbelievable

Lesson 57

1
a. 2   c. 5   e. 3
b. 6   d. 1   f. 4

2
2. That's wrong.   5. That's right.
3. That's right.   6. That's wrong.
4. That's wrong.

3
1. Yes.   2. Yes.   3. No.   4. No.

Lessons 58–59

1
POSSIBLE ANSWERS
B What I'd like to do is some fishing,/Some fishing is what I'd like to do, . . .
A Where I'd rather go is the Senegee River./The Senegee River is where I'd rather go.
B Who I'd like to see go is my brother./My brother is who I'd like to see go. . . . What he needs is more experience./More experience is what he needs.

2 Answers will vary.

3 Answers will vary.

4
1. didn't like   5. liked
2. liked, didn't like 6. liked
3. liked, didn't like 7. didn't like; liked
4. liked; didn't like 8. didn't like, liked

5 Answers will vary.

6
POSSIBLE ANSWERS
2. Well, it has to grow on you. I didn't care for it myself at first.
3. Try it, you'll like it.
4. It takes time getting used to.
5. It's not your cup of tea, I guess.

7
POSSIBLE ANSWERS
B Mr. Delon said that while I'd been doing good work, he had to let me go. In a way, I wasn't surprised, yet it was still a shock. I knew I was doing O.K. However, the company's been losing money.
A You'd indicated that. Nevertheless, I didn't realize your job was in danger. Whereas you may have lost this job, you shouldn't have any trouble getting another one.
B I hope not. On the other hand, I still don't look forward to job hunting again. While it's no fun, maybe I'll get an even better job this time.

Lesson 60

Answers will vary.

Review of units 7–12

1
Paragraph 1: in spite of/despite; However/ Nevertheless/Nonetheless/On the other hand, yet, however/nevertheless/ nonetheless/on the other hand
Paragraph 2: Whereas/While, however/nevertheless/ nonetheless/on the other hand

2
2. he will have had seven different positions with the company.
3. he will have worked for three generations of the Field family.
4. they will have lived at three different addresses.
5. they will have been living at their present home for 43 years.
6. they will have seen a lot of changes in their neighborhood.

3
2. You can either choose our ordinary savings rate or our extraordinary rate ($1,000 minimum deposit).
3. We give you not only the highest interest rates, but also we give you the lowest rates on loans.
4. We're neither too large to know you personally nor too small to give you full service.

4
POSSIBLE ANSWERS
2. If he weren't so absent-minded, he wouldn't have forgotten to apply for a promotion he might have gotten.
3. He'd have money if he hadn't spent his income foolishly.
4. He wouldn't have bought a videocassette recorder last month if he were more practical.
5. If he'd saved some money, he'd be able to buy some of the other things he wants now.

5
2. B I guess it would be all right, but where I'd rather go is Westfield.
   B I guess it would be all right, but Westfield is where I'd rather go.
3. B Actually, who I'd like to see is Cary Cable.
   B Actually, Cary Cable is who I'd like to see.
4. B That wouldn't be bad, but what I'd prefer to see is *Night Fright* if it's still around.
   B That wouldn't be bad, but *Night Fright* is what I'd prefer to see if it's still around.

6 *Deserted,* which opened at Cinema City last night, is one of the best movies of the year. It's the second film directed by Tienne Dubois, who's the most exciting director now working. It stars Patricia Wen and Leonardo Amato, who's Ms. Dubois's husband in real life. *Deserted,* which is advertised as a mystery, is also a moving love story. Patricia Wen, who gives the performance of her career, plays a woman whose husband suddenly and mysteriously disappears. Alone, she begins her search for her husband, which takes her to North Africa. In Marrakesh, she is joined by her husband's brother, about whom her husband never told her. The identity of this "brother" is only one of the mysteries in this "must see" movie. Don't miss it!

7 POSSIBLE ANSWERS
1. b. I'm awfully sorry to ask you to do this, but there's no one else with your experience who could do a better job.
   c. If you teach this class, you won't have study hall or cafeteria duty.
2. a. Help me, or I'll tell Mom and Dad what you did yesterday.
   b. You're so good at English that it would be easy for you to help me.
   c. If you'll help me with this, I'll help you with the dishes.

8 POSSIBLE ANSWERS
1. I wonder if I could ask a favor. Would it be all right if I had someone else take my 9:00 class? I have to do something very important.
2. Could you take my 9:00 class for me? I know you're free then. I'll take over for you some time.

9 Answers will vary.